W9-BCL-335

MILTON STUDIES

XVII

MILTON STUDIES
James D. Simmonds, Editor

GRACE LIBRARY, CARLOW COLLEGE
PITTSBURGH, PA. 15213

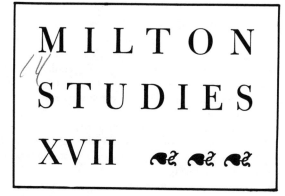

MILTON STUDIES XVII

Composite Orders

The Genres of Milton's Last Poems

Richard S. Ide

Joseph Wittreich

Guest Editors

PR
3579
M5
V·17

UNIVERSITY OF PITTSBURGH PRESS

CATALOGUED

MILTON STUDIES

is published annually by the University of Pittsburgh Press as a forum for Milton scholarship and criticism. Articles submitted for publication may be biographical; they may interpret some aspect of Milton's writings; or they may define literary, intellectual, or historical contexts—by studying the work of his contemporaries, the traditions which affected his thought and art, contemporary political and religious movements, his influence on other writers, or the history of critical response to his work.

Manuscripts should be upwards of 3,000 words in length and should conform to the *MLA Style Sheet*. Manuscripts and editorial correspondence should be addressed to James D. Simmonds, Department of English, University of Pittsburgh, Pittsburgh, Pa. 15260.

Milton Studies does not review books.

Within the United States, *Milton Studies* may be ordered from the University of Pittsburgh Press, Pittsburgh, Pa. 15260.

Overseas orders should be addressed to Feffer and Simons, Inc., 100 Park Avenue, New York, N.Y. 10017, U.S.A.

Library of Congress Catalog Card Number 69-12335

ISBN 0-8229-3473-6 (Volume XVII)

US ISSN 0076-8820

Published by the University of Pittsburgh Press, Pittsburgh, Pa. 15260

Copyright © 1983, University of Pittsburgh Press

All rights reserved

Feffer & Simons, Inc., London

Manufactured in the United States of America

To the Memory
of
Joan Malory Webber

Words fall to the dark, to the light, poems
Are born . . .

"Does it make more light for all of us?"
More light, more pain. It gives
Those places names, clears the map.

                    —*Joan Malory Webber*

CONTENTS

Contents

PREFACE

The kinds, taken as a whole, can make up the furniture of a man's mind, can represent his whole culture. . . . [They] can easily be seen as tiny subcultures with their own habits, habitats, and structures of ideas as well as their own forms. . . . As subcultures continually melt into and are absorbed by a neighboring culture, so did the kinds . . . melt into one another—often to enrich the possibilities of literature taken as a system.
                    —Rosalie Colie, *The Resources of Kind*

The history of Western poetics teaches that a few texts have habitually enjoyed exceptional status because they were reputed to contain—or to transcend—all known and possible genres.
                    —Michel Beaujour, *Glyph*

THE TITLE for this volume derives from William Wordsworth. While sorting the "kinds" into larger generic categories and then organizing those categories into a literary system, Wordsworth points to the propensity of certain poets, Young and Cowper most notably, for constructing a "composite order" out of the various generic categories.[1] A decade later, William Hazlitt extends this conception to Raphael and Milton: "Their productions were of the *composite order;* and those of the latter sometimes even amount to centos."[2] Like so much of the supposed revolution in Romantic poetics, this piece of Romantic critical idiom is rooted in the Renaissance, both in Renaissance scriptural exegesis, especially in England, and in Renaissance literary and aesthetic theory, evolving in Italy and finding embodiment in the visual as well as the verbal arts. Hence E. H. Gombrich's conception of "total form" is of a piece with Rosalie Colie's of *genera mixta,*[3] each directing attention to assumptions that are fundamental to Renaissance critical theory and artistic practice and that bear special relevance to the great poetic achievements in England: the epic-romance of Spenser, the tragedies and tragicomedies of Shakespeare, and, what is of particular concern here, the last poems of Milton.

All three of these poets write in a period when reflection concerning literary genres is intensified. But Milton especially, arriving late in the Renaissance and beginning his major poems late in life, has a privileged vantage on a tradition in which genres that are intricately defined and codified in theory are boldly reconstituted and redeployed in practice, as if to sponsor a proposition like Irving Wohlfarth's: "Art is a coherent continuum of forms which immanently tend toward . . . self-dissolution in higher, more reflexive forms that better approximate to the idea of art, with which the absolute work of art will finally coincide."[4] Thus, even if Milton's last poems can be anatomized into parts and the parts given a generic identity, these individual generic components belong finally to what Rodolphe Gasché calls a "global order" and Angus Fletcher a "transcendental form."[5] Indeed, in the very act of pressing beyond generic limitations to create new composite orders, Milton's last poems advance toward an aesthetics of *the beyond*.

Paradise Lost, Paradise Regained, and *Samson Agonistes* are landmarks in the history of their genres and central documents in the history of poetics. These poems bear witness to the Coleridgean dictum that "art would or should be the abridgement of nature. Now the fulness of nature is without character, as water is purest when without taste, smell, or color; but this is the highest, the apex only,—it is not the whole. The object of art is to give the whole *ad hominem;* hence each step of nature hath its ideal, and hence the possibility of a climax up to the perfect form of a harmonized chaos."[6] In the case of Milton, as Coleridge well understood, different steps of the ideal are achieved by the lyric poems: his ode on Christ's Nativity, his pastorals and sonnets for various occasions, his masque for Michaelmas Feast, and his elegy for Edward King. But if the early poems thus raise their respective kinds to a new key of perfection, the climax is reserved for Milton's last poems, each a gathering of multiple forms, each a generic chaos harmonized.

All the essays in this volume are concerned with the nature of this achieved harmony, either with the "whole" that Milton presents to us or with its constituent parts. Earl Miner suggests that in *Paradise Lost* the harmony proceeds from the poem's firm generic subordination in which, among the three grandfather genres, narrative dominates drama and lyric even as it exploits the resources of those same subordinate kinds. O. B. Hardison's examination of Milton's puzzling, risky decision to begin *Paradise Lost* with a towering portrait of Satan is similarly predicated on the assurance that the poem is firmly lodged in the epic tradition and, for that reason, that the convention of *in medias res* provides special access to its problematical beginning. And Barbara Lewalski's evaluation of *Paradise Lost* as a *genera mixta* poem in which recognizable genres, with their established assumptions and values, are used to convey to the reader Milton's own range of perceptions also posits for the poem a secure generic hierarchy.

A dominant or containing form, definitive subordination, and contributory functions for the lesser genres—although these are important elements in Milton's composite ordering, none of these critics would wish to imply that Milton's approach to genre is staid, or predictable, or strictly determinate. On the contrary, it is innovative, exciting, and distinctive, whether the distinctiveness resides in the unique use of the reliable narrator, bold exploitation of *in medias res*, or exceptional diffuseness of his epic form. Indeed, the essay on *Paradise Lost* by Richard Ide and on *Samson Agonistes* by Mary Ann Radzinowicz depend upon one's recognizing the distinctive treatment of genre in those works. Because Milton is engaged in transvaluating traditional epic subject matter in *Paradise Lost*, he incorporates aspects of Elizabethan tragedy and tragicomedy into his poem to characterize Satan's epic behavior as false heroism and Adam and Eve's "better fortitude" as true heroism. And it is owing to the distinctive recapitulative structure of *Samson Agonistes* that Milton is able to incorporate lesser poetic genres into his tragedy— the "character," the *récit*, the debate, and the narrated play-within-a-play—to support the development of theme and character.

If these five essays share a common point of departure, that being the identification of the work's subsuming genre or the hazarding of the generic "guess," as E. D. Hirsch might say,[7] John Shawcross would raise an anterior question in regard to the genres of *Paradise Regained* and *Samson Agonistes*. His essay on the advantages to be gained by juxtaposing these two works in a single volume is additionally an essay in generic redefinition: what should one understand by the term *brief epic*, and how does one respond to a drama that is intended to be read as a poem?

Not all the contributors to the volume, however, would be comfortable with the notions of firm generic subordination and sharp definition, nor with the metaphor of harmony insofar as it implies tranquility. For them, Milton's late poems, in their very absorption of the kinds, self-consciously recognize the partiality and hence the inadequacy of each kind taken by itself and remind one, with Coleridge, of the "difference between form as proceeding, and shape as superinduced; the latter is either the death or the imprisonment of the thing;—the former is its self-witnessing and self-effected sphere of agency."[8] Generic mergers in *Paradise Lost* and *Samson Agonistes* occasion generic strife, militating against the genres' peaceful coexistence and producing a vision that, while it may be unified, is not likely to seem harmonious, and certainly not tranquil. This is not to say that generic tension cannot be creative, however. As Balachandra Rajan argues in this volume, from the seeming cross-purposes of the tragic Fall and epic recovery in *Paradise Lost* issues a creative tension that, though it confronts one's formalist tendencies with a recalcitrant irresolution and uncertainty, is itself true to the reality of our own experience in an uncertain world.

Fredric Jameson has argued powerfully for the position that "genre theory must always in one way or another project the coexistence or tension between several generic modes or strands: and with this methodological axiom," he concludes, "the typologizing abuses of traditional genre criticism are defiantly laid to rest."[9] Generic strife asks new questions of criticism and places new obligations on critics. In Milton's last poems, literary categories do not seem to rest comfortably side by side as constructive parts of a whole but to jostle with one another, to challenge one another's assumptions and values, and to compete with one another. We must learn, with Claudio Guillén, to reckon with a system of counter-genres, to rethink the notion of containing or subsuming form, perhaps even to redefine the idea of organic form.[10] Is the latter simply a measure of the integration of form and content within a work, or is it more descriptive of a dynamic, evolving, organic process of generic contention that comes to define form "as proceeding," that is, form as the work's own "self-witnessing and self-effected sphere of agency?"

Thomas Amorose suggests that this dynamic conception of form is writ small in Milton's handling of history in Books XI and XII of *Paradise Lost*. Here Milton brings competing theories of history into dialectical conflict from which emerges his own peculiarly apocalyptic vision of history (itself indicative of the prophetic cast Milton gives to the entire epic). More explicitly, Joseph Wittreich argues that Milton's method of psychologizing the council scenes in *Paradise Lost* epitomizes not only the way epic and prophecy compete in the poem but the way Milton uses the conventions of the former to advance the purposes of the latter. Similarly, John Ulreich suggests that the generic tension between competing conceptions of tragedy in *Samson Agonistes* helps to shape its subsuming form of prophetic tragedy, for which the Book of Amos is Milton's model.

Each of these essays points out how Milton presses beyond restrictive generic conceptions—sometimes building from them, sometimes rejecting them—in creating a new composite order appropriate to his distinctive vision. The relationship between the newly emergent form and its inadequate predecessor may be corrective but is more likely to seem subversive. In this respect, the essays on *Paradise Regained* in this volume comprise a kind of triptych, each testifying to the brief epic's subversive treatment of the genre and subgenres that seem to stand squarely in its tradition—narrative, romance, and epic.

Stanley Fish argues that Satan's temptations issue from assumptions about time and worldly values that are precisely the constitutive assumptions of narrative plot; Jesus rejects the temptations and in so doing forces the reader to reject his or her own traditional assumptions about what constitutes action, value, even reality in this world. Annabel Patterson's survey of Milton's changing attitude toward romance similarly concludes that while Satan may be given to romance assumptions and values, Milton's brief epic is finally a profound revaluation of romance tradition. And Stuart Curran's discussion of the ways *Paradise Regained* corrects the *Iliad*, the *Odyssey*, and the *Aeneid* likewise concludes by suggesting that Milton's brief epic demystifies the epic tradition, stripping it of its expansive settings, elaborate machinery, grand language, and worldly arguments in order to redefine the human aspiration at the heart of the heroic vision. Each of these essays, then, though different in approach and critical perspective, intimates that the artistic strategy of *Paradise Regained* is deconstructive, that the poem's assertion of its content undercuts the very assumptions of the form which would seem to contain it. These three essays, especially, raise questions about Milton's supposed allegiance to a generic hierarchy—and about his willingness to privilege any genre whatsoever. When a carpenter's son is the anointed hero of an epic and a juvenile delinquent the protagonist of a tragedy, one wonders if the revisionism does not point away from a hieratic toward an egalitarian conception of the genres.

As these prefatory remarks attempt to indicate, the range of the following essays is expansive, their approaches diverse, the conclusions sometimes in conflict with one another. Their apparent chaos is harmonized, however, by the questions that stand behind them: what is the nature of Milton's final vision, and what can genre tell us about it? Sadly, they are also harmonized by the spirit in which they were written: in tribute to the late Joan Malory Webber, who, in *Milton and His Epic Tradition*, addressed this area of criticism with singular success. More modest in scope and achievement, these essays written in tribute to Joan Webber presume to carry on her work.

Unless otherwise noted, citations for Milton's poetry are to the Columbia edition of *The Works of John Milton*, ed. Frank Allen Patterson, 18 vols. (New York, 1931–38), hereafter cited as CM. Whenever

Whenever possible, citations for Milton's prose are to the Yale edition of *The Complete Prose Works of John Milton*, ed. Don M. Wolfe et al., 8 vols. (New Haven, 1953–82), hereafter cited as YP, and in special cases to the Columbia edition.

R. S. I. and J. W.
May 1982

NOTES

1. Quoted from the 1815 Preface to *Lyrical Ballads*, in *The Romantics on Milton: Formal Essays and Critical Asides*, ed. Joseph Wittreich (Cleveland, 1970), p. 128.

2. Quoted from *The Plain Speaker* (1826), in *The Romantics on Milton*, ed. Wittreich, p. 397.

3. See Gombrich's *Norm and Form: Studies in the Art of the Renaissance*, 2nd ed. (London, 1971), and Colie's *The Resources of Kind: Genre-Theory in the Renaissance*, ed. Barbara K. Lewalski (Berkeley and Los Angeles, 1973).

4. "The Politics of Prose and the Art of Awakening," *Glyph*, VII (1980), 134.

5. See Gasché, "The Mixture of Genres, the Mixture of Styles, and Figural Interpretation," *Glyph*, VII (1980), 124, and Fletcher, *The Transcendental Masque: An Essay on Milton's Comus* (Ithica, N.Y., 1971), pp. 80–81.

6. *Biographia Literaria*, ed. J. Shawcross, 2 vols. (London, 1907), II, 262.

7. *Validity in Interpretation* (New Haven, 1967), pp. 76–77, 82–83.

8. *Biographia Literaria*, II, 262.

9. *The Political Unconscious: Narrative as a Socially Symbolic Act* (Ithaca, N. Y., 1981), p. 141.

10. *Literature as System: Essays Toward the Theory of Literary History* (Princeton, 1971).

MILTON STUDIES
XVII

THE REIGN OF NARRATIVE
IN *PARADISE LOST*

Earl Miner

I T IS obvious that *Paradise Lost* is the great English epic, a work of poetic narrative. It is only less obvious that the dominance of narrative does not preclude the presence of other genres in so long a poem. Deliberate misreadings—those that recognize the cost involved—of Milton's poem as a drama or a lyric are well worth attempting, showing us matters that a numbed narrative reading may have missed. But the dominant failure of Milton criticism this last century or two has been its inattention to the obvious and central. In what follows, I should like to explore some significances of the fact that in *Paradise Lost* narrative rules over dramatic and lyric elements.

I. A FEW THEORETICAL MATTERS

By now we are quite familiar with the proposition that seventeenth-century English poetry mingles genres, yielding *genera mixta*.[1] To be able to know that entities are mixed presumes that they can be known as single entities. Since there are very few works that we would think belong purely to one genre, we can only assume that our conceptions of genres involve abstractions from multiple literary experiences rather than abstractions from single examples. If tragedy be considered a genre, it is a capacious one, including many English examples with comedy as opposed to French examples without comedy and, for that matter, Greek examples that end happily, although the fact is usually ignored (even if not by Aristotle). Some people will hold to a conception of tragedy derived from pagan examples and so argue that Christian tragedy is impossible. Others will accept a Christian but rule out a Buddhist possibility. There is also a tendency, which flies in the face of the evidence, to limit generic conceptions to literature. If narrative is a genre, it may be found in some kinds of historical writing, the newspaper, or ordinary conversation. If tragedy is a genre, it will also be found in history, in the newspaper, and in ordinary conversation. In short, we are talking about abstractions with cognitive import.

3

Some people would hold that every identifiable literary kind is a genre: pastoral, comedy, tragedy, epic, satire, epigram, epithalamion, confessional poem, serial literature, and so forth. That position makes sense. But the conception followed in this essay involves a well-established triadic conception of genre: narrative, drama, and lyric. These are taken to be the radical kinds, whereas the others mentioned are examples of lesser kinds. Even within Western criticism, the triadic conception is by no means inevitable.[2] Chinese critics seem to be fine-tuners, in that they take varieties of lyric poetry, even those as similar as the shih and lü-shih, to be separate genres. Such a particularizing conception tends to emphasize the differences between literary cultures. With the Chinese conception, we consider that no Western tradition has a counterpart to the ornate fu (usually translated as "rhapsodies" or "rhyme-prose"). Again, Japanese linked poetry (renga, haikai) has no counterpart in Western literature.

The chief virtue of the triadic conception is not that it allows us to find resemblances (which may well serve valuable ends). Rather, the virtue lies in the explanatory power (by the rules of parsimony and adequacy) of the conception. The triadic conception allows us to account for, at least in theory, all literary examples, if we allow for the subsidiary hypothesis of generic mingling. Another justification for the triadic conception lies in its historical explanatory power.[3] Yet a third way of justifying the conception would be to uncover evidence that a given poet thought and practiced in such terms.

Milton appears to be the first English critic, as well as poet, to conceive of genres in terms of the triad of narrative, drama, and lyric, even if his account tends less toward the descriptive and more toward the normative. In a well-known passage in *The Reason of Church-Government* he mentions "that Epick form," "those Dramatick constitutions," and "those magnifick Odes and Hymns" for which he gives classical and biblical examples (YP, I, 813–15; see also YP, II, 404–05). His biblical examples (as of the Book of Revelation for a drama or the Book of Job as an example of a brief epic) may be personal, just as may be his comparison in *The Second Defense* of himself to "the epic poet" who lauds the "heroic achievement of my countrymen" (YP, IV, 685). It is curious that he seems to restrict his conceptions of the three genres to normative examples (narrative to epic rather than romance or satire, for example) and yet that he wishes to extend the normative conceptions to works that might cause us hesitation (the Book of Revelation as drama, or prose tracts as epic). I take it that there are good theoretical and historical reasons for concerning oneself with three genres, as also that those who would rather term narrative, drama, or lyric a "mode" or "a radical of presentation" will accept the concept of narrative (as mode if not genre) and presume that a given narrative work may draw on the resources of other kinds.

II. Some Non-Narrative Elements in Paradise Lost

In the long introduction to Book IX, Milton places his epic in the line of epic ventures before him. Already, in dealing with "Things unattempted yet in Prose or Rhime" (I, 16), a typically large assertion, he has laid claim to what the later induction makes clear. He asserts nothing less than that he is writing the true epic. Yet the earlier classical and modern epics that his poem displaces are truly epics, even if inadequately true.[4] Whatever his praise of these poems in his prose or his devaluation of them in explicit passages of his poem, he never says that earlier epics are not narrative.

Milton uses the word *drama* or *dramatic* nowhere in his poetry (although the subtitle of *Samson Agonistes* is *A Dramatic Poem*). And his uses of *play* are all in the sense of pastime or sport. Yet we need only look to *L'Allegro* (or common sense?) to discover that Milton knew and thought about the other two genres.[5] Some words used very sparingly by Milton have all the greater impact when they appear. Everyone feels the force of "I now must change / Those Notes to Tragic" in the induction to Book IX of *Paradise Lost* (5–6), although—or because—that is the sole use of the word *tragic* in his poetry. Similarly, in each of his three "major" poems, and nowhere else, he has a single and highly telling use of the word *theatre(s)*. In *Paradise Lost*, the singular of the word is used to characterize Eden (IV, 141), where the agon of the poem is to be staged. In *Paradise Regained*, the plural is used (IV, 36) to distinguish the pompous architecture of Rome. In *Samson Agonistes*, the Hebrew Messenger uses the singular to describe the Philistine temple (1605) where Samson undertakes his final act. This last example is especially nice, because it presents something of the converse of the generic constellation in *Paradise Lost*. The Hebrew Messenger uses the metaphor of the theatre in a narration of what has happened offstage. But that narration is a *dramatic* convention and is dominated by dramatic usage to dramatic ends.

Most readers of *Paradise Lost* have felt that Milton draws on drama most fully when he uses dialogue in critical or heightened situations. We shall later have cause to see that Homer had done the same before anyone knew of drama, but it will be clear enough that the poet who praised Shakespeare in a poem for the second Folio and who had intended to write a tragedy on Adam unparadised (and then thought better of it) was obviously well acquainted with dramatic usages.

In this initial survey, the counterpart lyric elements in *Paradise Lost* can also be readily specified. If it is a characteristic of lyric to celebrate a moment that abates action, then the epic similes of the poem offer (as they are usually thought to do) one example of lyric subgenre. The lyric character of the similes is sometimes heightened and sometimes compromised by Milton's making some of them longer than had been usual or by his seeking out negative versions. But there is no question that we have such elements in the poem. Another range of lyric will be found in various songs, prayers, apostrophes, and tributes spoken (or sung) by all the better characters in the poem—God, the Son, the good angels, Eve, and Adam. To Milton, their lyric was clearly the unfallen genre: narrative and drama explain the Fall, or account after the Fall for human experience.

There is also another kind of passage commonly thought lyric, although to me these intrusions by the narrator are rather ambiguous as to genre. (This will require fuller attention in a later context.) Insofar as they abate the action with attention to a subjective question, they can scarcely be ruled out as lyric. Insofar as they are narrator intrusions, they must by definition attest to the fact of narrative. In practice, various intrusions, or even parts of a given example, seem to me to be felt in varying ways. Let us consider the intrusion most neglected, Milton's last in the poem:

> How didst thou grieve then, *Adam,* to behold
> The end of all thy Ofspring, end so sad,
> Depopulation; thee another Floud,
> Of tears and sorrow a Floud thee also drown'd,
> And sunk thee as thy Sons; till gently reard
> By th' Angel, on thy feet thou stoodst at last,
> Though comfortless, as when a Father mourns
> His Children, all in view destroyd at once.   (XI, 754–61)

This intrusion offers a model of the modifications and yet dominance of narrative not only in narrator interventions but also in the inductions (or prologues) to Books I, II, IV, VII, and IX. Here the abatement of the narrative, the apostrophe to Adam, and the celebration of the moment by an affected speaker all testify to lyricism. There is also an attributive generic feature in the tragedy of the scene, for if this is not dramatic tragedy it nonetheless derives from theatrical tragedy a tragic emphasis. There may also be comic and satiric features in Satan's odyssey in Book

II and in the war in heaven (especially Book VI). And these attributive features of non-narrative genres have raised important questions about *Paradise Lost* from Dryden to this day.[6] We can also observe that the intrusion by the narrator quoted above concludes with a line and a half of simile, a procedure usually thought one of the lyric elements in the poem, and even more obviously that after the first two and a half lines the intervention presents its own narrative. In such terms does Milton's use of other genres, whether in proper or attributive versions of them, affect the narrative of the poem. And in such terms also does the narrator assert his rule.

III. THE NARRATIVE IMPERIUM

It seems natural enough that narrative should rule over the dramatic and lyric elements of Milton's epics. Epic was the highest genre, and narrative was sometimes associated with kings.[7] Yet in making the narrative not just primary but also complex, Milton made it, to some extent, problematic, both (as we shall see) in terms of the purity of his narrative and of the terms of rule. To be sure, the literary pleasures offered in *L'Allegro* are largely dramatic whereas those offered in the perhaps more definitive *Il Penseroso* are principally narrative, and even *Comus* and *Samson Agonistes* are more narrative than is typical of English masques and tragedies before Milton. All the same, narrative and drama are in some sense fabled stories, mere show, of some question— just as kingship is a problematic issue for the author of *Eikonoklastes* in replying to *Eikon Basilike*. The natural response by angels in *Paradise Lost* seems to be lyric, as is shown in two crucial episodes. In *Paradise Lost*, the angels' response to God's praise of the Son for undertaking "Humiliation" and "Manhood" (III, 313–14) is "Song" (369), a paean of no short duration (372–415). Similarly, after Jesus triumphs over Satan on the pinnacle of the Temple in *Paradise Regained*, the angels "Sung Heavenly Anthems of his victory" (IV, 594), once again a long tribute (596–635). Narrative and drama represent, in a real sense, the literary resources of the fallen world. The only adequate response to the glory of God and the love of the Son for ruined humankind is the lyric of praise and thanksgiving.

To point this out is another way of making the obvious point that *Paradise Lost* would have been superfluous if Adam and Eve had not fallen. But they did fall, and narrative (not drama, as Milton learned and Dryden after him) is the appropriate genre for dealing with the Fall. For that matter, in accounting for the angels' lyric exaltation of God and the Son or of Jesus, the poet in the fallen world finds it necessary to make their "Heavenly Anthems" conform to his narrative. In Book III, the angels recall an event that has not yet been fully narrated—the Son's triumph over the rebel angels, for God (the angels sing)

> by thee threw down
> Th' aspiring Dominations: thou that day
> Thy Fathers dreadful Thunder didst not spare,
> Nor stop thy flaming Chariot wheels, that shook
> Heav'ns everlasting Frame, while o're the necks
> Thou drov'st of warring Angels disarraid.   (391–96)

The same intrusion of narrative will be found in the angels' praise of the Son in *Paradise Regained*. This phenomenon of fallen narrative ruling even in heavenly lyricism (or Satanic drama) will be found throughout Milton's epics. There are numerous enough non-narrative elements in *Paradise Lost* and *Paradise Regained*, and no doubt it would be best if hymns were all that the race required. But given our fallen state, narrative is the essential genre for Milton.

The problem therefore becomes one of sorting out narrators or kings and of assessing those parts of *Paradise Lost* that are dramatic or lyric. A glance at a concordance would show how often kings are mentioned by Milton, as also how frequently they are inadequate. The problem lies in distinguishing between rival versions of kingship or of the hierarchy of genres, just as Milton's lifetime witnessed such disputes over sovereignty. *Paradise Lost* and *Paradise Regained* are, among other things, profoundly political poems.[8] When there are rival claimants, each person must choose the true one, since salvation depends on right choice. At the close of his third *Satyre*, Donne agonized over the matter, and Bunyan's Christian, in his confrontation with Apollyon, made his choice in a way that would justly infuriate an authority presuming any other king than "King Jesus." Milton was well enough aware of the problem, and he makes the distinction for us in one of the many speech-tags in *Paradise Regained:* "So spake *Israel's* true King" (III, 441). The true king is true by virtue of legitimacy as well as by virtue of power, as Milton knew long before the world heard of political science. It is remarkable how he presumes that the creatures may ascend from their given place (see Raphael's speech on "ontology," *PL* V, 469–505) and equally noteworthy that the passage begins "O *Adam*, one Almighty is." *Paradise Lost* posits one creator, one "true King," whose creatures or subjects may rise to great place but ought never aspire to godhead, as Eve does in falling: "nor was God-head from her thought" (IX, 790).

The distinction between true and false kingship requires comparable distinctions between subsidiary narrators in *Paradise Lost*. If even the angels in their hymns offer narrative, it is all the more true that other characters narrate. It is further true that we must distinguish between these many narrators in terms of their reliability. One of the poem's most generous surrogate narrators, Raphael, takes pains to be explicit about his *ars narrandi:*

> what surmounts the reach
> Of human sense, I shall delineate so,
> By lik'ning spiritual to corporal forms,
> As may express them best, though what if Earth
> Be but the shaddow of Heav'n, and things therein
> Each to other like, more then on earth is thought?   (V, 571–76)

This famous passage on "accommodation" deals partly with the problem of narrating to a human audience, even unfallen. The corollary is that God, even if he be thought a school divine, as Pope described him, is the only fully authoritative, truly omniscient narrator. To that extent, no other narrator among the poem's characters is wholly trustworthy, and since the words of God in the poem are presented by a fallen narrator who recognizes the need for accommodation to "human sense," even his narrative may pose some problem of reliability to the strict critic.

Yet Raphael's concluding question and his phrase, "more than on earth is thought," really refer to our thoughts as readers of the narrative, since it is not clear otherwise who "on earth," other than we, can be meant. We seem to have greater access to true narrative than strictures about our fallen state would appear to allow. For Milton, the Bible is exemplary of true narrative. The "sacred penmen"—as Dryden calls Moses, the Gospel writers, and other authors of books of the Bible—offer a trustworthiness that only divine inspiration can confer. Their narration is not by God, but it is wholly trustworthy. (See Milton's very Protestant use of biblical proof-texts in *Of Christian Doctrine*.) The problem for *Paradise Lost* therefore necessarily entails our distinguishing unreliable from reliable narrators, or, in strict construction, less from more reliable narrators. In a poem so extraordinarily given to retrospection, there are as many narrators as characters. Whether making such distinctions among them is an easy or difficult matter depends on the poem's interpreters, who have not come to the same conclusions.

We may begin with Milton on himself as "interpreter & relater."

I apply'd my selfe to that resolution which *Ariosto* follow'd against the perswasions of *Bembo*, to fix all the industry and art I could unite to the adorning of my native tongue; not to make verbal curiosities the end, that were a toylsom vanity, but to be an interpreter & relater of the best and sagest things among mine own Citizens throughout this Iland in the mother dialect. (YP, I, 811–12)

The sentence can be read: I determined to write and excel in English. But Milton has anticipated any possible deconstructor by rejecting "verbal curiosities" and by claiming to act as "interpreter & relater," and indeed of "the best and sagest things."

The role of an interpreter and relater is the role of narrator. The words *interpreter* and *interpret* are used only three times in *Paradise Lost*. Satan is first user, in addressing Uriel as one "wont [God's] great authentic will / Interpreter through highest Heav'n to bring" (III, 656–57). Even if we take Satan to be dissembling—and he is—it is one of those instances when the devil speaks truth. In Book VII, Adam apostrophizes Raphael as "Divine interpreter" (72). The third instance is decisive, involving the Son's action as priest and mediator before God:

Now therefore bend thine ear
To supplication, heare his [Adam-Eve's] sighs though mute;
Unskilful with what words to pray, let mee
Interpret for him, mee his Advocate
And propitiation.   (XI, 30–34)

What follows is prophetic narrative by the Son and by God.

The word *relate* and its variants in *Paradise Lost* are fraught with greater complexity but issue in narrative certainty. The first appearance involves a familiar passage, the "Men call'd him *Mulciber*" simile (so-called), which concludes "thus they relate, / Erring" (I, 740, 746–47). The narrator, claiming to give a true relation, corrects the errancy of previous narrators. The second instance occurs toward the beginning of the last book when Michael shifts from teaching Adam by word and sight to teaching by word alone: "Henceforth what is to com I will relate" (11), so turning to prophetic narrative as the Son and God also do in another twenty lines.

Claims to truth imply possible falsifiability. The readiest exercise I know of in this regard is to read through Books I and II first attending only to what Satan says and then to read through attending to what the narrator says. Both cannot be right, and if the question hangs in balance, what follows in the poem answers it. In seeking to interpret and relate "the best and sagest things," Milton enters great claims for the reliability of his narration. His narrator invokes the same heavenly muse who was believed to have inspired Moses to write the Pentateuch (I, 6–10). The celestial light of God himself illuminates the narrator's darkness (III, 51). He names his muse—Urania, divine wisdom (VII, 1). It seems that the muse need not even be invoked, since she brings "Her nightly visitation unimplor'd" (IX, 22). Milton would have granted to God the sole title of omniscient narrator, but his assumptions about grace, faith, and regeneracy allow for an inerrant narrator of his poem. Dante's guides for his narrator are Virgil and the glorified Beatrice. Milton's guide seems to be the Holy Ghost, divine wisdom. It is not always observed that the guide for fallen but regenerate Adam and Eve is that very Providence (XII, 647) that the poem's argument asserts (I, 25).

Serious questions might be raised about Milton's claims for the reliability of his narration. How does Milton know what God said to the angels and Son before the world was created? What kind of mimesis allows him liberty to present an argument between Satan and Abdiel or the puns of Satan and Belial when they introduce artillery into the battle in heaven? It might appear that the voice to Job from the whirlwind spoke unheard by Milton.

Yet are the questions so difficult? The certainties of narration by Dante or Milton relate to the inerrancies of a Christian metaphysics. The problematics of Beckett or Borges imply another view of the world. There are also four specific matters that bear on the question: (1) In 1667 there appeared *Paradise lost. A Poem Written in Ten Books by John Milton*. This is a poem, so labelled by the author, over his name; it is not *De Doctrina Christiana*, whenever the connections between the two. (2) There is a varied but consistent tradition of Protestant English narrative in the seventeenth century that runs from Quarles to Thomas Ken's epics at the end of the century. (3) Reliable narrative requires a reliable hearer as well as relater, and both are assisted by that singular Protestant virtue, faith in grace. (4) The wide sense of narrative reliability involves the peculiar Protestant sense(s) of the inerrant literalness of Holy Scripture.

Such topics can be no more than mentioned in a chapter concerned with the more general subject of Milton's narrative. But two other, heuristic approaches can be added. One is to enter Marvell's professed uneasiness as expressed in his poem *On Paradise Lost* (prefixed to the second edition):

> The Argument
> Held me a while misdoubting his Intent,
> That he would ruine (for I saw him strong)
> The sacred Truths to Fable and old Song.[9]   (5–8)

Such distrust ends in concession: "But I am now convinc'd" (25). Another approach involves scaling down the apparent truth claims (the logicians should be allowed to enjoy the poem, too) to that moral reality that is the special province of narrative to relate and interpret. In this respect, it is not so much worth observing that God is an inadequate literary character in much of *Paradise Lost* as that we can tolerate God as a character at all or in fact know that the characterization is all serious rather than comic. One measure of the moral world or the reality that Milton creates is this: the history given in Books XI and XII exerts no greater claim to morality or reality than do the first two books, even though Books I and II include such remarkable passages as those on Sin, Death, Chaos, and Night.

Narrative rules over many dramatic passages and elements in the poem, then, by positing a reality and a moral order that are in turn founded on the reliability of the narrator relating religious matters believed true. It is worth recalling that many details in various poems by Milton's younger contemporary Dryden have been taken as representations of historical reality. Amnon's murder in *Absalom and Achitophel*, for example, is thought to reflect a covered-up homicide directed by the duke of Monmouth, and Achitophel's stated probity on the bench supposedly proves that Shaftesbury was a just judge.[10] No historical evidence has been found to establish either narrative reality. No evidence could be found in this world to establish numerous features of Milton's reality in *Paradise Lost*. Yet such concessions offer but another way of saying that narrative may establish the terms of its own reality and so carry conviction. We may long linger over what Shakespeare himself thought of the actions of the characters in his plays, and Milton's narration may similarly incorporate moments when dramatic features abate the process of narrative judgment. But those moments are part of a larger narrative in which judgment is persistent, is moral, and is constitutive of the reality of "the higher mimesis."

IV. Fallen Lyricism in Narrative

Although more particular things need be said later about certain dramatic features of *Paradise Lost*, there are also general and specific issues of lyric in the poem. The most important general issue concerns relative priorities. As we have seen, lyricism is the presumed prelapsarian genre. The morning stars sang together at the creation (Job xxxviii, 7), and once more at the birth of Jesus the angels sang (Luke ii, 13–14)—when, according to Christian legend, the music of the spheres, which had been silenced after the Fall, was briefly heard once more. As Milton explains in *At a Solemn Musick* (and in *Ode on the Morning of Christ's Nativity*), lyricism is now also fallen:

> disproportion'd sin
> Jarr'd against natures chime, and with harsh din
> Broke the fair musick that all creatures made
> To their great Lord, whose love their motion sway'd
> In perfet Diapason, whilst they stood
> In first obedience, and their state of good.   (19–24)

Yet these very lines praise solemn (fallen) music, as Milton's translations of certain Psalms honor God by representing biblical lyricism in English. The otherwise pertinent observation about the lines just quoted is, however, that they constitute a narrative.

The narrative that is a subgenre of *At a Solemn Musick* dominates in *Paradise Lost*, where Milton also deploys and exploits lyric to ends of relating and interpreting. In his epics, the lyric elements are at once numerous and quickly recognizable. Of the many examples of apostrophe in *Paradise Lost*, the two most important are the hymn to light (III, 1–55) and that to "wedded Love" (IV, 750–75), both of which contain narrative elements. Milton also makes considerable use of the set piece, or *descriptio* (a term which, like *narratio*, we owe to Cicero and the other rhetoricians, who used it with anticipations of modern meanings). Virgil's descriptions are normally introduced by formulae, such as *nox ruit* or *nox erat* in his night pieces in the *Aeneid*. The Roman poet uses such descriptions as resting points that nonetheless bear on the narrative. Sometimes the effect is consonance with the narrative (Night fell; all creatures sought rest, as did the Trojan heroes), and sometimes dissonance (It was night; all was peace—only Dido, restless in her love, and so forth). In *Paradise Lost*, Milton makes a good deal of night (the word is used a hundred times) and darkness (forty-three times). Sometimes the use is positive, especially when combined with references to the contrasting power of light: "Grateful vicissitude, like Day and Night" (VI, 8). The dominant usage, however, identifies darkness as an infernal contrast to "the sacred influence / Of light" (II, 1034–35). So strong is the identification of darkness with the infernal that a brief mention of it is likely to signal Satan on the move (for example: IV, 352–57; VI, 406–17; IX, 48–57).

The most studied of the lyrical elements in the poem are those referred to as epic similes.[11] If we accept the usual loose definition, there are perhaps fourteen similes in Book I. The usual definition is, however, not very precise, since it includes the famous "Men call'd him *Mulciber*" passage (I, 740–46), which is not properly speaking a simile at all, though it does include a simile, "Dropt from the Zenith like a falling star" (745; see also 730, another four-word simile).[12] Loosely or strictly construed, similes are most thickly sown in the first book, giving it a strong lyric subgenre, just as it and the second are also felt by readers to have a particularly strong dramatic subgenre.

The similes seldom give purely lyric repose. If Homer's similes "tend to move tangentially away from the narrative level in order to create a quiet grove from which the reader looks back on the physical action,"[13] Milton's seldom do so. A brief exception will be found in I, 708–09, but the rule is that the lyric similes that compromise the narrative are themselves usually compromised by four or five kinds of complexity. The first simile in the poem goes on for twelve lines (I, 197–208), joining elements by "or" alternatives and by adding the little narrative-in-simile of "Him haply slumbring on the *Norway* foam" and so on for five more lines. This simile is typically complicated and made complex by the introduction of a number of situations, by the recollection of earlier narratives, and by the incorporation of a miniature simile narration at its end. The best-known simile in Book I ("Thick as Autumnal Leaves," and so forth, 302–11) is also multiple in Milton's recollecting a range of similes from earlier epics.[14] It is also multiple in incorporating the narrative of the Book of Exodus within the simile. This lovely amalgam offers four of the five ways mentioned earlier by which Milton compromises the simple lyricism of his similes: multiplicity, recollection of earlier similes, recollection of narrative, and use of narrative in the simile.

The fifth technique for complicating can best be illustrated from Book I by the Mulciber passage:

> Men call'd him *Mulciber;* and how he fell
> From Heav'n, they fabl'd, thrown by angry *Jove*
> Sheer o're the Chrystal Battlements; from Morn
> To Noon he fell, from Noon to dewy eve,
> A Summers day; and with the setting Sun
> Dropt from the Zenith like a falling Star,
> On *Lemnos* th'*Aegean* Ile: thus they relate,
> Erring.   (740–46)

This passage recalls an account, a narrative, in the *Iliad* (I, 588–95) and is properly a narrative rather than a simile, although it includes a four-word simile (744), as has been observed. Yet if it is a narrative, and if it has no "as" or "like" to make it a proper simile, it has much the effect of a simile in that its narrative abates the narrative proper. We class this passage among the similes because it is a fifth kind of compromise of lyricism, what may be termed *dissimile*. Butler had published the first part of his *Hudibras* with many such dissimiles before *Paradise Lost* appeared. Milton differs from Butler, however, in using his dissimiles to distinguish between his truth and earlier falsehood: "thus they relate, / Erring." He often uses dissimile to such clarifying ends, as in the familiar gesture "to compare / Great things with small" (II, 921–22, and so forth; also small things with great). Dissimile becomes most explicit in another famous "simile," that characterizing Eden in Book IV, some seventeen lines beginning "Not that faire field / Of *Enna*" (268–84). This "simile" is multiple, it is recollective of narratives, it is narrative in some of its parts, and above all it is a dissimile. Because so many of these features belong to explicit or proper similes, it is quite natural that readers should think that an interruptive passage (however narrative or recollective) that behaves like the proper similes is itself a simile.

It is of great significance that we should think these last two examples rank with the others, that dissimiles without explicit signs of comparison should be thought to belong to the class of similes. For they make plain what otherwise would be missed: the similes testify to the presence of the narrator. Someone is *telling* that "thus they relate, / Erring," that the previous earthly paradises do not bear comparison with the true one, and that small things are being compared to great. This feature, this *factor* in the Latin sense, governs that other important class of passages we feel to have lyric quality—narrator intrusions, Milton's (or his narrator's) interruptions of the actions. To take but one example, the "hymn to Light" opening Book III contains a dozen first-person pronouns as well as narrative passages (for example, 9–12). Such lyric passages (the introduction to Book IX is another important example) bid us attend (in both the French and English senses) to the narrator. In short, the most lyric passages assert the truthfulness of the narrator and therefore the dominance of narrative in *Paradise Lost*.[15]

Other elements in the poem have also been thought lyric. One such is the pastoral. It seems likely that many of the instances given are probably georgic, as the next century would discover and explore. But in any case, Hobbes, Marvell, and Dryden seem to have assumed that pastoral is narrative rather than lyric in nature.[16] Yet there are pastoral passages in *Paradise Lost* that anyone would consider lyric, such as Eve's beautiful love song to Adam (IV, 639–56); I make no claims for the view of women immediately preceding.

> With thee conversing I forget all time,
> All seasons and thir change, all please alike.
> Sweet is the breath of morn, her rising sweet,

With charm of earliest Birds; pleasant the Sun
When first on this delightful Land he spreads
His orient Beams, on herb, tree, fruit, and flour.
Glistring with dew; fragrant the fertil earth
After soft showers; and sweet the coming on
Of grateful Eevning milde, then silent Night
With this her solemn Bird and this fair Moon,
And these the Gemms of Heav'n, her starrie train:
But neither breath of Morn when she ascends
With charm of earliest Birds, nor rising Sun
On this delightful land, nor herb, fruit, floure,
Glistring with dew, nor fragrance after showers,
Nor grateful Eevning mild, nor silent Night
With this her solemn Bird, nor walk by Moon,
Or glittering Starr-light without thee is sweet.

Like the angels' song to God and the Son in Book III, these lines present in fallen narrative a version of prelapsarian lyricism. It is the highest moment of human lyricism in the entire poem. Eve's "conversing" with Adam means "living together; commerce; intercourse, society, intimacy." The word Eve uses also implies our modern sense of talking together and foreshadows "sexual intercourse or intimacy" (definitions from the Oxford English Dictionary, s.v. "conversation"). This is to say that her lyric refers in narrative fashion to the little time she has had with Adam ("I forget all time") and forecasts the "wedded Love" hailed by the narrator. If we doubted that this lovely lyric serves the interests of narrative, we should recall that her forgetting all time involves her singing of the only time she has known, the diurnal. She twice runs through (641–49, 650–56) a lyric narrative of a day from dawn to night. Just as the similes incorporate narrative to make them merge with the dominant narrative of the poem, so does this beautiful song, both in Eve's recollecting time as she forgets it and in the implication of what she says about "conversing" with Adam.

The other major lyric passage not assumed by previous categories is the description of Eden earlier in Book IV (214–68). Too lengthy for quotation, it obviously owes much to other descriptions of the earthly paradise or *locus amoenus*.[17] The passage begins in narrative fashion: "in this pleasant soile / His farre more pleasant Garden God ordaind" (214–15). This statement is a dissimile for what immediately precedes—Satan's desecration of the scene in Eden. It is narrator comment such as the interjection "and next to Life / Our Death the Tree of knowledge grew fast by, / Knowledge of Good bought dear by knowing ill" (220–22).

In what we may term the first sentence of this description (214–22, including the passages just quoted), we are given in proper psychological fashion an initial cognitive grasp of the whole. The verbs are static (e.g., "stood," "grew"), the perception general, holistic. In what may be termed the next sentence (223–46), Milton sets the scene into motion, as if we were observing the vitality, the narrative of what we had hitherto taken in as a static, lyric picture. He switches, therefore, to active verbs: "went," "pass'd," "thrown," "Rose," "fell," "Runs divers, wandring," "Rowling," "Ran," "visiting," "Powrd," "smote," and others of like effect. The sense of action gives the lyric description a narrative cast. The rest of the description maintains the active verbs but involves the different senses successively until finally we are unable to say which sense or senses are activated:

> The Birds thir quire apply; aires, vernal aires,
> Breathing the smell of field and grove, attune
> The trembling leaves, while Universal *Pan*
> Knit with the *Graces* and the *Hours* in dance
> Led on th'Eternal Spring.   (264–68)

Sound is smell and smell is sound in a lyric that eases into narrative: Pan knits with the Graces and the Hours (giving time, place, and actors in action—the usual constituents of narrative), and the narrator's presence is asserted by the past tense: "*Knit* with the Graces," "*Led* on th'Eternal Spring."

If the dominance of narrative were not clear from this ending after that beginning, we should recall that this description presents what we are led by the narrator to see (hear, smell, feel) as Satan sees from his vantage point while he gazes on the garden in the guise of a cormorant perched, as the narrator tells us, "on the Tree of Life, / The middle Tree and highest there that grew" (194–95). This position, this place is at once typological and proleptic in Milton's narrative. The "middle Tree" is a type of the cross on which the Son of God was crucified between two thieves, the tree that would bring the race salvation. From the examples just given, it can be seen that the undoubted lyricism of this *descriptio* enriches rather than compromises the narrative of the poem. In all such extended lyric passages, Milton takes deliberate measures, as he does in his similes and in Eve's song, to ensure that lyricism be subordinated to narrative.

V. DRAMA AND THE NEW NARRATIVE OF PARADISE LOST

The inconsistencies of a great critic illuminate serious issues. In his life of Waller, Dr. Johnson stigmatized poetry on sacred subjects: nothing can be said that is both true and new, and there is always the risk of blasphemy. Given such warnings, or apprehensions, it is of great significance that in his life of Milton Johnson does not raise the issue. He might have thought Milton a vile Whig; he might find the pastoral of *Lycidas* too simple, too hackneyed, and therefore distasteful; he might indeed prefer to praise *Paradise Regained*, in an age that extolled *Samson Agonistes* while slighting Milton's brief epic. But Johnson's preferences also show that what he could not abide in Waller's lyrics or depreciated in Milton's "Dramatick Poem," he nonetheless found acceptable in narrative. This inconsistency can be taken to testify to a consistent prejudice in favor of narrative as a means of dealing with sacred matters. And it can also be taken as testimony to the integration (and subordination) of dramatic elements into narrative by Milton in a fashion that is new.

Homer and Thucydides taught subsequent Western writers of narrative an art unifying speech and action, a *lexis* and *praxis* essential to each other and to narrative integrity. The *Iliad* represents the copybook model of unity with such means, the *Odyssey* gives a more episodic example, and the *Aeneid* of course offers something of each. Erich Auerbach seems very right in his analysis of the styles and foregrounding of Homer (as opposed to the more paratactic style of the Bible with its background of the divine),[18] but already in the *Odyssey* we observe that retrospective narration like Odysseus' in Phaeacia gives more backgrounding than does simple narration, and with the change comes greater emphasis upon psychological states, even if Homer seems almost unaware of any formulation other than those of the role of Athene and telling of one's past. Virgil's increase in psychological concern involves earlier use of retrospection and (showing that he understood its potential), in particular possibilities of applying the Odyssean procedure to romantic love. (So Eve recalls her brief past for Adam.) Virgil also takes a hint from Tiresias' prophecy of Odysseus' end in Book XI of the *Odyssey* to give a full-scale prophecy of Roman and world history as then understood (Book VI). In each case, the future is learned in the underworld and does not seem to belong to the light of day. Milton learned many ways of handling and of reinforcing these classical ends of narrative from Ovid, Italian Renaissance poets, Spenser, Cowley, and others. But his new narrative, which stands in a fresh relation to drama as well as to lyric, essentially poises the classical means and ends with biblical means and ends, so that its techniques, somewhat like his angels, "when they please / Can either Sex assume, or both" (I, 424–25).

To simplify in the terms of the passage given earlier from *The*

Reason of Church-Government, in becoming an "interpreter & relater of the best and sagest things," Milton followed the classical patterns of narrative in the style and method that he used as relater, whereas he followed the biblical patterns as interpreter both of best things and all things important, constantly insisting on discrimination—by drawing on biblical authority—of what is real, what true. As relater, he retains, he even exaggerates, many features of classical epic narrative. As interpreter, he constantly brings classical presumptions into biblical order, as the accounts of Mammon and of Eden have shown in dissimiles.

A few examples will show what Milton is up to. His use of overlying "levels" of retrospection over present-order narrative far exceeds that in the *Odyssey* and *Aeneid* in both proportion and complexity. When Satan and Abdiel offer rival narrative retrospections on their past, their narratives are presented as being told by Raphael to Adam, and the presenter is of course the general narrator of the poem. As we have seen, even the lyric moments—similes, authorial intrusions, Eve's song—are given their own narrative elements by incorporating allusions to earlier narratives and subordinating lyricism to narrative. Before Book IX, each (as it were) present narrative seems set in some other narrative. Milton managed clarity here only by extraordinary control, that is, by commitment to the ends of biblical narrative. The biblical end somewhat diminishes the psychological potentiality of so much retrospection, but his handling was as necessary to render everything intelligible as the retrospection was to include everything important. Analysis of the opening lines of the poem for their use of parataxis and hypotaxis would show how much the ordering within little (the "style") is identical to that within great (the "structure").

Whereas to Homer and Virgil prophecy belongs to underworld scenes, Milton makes it part of divine revelation. It is from God (in Book III) that the angels learn that humankind will fall—and ultimately have grace to be redeemed. The major "historical prophecy" comes, moreover, not toward the middle of the poem, as in the *Odyssey* and the *Aeneid,* but at the close. Milton's millenarian and political hopes had suffered, but this made the ends of prophecy and apocalypse the more important for being delayed.[19] Milton honors the convention of the descent to the underworld in typical fashion—overdoing it (two books instead of one, at the beginning instead of at the middle) and ultimately dismissing it (there is no good, no truth to be found there). Echoes of the *Odyssey,* verbal and allusive, are strongest in the first two books. If we can trust Gillies and Bishop Newton, parallels to the *Aeneid* continue to the end of the poem, probably because it has always been easier to moralize (interpret) Virgil than the Homeric poems. (Gillies extracted from Thomas Newton's three-volume edition, London, 1749–52.) In any event, these commentators notice not a single echo of either Homeric poem in the last three books. Milton's poem has many principles of organization, but this displacement and enlargement of the classical middle part of prophecy is a central one, and from that displacement Milton derived another. The second half of his poem begins, as does the Bible, with Creation, and it ends, as does the Bible, with a vision of apocalypse. There are many other orderings in the poem besides these, but these will illustrate some of the ways Milton has interpreted the classical relaters.

A last example of the renovation of epic narrative shows Milton's debt to the moderns: Eve's importance. Here again, Milton honors the classics—Helen, Dido, Cleopatra are precedents. But he gives Eve an importance such as only the modern poets had been willing to concede women. And her importance transcends that of earlier epics to the extent that Books IX and X constitute an Eviad. She is first to sin. She is first to recover humility, penitence, and that charity for Adam that gives them hope and faith as well. More striking perhaps even than that, given epic tradition, it is Eve who makes the last speech in the poem (XII, 610–23).

This new narrative could only make a different use of dramatic elements than had earlier epic narrative. Two important instances will show the strong measures Milton devised to control, to direct dramatic elements to his ends. A set of other examples will show how he sometimes allows drama to exert a powerful counterforce that only the strength of his narration can direct.

The two examples of rigorous narrative control are those from sections often thought particularly dramatic: among various possibilities, there are the speeches in Book I and the encounter of Satan with Sin and Death in Book II. Book I has seven speeches of no little length. Five are by Satan (84–124, 157–91, 242–70, 315–30, 622–62) and two by Beelzebub (128–55, 272–82). These are long and affective speeches, but "when all is said" they make up only just over one line in four in Book I, constituting but 221 lines out of the 798 in the book. The rest, with some lyric elements, is predominantly narrative.

It is easier to anatomize the example in Book II, because it is briefer. Satan's encounter with Sin and Death takes up about 242 lines (II, 648–889). Once again there are seven speeches, all but one much shorter than those in Book 1, and the narrator's comments between them are also far briefer. Since the speeches constitute some 157 lines of dialogue, they take up a far higher proportion of the whole passage than the speeches in Book I. Here is the pattern:

		Narrator:	648–80 (33 ll.)
1.	Satan to Death:		681–87 (7 ll.)
		Narrator:	688 (1 l.)
2.	Death to Satan:		689–703 (15 ll.)
		Narrator:	704–26 (23 ll.)
3.	Sin to Satan:		727–34 (8 ll.)
		Narrator:	735–36 (2 ll.)
4.	Satan to Sin:		737–45 (9 ll.)
		Narrator:	745 (1 l.)
5.	Sin to Satan:		746–814 (69 ll.)
		Narrator:	815–16 (2 ll.)
6.	Satan to Sin and Death:		817–44 (28 ll.)
		Narrator:	845–49 (5 ll.)
7.	Sin to Satan:		850–70 (21 ll.)
		Narrator:	871–79 (9 ll.)

The longest speech, the fifth, by Sin, provides what might be regarded as the basis for a little drama of recognition and reversal. By it Satan is led to recognize Sin as his daughter and wife and to change his tune about the foulness of her and their offspring Death. This feature of the episode combines with such others as the shorter speeches to give a genuine dramatic effect within the narrative. But its drama is appreciably reduced, or rather controlled, by virtue of the fact that Sin's long speech is a retrospective narration.

In *Paradise Lost*, Milton also drew upon drama in a way that ran higher risks for higher stakes. Since his actions deal with choice, he must supply adequate motivation, and since the main choices in the poem are to do wrong, he must convey the psychology of error. For most of the poem, he draws on resources that are dominantly narrative. But as perhaps has not been noted, he also uses a series of equivalents of the villain's soliloquy as it was practiced in English drama. The purpose of the convention is to reveal evil intention, the psychology behind an act or an omission to act where one should. Anyone will recall such familiar examples as Claudius in *Hamlet* (III.iii), Iago in *Othello* (I.iii), and Mosca in *Volpone* (III.i).

Of the passages resembling soliloquies, the one best known in that guise is also the first and longest, Satan's apostrophe to the sun and meditation on his condition, resolving, "Evil be thou my Good," and on his ambition to hurt God by seducing Adam and Eve (Book IV). This

long passage, following hard upon the narrator's intrusion at the beginning of Book IV (1–31), covers lines 33 to 113. Satan has two other
soliloquies in Book IV. The next (358–92) exclaims over the impressive-
ness of Adam and Eve and their world, presenting his envy by an ironic
offer of concord:

> League with you I seek,
> And mutual amitie so streight, so close,
> That I with you must dwell, or you with me
> Henceforth.   (375–78)

He would not, he says, do what he is about to, except that (as the
narrator comments immediately after) he excuses his evil "with necessi-
tie, / The Tyrants plea" (393–94). In Satan's third soliloquy (505–35), he
reacts with jealousy, prurience, and insatiable lust to the sight of Adam
and Eve embracing. He has overheard them, learned about the interdicted tree, and by such means resolves to gain revenge. It is remarkable that these three soliloquies make a treble pattern. Each makes
known to us the evil psychology behind Satan's actions. In sequence,
the soliloquies grow shorter, as if we are approaching some climax. And
the three differ by virtue of distinguishing temporal emphasis. The first
is distinguished by its emphasis of the past, the second the present, and
the third the future (although the elements exist in all three). Such
patterns order the strong dramatic force of these passages in the larger
pattern of the new narrative.

The soliloquies in Book IV are but half those in the poem, since
there are three in Book IX. In the first of these, Satan responds to the
sight of Eve working alone, at first abstracted "From his own evil, and
for the time . . . Stupidly good" (464–65). But when he muses, it is
with the purpose of clarifying his resolution to act "her ruin" (493). The
other two soliloquies of the book introduce the motives of two other
characters, Eve and Adam, and their soliloquies come at exactly parallel moments. Having been led to the forbidden tree, having told Satan
that it was expressly interdicted, she yields to his lies and persuasions
enough to muse to herself (745–79). She dwells on Satan's central lie:
that he is the serpent (actually, he is only the intelligent soul informing
the serpent); that he has eaten the fruit; and that that has raised him as
supposed serpent from the lower order of animals to the human level
of speech. By analogy, a human creature eating the fruit might aspire
to grand status indeed—if the logic were not false at each step. And so
she eats the fruit, the sign of disobedience. Adam's soliloquy comes at
a comparable moment (806–16). When Eve returns with the fruit and

guile, he sees at once what has happened. He knows the issues involved. Yet he makes clear that he is motivated to do wrong, knowing it to a degree that deceived Eve could not. So he also sins. The parallelism of their two soliloquies generates narrative pattern in sequence, but that pattern is at variance from the pattern of Satanic soliloquy continued into Book IX, and so in this book we feel a very powerful dramatic energy being brought into the narrative. Had we not come so far in the poem, did we not have the previous eight books bearing on this one, that energy might well put the narrative strength at hazard. As it is, it makes a fitting climax to a poem beginning, "Of Mans First Disobedience, and the Fruit [sic] / Of that Forbidden Tree."

The soliloquies offer Milton some of the resources of drama to illuminate the motives of characters. Of course speeches and actions also reveal motives, but often less directly. In any event, the soliloquy is a chief means by which Milton conveys intent to do evil—repeatedly by Satan, momentously by Eve and then Adam. When people mean to do good in *Paradise Lost*, they either do it or speak to others of doing it. To that extent, the quasidramatic soliloquies offer a potential for evil grounded in and enclosed by a narrative of speech and action. Ironically, the dramatic soliloquies closely resemble those passages in which the narrator is most self-insistent as to his being narrator. The dramatic is poised against the lyric in *Paradise Lost* to do the service of the new narrative.

Milton was to renovate yet farther in *Paradise Regained*. The poem is not my present concern, but a remark or two concerning it will cast a final light on certain elements in the narrative of *Paradise Lost*. The brief epic has far less retrospection, and much of its action consists of the Son doing the same thing over and over while Satan does different things. Both features simplify the narrative, making the biblical features in it more prominent by far than in *Paradise Lost*. The terms on which drama and lyric are employed also differ, and among the distinctions is the use of soliloquy. In *Paradise Regained* the convention adapted is that of the hero's, not the villain's, soliloquy. The first example is a speech by the Son (I, 196–293), the second one by Mary (II, 66–104). Again the soliloquies give an account of motivation, an "account" because they are far more narrative in cast than the soliloquies in *Paradise Lost*. And since they show goodness, there is a reversal of the balance in *Paradise Lost* that made soliloquy suspect, while action and speech might be good things. For many such reasons, *Paradise Regained* is, as they say, another story. In it Milton continued as interpreter and relater of best things to levy as if for tribute on the resources of other genres for the narrative imperium.

Princeton University

NOTES

I wish to record my gratitude to William Brennan and Michael Seidel for their comments on an earlier version of this essay; their assistance has been material.

1. Rosalie Colie has done most to instruct us in the prevalence of generic mixture in seventeenth-century writing. See *"My Ecchoing Song": Andrew Marvell's Poetry of Criticism* (Princeton, 1970); *The Resources of Kind: Genre-Theory in the Renaissance*, ed. Barbara K. Lewalski (Berkeley and Los Angeles, 1973); and *Shakespeare's Living Art* (Princeton, 1974).

2. The best acount of traditional Western concepts of genre and their vicissitudes is surely that by Irene Behrens, *Die Lehre von der Einteilung der Dichtkunst*, in *Beihefte zur Zeitschrift für romanische Philologie*, XCII (Halle, 1940).

3. As I have tried to show in an essay "On the Genesis and Development of Poetic Systems," *Critical Inquiry*, V (1979), 339–53, 553–68. This also relates to the next paragraph of this chapter.

4. This old subject has been well renovated by Joan Malory Webber, *Milton and His Epic Tradition* (Seattle, 1979), and by Francis C. Blessington, *"Paradise Lost" and the Classical Epic* (Boston, 1979).

5. *L'Allegro* mentions "mask" (128), Jonson (132), and Shakespeare (133), as also shortly thereafter the lyric—"*Lydian* Aires." There are a few uses of the word *lyric* in Milton's verse and a very large number of references to *song(s)* and *air(s)*.

6. Seeking to "take Mr. Rymer's work out of his hands," that is, to forestall the great reductionist's promise to demolish Milton, Dryden enters criticism that *PL* is unprecedentedly tragic: the "event [outcome] is not prosperous, like that of all other epic works" (*Of Dramatic Poesy and Other Critical Essays*, ed. George Watson, 2 vols. [London, 1962], II, 84.) He enters other criticisms but justifies Milton as another Homer. For a recent view of Renaissance theory, see John M. Steadman, *Epic and Tragic Structure in "Paradise Lost"* (Chicago, 1976).

7. Of course the topos of narrative as king, prince, or monarch is but one version for any kind of poet, including the lyric poet, as Carew's conclusion to his elegy on Donne shows in Milton's time.

8. Even if he is not aware of some other important matters, Christopher Hill has shown that political considerations cannot be disregarded as integral features of the poem in his *Milton and the English Revolution* (London, 1977).

9. CM, II, Pt. 1, p. 3, ll. 5–8.

10. As I have discussed in "The Higher Mimesis," pp. 343–64, in *The Restoration Mode from Milton to Dryden* (Princeton, 1974).

11. Some readers seem to feel that the entire presentation of Eden is fundamentally lyric in nature. There are, however, excellent studies showing its narrative quality. See A.

Bartlett Giamatti, *The Earthly Paradise and Renaissance Epic* (New Haven, 1966); Harry Levin, *The Myth of the Golden Age in the Renaissance* (Bloomington, Ind., 1966; Joseph E. Duncan, *Milton's Earthly Paradise: A Historical Study of Eden* (Minneapolis, 1972); and of course, on the topic of the *locus amoenus*, E. R. Curtius, *European Literature and the Latin Middle Ages* (Princeton, 1967).

12. The best detailing of the similes of which I know is that in the index (sig. S6ʳ–7ᵛ) of John Gillies' edition, *Milton's "Paradise Lost,"* 2d ed. (London, 1793). He does not include the Mulciber passage as a simile.

13. From an unpublished essay by Joseph L. Greenberg, "The Simile in *Paradise Lost.*"

14. Editors refer to Homer, Bacchylides, Virgil, Dante, and Tasso.

15. On "Milton's presence in the poem," see William G. Riggs, *The Christian Poet in "Paradise Lost"* (Berkeley and Los Angeles, 1972).

16. For Hobbes, see his "Answer to Davenant" in *Critical Essays of the Seventeenth Century*, ed. J. E. Springarn, 3 vols. (Bloomington, Ind., 1957), II, 55; for Marvell, see *Upon Appleton House* and stanzas 4–6 of *The Garden*. For Dryden, see "The Dedication of the Pastorals" (of Virgil) in *The Poems of John Dryden*, ed. James Kinsley, 4 vols. (Oxford, 1958), II, 870–71, and also *To the Dutchess of Ormonde* and *To My Honour'd Kinsman* in *Fables*, IV, 1463–67, 1529–35.

17. See n. 11.

18. *Mimesis* (Princeton, 1953), especially the first chapter.

19. In his *Visionary Poetics: Milton's Tradition and His Legacy* (San Marino, Calif., 1979), Joseph Wittreich has recovered prophecy as a central Miltonic concern.

IN MEDIAS RES
IN PARADISE LOST

O. B. Hardison, Jr.

N ORMALLY, OUR efforts to understand the artistic motives of Renaissance poets are based on conjecture. Historical criticism attempts to fill gaps in our knowledge by pointing to influences that affect a given work, but our uncertainty is often increased by the very process that seeks to reduce it. As the number of possible influences grows, how do we decide which influence is the most important? In the case of *Paradise Lost*, however, the historical record is unusually clear. We know a good deal about Milton's reasons for beginning *Paradise Lost* where he did, and this information provides several useful insights into the motives that determined the poem's final shape.

In medias res is the familiar prescription given by Horace for beginning an epic poem. It is usually considered no more than that—a formula that eventually led to a standard literary convention. We know, however, that the formula is closely related in classical literary criticism to the problem of poetic unity. We also know from Milton's numerous references to Aristotle and Horace that he was thoroughly familiar with the *Poetics* and the *Ars Poetica*, as well as with the efforts of Renaissance critics to reduce these works to a series of rules for various genres.[1]

In addition to our knowledge of Milton's interest in critical theory, we have direct evidence that he considered several points of entry into his material before he decided to begin *Paradise Lost* with the demonic conclave. This evidence can be supplemented with the less firm but still considerable information concerning the stages in the composition of the poem offered by Allan Gilbert in *On the Composition of "Paradise Lost."*[2]

I

In Chapter VIII of the *Poetics*, Aristotle discusses the problem of unity. He is primarily interested in tragedy, but he approaches tragedy in terms of epic. The best epic plots, he believes, are those which have the same tightly unified structure as tragic plots. Poets identified by Aristotle as "cyclic" produced loosely unified poems which he illustrates by citing cradle-to-grave celebrations of heroes like Hercules and Theseus. Homer

27

showed what proper epic plots should be: "In producing the *Odyssey* he
did not make it concern all that happened to Odysseus, e.g. his being
wounded on Parnassus or pretending to be mad. . . . Instead he constructed the *Odyssey* and similarly the *Iliad* around one action."[3] Later
(XVII), Aristotle summarizes the plot of the *Odyssey*. The plot is limited
to the return of Odysseus, from his departure from Calypso's island to the
time when he slays the suitors and is reunited with Penelope. "Everthing
else," says Aristotle, "is episode." By episode Aristotle means something
like "digressive episode." Evidently, the story of the wanderings of Odysseus, which occupies four books of the *Odyssey* (IX–XII), is a case in
point. Later still, in Chapter XXIV of the *Poetics*, we are told that such
digressive episodes are proper to epic, lending it a characteristic grandeur
and variety. In sum, Aristotle recommends that the epic have a short,
tightly unified frame plot based on a small segment of a larger story with
extended digressive episodes used as ornament. He does not use a Greek
phrase equivalent to the Latin *in medias res*, but the corollary of his
remarks about the *Odyssey* is that the epic poet *must* begin "in the
middle" of his story and introduce prior events and secondary actions
through the "episodes."

Memories of these ideas linger in the *Ars Poetica*. Horace places
great emphasis on the need for a proper beginning. He contrasts
Homer's method of beginning to the lame opening line of an anonymous
cyclic poet. The cyclic poet begins by promising to "sing the fate of
Priam and the famous Trojan war." Evidently this is a poor beginning
because it promises two actions, one of them (the fate of Priam) personal
and tragic and the other (the Trojan War) social and heroic. The poet's
object, says Horace, should be "to fetch light from smoke, not smoke
from a flash of light." This leads to a more general comment on poetic
beginnings:

The epic poet does not date the return of Diomedes from the death of Maleager
or the Trojan war from Leda's twin egg. He hastens to the climax and catches
the reader in the midst of the events as though they were already familiar. What
he cannot make brilliant he omits and he uses fiction and mixes the false with
the true so that the middle is consistent with the beginning and the end with the
middle.[4]

Long after Horace's death, medieval and Renaissance scholiasts glossed
these observations in various, often inconsistent ways. Since epic and
tragedy were both supposed to be based on history, it was conventional to cite *in medias res* as a distinction between the poet and the
historian. The historian was supposed to use chronological, or "natural"

order (*ordo naturalis*), while the poet used "artificial" order (*ordo artificialis*) and, in the words of Rudolphus Agricola, "usually re-arranges events and begins in the middle and then brings in prior events by the device of a character or some comment or other."[5] In his "Letter to Raleigh" explaining *The Faerie Queene*, Edmund Spenser summarizes this distinction:

The Methode of a Poet historical is not such, as of an Historiographer. For an Historiographer discourseth of affayres orderly as they were donne, accounting as well the times as the actions, but a Poet thrusteth into the middest, even where it most concerneth him, and there recoursing to the thinges forepaste, and divining of thinges to come, maketh a pleasing Analysis of all.[6]

Milton, of course, knew this tradition thoroughly. In *Of Education* he commends "that sublime art which in *Aristotles Poetics*, in *Horace*, and in the *Italian* commentaries of *Castelvetro, Tasso, Mazzoni*, and others, teaches what the laws are of a true *Epic* poem, what of a *Dramatic*, what of a *Lyric* . . ." (YP, II, 404–05). In *The Reason of Church-Government* Milton balances the laws and rules of the critics against the idea that the poet should follow nature, an option to which he had alluded long before in his image of Shakespeare warbling "his native woodnotes wild" ("L'Allegro," 133) in contrast to the learned Ben Jonson. He asks whether in epic poetry "the rules of *Aristotle* herein are strictly to be kept, or nature to be follow'd, which in them that know art, and use judgement is no transgression, but an inriching of art" (YP, I, 813).[7] This is a liberal, almost an anticlassical position. Twelve years later, in *The Second Defense*, Milton sounds much more classical. Paraphrasing *Poetics*, Chapter VIII, he announces that the epic poet, if he adheres strictly to established rules, "undertakes to extol, not the whole life of the hero whom he proposes to celebrate in his verse, but usually one event of his life (the exploits of Achilles at Troy, let us say, or the return of Ulysses, or the arrival of Aeneas in Italy) and passes over the rest" (YP, IV, i, 685). Finally, in the argument to Book I of *Paradise Lost*, Milton explains, "the Poem hasts into the midst of things, presenting *Satan with his Angels now fallen into Hell*." "Hasts into the midst of things" is simply a slightly modified quotation from memory of Horace's *festinat et in medias res*.

II

To relate Milton's theory to his practice, we need first to establish an approximate chronological sequence for the major events in the poem. The initiating event is God's elevation of Christ, which Milton witholds until Book V of *Paradise Lost*. Christ's elevation leads to Satan's rebellion and the War in Heaven (Books V–VI) and the fall of Satan (Books VI, I). While the bad angels are falling toward Hell, the Creation occurs (Book VII) and evidently the creation of man and Adam's earliest experiences (Book VIII). The demonic conclave (Books I–II) leads to Satan's flight to earth (Books II–III), which is simultaneous with the debate between God and Christ (Book III). With Satan's arrival (Book IV) the story settles down to a straightforward action extending from the nuptials of Adam and Eve to the expulsion. There is one long interruption (Books V–VIII) devoted mostly to retrospective narrative and one inversion (Michael's prophecy of human history, Books XI–XII). I consider this an inversion because it precedes rather than follows the expulsion from the garden. Clearly we are dealing with a quite sophisticated manipulation of a fairly simple set of events.

I will call the complete sequence of events from the elevation of Christ to the Last Judgment Milton's *inclusive plot*. Most of the inclusive plot is told by narrators who are also dramatic characters, but three episodes—the demonic conclave, the debate in Heaven, and Satan's return to Hell to announce his victory—are presented by the epic poet himself. At the same time that *Paradise Lost* has an inclusive plot, the convention of *in medias res* gives it what I will call a *dramatic plot*. This is its plot in the Aristotelian sense endorsed by Milton in *The Second Defense*. The dramatic plot centers on a "particular action" in the life of the hero—the Fall—and extends from the entry of Satan into the newly created world to the expulsion. Material from the inclusive plot is introduced into the dramatic plot by Milton's characters, and because this material is part of a "particular action" it becomes functional in the dramatic plot. For example, Raphael's story of the War in Heaven provides interesting historical information, but its dramatic function is to instruct Adam in the need for obedience. Again, Michael's prophecy (Books XI–XII), which C. S. Lewis once called an "untransmuted lump of futurity,"[8] is explicitly identified in the poem as a form of consolation for Adam after the Fall.

As far as the convention of *in medias res* is concerned, any action except the elevation of Christ would have been a suitable point of entry into the story. If Milton had followed Aristotle or a Renaissance critic like Girolamo Vida, he might have begun late in the story, perhaps after the Fall had occurred. On the other hand, if he had followed Spenser he might have begun with the War in Heaven, the second event, while reserving the first event, the elevation of Christ, for a "discovery" scene at the very end. Given the varieties of Renaissance critical theory, the precedents of Homer and Virgil could have been cited to justify almost any episode between these extremes.[9]

One other theoretical consideration. All Renaissance critics who discuss the problem of epic unity, including advocates of romantic epic like Cinthio and Tasso, as well as the Aristotelians, agree that epic needs a central action to which all secondary episodes are ultimately related.[10] In other words, as far as Renaissance criticism is concerned, what I have called the inclusive plot should always be subordinate to the dramatic plot. We know from the opening lines of *Paradise Lost* that Milton's "particular action" is "Mans First Disobedience, and the Fruit / Of that Forbidden Tree." This being the case, Milton's decision to begin with the demonic conclave and the debate in Heaven of Books I through III is something of an anomaly. The episodes in Books I through III are not subordinated to the dramatic plot as is the narrative of the War in Heaven. They are not recounted by a character in the dramatic plot, nor do they have any functional relation to Adam's experience, since Adam never hears of them. They are narrated by the inspired poet and are addressed directly to the reader. They are episodes that Aristotle would have called "outside of the action"—a prelude to it but not part of it. In addition, unlike most of the rest of *Paradise Lost,* Books I and II are fictional in the sense that they are not based on scriptural history or a well-defined literary tradition.

I will return to this point later. For now I will only point out that the practical result of beginning with Satan and his cohorts in Hell has been a long history of confusion about who the hero of the poem really is, which is ultimately a confusion about whether Milton was writing to narrate the trials of Adam or to glorify Satan. Since Milton deliberated long and chose late, I think it is reasonable to assume that these problems occurred to him long before they were debated by critics: that he eventually decided to begin with Satan in spite of the obvious liabilities and inconsistencies inherent in this approach.

III

To turn now from theory to history, we have considerable information concerning the various places in the story that Milton at one time considered appropriate points of entry. This evidence underscores the close relation between tragedy and epic in Aristotle's—and in Milton's— thought and also does much to explain the prominence of tragic elements in the completed poem, observed, for example, by James Holly Hanford, Helen Gardner, and Arthur Barker.[11]

One important piece of evidence comes from Milton's nephew Edward Phillips. In the biography of Milton which he published in 1694, Phillips wrote: "The subject was first designed a tragedy, and in the fourth book of the poem there are six verses, which several years before the poem was begun, were shown to me and some others, as designed for the very beginning of the said tragedy."[12] Phillips quotes not six but ten lines from the soliloquy of Satan at the beginning of Book IV, beginning "O thou that with surpassing glory crown'd." Whether Phillips' reference is to a time before or after the outline of tragedies in the Trinity manuscript was made will probably never be known.[13] What is important is that at an early stage in Milton's thinking about the literary possibilities of the Fall, he chose as his "very beginning" the lines that introduce what I have called his dramatic plot.

The choice is a natural one. Beginning with this soliloquy moves us directly toward the major crisis of the plot—the temptation. It also ensures that any parts of the inclusive plot introduced later will be subordinate to the dramatic plot. This would be true by definition in a tragedy, where the poet speaks only through characters; it would also be true, though to a lesser degree, in what ancient and Renaissance critics called the "mixed" form of epic, which involves narration by the author as well as speeches by characters.

Satan's soliloquy is just that. It is a true soliloquy. It is not a defiant oration but an anguished private expression of doubt, torment, resentment, and, ultimately, defiance born out of despair. There is nothing quite like it in Greek or Senecan drama. Allan Gilbert remarks, "Satan's address to the sun in *Paradise Lost* IV, 32–41, could not have been the beginning of a formal prologue like that of ['Adam unparadiz'd']. It is rather a plunge directly into the action more violent than that beginning *Samson Agonistes*" (p. 17). Helen Gardner is therefore right, I think, in looking not to ancient drama but to the Elizabethans for its antecedents. Choosing *Macbeth*, *Dr. Faustus*, and *The Changeling* as typical dramas of tormented villainy, she writes: "It is not suggested that . . . when Milton drew his Satan he had one of these great tragic figures in mind. What is suggested is that Satan belongs to their company, and if we ask where the idea of damnation was handled with seriousness and intensity in English literature before Milton, we can only reply: on the tragic stage."[14]

I would add to this point that there is a structural as well as a psychological link between Milton's projected tragedy and the Elizabethan theater. Several Elizabethan plays begin with soliloquies by villainous characters, *The Jew of Malta* and *Richard III* being two obvious examples. Although I agree that the content of Satan's soliloquy is closer to *Macbeth* than *Richard III*, the opening strategy of the work described by Phillips resembles *Richard III*, which, incidentally, is one of the few Shakespeare plays directly quoted by Milton.[15]

The conclusion suggested by these observations is that at an early stage in his thinking, Milton saw the Fall in terms of Elizabethan tragedy. Since the word *revenge* is repeatedly used by Satan and his cohorts to explain their motive,[16] we can be more specific. The genre closest to Milton's intention is the revenge play. The play Milton seems to have had in mind would have been simpler than an Elizabethan play. It would have presented a psychologically complex, tormented antagonist pitted against an innocent and sympathetic protagonist, and the success of the antagonist would have been balanced against his own damnation and the eventual salvation of his victim. Whether the form would have been classical or Elizabethan is beyond saying, but it is surely worth remembering that when Milton referred to Aristotle's rules in 1642, he immediately added that following nature was "no transgression, but an inriching of art." Evidently he was keeping an open mind regarding nonclassical form. At any rate, we know from Arthur Barker's study of the structure of *Paradise Lost* that Milton's interest in tragedy extended as far as the first edition of *Paradise Lost*, which was in ten books having a five-act structure rather than the more conventional twelve books created by Milton's revisions in the second edition of the poem.

Although Milton evidently was interested in Elizabethan drama, there is no doubt that classical form and the "rules of Aristotle" exerted an equal or greater fascination. The evidence for this is the series of four outlines in the Trinity manuscript which Milton made for dramas on the Fall. Critics have generally lumped Phillips' comment with the Trinity outlines as evidence of Milton's interest in a dramatic version of the Fall. But if the evidence is taken seriously, the Trinity outlines can be seen to point to a kind of drama somewhat different from the revenge play suggested by Phillips. In the first place, Phillips is quite explicit in stating that Satan's soliloquy was to be the "very beginning" of the tragedy he discussed with Milton. In none of the Trinity outlines does Satan appear at the beginning, and in the last two, which are the only two with sufficient detail to allow firm conclusions, Satan does not appear until the third act.

All four outlines begin with a prologue spoken by a divine agent. In the first three, the prologue is followed by characters representing divine concern for man—"Heavenly Love" or the allegorical figures of Justice and Mercy are to initiate the action. The point of entry of the first three Trinity dramas thus corresponds not to the beginning of Book

IV of *Paradise Lost* but to the debate between God and Christ at the beginning of Book III.

"Adam unparadiz'd" is the most detailed of the outlines. Gabriel serves as prologue and begins the play with an evidently lengthy description of Paradise. The chorus then appears to show "the reason of [Gabriel's] comming to keep his watch in Paradise after Lucifers rebellion" (CM, XVIII, 231). The chorus's references in Act I to "Lucifers rebellion" would have to be brief, since the chorus is required to sing "of the battell, & victorie in heavn against [Satan], & his accomplices" after Act II. The emphasis of the first act of this version of the play, therefore, would have to be on Gabriel's description of Paradise—in other words, material corresponding to passages in the middle of Book IV of the finished poem. The beauty of the garden would be untouched by the sinister figure of Satan, because Satan does not begin the play. In fact, he is not allowed to enter the outline of "Adam unparadiz'd" as a character until Act II. Although Lucifer explicitly states that he "seeks revenge" in his first speech, the form and general effect of this version are quite different from that of the revenge play remembered by Phillips. Second, and very striking I think, the heart of the revenge play and of what we have in the finished poem is missing in the Trinity outlines. The first outline includes the serpent in the cast of characters, but after this all traces of the temptation scene disappear. In the third outline Satan appears in Act III "contriving Adam's ruin," and by Act IV the Fall has already occurred. In "Adam unparadiz'd," when Adam and Eve first appear in Act III they are represented as "having by this time bin seduc't by the serpent" (CM, XVIII, 231). Thereafter they quarrel, are shown the future of the race by Mercy, and leave the garden reconciled to their fate. The dramatic action of "Adam unparadiz'd" is thus focused on the material which appears in *Paradise Lost* from the end of Book IX to Book XII.

This is such a startling fact that one wonders why more has not been made of it. Gilbert attributes it to Milton's reluctance to present a serpent onstage. Perhaps, but he showed no reluctance about bringing Comus and his half-bestial followers onto the stage at Ludlow Castle. A better explanation is the Horatian decree that exceptionally violent or shocking actions should occur offstage, an injunction that Milton scrupulously followed in *Samson Agonistes*. Only a determination to be thoroughly classical and to follow "Aristotle's (and Horace's) rules" can explain why Milton would have banished the most intensely dramatic moments of the Fall from his proposed drama.[17]

Third, "Aristotle's rules" called in the seventeenth century for observance of the unities of time, place, and action—and for the use of prologue and dramatic chorus. Elizabethan drama was under no such constraints. A play in the Elizabethan mold could have begun directly with Satan's soliloquy (skipping the prologue); it could have presented the temptation and Fall onstage; it could have moved freely in space and time; and it could have minimized or done without a chorus.

What the Trinity manuscript therefore shows is that Milton considered four classicizing (i.e., non-Elizabethan) dramas on the Fall. They were not similar to the revenge play suggested by Phillips' comment; they were alternatives to it. Elements of morality play and masque can be found in the Trinity outlines. The only element conspicuous by its absence is precisely the element suggested by Phillips and found lingering in the finished poem by Helen Gardner—the Elizabethan revenge tragedy.

To return to *in medias res*, it is clear that Milton considered three points of entry into his material—Satan's arrival in the newly created world, now part of Book IV (the Phillips version); a debate on man's destiny resembling the debate between God and Christ now part of Book III (the early Trinity outlines); and a description of Paradise *sans* Satan, now part of Book IV (the Trinity outline titled "Adam unparadiz'd"). The first point of entry is associated with a straightforward dramatic presentation of the Fall and heavily influenced by the tradition of the revenge play. The second and third are associated with a more formal and classical treatment of the theme and have the effect of emphasizing the ultimate goodness of man's fate rather than creating suspense by emphasizing his peril. All three points of entry rest solidly on Scripture. They are free elaborations, but they are not inventions. The first and third are developed out of scriptural history, while the second, the debate on man's ultimate fate, dramatizes scriptural theology and is based on the convention of the debate of the Daughters of God going back to the Middle Ages.

Yet instead of choosing one of these points of entry, Milton eventually rejected them all. In their place he created two books which are fictional in the sense that they are neither based on Scripture nor are they dramatizations of scriptural theology.[18] Milton could have defended this practice by citing Horace's advice to "use fiction and mix the false with the true," but the *Ars Poetica* hardly explains why he chose to exercise poetic license at such a critical moment as the poem's first episode.

To review this history is to be impressed with the fact that nothing we know of Milton's plans implies the demonic conclave. Here we move from hard evidence to conjecture. In *On the Composition of "Paradise Lost,"* Allan Gilbert argues that *Paradise Lost* took shape in several stages.[19] Its earliest form after it was recast from dramatic to epic form was chronological rather than artificial. That is, it began with the first episode of the inclusive plot, the elevation of Christ, and continued with the War in Heaven and the Creation. At a later date Milton came to feel that the chronological version was loose in structure. He therefore revised it by moving the War in Heaven and the creation to their present location in the middle of the poem and adding the demonic conclave, Books I and II.

The chronological poem that Gilbert describes is so far from "Aristotle's rules" and Milton's own poetic tendencies that I seriously doubt whether it ever existed. Whether it existed or not, however, at some point before the creation of Books I and II the action of Milton's poem must have resembled the revenge tragedy suggested by Phillips, presented now in the "mixed form" of epic narrative and expanded with the "episodes" which according to Aristotle lend epic its special gradeur and variety. It might have begun with Satan; more probably, it began with the debate in heaven. The point is that it was complete: it followed "Aristotle's rules"; it began *in medias res;* it included a representation of the temptation and Fall; and it had the unity commended by Milton when he wrote that "the epic poet, who adheres to all the rules of that species of composition, undertakes to extol, not the whole life of the hero whom he proposes to celebrate in his verse, but usually one event of his life" (YP, IV, i, 685). Why was the demonic conclave necessary at all?

IV

We have reviewed the liabilities involved in Books I and II. The demonic conclave diverts attention from the main action, the Fall; it is fictional, rather than a free variation on scriptural sources; it is narrated by the poet rather than by a character in the dramatic plot; and, as we know from sad experience, it invites confusion about the status of Satan in the poem. The obvious question is what Milton gained by it that was important enough to offset its liabilities.

It would be easy to explain Books I and II in terms of their splendid imagery and their ability to engage the reader's interest, but I suspect that these explanations may be too easy—that the imagery and the play on reader psychology are by-products of revision rather than basic motives.

The primary difference between Milton's earlier plans and *Paradise*

Lost as we now have it is that all of the earlier plans begin with assertions of divine goodness or power. This is obvious in the case of the dramatic outlines that begin with speeches by Heavenly Love, or Justice and Mercy, or with a description of Paradise. Note that it is also true of the tragedy which Phillips recalled that began with Satan's soliloquy. The end of the passage which Phillips quotes is as follows:

> to thee I call,
> But with no friendly voice, and add thy name
> O Sun, to tell thee how I hate thy beams
> That bring to my remembrance from what state
> I fell, how glorious once above thy Spheare;
> Till Pride and worse Ambition threw me down
> Warring in Heav'n against Heav'ns matchless King.   (IV, 35–41)

This is not an expression of heroic defiance. It is a confession. The Satan of these lines is closer to Shakespeare's anguished Claudius than to the defiant rebel of Books I and II. He is sympathetic, but he is sympathetic because he admits the major premise of the Christian view of the poem: that he fell because of his own "Pride and worse Ambition," and that God is "Heav'ns matchless King." In other words, Satan admits that this fall was deserved, that God is good, and that God is all-powerful.

A speech of this sort would be a superbly effective beginning for a tragedy limited to the visible world. I doubt that Milton at any stage planned to limit himself entirely to the visible world, but certainly when he decided on an epic rather than a tragedy he did so with the intention of exploiting fully what Renaissance critics usually called "the Christian marvelous."[20]

We are dealing here with much more than a pretty convention. A poem that moves between the invisible and the visible world offers two perspectives. What Aeneas experiences as a bad storm, for example, becomes, when we move to the invisible world, an episode in a long-standing feud between the gods. In *Paradise Lost* the perspective of the invisible world is more important than that in the *Aeneid* by exactly the degree to which the actions of Milton's Christian God command more authority than the actions of pagan deities.

This is the crux of the problem created by Milton's material. *Paradise Lost* is committed to two perspectives, and both of them are valid. According to the first, the divine perspective, God is "matchless"—that is, omniscient, omnipotent, and benign. From this perspective evil is a part of God's larger plan for creation. The worst that evil can accomplish is the Fall, which we eventually recognize as a Fortunate Fall rather

than an unqualified victory of evil over good. This perspective is dramatized by Milton in the debate between God and Christ, in the humiliat-
ing defeat of the rebellious angels, in Satan's soliloquy and in his progressively more degraded disguises, and in numerous other passages. As
Belial tells his cohorts in Hell, from the divine perspective the efforts of
the fallen angels are futile, almost trivial:

> he from heav'ns hight
> All these our motions vain, sees and derides;
> Not more Almighty to resist our might
> Than wise to frustrate all our plots and wiles.   (II, 190–93)

From the limited perspective of human history, however, evil is anything but trivial. It is powerful. It threatens at every moment to gain a
decisive advantage over good. Milton lived through enough history to
recognize this in fact as well as in theory, and his experience is distilled
in Michael's gloomy resumé of human experience in Book XII: "so shall
the World goe on, / To good malignant, to bad men benigne" (537–38).

In an extremely perceptive article William McQueen points out
that the two perspectives in *Paradise Lost* are antithetical.[21] According
to the first, God is omnipotent and evil is weak. Belial rightly fears that
the fallen angels may not appear menacing, only ridiculous. At the same
time, evil as experienced is terrifying. The easy optimism of "God's in
his heaven, all's right with the world" would be fatal to *Paradise Lost* if
it cancelled our sense of the dark presence of evil in human history and
human experience.

Seen in these terms, Milton's problem was almost the reverse of
what it is usually considered to be. He did not want, either consciously
or unconsciously, to make a hero out of Satan, but at the same time he
could not allow Satan to be weak or insignificant. All of the early plans
concerning which we have any evidence, however, diminish Satan
either by emphasizing divine power and love or by beginning with a
Satan who honors God as "Heav'ns matchless King" and confesses to
"Pride and worse Ambition." If Allan Gilbert's chronological epic ever
existed, it compounded the problem by beginning with the elevation of
Christ and the ignominious defeat of the rebel angels.

The conclusion to which we are led by these observations is that the
basic function of Books I and II—and the reason why Milton needed
them in spite of their liabilities—is to make Satan a credible example of
evil by offsetting the later episodes which stress God's supreme and
benign power. To do this, Milton isolated Satan and his followers in a
Hell separate from earth and in some sense opposite to Heaven. Admit-

tedly, Milton was not entirely consistent. At times in the first two books the voice of the narrator reminds us that Satan is not all-powerful, that his "dark designs" will ultimately serve God's plan. In spite of these intrusions, however, the predominant effect is splendidly, almost embarrassingly successful. An image of titanic vitality and heroic perseverance is created at the outset of the poem which remains with the reader until the closing lines. It is so powerful that for many readers it has overshadowed the later passages emphasizing Satan's weakness.

In sum, Milton could not resolve the contradiction between the invisible power of God and the visible power of evil. He could only arrange *Paradise Lost* so that both elements would exist in the poem in something like a balance. To do this, he presented the inherently weaker elements, the characters symbolizing evil, first, and in a setting where their weakness would not be immediately exposed. Only after the image of evil was firmly established did he introduce characters representing the power of God, and he delayed the War in Heaven, which ends with the open defeat of evil, until Books V and VI.

Milton's problem was not keeping Satan under control but creating an effective symbol of evil in a poem that proclaims the omnipotence of God and the ultimate redemption of fallen man. He solved it by a creative and, I think, an artistically daring use of the convention of *in medias res*. At the very beginning of his poem he drew on Horace's license to use fiction and mix "the false with the true so that the middle is consistent with the beginning and the end with the middle." In doing this he also succeeded in the difficult task set by Horace for the epic poet. In Ben Jonson's translation:

> He thinks not now to give you smoak from light
> But light from smoak, that he may draw his bright
> Wonders after.

The Folger Shakespeare Library

NOTES

1. Cf. Marvin T. Herrick, *The Fusion of Horatian and Aristotelian Literary Criticism, 1531–1555* (Urbana, 1946). Milton's critical theory is analyzed and the important passages are collected in Ida Langdon, *Milton's Theory of Poetry and Fine Art* (New Haven, 1924).

2. Chapel Hill, 1947.

3. I have used the translation by Kenneth Telford (Chicago, 1965). For my own interpretation of these and related passages, see Leon Golden and O. B. Hardison, Jr., *Aristotle's Poetics for Students of Literature* (Englewood Cliffs, N.J., 1968). The key chapters for epic unity are VIII, XVII, XXIII, and XXIV. Aristotle is remarkably consistent on the subject, even to the extent of repeating key ideas and phrases.

4. Horace, *Opera Omnia*, ed. Hans Farber (Munich, n.d.), pp. 146–52.

5. *De dialectica disciplina* (Louvain, 1515), fol. b viv: "plerumque perturbat eas [res] atque a mediis orditur rebus: deinde quae primae fuerant carminum: posterius personae colore alicuius aut alio quovis commento infert mentionem . . . iam videmus contrarium naturali: id est artificialem ordinem esse. . . . Historie cuius prima laus est veritas: naturalis ordo convenit." Cf. comment on this distinction in Bernard Weinberg, *A History of Literary Criticism in the Italian Renaissance*, 2 vols. (Chicago, 1961), I, 40–43.

6. Spenser's *Faerie Queene*, ed. J. C. Smith, 2 vols. (Oxford, 1909), II, 486.

7. The art/nature contrast is evident in Milton's well-known contrast between "Jonson's learned sock" and "sweetest Shakespear fancies childe" in *L'Allegro*, 132–33 (cited in the text); and also in the verses Milton contributed to the Second Folio: "whilst to th' shame of slow-endeavoring art, / Thy easie numbers flow" (*Of Shakespear* [9–10]).

8. *A Preface to "Paradise Lost"* (New York, 1960), p. 129.

9. Classical precedent is confusing. The *Odyssey* and the *Aeneid* clearly begin *in medias res*. The *Iliad* is ambiguous. The *Pharsalia* and the *Thebaid* are chronological. Vida and Spenser, along with Ariosto, followed Horace. Trissino not only wrote *Italia Liberata dai Gotti* in "the order of nature" but argued in his introduction that he was following the precedent of Homer's *Iliad* and that this procedure was quite in accord with the *Poetics*. Cf. Gilbert, *On the Composition of "Paradise Lost,"* pp. 59–61. For Vida, see A. S. Cook, *The Art of Poetry* (Boston, 1892), pp. 39–156.

10. In the special case of a chronological epic like *Italia Liberata* the inclusive plot is identical with the dramatic plot.

11. Gardner, "Milton's Satan and the Theme of Damnation in Elizabethan Tragedy," in *Essays and Studies*, N.S. I (1948), 46–66; Barker, "Structural Pattern in *Paradise Lost*," *PQ*, XXVIII (1949), 16–30. Cf. also Hanford, "The Dramatic Element in *Paradise Lost*," *SP*, XIV (1917), 178–95; W. A. Wright, *Facsimile of the Manuscript of Milton's Minor Poems* (Cambridge, 1890); and Gilbert, *On the Composition of "Paradise Lost,"* pp. 11–26. I have used *The Student's Milton*, ed. Frank A. Patterson (New York, 1947) for the text of Phillips' *Life*.

12. *Student's Milton*, p. xl.

13. Hanford, *A Milton Handbook* (New York, 1946, p. 187), suggests merely "circa 1642." Gilbert argues that the tragedy described by Phillips came after the Trinity outlines and calls it the "Fifth tragedy" (*On the Composition of "Paradise Lost,"* pp. 21–23). If we consider the Phillips tragedy as an alternative to the Trinity outlines, Phillips' reference could be to a time before or after them. The Trinity manuscripts are printed in CM, XVIII, 228–45. "Adam unparadiz'd" is on pp. 231–32.

14. "Milton's Satan," as reprinted in Arthur Barker, ed., *Milton: Modern Essays in Criticism* (Oxford, 1965), p. 208. Compare Gilbert, *On the Composition of "Paradise Lost,"* pp. 17, 20–21.

15. In *Eikonoklastes* (YP, III, 361–62), as an example of villainous hypocrisy.

16. E.g., *PL*, I, 35, 107, 148, 170; II, 107, 330; IV, 386; IX, 168, 171; X, 374. The word *revenge* is used ten times in Books I and II, and twenty-one times in the poem as a whole.

17. Cf. Gilbert, *On the Composition of "Paradise Lost,"* p. 22: "To write a dramatic

Paradise Lost without showing the taking of the fruit seems like playing around the main action without actually touching it . . . It may be that in the last plan [i.e., Gilbert's "Plan Five," the Phillips tragedy] the serpent did again come on the stage."

18. There are numerous "demonic councils" in the poems of the "celestial cycle" which are analogues for the council in *PL*, but they are not sanctioned by Scripture as are the arrival of Satan in Paradise or the theology of redemption dramatized by the debate of the Daughters of God. They are free inventions. Milton drew extensively on literary tradition in Books I and II. At the same time, his treatment is unique in both its setting and its combination of details. Discomfort with the "fictional" quality of the demonic conclave has a long history and was expressed, for example, by Defoe in the eighteenth and Coleridge in the nineteenth century.

19. Cf. esp. pp. 101–06, and the charts showing the order of composition and disposition of materials, pp. 85–87 and 152–55.

20. The primary source for this idea in the later Renaissance is Tasso's *Discourses on the Heroic Poem* (1594). See Allan Gilbert, *Literary Criticism: Plato to Dryden* (New York, 1940), pp. 478–81. Also, Weinberg, *History of Literary Criticism*, II, index, s.v. "marvelous."

21. "Point of View in *Paradise Lost*," in *Renaissance Papers*, ed. Peter G. Phialas (Chapel Hill, N.C., 1968), pp. 85–92. Compare Gilbert, *On the Composition of "Paradise Lost*," p. 74; and Coleridge, *Lectures on Shakespeare* (London, 1951), p. 185.

"ALL ANGELIC NATURES JOINED IN ONE": EPIC CONVENTION AND PROPHETIC INTERIORITY IN THE COUNCIL SCENES OF *PARADISE LOST*

Joseph Wittreich

> Every epic contains prophecy.
> —Joan Malory Webber

"**I** HAD READ Book II of *Paradise Lost* a great many times before I fully understood the infernal debate,"[1] C. S. Lewis confided to an earlier generation of Miltonists, in a context that would secure for the poem a central place within the venerable tradition of epic. Still, the fullness of Lewis' understanding is achieved quite apart from a scrutiny of this particular epic convention, of its counterparts in both classical and Christian literature, and quite apart, too, from a recognition that epic is a *mixed kind* which from Milton's point of view finds its subsuming form in prophecy. Milton's efforts, always, are directed toward bursting the boundaries of received forms; in *Paradise Lost*, those efforts express themselves in the intention to make this poem "not less an epic, but more than an epic"—as A. S. P. Woodhouse explains, to create "a theodicy" along the lines of "Christian revelation."[2] In the process, an epic undertaking is absorbed into a prophetic vision, with the consequence that the conventions of one genre become adjusted, sometimes radically so, to fit the purpose of another.

The generic experiment of *Paradise Lost* finds clarification in *Paradise Regained*. Lyric odes and epics, tragedies no less than orations—all are now construed to be "false, or little else but dreams, / Conjectures, fancies built on nothing firm" (IV, 257–61, 291–92). "*Greece* from us these Arts deriv'd," says Jesus, and so "Ill imitated" them that whereas Christian song teaches the virtues, classical song teaches the "vices" of its deities. The highest order of Christian song, for Jesus, is prophecy, which better teaches "Then all the Oratory of *Greece* and *Rome* . . . /

43

What makes a Nation happy, and keeps it so, / What ruins kingdoms, and lays Cities flat" (IV, 356–63). In such passages, *Paradise Regained* simply brings out of concealment a set of aesthetic suppositions it shares with *Paradise Lost*. In *Paradise Lost* Satan is portrayed as a perverter of prophecy who, as he tells his cohorts, seeks "Deliverance for us all" (II, 464); and they, in turn, are represented as the progenitors of heroic song, "sing[ing] / With notes Angelical to many a Harp / Their own Heroic deeds" (II, 548–49). A poem that for so many has seemed to exalt Satan at God's expense, to be bent upon exposing the virtues of the former, the vices of the latter, through a clever sleight of hand reverses the direction of its classical antecedents so as to hymn the praises and proclaim the virtues of a deity who is the true agent in man's deliverance, the real instigator of heroic song.

All the literary forms, the disfiguration of which continues through the reign of classical literature, are absorbed into, exist in their purified state within, the genre of Christian prophecy. Prophecy, not epic, is the containing form of *Paradise Lost*. As with theological, so with literary systems: they are produced and propounded, according to *De Doctrina Christiana*, as part of an effort to achieve "further purification," with Milton's attempts at restoring the genres being paralleled here by "the process of restoring religion to something of its pure original state" and so wiping away tyrannical systems, religious no less than aesthetic, from human life and the human mind (YP, VI, 117–18).

Prophecy, as represented by the Book of Revelation and as understood by its Renaissance commentators, offers the best analogy for the generic merger attempted and achieved in *Paradise Lost*. In comparison with epic and tragedy, both of which had become enmeshed by rule, prophecy was a relatively unfettered form and, ideologically more like oratory, had the capacity to uproot the old and implant new ideas, to advance mankind beyond what was current and bring it closer to ideal existence. The Apocalypse, as Heinrich Bullinger anatomizes it, was both an oration and a prophecy and so was structured according to the principles of both genres (others had set forth the visionary design of that prophecy; hence Bullinger proceeds to explain its rhetorical procedures and organization).[3] Yet Bullinger, like most other of his contemporaries, perceives the epical character of that book, representing as it does a great swath of history reaching from the First to the Second Coming—a book that was finally, as Milton himself allowed, "the majestick image of a high and stately Tragedy" (YP, III, i, 238); was acknowledged to be such not only by David Pareus (the authority whom Milton cites) but by thinkers ranging from Bernardo Ochino and Jean

Baptista van der Noot in the sixteenth to Henry More in seventeenth century.[4] As a prophecy shaped according to the Revelation model, then, *Paradise Lost* would be a mixed-genre poem containing a sequence of visions, along with an oration, a "great Argument" (I, 24), folded into and explanatory of those visions, which, epic in their dimension, would also be here tragic there comedic in both design and implications. *Paradise Lost* would be, therefore, the great epic of history, ranging from the Creation to Apocalypse, but with its accents (they would change in *Paradise Regained*) striking the tragedy of history: the fall of Satan, the fall of Adam, the Fall of every man. The swirl of that history would be inward.

As *prophetic* history, *Paradise Lost* would use the outward, chronicled events of world history to explore the interior life, the spiritual history of every man. Sometimes sheer opposites, epic and prophecy eventually are reconceived as contraries, and their convergence, especially during the Renaissance, signals a new orientation for heroic song. The tug is now inward; the field of inquiry, the human mind. Tasso, in attempting to redeem his poem from its critics, devised a mind-centered allegory through which he may have anticipated the psychological orientation of Milton's poem, and Spenser, by portraying Arthur and Gloriana through an array of figures surrounding them, surely anticipates one of Milton's most important yet unstudied strategies of character delineation. Yet each of these seeming advances within the epic tradition is actually an aspect of the generic convergence involving epic and prophecy, of a convergence wherein the conventions of one genre become modified under the pressures exerted by another.

Milton's handling of the traditional epic council scene illustrates the point: here he exploits a narrative device for character delineation, in the process interiorizing and psychologizing a convention of epic poetry so as to make it integral and responsive to the demands of prophetic song. "It was by means of his infernal council," says Mason Hammond, "that the transformation of *Paradise Lost* to the epic form was accomplished."[5] I am arguing otherwise: that by means of both the infernal council of Book II and the heavenly council of Book III *Paradise Lost* achieves its prophetic character. "The origins of Satan, considered as the universal personification of evil," according to Arturo Graf, "are far less epic and at the same time far more remote and profound. Satan is anterior . . . ; he did not fall headlong from heaven, but leaped forth from the abysses of the human soul."[6] The major Christian texts for the evolution of his character are prophetic in nature; within the province of prophecy, Graf might have argued, Satan achieves fullness of being. In

the course of my own argument, I shall examine not only the consequences of allowing prophecy to invade epic and modify its conventions
by intensifying a latency within them ("epic has consistently turned
inward," says Joan Webber)[7] but the implications of Milton's reverting
to prophecy in the first place, especially to the Revelation prophecy of
St. John which possesses natural affinities with Milton's poem.

I

What we have within, that only can
we see without.
—Samuel Taylor Coleridge

In the pairing of his council scenes, infernal and divine, Milton has
juxtaposed the matter of classical antiquity and of Christianity—through
a shorthand, as it were, has created emblems of the generic confrontation between epic and prophecy that occurs within his poem. The councils of the gods in both the *Iliad* and the *Aeneid* establish a pattern, as
well as provide much of the machinery, for such scenes in later poetry.
While in *Paradise Lost* many conventions of epic are eroded or ex-
ploded, this one is held intact, its external features observed even as it is
being transformed from within.

The surprisingly little attention accorded the convention of the epic
council has yielded this much information about it.[8] There are two kinds
of scenes, active and deliberative, in epic poetry. Council scenes typify
the latter and, as in Books II and III of *Paradise Lost*, may be balanced
against the former: the council scene in hell paired with Satan's flight
though Chaos in the first instance, and the corresponding scene in
Heaven juxtaposed with his flight through air. The effect of such scenes
is to relax the intensity of action, to induce contemplation, and thereby
to improve apprehension of the main action (as happens with God's
council in Book III) or even sometimes to instigate that action (as happens in Satan's council of Book II).

These moments of reflection in epic poetry tend to be allegorical
centers as well, with, for example, Belial, Mammon, and Moloch em-
blematizing the master categories of sin (lust, avarice, and pride, respectively), or the Father and Son dividing the justice and mercy of deity
between them. Yet here in *Paradise Lost* such scenes, intensely emblematic but never monolithically simple, are perhaps more exactly, like
those in Dante's *Inferno*, "*quasi*-allegorical, or conceived," as Coleridge
explains, "in analogy to pure allegory."[9] In *Paradise Lost*, such scenes
are sublime allegories wherein literal and figurative levels are both

meaningful, responding respectively to the claims of narration and characterization, and wherein allegorical personages become so strongly individualized that they take on the character of symbols, do so by exhausting allegory in order that they may become figures. Owing to these scenes, then, Milton's poem is remarkably richer in symbolic significance—is so because it fully realizes that "the nature of allegory or emblem requires continuity," according to Johann Gottfried Herder's principle: first, that "every part of the emblem shows us that it is not an insulated, but a general, connecting symbol" and second that if the allegory to which it pertains "is not a whole it is lost."[10] In the council scenes, both in Hell and Heaven, there is an unceasing reference of all thoughts and all characters to the figure—either of Satan or God—in whom they will terminate.

Henry Boyd understood something of this when, by way of illuminating Milton's genius, he suggested that the devils in *Paradise Lost* are "pictures of human nature, or at least of human passions, personified with aggravated features indeed, but still preserving their original lineaments." Boyd acknowledges as well that his "observations" about Satan and those about his associates are to some extent interchangeable: "As the first impulse came from him, and he may be said to have given them all a certain tincture of his own character: This similarity will enable us to apply, in a certain sense to *him*, what we shall further remark with regard to *them*."[11] The portraits of the devils in council are thus mutually reflective and illuminating, bodying forth the inward state of their speakers but also revealing Satan by giving external form to the malignancy of his will. Milton may have no biblical authority for the council scene per se, but he has some precedent for this particular assemblage of devils in dramatizations of both Christ's temptation and the Harrowing of Hell, where customarily Satan, Belial, and Beelzebub all appear. In its divine gatherings, the Book of Revelation, of course, provides a sanction for the council scene in Heaven.

Traditionally such council scenes are highly structured according to a pattern that proceeds from an opening speech into a debate marked by images of contention and division toward a conclusion or resolution.[12] Thus the infernal council in *Paradise Lost* commences with an opening speech given to Satan, continues with a debate whose chief spokesmen are Moloch, Belial, and Mammon and whose divisions of opinion are figured by "blustring winds" and the "hoarse cadence" of the sea (II, 286–87). Beelzebub brings the debate to resolution by appointing Satan the protagonist of the undertaking, by raising him "Above his fellows" in glory (II, 428). The debate thus ends where it began—within Satan:

"The Consultation begun, *Satan debates* . . ." (II, Argument; my italics). The implied strategy here is that of Virgil in the tenth book of his *Aeneid* where Venus and Juno, the participants in the debate, are used to reveal the turmoil in the mind of Jupiter. So in *Paradise Lost,* in both Books II and III, internal debate, the arena for which is first Satan's mind, then God's, is exteriorized, and here, as in *The Aeneid,* the element of prophecy is introduced: the council scene is occasioned by as well as responsive to a situation arising out of a prophecy fulfilled or about to be fulfilled. There is that "ancient Prophesie" of a new world: "To find out the truth of this Prophesie, and what to determin thereon he [Satan] refers to full Councel" (*PL* I, Argument). Beyond these features is the Homeric device of pairing, for purposes of contrasting, a human and divine assembly, the first ending in contention, the second in harmony. Such contrasting parallels are analogous to Milton's wherein an accumulation of details defines differences between Hell and Heaven, God and Satan, and as Don Cameron Allen has noticed, in the Homeric epics especially are to be found multiple "counterparts" for Milton's demonic heroes, whose speeches resemble those their literary ancestors made in Troy.[13]

In his council scenes, then, Milton "has followed a well established Epic Tradition,"[14] but has also modified that convention in accordance with the dictates of prophetic song. Epic tradition supplies the convention, provides the device, but prophetic tradition determines the use of that convention, activates the device. The council scenes in *Paradise Lost* constitute a still point, but not a silence, in the poem: ostensibly instigating action, advancing narrative, they actually (far more important) reveal character by fragmenting it into its component parts; they are revelations of God and Satan—objectifications of inner turmoil and emblems of mental divisions, as well as explorations through God and Satan of the nature of good and evil. As early as Homer, a function of the council scene had been character delineation, but not until Milton is that function exercised so prominently or so probingly in order to reveal, as C. S. Lewis might put it, "the emergence of mental facts into allegory" as well as the fact that the gods "died into allegory" and that allegory, in turn, became a means for painting their "inner world."[15]

On the logic that pagan heroes and deities are equivalents of Christian villains and demons, the assembly of gods in the classical epic provides the prototype for the infernal councils of Christian epic, important manifestations of which are the council scenes in the Gospel of Nicodemus and in the hexameral literature of the Middle Ages and early Renaissance. By the time of Milton, such scenes, often personifying vices and allegorizing qualities or states of mind, have become fixtures of epic poetry, yet within *Paradise Lost,* as Burton O. Kurth observes, this "set piece . . . is brought into full perspective as an essential element, not as a convenient piece of epic machinery,"[16] Here all the gods of antiquity are distributed between and summed up in God and Satan. Tasso may have pointed the way in his allegorization of *Gerusalemme Liberata* by insisting that his devils "are both a figure, and a thing figured"—and Camoens, too, by presenting a set of symbolic gods who, as C. M. Bowra has explained, "figure different activities of one supreme God . . . even aspects of Him."[17] Only incidentally a function of plot now, the council scene has become chiefly a device for characterization, for mental exploration—for interiorizing the space of epic poetry so as to create, by extending its boundaries, landscapes of the mind. Even as such scenes have acquired this new significance, they have maintained their historical importance of foreshadowing events in the life of Christ, in this instance of both his First and Second Comings, by representing within a demonic perspective all the ironies that attend upon a scrutiny of Satan's motives in the light of Christ's. Man-slaying is "the end of all Sathans Counsels"; man–saving, the end of Christ's.[18] Literarily modeled on the council scenes of precursor epics, the infernal council as represented by Milton is itself the precursor of all such scenes in history when "Gray-headed men and grave, with Warriours mixt, / Assemble, and Harangues are heard" from which "violence / Proceeded, and oppression, and Sword-law" (XI, 662–73).

The strategies of John's Apocalypse have particularly profound consequences on the formation and function of such scenes in *Paradise Lost* and *Paradise Regained,* moving the convention in directions only hinted at by Virgil's use of it in the *Aeneid.* As to why the Apocalypse should have so important a bearing here, it is worth remembering, first, why it had such a commanding hold on the imagination of Milton going back to the time of *Lycidas* and, second, what its natural affinities are with a poem whose intentions and objectives are to assert "Eternal Providence, / And justifie the wayes of God to men" (I, 24–25); to show God, "whose wisdom had ordain'd / Good out of evil to create" (VII, 186–87), with "Good / Still overcoming evil, and by small / Accomplishing great things" (XII, 565–67). Like its scriptural antecedent, *Paradise Lost* responds to a world turned upside down by Satanic forces that hope "out of good still to find means of evil" (I, 165) and, in travesty of God, expect "great things of small . . . [to] create" (II, 258, 260). It is a poem, though, which like St. John's persists in its hope that such a "world shall burn, and from her ashes spring / New heav'n and earth . . . golden days, fruitful of golden deeds, / With joy and love triumphing, and fair truth" (III, 334–38).

Herder reminded another century that "every Christian poet has drawn from this source [i.e., the Book of Revelation]: . . . we may trace its hallowed sounds through Dante, Petrarch, [and] Milton" especially— and incidentally suggested why: "The object of the book, taken as a whole, and without which the whole is inexplicable" is the revelation and explication of the Christian deity not only through his Son but through his chief perversion who is Satan.[19] This understanding had already asserted itself in the Renaissance when the Apocalypse was regarded as the culmination of prophecy, in part because, whereas earlier prophecy declared, this prophecy demonstrated—justified—the ways of God to men. Its master theme is God's Providence. All its visions, according to Augustin Marlorat, reveal "the certaintie of God's providence"[20]: he is the orderer and disposer of evil, turning all evils into good. The same understanding caused Bartholomew Traheron to proclaim that John's prophecy "leadeth us to a consideration of gods . . . ordering of all things"; God's will, he insists, is to turn Adam's sin to good, to bring good out of his evil.[21] This is the scriptural book for all the Revelation commentators that affords so many compelling arguments in behalf of God's Providence, love, and truth—the book that makes the seemingly incomprehensible comprehensible. In the words of George Gifford, the Apocalypse is where we come "to know the wayes of God."[22] Or as Henry More will say in Milton's own century, John's prophecy is Scripture's greatest "Argument for Providence"—that is "the First great Fruit and use"[23] of this book designed as consolation for men living in hard times and providing a fulcrum for such theological conceptions as free will and grace, as well as a new heroism wherein God and man act cooperatively to achieve a common goal. The substantive center of Milton's poem is identical to that of John's prophecy; for that matter, so are the actual centers of these equally Christocentric works, each revolving around the story of War in Heaven, two of whose reference points are the Crucifixion and the Wilderness experience. The point is emphasized in the Book of Revelation by framing the celestial battle with the stories of the two witnesses who lie slain in the streets only to be resurrected and the woman who flees into the Wilderness, a place of trial prepared for her by God. Hidden in Milton's account of the Battle in Heaven, as William B. Hunter has shown,[24] is the Crucifixion story, and emanating from the center of this epic is the drama of *Paradise Regained*. The strategies of both John's prophecy and Milton's for protraying God and Satan are the same, and within the divine comedy of each work is contained the tragedy of Antichrist.

The great map of God's Providence, the Book of Revelation is also the Bible's fullest revelation of both God and Satan, achieved through strategies hinted at in the Gospels and Epistles. The Son acknowledges in the Gospel of John, "If ye had known me, ye should have known my Father also: and from henceforth ye know him, and have seen him" (xiv, 7); and in Matthew it is said, "No man knoweth the Son, but the Father; neither knoweth any man the Father, save the Son, and he to whomsoever the Son will reveal *him*" (xi, 27). It is the Son, we are told in the Epistle to the Hebrews, who is "the brightness of *his* glorie, and the express image of his person" (i, 3)—who is according to Colossians, "the image of the invisible God" (i, 15). In *De Doctrina Christiana*, Milton ascribes to John of Patmos the technique of holding the Father and the Son distinct and separate and, having already explained that the Son is the "image of the Father" (YP, VI, 237), attributes to John's prophetic style the device of using angels as "representatives of the divine presense and person": "angels often take upon them as their own name, the person and very words of God and Jehovah" (YP, VI, 251, 255). Moreover, Milton acknowledges that God typically "reflects outside himself something he has decreed within himself"—what is internal is thus represented as external (YP, VI, 204–05), and Milton suggests that Christ be understood as a composite figure: "Understand the name of Christ as meaning also Moses, and the prophets who foretold his coming, and the apostles who he sent" (YP, VI, 126). Christ is the spirit of prophecy and the summation of the prophets, who, with the Apostles, reveal him just as he is also revealed by the angels and, with them, is a revelation of deity. Milton formulates the belief here that Satan has obtained various names corresponding to his actions, and associates him with Beelzebub, Abaddon, Apollyon, and other figures of evil, especially in the Apocalypse (YP, VI, 349–50). These names, as Merritt Y. Hughes perceives, "suggest an identity as elusive as the multiple forms of evil itself."[25] If there is a literary precedent for Milton's conception, it is probably to be found in Spenser, whose Satan is "much like Milton's" in that he is represented as a multiplicity of forms.[26]

John's suppositions and strategies for the depiction of deity, heavenly and infernal, are those deployed by Milton in his characterizations of God and Satan in *Paradise Lost*. Thus in Book III:

> on his right hand
> The radiant image of his Glory sat,
> His only Son.   (62–64)

in Mercy and Justice both,
Through Heav'n and Earth, so shall my glorie excel,
But Mercy first and last shall brightest shine.   (132–34)

Beyond compare the Son of God was seen
Most glorious, in him all his Father shon
Substantially express'd, and in his face
Divine compassion visibly appeered,
Love without end, and without measure Grace.   (138–42)

his meek aspect,
Silent yet spake, but breath'd immortal love
To mortal men.   (266–68)

Begotten Son, Divine Similitude
In whose conspicuous count'nance, without cloud
Made visible, th'Almighty Father shines

on thee
Imprest th' effulgence of his Glorie abides,
Transfus'd on thee his ample Spirit rests.   (383–89)

Again in Book VI:

Effulgence of my Glorie, Son belov'd,
Son in whose face invisible beheld visibly,
What by Deitie I am.   (680–82)

he all his Father full exprest.   (720)

I . . . Image of thee in all things.   (734–36)

And in Book VII:

the Son
. . . now appear'd,
Girt with Omnipotence, with Radiance crown'd
Of Majesty Divine, Sapience and Love
Immense, and all his Father in him shone.   (192–96)

Milton's thinking is identical with Alexander Ross' (Christ is "the express and essential image of his Father"[27]) and is summed up in Book X of *Paradise Lost:*

on the Son
Blaz'd forth unclouded Deity; he full
Resplendent all his Father manifest
Express'd.   (64–67)

For Revelation's commentators, the strategy for characterization here parallels the representation of pagan deities, especially of Mars and

Venus, who are manifestations of Zeus or Jupiter—revelations, respectively, of his wrath and love. In its Christian application, this strategy, perfected by John of Patmos, reveals Christ to be "the clearest, the express image" of God, "the likeness of the Father, and the ingravers Character of his image"; and by extension, the angels themselves, who are revelations of Christ, are also manifestations of the Father.[28] Similarly, the false prophet, the beast, and the dragon are interdependent figures in the Apocalypse, the false prophet (according to David Pareus) making apparent "the character of the Beast" and thus being the express "Image" of him.[29] God is revealed in the Apocalypse, then, not only by his thesis but by his antithesis, by Christ *and* Satan.

Just as the Son and the angels bear the Father's image, so Satan's cohorts "bear the image of this father devil," says George Gifford in a statement that will be expanded upon by Thomas Brightman as he proposes that God has his double in the Son; the Son his in Michael; and Satan his in Beelzebub.[30] This is all by way of confirming a hypothesis like Gifford's, that as the angels are figured in Christ so the devils are all comprehended in Satan and by the dragon of Revelation. "By this Dragon," says Gifford, "the Kingdom of devils is represented"; he is "a head or a master devil" in whom all other devils "do joyne in one": "all of them so joyne together . . . as if they were but one, not manie devils. Their malice, their power, their craftiness, and their indeavors, do all concurre. Our Saviour teacheth, that Satan's kingdom is not divided."[31] There is, moreover, "a kind of order amongst devils,"[32] according to Thomas Taylor, so that the three orders and nine degrees of angels and devils are parallel. Yet the Book of Revelation also tends to blur orders and degrees into sameness by implying that the relationship between the dragon and the beast is closer, more intricate than that of chief devil to subordinate demon—as John Count recently has noticed, "is more like the merging of one diabolical image or manifestation into another."[33] In early Christianity, Antichrist was an emissary and ally of Satan yet quite distinct from him,[34] but by the Renaissance, due largely to the sway of John's Apocalypse, Antichrist and Satan became knotted in a conception that, during the seventeenth century, would be unravelled by fragmenting Antichrist into various persons, causes, even institutions. These limbs of Antichrist, or of Satan, did not provoke a new separation of concepts but instead provided for an elaborate elucidation of them. The proposition derives from Tyconius, who analogized "the Lord and his body" and "the devil and his body," thereby suggesting, as Richard Bauckham points out, that "the whole mystical company of the reprobate [is] the mystical body of Satan" and so leading to the counsel:

"Make not your body, which is a member of Christ, a member of Antichrist."[35]

The volume compiled and introduced by Samuel Hartlib, the friend to whom Milton dedicated *Of Education*, is useful here in drawing together diverse threads of this interpretation even as it suggests the possibilities for further interiorizing such a reading. The Book of Revelation is said to be "a Revealing" both of Christ and of God through him, and of Satan; it is, more profoundly, a revealing of man—of what is within him: "the Beast [is] with ourselves," but so is God[36]; we possess both their natures—Satan's which divides and fragments, God's which harmonizes and unifies us. Commentators came to stress not only the complexity and interiority of John's portrayals but also their deviousness. False prophets appear as angels, rather as Satan appears to Uriel in Book III of *Paradise Lost*, the emphasis here being on the deceptiveness of appearance, the elusive quality of evil. As Alexander Ross says, "The Divel is never more dangerous, than when he transformes himself into an Angel of light"[37]; and Milton underscores the point by having St. John's angel in the sun, "The sharpest-sighted Spirit of all in heav'n" (III, 691), be fooled by this false dissembler. There is "a certain theatricality" here: "evil playacting good, Satan disguising himself as an angel of light"; and if, as Bauckham argues, "the theological surface of the idea was barely scratched in the sixteenth century thought, its theatrical potential is somewhat obvious"[38]—is there, it should be added, to be exploited by Milton. Revelation's is a topsy-turvy world, like that of *Paradise Lost:* in the former the beast is internally a dragon, externally a lamb; in the latter Satan appears to be angelic, God (to some) to be demonic, and both thereupon are revealed to be other than they seem. John's strategies, and Milton's, are indebted to Mark vii, 15, where the false prophet comes in sheep's clothing, although inwardly he is a ravening wolf, and are a reflex of the problem of a prophet's living in and bestowing knowledge upon a fallen world. "Knowing good and evil," says Thomas Taylor, "is essential to fallen man, yet his problem derives from the fact that he knows such things not as Gods, but by a miserable and experiential knowledge in the want of good, and presence of evill."[39] In almost identical language, Milton addresses the same problem in *Areopagitica* and thereafter dramatizes it in his portrayals of God and Satan in *Paradise Lost*.

In this context, we may recall Coleridge's complaint about Milton's "addition of Fiction" to his account of the fallen deities: "Readers have learnt from Milton alone, that Satan & Beelzebub were different Persons (in Scriptures they are different names of the same Evil Being) it produces an effect too light, too much savoring of capricious Invention, for the exceeding Solemnity of the Subject."⁴⁰ This is the same complaint that nearly a century before was registered by Daniel Defoe: "I admire Mr. *Milton* as a Poet, yet . . . he was greatly out in matters of History and especially the History of the Devil." The truth is, Defoe continues, "all the antient names given him, of which the Scripture is full, seem to be originals derived from and adapted to the several steps he has taken, the several shapes he has appeared in to do mischief in the world." For Defoe, the Devil epitomizes all evil things in the world, all evil personages, and signifies "not persons only, but actions and habits"; and so Defoe concludes: all the actions, performances, and achievements of the lesser devils "are justly attributed to him [Satan], not as the prince of *Devils* only, but the Emperor of *Devils:* the prince of all the princes of *Devils.*" In Scripture, Satan comprehends all the other devils; there Beelzebub and Belial, Moloch and Mammon, "are all names proper and peculiar to *Satan* himself."⁴¹ And not only in Scripture, Defoe might have posited, but in *Paradise Lost* this is the case as well.

The suppositions about portraying Satan that lie behind Defoe's remarks, and Coleridge's, derive from Revelation exegesis wherein Milton himself would have encountered what Coleridge elsewhere regards as his own "*perfectly new observation* / that the Devil and Devils among Christians form precisely the same System, with the same Feeling, of *one* and at the same time *many*" as one finds among the pagans. In depictions of "Jupiter and his variously subordinated gods," says Coleridge, an "obscure feeling of unity remained . . . So with our Evil Spirit / —the *Devil* / —and this again into Satan and his Subordinates."⁴² Coleridge's "new observation" not only would have been imparted to Milton by biblical exegetes but is formulated as a theological dictum, with reference to both God and Satan, in *De Doctrina Christiana* and is then given poetic expression in both the infernal and heavenly council scenes of *Paradise Lost*. In these council scenes, the claims of theological tradition and prophetic song harmonize in a chord.

II

All hell's dire agents in one form combin'd
To fire the globe, and demonize mankind.
  —William Hayley

The theological tradition referring to Satan in Milton's time corresponds with the one familiar to Defoe and Coleridge. Hence if Comte Du Lude contends in the eighteenth century that "the Holy Scripture speaks but of one Devil," all others being but personifications of Satan's interior evil, that "we are to believe . . . there is but *One Serpent, One Satan, One Devil*," in Milton's century Lucas Jacobson Debes proposes that the various devils are "Spectres" of Satan, the same spirit in a different "outward shape."[43] John Deacon and John Walker similarly insist that Satan reigns over all the devils, that the different princes of the various orders are "all joyntly *combined* together in *Satan* himself," that "what *powers* soever the infernall spirits so doe joyntly execute, *power* is onely in Satan himselfe."[44] Furthermore, Deacon and Walker urge that any attempt to portray the Devil and through him to project a conception of evil should employ the devices of allegory and metaphor, so as to push meaning beyond what is literally expressed. Both council scenes in *Paradise Lost* are observant of such instructions. Insofar as they represent embryonally an element of theological history, they appear to claim, as C. S. Lewis might say, that monotheism is not the "rival" of polytheism but its "maturity," representing the gods of paganism as "aspects, manifestations, temporary or partial embodiments of the single power[,] . . . personifications of the abstracted attributes of the One."[45] In *Paradise Lost*, an allegorical conception of Hell is extended to Heaven and allowed to envelop the inhabitants of both places; here allegory is as much a technique of composition as a device for interpretation.

Not until the final books of Milton's epic does Satan assert his presence as an historical conception and then in a series of visions replete with figures who are his human representatives, just as the initial books of the poem are filled with his mythical representatives. In the early books, of course, it is Satan as theological and as poetical conception that commands attention, the two traditions preying upon, also playing off against one another in such a way as to create a figure dependent upon tradition yet not circumscribed by it. The theological tradition has its base in Scripture—is founded upon renderings of Satan in the Old and New Testaments and upon relationships defined in the one testament, then redefined in the other.[46]

In the Book of Numbers (xxii, 22), for example, Satan becomes a divine, mythological concept, the emissary of God, identical with Yahweh but not Yahweh in his all-embracing totality. Satan is one manifestation of Yahweh, is representative of one aspect or function of his being. So too in *Paradise Lost:* Satan is not the opposite of God but a perversion of him, in Book VI startling Abdiel by the fact "that such a resemblance of the Highest / Should yet remain" (114–15). If there is identity in Numbers, there is distinction in the Book of Job (i, 6–12; ii, 1–7), where, in a process of differentiation, Satan, still an emissary of the Lord, represents one of the opposing sides of his will and so comes to figure forth an inner conflict in deity. The process of differentiation is more evident still in the Book of Zechariah, where in the fourth vision (iii, 1–10), the trial of the high priest Joshua, Satan functions as accuser, Yahweh as defender, and Yahweh prevails. In the first Book of Chronicles (xxi, 1), Satan is the instigator of an impious action and the opponent of both the divine will and law. If elsewhere he is an aspect of deity manifesting a specific quality or function of God, here he is the antithesis, defining God only negatively. On the one hand, then, the Satan of the Old Testament is a projection, albeit of the dark side, of deity, while such pagan gods as Moloch, Belial, and Beelzebub define the evil that, especially in the New Testament, Satan will come to represent. On the other hand, Satan does emerge in the Old Testament, however tentatively, as the evil figure that he becomes in the New Testament. A similar process involves both God and Satan: initially a multiplicity, each becomes a unity and thereupon is subject again to differentiation by way of anatomizing good and evil, dissecting each into its constituent parts. In this process, God becomes differentiated into three persons; Satan, into various of the pagan deities including Moloch and Mammon, Belial and Beelzebub.

The two traditions exist side by side in the New Testament, with Satan here identified with, there distinguished from these other devils. The two traditions sit alongside one another in *Paradise Lost* as well, where at the literal level there is distinction and at the symbolic level identity between characters. Indeed, it is this double tradition pointing now to multiplicity, now to unity that enables Milton to render his council scenes, both in Hell and Heaven, dramatically in dialogue and still remain within the realm of doctrinal propriety. In this Milton is responsive to the claims of contending theological and even aesthetic traditions and, as regards the latter, especially to the Renaissance tendency to particularize the emblem so that it is simultaneously individual and symbol. There is a sense, then, in which Milton invites the confident declaration of Merritt Hughes that he "did not allegorize his devils," hence any treatment of them as "deliberately patterned examples or embodiments of the seven deadly sins, or of any other traditional abstractions of theology is to violate their essence as individuals" even if ultimately Milton disallows such a declaration by also inviting praise for drawing "with exactitude the individual physiognomies of many of the satellites of Satan,"[47] for doing verbally what artists of the Renaissance were doing visually—anatomizing evil into different aspects that eventually are all identified with *and within* Satan. The processes of mythic differentiation and condensation operative in the Bible no less than in Milton's poem find sanctions in multiple traditions, sacred and secular, iconographic and occult, all of which press strategies for characterization onto *Paradise Lost*.

When St. Paul writes, "And what concord hath Christ with Belial? or what part hath he that believeth with an infidel" (2 Corinthians vi, 15), Calvin responds, "Paul has employed the word [Belial] here to mean devil, the head of all wicked persons [Satan]."[48] Or where it is written, "Ye cannot serve God and mammon" (Matthew vi, 24; Luke xvi, 13), the name of Mammon is construed by Gregory of Nyssa and others as yet another name for Beelzebub or Satan.[49] In the case of Moloch, there is the scriptural association of him with Malcham, Milcom, and Remphan, which, as John Diodati explains, is the basis for the commonplace notion that Moloch and the Devil are one and the same.[50] In the Kabbalah, not only is Moloch identical with Satan but so is Beelzebub. If the latter's name and Satan's are used interchangeably in the New Testament, where Beelzebub is called "the prince of the devils" or "the chief of the devils" (Matthew xii, 24; Mark iii, 22; Luke xi, 15), those names are nonetheless distinguished from one another in the Gospel of Nicodemus, which records a quarrel between Satan, "the prince and captain of death," and Beelzebub, "the prince of hell" (xv, xvii, 14). Here Beelzebub upbraids Satan for persecuting Christ and bringing him to Hell, and Christ, in return for being able to rescue Adam and his sons from Hell, gives Beelzebub dominion over Satan, whom Beelzebub describes as "prince of destruction, author of . . . defeat and banishment, . . . prince of all evil, author of death and source of all pride" (xviii, 1, 2).

Not just with Beelzebub but with all the devils, there are two traditions: one that identifies them with, the other that discriminates them from Satan. During the Middle Ages the first tradition gained predominance because of the authority assigned to the scriptural tradition and because of the pressure such authority exerted on literary tradition. Beelzebub, for instance, is the name by which Dante refers to Satan in the *Inferno* (XXXIV, 127). This same tendency persists with equal authority in the Renaissance. Thus in *Gerusalemme Liberta* where Tasso writes "Belzebú," Fairfax translates "Satan" (VII, 99). Yet beside this tradition is the incidental one, fostered by occult literature, wherein Beelzebub is distinguished from Satan.

Once they differentiate the various demons, the occultists proceed to rank them in a hierarchical order that parallels the divine order from which they have fallen and which, in the process, they have perverted.

This practice, authorized by the Book of Enoch and encouraged by Thomas Aquinas, was popularized in the seventeenth century by Robert Burton and Thomas Heywood. Beelzebub is now assigned the highest rank, presiding over the false gods whom the gentiles adored as idols, followed by Apollo Pythius who rules the liars and equivocators and Belial who presides over the "vessels of anger . . . [and] fury"— the "inventors of all mischief." The fourth order of devils—the "malicious revenging Devils"—is ruled by Asmodaeus, and the fifth order representing the "cozeners . . . Magicians and Witches," by Satan. The next rank, the aerial devils, is ruled by "the Prince of Air"; then come the destroyers, who cause war and tumult, represented by Abaddon; the "accusing or caluminating Devil" called Diabolos who "drives men to despair"; and finally "those tempters in several kinds" whose prince is Mammon.[51] The notion of an infernal hierarchy so widely interested the Protestants of the Renaissance that Calvin, while clearly taking Beelzebub to be another name for Satan, explains that the phrase "prince of devils" implies that "the reprobate have a head, in the same manner as Christ is the Head of the Church."[52] And such a notion clearly stands behind the catalogue of pagan deities in Book I of *Paradise Lost*.

Related to the occult tradition of ranking the devils in a hierarchy is the iconographic tradition of representing the Devil with three faces—a tradition that was engendered by the Gospel of Nicodemus and the Good Friday Sermon of Eusebius of Alexandria. The various addresses to the Devil as "three-headed Beelzebub" find analogs in other trinitarian conceptions of evil: the three-headed Hecuba, the three-headed monsters, the three-headed Cerberus. In Christian art the diabolical trinity is developed as a parallel to and parody of the heavenly Trinity. The three-headed Lucifer, "a sort of antithesis or reverse of the Trinity," as Arturo Graf explains, "appears in works of sculpture, in paintings on glass, in manuscript miniatures," the tradition culminating in Dante's *Inferno* where Lucifer is portrayed with three faces (XXXIV).[53] The Devil is not only given three faces in the typical depictions of him, but additional faces, all of them with a different character recalling the hierarchy of the devils, are often fixed to his shoulders and knees, and the most grotesque of the faces, usually with mouth open and tongue extended, is used as covering for the genitalia. Yet even here two traditions are converging, the different physiognomies recalling the tradition that would distinguish the various devils and their superimposition on the form of Satan invoking the tradition that treats the various devils as extensions or emanations of Satan revealing in caricature the multiple facets of his evil nature. In the Renaissance, those contending traditions conflate. Thus Burton, having described a hierarchy of devils that places Beelzebub above Satan, proceeds to talk about the "several shapes" and "several names" by which the devil "hath deceived the inhabitants of the earth" and thereupon relates Beelzebub and Milcom (Moloch) to Satan.[54]

These same two traditions exist alongside one another in *Paradise Lost* but not with equal authority, Milton believing (as Dr. Johnson once told Boswell in a different context) that what philosophers report to us on this subject is probable: what scripture tells us is certain. In *De Doctrina Christiana*, Milton's views are summarized in successive statements: "The devils have their prince. . . . They also keep their ranks. . . . The chief is the author of all wickedness and hinders all good . . . he has been given numbers of titles, which suit his actions. He is frequently called Satan" (YP, VI, 349–50). In *Paradise Lost*, then, two traditions not only converge but are brilliantly reconciled within a succession of exegetical levels that allow for identity and distinction even as they give priority to the claims scriptural tradition has on the former tradition. It is not without significance that the speech of Satan to Beelzebub, "Both waking *we were one*" (V, 678; my italics), is lodged between speeches of the Father to the Son emphasizing their oneness and their similitude. Thus, the Father to the Son: "abide / United as one individual soul" (V, 609–10), and again: "thou in whom my glory I behold / In full resplendence" (719–20). Neither is it a coincidence that Satan's first speech in *Paradise Lost* should assert an identity between himself and Beelzebub, speaking of their "mutual league, / United thoughts and counsels"—"Joined with me once, now . . . joined," says Satan to his nearest mate (I, 87–88, 90). Nor should it be forgotten that the initial chronological event of the poem, situated in the midst of its narrative, is God's construing his Son as other and same. Satan's words to Beelzebub both parallel and parody God's to the Son. The begetting of the Son is a differentiation of him from deity—in Thomas Maresca's words, is "an extrusion of him from the unity of the deity or an elaboration of unity into multiplicity."[55] As with the Son, so with the angels and their "radiant forms / Divine effulgence" (V, 457–58), and so too with Beelzebub and other of the fallen deities: they explicate Satan as the Son and angels explicate the Father—are "the unfolding of Sameness and the infolding of Otherness," as the council scenes declare and demonstrate.[56] There is a sense, then, in which the chronology of events that comprises Milton's epic and the narrative ordering of those events are contiguous if not exactly correspondent: the dissolving of unity into multiplicity, the effect of Christ's and of Satan's "begettings," implies the return of that multiplicity to unity which is the subject of the council scenes in Books II and III. In *Paradise Lost*, everything tends to unity, in Hell no less than in Heaven: if God is All in All (III, 341) so too, albeit in an ironic sense, is Satan.

Milton acknowledges an infernal hierarchy, but his strategy is immediately to confuse the usual order, to blur the divisions codified by Burton and Heywood. Milton makes Beelzebub a subordinate of Satan and makes Satan the "Prince of the Aire" (X, 185); he allows Moloch to represent the first rank of devils, the false Gods, as part of the displacement of Beelzebub, but at the same time will associate Moloch with the third rank, the vessels of anger and of fury, as well as with the seventh rank, the destroyers who instigate war. Milton then has Belial represent the second rank, the liars and equivocators, but also maintains the association of Mammon with the last order. Other classes—the malicious and revenging devils, cozeners and magicians and witches, the accusers and calumnators, those who drive men to despair—are represented by all the devils participating in the council scene and are thereupon gathered up into the figures of Beelzebub and Satan. By seeming to confuse the various orders and the devils associated with them (in the council scene, both Moloch and Belial are associated with violence, and both Belial and Mammon are associated with the temptations of the world and the method of proferring them by fraud and persuasion)—in this way Milton creates the impression that at different times the infernal deities engage in all these activities. Indeed, by identifying Beelzebub and Satan, Milton suggests that the arch-fiend and his subordinate epitomize the various aspects of evil represented by the lesser devils. The first two books of *Paradise Lost* thereby render in dramatic terms Milton's belief that Satan has obtained many names corresponding to his actions; in Book I, Beelzebub and Belial, Moloch and Mammon may only be aligned with Satan's evil, but in Book II each becomes identified with Satan himself and so appears as an element of his personality, an aspect of his being. The initial books of Milton's poem, simply, are an exploration of the Satan archetype. What Satan says to Beelzebub he might just as well have said to the other fallen deities: *we are one*. It is only when we come to see all in relation to Satan that we recognize the richness and resonance of these portraits for all the poem, recognize their participation in a strategy neither of degeneration nor degradation but of exposure.

The council scenes are presented, then, rather like the one in Night I of Blake's *The Four Zoas*, with double vision: "contracting their ex-

alted senses / They behold Multitude or Expanding they behold as one /
As One Man all the Universal family . . . / . . . they in him & he in
them . . . / Consulting as One Man" (2–7).[57] Blake's observation here
reflects upon *Paradise Lost*, where, in the council scenes, divine and
infernal, we behold God and Satan, at one level at least, "as One . . .
Consulting as One." These council scenes constitute a focal moment
wherein we see all characters in relation to Satan and God respectively,
and then God and Satan in relation to each other. Milton's critics have
approached this perception, with Thomas Kranidas describing Raphael
as "a minor projection of Deity . . . brought forward temporarily," with
Arnold Stein representing Moloch as an integral part of Satan, "the
Satan of the 'fixt' mind and absolute courage, unafraid of death," and
with Robert C. Fox arguing that "Moloc reflects the wrathful side of
Satan's soul."[58] Yet as Fox astutely observes, none of the devils within
Milton's allegory is a "static symbol of a single vice"; rather, each is "a
dynamic figure in whose soul . . . [a vice] develops and expands until he
partially progresses beyond the limits of the original . . . to embrace the
more comprehensive vice"; and as Stein astutely perceives, "there are
significant relationships in personality as well as consciousness" between
Satan and his followers.[59] As this vice is absorbed into that one, this
devil merges into that one until eventually all merge into and are contained by Satan. In *Paradise Lost*, all forms—divine and infernal, human
and even literary—search out and discover their ultimate subsuming
form.

   The council scene in Hell, at least on its surface, is more conten-
tious than that in Heaven—presumably to pay lip service to the Augustinian notion that it is the demons, not the gods, who are divided into
parties and engaged in strife. Such a notion is furthered when subsequent to Satan's departure the devils dispute such matters as "providence, foreknowledge, will and fate" and "Of good and evil much they
argued then" (II, 559, 562) and when Chaos, described as a place of
"Tumult and Confusion . . . / And Discord" (II, 966–67), becomes a
mirror reflecting upon Satan, who, for the moment, "falls into many
doubts with himself" (IV, Argument). Yet, for the duration of the council
scene, this suggestion is subdued by another, for that scene is less a
genuine debate than an imaginative rendering of what Calvin describes
as the "subtle methods Satan employs, presenting all the while an appearance of discord, in order to entrap the minds of men." Though he
may pretend to fight with himself, says Calvin, "whenever Satan enters
into collusion with himself . . . it is himself that triumphs."[60] Satan, with
no small irony, makes the point early: "where there is . . . no good / For

which to strive, no strife can grow up there / From Faction"; unlike Heaven, he says, Hell is a place of "union . . . , and firm accord" (II, 30–32, 36). Within the allegory of Book II, this is the point of view that Milton adopts: "men only disagree / . . . live in hatred, enmity, and strife / Among themselves"; in contrast, "Devil with devil damned / Firm concord holds" (496–97, 500–01). And in Book III we are reminded that for some duration there is contention in God himself, "the strife of mercy and justice in thy face discerned" (406–07). The respective council scenes, as John Peter has noticed, are less "an actual discussion" than "a train of thought": if "on one level [the literal] the debate can be accepted as a debate, on another level [the symbolic] it can also be accepted as a dramatized account of Satan's inner motives."[61] The various proposals advanced here, then, are not so much different alternatives as "the processes through which [Satan's] own mind has been moving"—a point that Milton himself emphasizes by saying in the argument to Book II not that the devils debate but that *Satan debates*.[62] It may be that these council scenes are more like the one in *Paradise Regained* than Thomas Newton would allow when he asserted that in the brief epic there "is a council scene without a debate; Satan is the only speaker."[63] Here it should be remembered that the infernal council scene in *Paradise Regained* stipulates the chief discovery of the divine council of *Paradise Lost*—that in the face of Jesus "The glimpses of his Father's glory shine" (I, 92); that the infernal council here is reconvened in order that Satan can choose from among the assemblage those "likest to himself," should there be "cause . . . to unfold some active scene / Of various persons" (II, 236–40); that, as in *Paradise Lost*, there is a disarmingly deceptive display of discord, with Satan now belittling Belial for the suggestion "Set women in his eye and in his walk" (II, 153), only to do later what Belial had proposed:

> now solemn stood
> Nymphs of Diana's train, and Naiades
> With fruits and flowers . . .
> And ladies of th' Hesperides, that seemed
> Fairer than feigned of old, or fabled since
> Of Fairy damsels met in the forest wide
> By knights.   (II, 354–59)

In both epics, if the participants in the heavenly council scene are what Coleridge might call unfolded fragments of the deity, those in Hell are splinterings of the fallen Lucifer, psychological fragments of him, reflections of his consciousness and its range of awareness.

III

The boundaries . . . blur, episodes are transformed into different
episodes . . . , and the interpretations of whole poems take on new
depths in the changing flow and play of consciousness from age to
age.

—Joan Malory Webber

It was said long ago that the infernal council scene is *Paradise Lost*
signals "the mode of reading" Milton.[64] In one sense, this is only to
acknowledge that all epics contain episodes that reflect and interpret
their larger meaning, that are miniatures of the total poem, but it is also
to attribute a crucial importance to this particular episode, which possesses a local significance yet exerts a pressure that is felt throughout
Milton's poem, especially upon the system of epic conventions that is so
fundamentally a part of its meaning and design. The very books that are
sometimes thought to exalt Satan to the status of epic hero, through
allegory initiate a process of exposure that, persisting through the entire
epic, aligns Satan not only with the serpent in the Garden but with the
Antichrist in history—the dragon of the Apocalypse. The allegory here is
like that "in Scripture [where] an *Allegory* is a drawing of words from a
plain *natural* sense to a *Spiritual Mystical* sense"[65] so as to produce an
unfolding revelation. In such allegories, meaning gradually emerges, as
light comes out of darkness and quickens into revelation. Allegory can
thus be a strategy of exposure that, in *Paradise Lost*, is a part of a larger
strategy of deception wherein figures appearing to be one thing are
revealed to be another: in Book II Satan appears to be heroic, even
angelic; in Book III God, who has seemed demonic to some and to
others simply boring, is revealed by Christ and the angels, who manifest
his goodness, to be more than heroic—above heroic. The meaning of the
latter council scene, as Irene Samuel shrewdly states, "depends in large
part on the continuity of the poetic fabric,"[66] the scene in Hell indicating
how we are to regard the corresponding one in Heaven. The extended
scene in Book II thus makes possible the more abbreviated one in the
next book whose meaning it both parodies and probes, even as it anticipates the strategy of characterizing Adam through Eve in Book V: "O
sole in whom my thoughts find all repose, / My glory, my perfection"—
"Best image of myself" (28–29, 95). The portrayal of Satan in Book II in
terms of the master categories of sin foreshadows the later depiction of
him in relation to the seven deadly sins of which the various animal
disguises are emblematic, and the association of Satan with the threefold
temptation process implicit in the characterizations, as well as the spe-

cific proposals of Moloch, Belial, and Mammon, anticipates the strategies of temptation (if not exactly their content) that will be utilized first when Satan inspires Eve's dream and later when the formal temptation commences. The portrayals of evil here glance ahead to its operations in the fallen world of Books XI and XII. In this way, the whole of *Paradise Lost* is mirrored in a part.

Finally, though, Milton's intellectual triumph may be more compelling than his poetic success, for it is in this area especially that Milton may be said to have participated decisively in a task begun by John of Patmos, that of "conquer-[ing] Hell and . . . redeem[ing] us from the Devil"[67] by both redefining and relocating place and person. In this regard, one needs only turn to a work like the *Dictionnaire infernal* (Paris, 1818) to assess the degree to which Milton's infernal council has had a shaping influence on subsequent conceptions of the devil—or to an edition like William Cowper's to ascertain the extent to which *Paradise Lost* was perceived as shaping a new version of Christianity. "How new" some of these current ideas are, says Cowper, "Milton is a witness."[68] Indeed, Milton probably understood as well as some in our own century that "the Apocalypse prescribes, calls for, and demands a new religion; that is its essence"[69]—and the essence of any poem that would truly follow it as a model. The extent to which *Paradise Lost* observes such a model was suggested long ago by George Gregory, the translator of Bishop Lowth's lectures, as he proclaimed that

The whole fabric of *Paradise Lost*, except the more naked narrative of the Fall, is founded upon the most slender authority imaginable, two or three short, obscure, and ill-understood passages, chiefly in the Epistle of St. Jude; and yet it forms at present a part of our popular theology. Our grandsires, and even perhaps many grave Doctors of Divinity, would exclaim against the impiety of that man who would dare to question a syllable of the authenticity of all that he has related, of the war in heaven, of the rebellious spirits, etc. etc. This is a new proof of the preponderancy of Milton's genius, as well as of his popularity.[70]

Milton has used the full apparatus of the Christian mythology to expose its naiveté: he has turned its geography into metaphor and its actors into symbols, in the process showing that what has been conceived as outside is actually within. *The mind is its own place*—there Christ and Satan enthrone themselves, there Heaven and Hell are discoverable as projections of the human mind—as places into which the poet, internally, may ascend or descend. *Into himself descended*—the phrase is as apt a description for the experience of Jesus in the Wilderness as for the poet in his poem. The characters of *Paradise Lost* are in

Milton as he is in them: as Coleridge once said, the poem is ultimately a revelation of Milton's own mind; "It is Milton himself whom you see; his Satan, his Adam, his Raphael, almost his Eve—all are John Milton."[71] A similar perception, probably gleaned from his reading of Blake, caused Denis Saurat to speculate that the poet is himself the real hero of *Paradise Lost:* "Milton brings his own self into the poem just as he did in the pamphlets . . . [;] he has a personal share in the fighting. He it is, and not God or the Son, that overcomes Satan. He follows him in all his enterprises. . . . What need has Milton of a hero in his poem. He is his own hero."[72] Perhaps more exactly, Saurat might have said: it is the Son in Milton who overcomes the Satan in Milton. Like its Revelation model, then, *Paradise Lost* is a great turning inward, taking many of its cues from Revelation as Milton moves toward the completely interiorized visionary drama of *Paradise Regained*. By the Renaissance, the temple of Revelation was perceived as a temple of the mind; the garment imagery in that prophecy as referring to a universe within; Jerusalem and the Church and Christ's kingdom as inward states; God and Satan as dwelling within the human soul where the celestial battle is fought; history itself, not so much as the outward history of civilizations as the spiritual history of individual men and of human consciousness.

The tendency among Revelation's commentators of the 1640s to interiorize Christ is a response to an earlier tendency to interiorize Antichrist. Augustine Marlorat, for instance, argues that Satan, the false prophet and Antichrist, does not exist apart from the faithful but is to be found within their company; driven into the hearts of God's children during the Battle in Heaven, Satan now resides there.[73] John Napier draws similar conclusions: the meaning of the War in Heaven is that Satan rises up within the minds of the elect, which then and now are his battleground.[74] For Patrick Forbes, Antichrist "is no forraine invader, but an inward Traitor"; or as Thomas Taylor will say, he is a power "within"— "a bosome enemy."[75] By the middle of the seventeenth century, such readings of the Book of Revelation are ubiquitous: according to Roger Bacon, Lucifer is "*in All*"—king, Parliament, Army, *all;* and from the viewpoint of Richard Coppin, "Antichrist . . . exalts and sets up himself in the mind of man," but so does Christ—the former inhabiting the natural, the latter the spiritual man.[76] The Christian journey is thus represented by Coppin as a passage through three states: that of Satan, that of Christ in the flesh, and that of Christ in the spirit. James Nayler argues similarly that Christ and Satan are in everyman, and William Guild cautions that Christians "mis-know" both Christ and Satan and never will know either rightly until they begin to look for each within.[77]

Again, Milton's friend Samuel Hartlib provides a convenient summary of such interpretations in a set of related propositions, all predicated on his belief that the real mystery of the Apocalypse will be discovered only by relating outward events to man's interior life. Christ in man, says Hartlib, must triumph over Satan in man; when that victory occurs, Jerusalem will be erected within the human mind and thereupon, extended beyond man, will become the condition of mankind's new society.[78] A vision of Christ within and of Satan within is thus corollary to the idea that Heaven and Earth, Hell and Paradise are places within the human mind and states of the human soul.

The council scenes in *Paradise Lost* not only look beyond themselves to other episodes in the poem: they point to other of the epic conventions that share with them a profound interiority. To illustrate the point, we may turn to beginnings, middles, and endings in epic poetry long enough to observe, first, that with reference to *Paradise Lost* each of these moments in the narrative structure is marked by a striking inversion and, second, that the inversion functions as an intensifier or a punctuation mark underlining a movement inward. "The *descensus ad infero*," says Thomas Maresca, is "a mainstay of the epic poem," on the one hand focusing the paradox of descending so as to rise into knowledge and on the other centering the poem in processes of "unfolding . . . unity into multiplicity" and of "infolding . . . multiplicity into unity."[79] Not only has Milton rearranged the epic components in *Paradise Lost*, but he has arranged them in such a way as to involve the council scenes in that paradox and to figure through them those processes. Here, their order inverted, epic conventions merge and become intervolved, each sharing in and furthering the functions of the others. Milton's epic prophecy begins with a descent into Hell rather than with the usual council scene or debate; at its center is the story of the celestial battle, transferred from the end of time to a point in time before Creation; at its end is a prophecy of future history followed by an expulsion of Adam and Eve into that history, rather than vice versa. Through such marked inversions, attention becomes fixed upon a beginning where the descent into Hell is transmuted into a descent within the human mind, of which Hell is a projection; upon a middle where an external battle is translated into a gigantic metaphor portraying an interior battle; upon an ending wherein history, paradoxically, finds its meaning in terms of a mind assimilating its drama and participating in, with the hope of transforming, that history.

Such inversions are even more sharply focused by the recognition that the usual beginnings, middles, and endings of epic poetry have been preserved only superficially, it appears, and then only so that they might be challenged from the inside. Epics typically begin in debate or contention, proceed toward a middle marked by a descent into the underworld, and conclude, as Joan Webber would have it, in an embrace.[80] Such a pattern is dimly visible in *Paradise Lost:* there are the council scenes of the early books, but in them the debate is feigned; there is Satan's descent into Hell and Christ's into Chaos in the middle books, but at this epic's actual midpoint is Christ's ascent; there is the embrace—"they hand in hand" (XII, 648)—in the concluding lines but an embrace most notable for marking the divorce of Adam and Eve from Eden and only hinting at a marriage at the end of time when they can wipe the tears now being shed from their eyes forever. There is early in Milton's poem, however, a striking point of convergence, a moment in which conventional beginnings, middles, and endings are synchronized: the council in Heaven of Book III promises a descent into the *under*world for the Incarnation and ends in the embrace of the Father and the Son—the most memorable embrace in all of Milton's poetry, certainly, and, with the possible exception of those many embraces in the climactic plates of Blake's *Jerusalem,* the most memorable in all of epic poetry. That convergence quietly reinforces the point, "I am the Alpha and the Omega, the beginning and the ending" (Revelation i, 8; cf. xxi, 6, xxxii, 13), even as it wittily draws attention to the logic of a poem that "hastes into the midst of things," appropriating for its beginning the descent into the underworld customarily situated at the midpoint of an epic poem. Moreover, that convergence has the effect of thrusting into the poem's middle an event that ends time and, as Milton would have it, begins time as well. In this way, beginnings and endings collapse into the middle of *Paradise Lost,* this time according to the logic that the Battle in Heaven is a perpetually recurring event—a metaphor for a struggle that repeats itself unendingly through time. Beginnings, middles, endings—in *Paradise Lost* each reduces to the same symbolic event (a battle) and is figured in the same pattern (a descent).

It has been said that "the real mirrors of *Paradise Lost* are the first and last units of the poem, and what they mirror is the center."[81] The beginning and end of history are mirrored at the center of *Paradise Lost,* which, in turn, mirrors and is mirrored by the beginning and end of the poem. Near the end of Book VI is Satan's descent actualized in the vision of Books I and II; near the beginning of Book VII is Christ's descent accomplished within the history envisioned by the final books.

In the first and last books there is the feigned contention of pandemonium, as well as the pandemonium that produces contention in human history; in both instances the field for contention is located within the human mind: "Satan debates" (II, Argument) and "Dream not of thir fight, / As of a Duel, or the local wounds / Of head or heel" (XII, 386–88). In both instances, that is, the epic warfare is spiritualized, internalized, thereby suggesting the nature of the warfare that is reported in Book VI. At the same time, the epic descent which has always constituted the heart of epic poetry remains that in *Paradise Lost* but now becomes, additionally, the "frame" and "skeleton" for the genre as well.[82]

The descent, by tradition, is preliminary to both illumination and ascent, the latter constituting the great moments of revelation in both of Milton's epics. In *Paradise Lost* Satan and God confront themselves in their cohorts and thereupon are confronted by Milton's readers, who, piercing the veils, can proclaim with the Jesus of *Paradise Regained:* "I discern thee other then thou seem'st"; "plain thou now appear'st" (I, 348; IV, 193). In *Paradise Regained* Jesus confronts his manhood on the mountaintop, his godhood on the pinnacle. No less than in the brief epic, in *Paradise Lost* moments of revelation are linked to ascents: on Mount Niphates Satan perceives himself as evil and recognizes the "Hell within Him," that "within him hell / He brings": "Which way I flie is Hell; myself am Hell," (IV, 20–21, 75); and atop the Mount of Vision in the concluding books of the poem, Adam learns of "A Paradise within . . . happier farr" (XII, 587) than the one from which he is being exiled. As the poet and his characters turn inward in Milton's epics, they discover the geography of Christianity, as well as its actors; they find a center there opening upon a drama that, beginning to unfold within man, completes itself in history, the major reversal of which occurs during Christ's journey into the Wilderness. A poem about origins, *Paradise Lost* is also a poem that heralds the new beginning inaugurated by *Paradise Regained*.

The process depicted in an epic and enacted by its narrative has been called *centroversion*, which, as Maresca explains, is "the raising to consciousness of what has previously been latent."[83] This process is visible within *Paradise Lost* in the way that the poem responds to and elaborates upon tradition, both literary and theological; within Milton's canon in the way that *Paradise Regained* emerges out of and brings to fulfillment the tendencies of *Paradise Lost*; and, finally, within the tradition of epic-prophecy itself especially by those manifestations of the tradition that are inspired by Milton's last poems. If *Paradise Regained* is a centering of the vision of *Paradise Lost*, many of the long poems of the Romantic period are equally centerings of the vision advanced by Milton's brief epic—Blake's *Milton*, certainly, and perhaps even more notably, *The Prelude*.

It has been argued by James Rieger that *The Prelude* enables Milton to appear today as a more modern poet than he really was and conversely by Isabel MacCaffrey that this poem reveals *The Faerie Queene* to be a more modern, Wordsworthian poem than anyone had previously dreamt.[84] By its greatest critic, Romanticism has been said to mark the beginning of a major change in the Christian mythology, and what this change involves, according to Northrop Frye, is the transposition of the Christian universe, the internalization of what previously had been exteriorized: "In Romanticism the main direction . . . tends increasingly to be downward and inward,"[85] and as the universe alters so too do the genres of poetry that are mirrors of it. Wordsworth would seem to offer the surest poetic testimony of Frye's belief, were it not that, in the very act of setting himself apart from Milton, Wordsworth establishes a knit of identity with him. In *The Recluse*, invoking Urania only to suggest that he may need "a greater Muse" to support his new undertaking, brilliantly but unwittingly Wordsworth describes the direction of Milton's own poetic achievement: "I must tread on shadowy ground, must sink / Deep—and, aloft ascending, breathe in worlds / To which the heaven of heavens is but a veil" (781–83). As in Milton, the turn is inward, albeit more radically so, to "the Mind of Man— / My haunt, and the main region of my song" (793–94). The difference in their respective poetry is not in kind but in degree: it is poetry, in Milton's words, "Differing but in degree, of *kind* the same" (V, 490; my italics). The essential genre for both poets is prophecy, and in their major poems the field of vision is insistently the human mind. To "know" Milton's achievement is thus to know something essential about the character and achievement of Romantic poetry, about a new interiority for poetry that Milton fosters and the Romantics further. To place the major poems of English Romanticism—*Milton* and *Jerusalem*, *The Prelude*, *Prometheus Unbound*, even *Don Juan*—within the context of Milton's epic-prophecies is finally to bear witness to an essential truth of literary criticism; that "the transgression of genre . . . does not do away with *norms*. On the contrary, the transgressive work [or works] will become a new norm or a generic paradigm in its turn, thus establishing a new taxonomy of kinds."[86]

University of Maryland

NOTES

1. *A Preface to "Paradise Lost"* (1942; rpt. New York, 1961), p. 104.

2. *The Heavenly Muse: A Preface to Milton*, ed. Hugh MacCallum (Toronto, 1972), p. 182.

3. *A Hundred Sermons upon the Apocalypse of Jesu Christ*, trans. John Day (London, 1573), esp. pp. 5ᵛ–6.

4. See Pareus' *A Commentary upon the Divine Revelation of the Apostle and Evangelist John*, trans. Elias Arnold (Amsterdam, 1644), esp. pp. 20, 23, 26 (commentary); and also Orchino's *A Tragoedie or Dialoge of the unjuste usurped Primacie of the Bishop of Rome* (London, 1549), and van der Noot's *Theatre for Worldlings* (London, 1569). Cf. John Foxe, *Christus triumphas, comoedia Apocalyptica* (London, 1551). And finally see Henry More, *An Explanation of the Grand Mystery of Godliness* (London, 1660), p. 201.

5. "*Concilia deorum* from Homer through Milton," *SP, XXX* (1933), 25.

6. *The Story of the Devil*, trans. Edward Noble Stone (New York, 1931), pp. 3–4, 13.

7. *Milton and His Epic Tradition* (Seattle, 1979), p. 10.

8. See Olin H. Moore, "The Infernal Council," *MP, XVI* (1918–19), 169–93; Hammond, "*Concilia deorum*," pp. 1–16; Burton O. Kurth, *Milton and Christian Heroism: Biblical Epic Themes and Forms in Seventeenth-Century England* (1959; rpt. Hamden, Conn., 1966), esp. pp. 44–47; Thomas M. Greene, *The Descent from Heaven: A Study in Epic Continuity* (New Haven, 1963), esp. pp. 19–22; William J. Knightley, "The Perfidy of the Devil's Council," *University of Mississippi Studies in English*, V (1964), 9–14; John M. Steadman, "Pandemonium and Deliberative Oratory," *Neophilologus*, XLVIII (1964), 159–76, and "*Ethos* and *Dianoia*: Character and Rhetoric in *Paradise Lost*," in *Language and Style in Milton*, ed. Ronald David Emma and John T. Shawcross (New York, 1967), p. 201.

9. *The Literary Remains of Samuel Taylor Coleridge*, ed. Henry Nelson Coleridge, 4 vols. (London, 1835), I, 157.

10. *A Brief Commentary on the Revelation of St. John* (London, 1821), pp. 156, 203.

11. "Observations on the Characters of the Fallen Angels of Milton," in *The Poetical Works of John Milton*, ed. Henry John Todd, 7 vols. (London, 1809), II, 259, 265–66.

12. See Hammond, "*Concilia deorum*," pp. 1–16.

13. *Mysteriously Meant: The Rediscovery of Pagan Symbolism and Allegorical Interpretation in the Renaissance* (Baltimore, 1970), p. 294.

14. Hammond, "*Concilia deorum*," p. 14.

15. *The Allegory of Love: A Study in Medieval Tradition* (New York, 1936), pp. 63, 78, 113. On the development of allegory, see also D. W. Robertson, Jr., *A Preface to Chaucer: Medieval Perspectives* (Princeton, 1963), esp. p. 209. Another discussion of allegory that has application here is Rhodes Dunlap's "The Allegorical Interpretation of Renaissance Literature," *PMLA*, LXXXII (1967), 39–43.

16. *Milton and Christian Heroism*, p. 92.

17. See Tasso's explanation of his poem's allegory in *Godfrey of Boulogne: or the Recovery of Jerusalem*, trans. Edward Fairfax (London, 1624), sig. Aᵛ–A², as well as Bowra's remarks in *From Virgil to Milton* (1945; rpt. London and New York, 1965), pp. 118–20.

18. Giacomo Aconcio, *Satans Strategems, or the Devils Cabinet-Councel Discovered* (London, 1648), p. 40.

19. *Brief Commentary*, pp. 273, 280.

72 MILTON STUDIES

20. *A Catholike Exposition upon the Revelation of Sainct John* (London, 1574), sig. Aiii.

21. *An Exposition on the Fourth Chapter of S. Johns Revelation* (London, 1577), sig. Aiii^v, Avi^v, Ciiii–Cv^v, Dviii.

22. *Sermons upon the Whole Booke of the Revelation* (London, 1599), p. 20; see also Pareus, *Commentary*, p. 369 (commentary).

23. *An Explanation*, pp. 201, 205.

24. "Milton and the Exaltation of the Son: The War in Heaven in *Paradise Lost*," *ELH*, XXXVI (1969), 215–31.

25. *Ten Perspectives on Milton* (New Haven, 1965), p. 167. Hughes' note on *Paradise Lost*, X, 249–63 in *John Milton: Complete Poems and Major Prose* (Indianapolis, 1957), p. 412, is pertinent here.

26. See *The Works of Edmund Spenser*, ed. Edwin Greenlaw et al., 16 vols, (Baltimore, 1953), II, 428.

27. *Pansebeia: or, a View of All Religions in the World*, 4th ed. (London, 1672), p. 316.

28. See William Erbery, *The Lord of Hosts* (London, 1648), p. 4; William Guild, *The Sealed Book Opened* (London, 1656), p. 133; and Theodore Haak, *The Dutch Annotations upon the New Testament* (London, 1657), sig. Mm3.

29. *Commentary*, p. 495 (commentary).

30. Gifford, *Sermons*, p. 243; Brightman, *The Revelation of S. John* (Leyden, 1616), pp. 150–51.

31. *Sermons*, pp. 220, 230.

32. *Christs Victorie over the Dragon: or Satans Downfall* (London, 1633), p. 343.

33. *Myth and History in the Book of Revelation* (London, 1979), p. 111.

34. Herder, *Brief Commentary*, p. 119.

35. *Tudor Apocalypse: Sixteenth-Century Apocalypticism, Millennarianism and the English Reformation* (Appleford, England, 1978), pp. 56–58.

36. *The Revelation Reveled by Two Apocalyptical Treatises* (London, 1651), pp. 28, 45–46, 69.

37. *Pansebeia*, p. 509.

38. *Tudor Apocalypse*, p. 105. The immediate context for this disguise—the antipapal satire implicit in the Paradise of Fools episode—is likewise relevant here, particularly in view of Bauckham's insistence that "the Protestant image of the papal Antichrist was . . . an extraordinary vision of the devil disguising himself as an angel of light" (p. 104).

39. *Christs Victorie*, p. 149.

40. Quoted from *The Romantics on Milton: Formal Essays and Critical Asides*, ed. Joseph Wittreich (Cleveland, 1970), p. 211.

41. *The History of the Devil*, 2d ed. (London, 1727), pp. 27, 41–43.

42. *The Notebooks of Samuel Taylor Coleridge*, ed. Kathleen Coburn, 3 vols. New York, 1957–), entry for March 1805, no. 2469: 17. 43, II, text.

43. See De Lude's ΔΑΙΜΟΝΟΛΟΓΙΑ: *or, a Treatise of Spirits* (London, 1723), pp. 78, 88, 92–93, 175); and Debes' *Foeroe, and Foeroa: That Is a Description of the Islands and Inhabitants of Foeroe*, trans. John Sterpin (London, 1676), pp. 365–70.

44. See both *A Summarie Answere to All the Material Points in Any of Master Darel His Bookes* (London, 1601), p. 149, and *Dialogicall Discourses of Spirits and Devils* (London, 1601), p. 110.

45. *Allegory of Love*, p. 58.

46. The following are essential readings: Edward Langton, *Satan, a Portrait* (London,

1945); Rivkah Schärf Kluger, *Satan in the Old Testament*, trans. Hildegard Nagel (Evanston, Ill., 1967); Moncure Daniel Conway, *Demonology and Devil-Lore*, 2 vols. (London, 1880); L. W. Cushman, *The Devil and the Vices in English Dramatic Literature before Shakespeare*, Studien zur Englischen Philologie, VI (Halle, 1900); Paul Carus, *The History of the Devil and the Idea of Evil* (Chicago and London, 1900); R. Lowe Thompson, *The History of the Devil: The Horned God of the West* (London, 1929); and Graf, *Story of the Devil*. Carus observes that "the Protestant Devil . . . received his finishing touches from Milton" (p. 351). See also *S.V.* "Beelzebub," "Belial," "Mammon," and "Moloch," in *A Milton Encyclopedia*, ed. William B. Hunter, Jr. et al., 8 vols. (Lewisburg, Pa., 1978–80), I, 133–38, 138–40; V, 60–62, 150–52. In these entries I include details germane to this essay.

47. Hughes, "Devils to Adore for Deities," in *Studies in Honor of DeWitt T. Starnes*, ed. Thomas P. Harrison et al. (Austin, Texas, 1967), pp. 250–51, and Emile Grillot de Givry, *Witchcraft, Magic, and Alchemy*, trans. J. Courtenay Locke (London, 1931), p. 126.

48. *Commentary on the Epistles of Paul the Apostle to the Corinthians*, trans. John Pringle, 2 vols. (Edinburgh, 1849), II, 259. Cf. Calvin, *Commentary on the Four Last Books of Moses, Arranged in the Form of a Harmony*, trans. John Pringle, 4 vols. (Edinburgh, 1852–55), II, 86. See also T. H. Gaster's remarks in *The Interpreter's Dictionary of the Bible*, ed. George Arthur Buttrick et al., 4 vols. (New York and Nashville, 1962), I, 374, 377.

49. See Gustav Davidson, *A Dictionary of Angels Including the Fallen Angels* (New York and London, 1967), p. 182.

50. *Annotations upon All the Books of the Old and New Testament*, 3d ed. (London, 1657); see esp. the notes to Acts vii, 43, Amos v, 26, 1 Kings xi, 5, and Leviticus xviii, 21 and xx, 2.

51. See Burton's *Anatomy of Melancholy*, ed. Floyd Dell and Paul Jordan-Smith (New York, 1931), I, ii, I, 2. Cf. Heywood, *The Hierarchie of the Blessed Angells . . . The Fall of Lucifer with His Angells* (London, 1635), and Henry Cornelius Agrippa, *Three Books of Occult Philosophy*, trans. J. F. (London, 1651), pp. 397–99. On Milton's allegiance to such traditions, see Grant McColley, *"Paradise Lost": An Account of Its Growth and Major Origins* (Chicago, 1940), p. 121; Robert H. West, *Milton and the Angels* (Athens, Ga., 1955), esp. pp. 69, 125; and C. A. Patrides, *Milton and the Christian Tradition* (Oxford, 1966), p. 93.

52. *Commentary on a Harmony of the Evangelists, Matthew, Mark, and Luke*, trans. William Pringle, 3 vols. (Edinburgh, 1845–46), II, 66.

53. *Story of the Devil*, p. 29.

54. *Anatomy of Melancholy*, III. iv. I. 2.

55. *Three English Epics: Studies in Chaucer, Spenser, and Milton* (Lincoln, Neb., 1979), p. 105.

56. Ibid., pp. 105–06.

57. P. 21, ll. 2–7. of *The Four Zoas*, is quoted from *The Poetry and Prose of William Blake*, ed. David V. Erdman, rev. ed. (New York, 1970), p. 306.

58. See Kranidas' *The Fierce Equation: A Study of Milton's Decorum* (The Hague, 1965), p. 145; Stein's *Answerable Style: Essays on "Paradise Lost"* (Minneapolis, 1953), p. 51; and Fox's "Satan's Triad of Vices," *TSLL*, II (1960), 275.

59. "The Character of Mammon in *Paradise Lost*," *RES*, N.S. XIII (1962), 39, and *Answerable Style*, p. 50.

60. *Commentary on a Harmony of the Evangelists*, trans. Pringle, II, 68.

61. *A Critique of "Paradise Lost"* (Ithaca, 1960), p. 42.

62. Ibid. Still the best theoretical guide to Milton's strategies for depiction of character in the council scenes is Maud Bodkin's *Archetypal Patterns in Poetry: Psychological Studies of Imagination* (1934; rpt. New York, 1958). Allan H. Gilbert's *On the Composition of "Paradise Lost"* (Chapel Hill, N.C., 1947) puts a somewhat different construction on the phrase from Milton's Argument, using it to suggest that the remark is at odds with the poem Milton has written (p. 102).

63. See Newton's annotation in *Paradise Regain'd* (London, 1785), p. 9.

64. Todd, *Poetical Works of John Milton*, II, 259.

65. H. Lukin, *An Introduction to the Holy Scripture* (London, 1669), p. 185.

66. "The Dialogue in Heaven: A Reconsideration of *Paradise Lost*, III. 1–417," *PMLA*, LXXII (1957), 602.

67. Graf, *Story of the Devil*, p. 225.

68. *Cowper's Milton*, ed. William Hayley, 2 vols. (Chichester, 1810), II, 431.

69. Vasily Rozanov, *The Apocalypse of Our Time and Other Writings*, ed. Robert Payne (New York, 1977), p. 236.

70. *Letters on Literature, Taste, and Composition*, 2 vols. (London, 1808), II, 295.

71. Quoted from *The Romantics on Milton*, ed. Wittreich, p. 277.

72. *Milton: Man and Thinker* (New York, 1948), p. 220.

73. *A Catholike Exposition upon the Revelation*, pp. 35ᵛ, 174ᵛ–75.

74. *A Plaine Discovery of the Whole Revelation of Saint John* (Edinburgh, 1593), p. 143.

75. See Forbes' *An Learned Commentarie upon the Revelation of Saint John* (Middleburg, 1614), p. 132, and Taylor's *Christs Victorie*, p. 468.

76. See Bacon's *The Labyrinth the Kingdom Is in* (London, 1649), p. 3, and Coppin's *Antichrist in Man Opposeth Emmannuel or God in Us* (London, 1649), pp. 36, 57.

77. See Nayler's *A Discovery of the Beast Got into the Seat of the False Prophet* (London, 1655), p. 4, and *Antichrist in Man, Christ's Enemy* (London, 1656), p. 2, and Guild's *The Sealed Book Opened*, sig. A4.

78. *Revelation Reveled*, sig. 4ᵛ.

79. *Three English Epics*, pp. 8, 88.

80. *Milton and His Epic Tradition*, p. 38.

81. Maresca, *Three English Epics*, p. 100.

82. Ibid., p. 139.

83. Ibid., p. 12.

84. See Rieger's "Wordsworth Unalarm'd," in *Milton and the Line of Vision*, ed. Joseph Wittreich (Madison, 1975), pp. 185–208, and MacCaffrey's *Spenser's Allegory: The Anatomy of Imagination* (Princeton, 1976).

85. *A Study of English Romanticism* (New York, 1968), p. 33.

86. Michel Beaujour, "Genus Universum," *Glyph*, VII (1980), 16.

THE GENRES OF *PARADISE LOST:* LITERARY GENRE AS A MEANS OF ACCOMMODATION

Barbara K. Lewalski

THAT *PARADISE LOST* is an epic whose closest structural affinities are to Virgil's *Aeneid*, and that it undertakes to redefine classical epic heroism in Christian terms are truisms about the poem's genre.[1] Widely recognized also is the importance of epic traditions and epic features other than Virgilian. *Paradise Lost* has an Iliadic subject involving the loss and woe resulting from an act of disobedience, together with an Achillean hero motivated by a sense of injured merit; that same hero is also an Odyssean hero of wiles and craft, who undertakes a perilous journey in order to find (like Aeneas) a new homeland.[2] *Paradise Lost* has also a Hesiodic gigantomachia with Homeric battle scenes; numerous Ovidian metamorphoses; an Ariostan Paradise of Fools; a pair of Spenserian allegorical figures (Sin and Death); a romance garden in which a hero and heroine must withstand a dragon of sorts; and a poetic hexameron in the tradition of Du Bartas.[3] Moreover, because heroic values have been so profoundly transvalued in *Paradise Lost,* the poem is sometimes assigned to categories beyond epic: pseudomorph, prophetic poem, apocalypse, anti-epic, transcendent epic.[4]

Within the epic or epiclike structure, many dramatic elements have also been identified, including some vestiges of Milton's early sketches for a drama entitled "Adam unparadiz'd," some structural resemblances to contemporary heroic epics in five acts such as Davenant's *Gondibert,* and a tragic figure (Adam) who falls from happiness to misery through *hamartia*. We find also tragic soliloquies by Satan and Adam which recall those of Dr. Faustus and Macbeth; a morality play "Parliament of Heaven" episode; a scene of domestic farce in which Satan first vehemently repudiates and then fawns upon his reprehensible offspring Sin and Death; scenes of domestic tragedy modulating to tragicomedy which present Adam and Eve's quarrel, fall, mutual recrimination, and later, reconciliation; and tragic masques or pageants portraying the sins and miseries of human history.[5]

Pastoral forms are hardly less important: landscape description; an Arcadian "happy rural seat of various view" (IV, 247); a pastoral idyl with Adam and Eve at their supper fruits engaging in eclogue-like dialogue; scenes of light georgic gardening activity.[6] Lyric forms of all kinds are also embedded in the poem and have received some attention: celebratory odes, psalmic hymns of praise and thanksgiving, epithalamia, love lyrics including Adam's aubade and Satan's nocturnal serenade to Eve, submerged sonnets, complaints, laments.[7] Rhetorical and discursive forms also abound: Satan's several speeches of political oratory; God's lengthy theological disquisition or sermon on free will; a parliamentary debate in hell over what to do next and another between Satan and Abdiel in heaven over God's right of governance; a treatise on astronomical systems; a dialogue about human nature between God and Adam and a dialogue about love between Raphael and Adam; an interpretative account of biblical history; and of course Satan's temptation speeches to Eve in the style and manner of "som Orator renound / In Athens or free Rome" (IX, 670–71).[8]

If we ask why Milton incorporated so complete a spectrum of literary forms and genres in *Paradise Lost*, a partial answer must be that much Renaissance critical theory supports the notion of the epic as a heterocosm or a compendium of subjects, forms, and styles. As Rosalie Colie has noted, Homer was widely recognized as the source and origin of all the arts and sciences—philosophy, mathematics, history, geography, military art, religion, oratory, hymnic praise, rhetoric, and much more—and by that token he was regarded as the source of all literary forms.[9] Out of Homer, said his great English Renaissance translator George Chapman (citing Petrarch), "are all Arts deduced, confirmed or illustrated," and by reason of this inclusiveness Homer can best instruct all kinds of people—kings, soldiers, counsellors, fathers, husbands, wives, lovers, friends.[10] For Scaliger as well, epic is both a mixed form and "the chiefest of all forms"; it is "catholic in the range of subject-matter," and it supplies "the universal controlling rules for the composition of each other kind." But for Scaliger the *Aeneid* is the supreme epic, presenting nature perfected—the very "*ideas* of things . . . just as they might be taken from nature itself," only more perfect.[11] Moreover, the Bible had long been regarded as epiclike in that it comprehended all history, all subject matters, and many genres—law, history, prophecy, heroic poetry, lyric, allegory, proverb, hymn, sermon, epistle, tragedy, tragicomedy, and much more.[12] Responding to this tradition, Torquato Tasso agreed that Homer and Virgil had intermingled all forms and styles in their great epics, but (with obvious reference to his own *Geru-*

salemme Liberata) he praised Renaissance heroic poems for their greater variety of matter, imaging that of the created universe itself:

The great poet (who is called divine for no other reason than that as he resembles the supreme Artificer in his workings he comes to participate in his divinity) can form a poem in which, as in a little world, one may read here of armies assembling, here of battles on land or sea, here of conquests of cities, skirmishes and duels, here of jousts, here descriptions of hunger and thirst, here tempests, fires, prodigies, there of celestial and infernal councils, there seditions, there discord, wanderings, adventures, enchantments, deeds of cruelty, daring, courtesy, generosity, there the fortunes of love, now happy, now sad, now joyous, now pitiful.[13]

In addition to this general idea of epic inclusiveness, many Renaissance theorists called attention to specific amalgams in the great poems of the tradition. Aristotle's close paralleling of epic and tragedy, together with his identification of the plot of the *Iliad* as "pathetic," laid the groundwork for the common Renaissance view of the *Iliad* as a tragic epic. William Webbe traced the origins of tragedy to the *Iliad* and the origins of comedy to the *Odyssey*. Giraldi Cinthio identified romancelike elements in the *Odyssey* and *The Metamorphoses* (characters, wonders, copia). Mazzoni discussed *The Divine Comedy* as both comedy and epic. Puttenham, following Scaliger, emphasized the historical dimension in the epics of Homer and Virgil, identifying these works as one species of a larger category of historical poems.[14] The most important English literary theorist of the Renaissance, Sir Philip Sidney, attributed a specific kind of teaching and moral benefit to each of the poetic kinds and defended their mixture: "if severed they be good, the conjunction cannot be hurtfull."[15] And the major English Renaissance narratives with claims to epic status before *Paradise Lost*—Sidney's *New Arcadia* and Spenser's *Faerie Queene*—were quite obviously mixtures of epic, romance, pastoral, allegory, and song.

This Renaissance theory and practice helps us understand how Milton came to resolve as he did the genre questions he was pondering in *The Reason of Church-Government* (1642):

Whether that Epick form whereof the two poems of Homer, and those other two of *Virgil* and *Tasso* are a diffuse, and the book of *Job* a brief model: . . . Or whether those *Dramatick* constitutions, wherein *Sophocles* and *Euripides* raigne shall be found more doctrinal and exemplary to a Nation, the Scripture also affords us a divine pastoral Drama in the *Song of Salomon* consisting of two persons and a double *Chorus*, as *Origen* rightly judges. And the Apocalyps of Saint *John* is the majestick image of a high and stately Tragedy, shutting up and intermingling her solemn Scenes and Acts with a sevenfold *Chorus* of halleluja's and harping symphonies: and this my opinion the grave autority of *Pareus* commenting that booke is sufficient to confirm. Or if occasion shall lead to imitat those magnifick Odes and Hymns wherein *Pindarus* and *Callimachus* are in most things worthy, some others in their frame judicious, in their matter most an end faulty: But those frequent songs throughout the law and prophets beyond all these, not in their divine argument alone, but in the very critical art of composition may be easily made appear over all the kinds of Lyrick poesy to be incomparable. (YP, I, 813–16)

Contemporary theory, it seems clear, gave Milton ample warrant to conclude that an epic incorporating the entire spectrum of kinds and subjects would be most doctrinal and exemplary and would also have the best claim to inclusion in the company he expressly sought for it—the *Iliad*, the *Odyssey*, the *Aeneid*, *Gerusalemme Liberata*, and the Bible.

Recognizing that Milton would want his poem to have the comprehensiveness attributed to the greatest epics, we need to ask a further question: just how did Milton employ generic inclusiveness to accomplish his specific poetic purposes? My general proposition is that for Milton, genre choices, changes, and transformations serve as a primary vehicle of artistic perception and of conscious accommodation to the reader, affording that reader a range of perspectives upon the Miltonic subject. This suggestion invites some revision in two currently fashionable views of Milton: that he saw himself as a prophet directly inspired by the Spirit of God, seeking to present his prophetic visions of divine truth to his audience; or, that he took on the role of rigorous and punitive teacher, engaging his reader in a strenuous dialectic intended to force the reader into frequent and inevitable mistakes in reading, thereby causing the reader to recognize and reenact his or her own fallenness. The formidable array of conventional genres in *Paradise Lost* indicates, I suggest, that Milton can only see and tell of things invisible by using the familiar forms art supplies to his own imagination and that of his readers. It also indicates that he can teach most effectively by building upon and letting his readers refine their developed responses to the values and assumptions about man, nature, language, heroism, virtue, pleasure, work, and love which have long been associated with the various genres and literary modes.

As a guide to Milton's poetic method and intention, I propose to examine the two poets/prophets/teachers he creates in the poem as subordinate narrators—Raphael and Michael. Both of them have to teach and to mediate divine truth to a sometimes not-so-fit audience, Adam and Eve, and both of them do so by literary accommodation, "inventing" precisely those literary genres which are most appropriate to their several subjects and to the special needs of the audience. Milton's angelic narrators invent the prototypes, as it were, of several genres we know, setting them forth in their pristine, ideal forms to teach, delight, and move Adam and Eve in the ways commonly attributed to those genres. The bard's audience, conscious of literary tradition as Adam and Eve are not, must learn from the angelic narratives in more complex ways, by comparing the angelic archetypal poems with their literary progenies in regard to the human goods and values presented.

Both of Milton's angelic narrators are prophets in the broad seventeenth-century sense of the term. According to the Cambridge Platonist John Smith, prophecy encompasses all forms of divine illumination of the mind, chiefly about divine things but sometimes about the natural order as well.[16]Citing Hebrew sources constantly, Smith identified several varieties and degrees of prophecy in Scripture, observing that angels often served as mediators of divine revelation, and underscoring the radical accommodation that prophets had often to make to their vulgar audiences: "Hence is that Axiome so frequent among the Jewish Doctors . . . Great is the power of the *Prophets,* who while they looked down upon these Sensible and Conspicable things, were able to furnish out the notion of Intelligible and Inconspicable beings thereby to the rude Senses of Illiterate people."[17] Going beyond this notion, Milton presents his angelic prophets as Renaissance poets who meet the problem of accommodation in part by inventing literary genres suited to their own capacities, the height and variety of the subjects they treat, and the needs and condition of the audience; like Milton himself, these angelic prophet/poets clearly believe that decorum is the grand masterpiece to observe.

Raphael is a prophet in Smith's most general sense: his understanding has been informed by God, he enlightens Adam about natural things as well as divine truth, but he is not himself dependent upon direct, continuous divine illumination, except (perhaps) in recounting the Creation story. God, we note, gave Raphael general directives concerning his manner, tone, and basic purpose: Raphael was to advise Adam about his own happiness and the threat to it from Satan. But God permitted the angel artistic license in devising appropriate forms of discourse to accomplish this mission:

> "Go therefore, half this day as friend with friend
> Converse with *Adam,* in what Bowre or shade
> Thou find'st him from the heat of Noon retir'd.

. . . .
and such discourse bring on,
As may advise him of his happie state,
Happiness in his power left free to will,

. . . .
tell him withall
His danger, and from whom.   (V, 229–39)

As a skillful teacher will, Raphael allows Adam's questions and initiatives
to determine the particular subjects discussed; and as a true poet must,
he finds for those subjects fitting generic forms which reinforce the
truths he is charged to set forth. At one point Adam accords Raphael the
title "Divine / Hystorian" (VIII, 6–7), recognizing thereby that the angel
discourses chiefly of past events and of the nature of things and that he
draws for the most part upon his own firsthand experience and observation—supplemented, we may suppose, by the reports of others, especially as regards the war in heaven. Since this is so, the poet Raphel
usually seems confident that his own knowledge is adequate to his subject matter, though worried at times about how to accommodate it to his
intelligent but inexperienced audience.

Responding to Adam's hospitable offer of food and queries about
the comparison of earthly and heavenly food, Raphael invents his first
literary work—a brief disquisition in verse on ontology, the nature of
things (V, 404–33, 469–505). Though its concepts derive from Plato's
Timaeus and from Lucretius, Lipsius, Fludd, and others,[18] its form, as a
miniature philosophic poem, is closest to Lucretius' De rerum natura.
Lucretius' poem (along with Empedocles' Περί φύσεως, Virgil's Georgics, and some others) became the basis for Renaissance critical disputes
about the status of the philosophical-scientific poem as poetry. Those
who followed Aristotle closely in making imitation the sine qua non of
poetry excluded such works; others, like Scaliger and Minturno, who
defined and categorized poetry according to verse forms or subject matter, identified Lucretius' poem as a philosophical epic or a variety of
heroic poem.[19] Puttenham ranked Lucretius and poets of his type who
treat "such doctrines and arts as the commonwealth fared the better by"
next after historical (epiclike) poems, noting that these poets employed
verse Exameter savouring the Heroicall."[20] Sidney proposed to leave to
grammarians the dispute as to whether such philosophical poems can
properly be termed poems or no, while he praised the "sweet food of
sweetly uttered knowledge" to be found in them.[21]

Lucretius' poem is a passionate and eloquent argument for the
philosophy of Epicurus, grounded upon a version of Democritean at-

omism. As the thematic statement in the first book indicates, the poem seeks to explain the nature of the universe, the origins of all life and change, the human condition, and human freedom as alike resulting from the constant, fortuitous collision of atoms, which, in various degrees of refinement, make up the substratum of all being, including the gods and the soul:

> nam tibi de summa caeli ratione deumque
> disserere incipiam, et rerum primordia pandam,
> unde omnis natura creet res auctet alatque
> quove eadem rursum natura perempta resolvat,
> quae nos materiem et genitalia corpora rebus
> reddunda in ratione vocare et semina rerum
> appellare suëmus et haec eadem usurpare
> corpora prima, quod ex illis sunt omnia primis.[22]

Lucretius' purpose is to free his addressee, Memmius, from superstition about the gods and from fear of death through knowledge of "the aspect and law of nature," so that he will base his choices in life upon true and profound understanding of man's place in the processes of nature:

> Denique caelesti sumus omnes semine oriundi;
> omnibus ille idem pater est, unde alma liquentis
> umoris guttas mater cum terra recepit,
> feta parit nitidas fruges arbustaque laeta
> et genus humanum, parit omnia saecla ferarum,
> pabula cum praebet quibus omnes corpora pascunt
> et dulcem ducunt vitam prolemque propagant;
> quapropter merito maternum nomen adepta est.
> cedit item retro, de terra quod fuit ante,
> in terras, et quod missumst ex aetheris oris,
> id rursum caeli rellatum templa receptant.
> nec sic interemit mors res ut materiai
> corpora conficiat, sed coetum dissupat ollis;
> inde aliis aliud coniungit, et efficit omnes
> res ita convertant formas mutentque colores
> et capiant sensus et puncto tempore reddant.[23]

Raphael's miniature *De rerum natura* recalls such statements both in its form and in its emphasis upon certain concepts—the heavenly source of all life, the common material substratum of all being, the ongoing processes of change in the universe. And Raphael also intends to lead his addressee, Adam, to make sound choices in life on the basis of a true apprehension of his place in nature. But Raphel's prototypical Lucretian epic is based on teleological rather than atomistic principles, recognizing God as the source and end of all the natural processes and emphasizing human choice rather than the fortuitous collision of atoms as a principal determinant of the direction of change:

> O *Adam*, one Almightie is, from whom
> All things proceed, and up to him return,
> If not deprav'd from good, created all
> Such to perfection, one first matter all,
> Indu'd with various forms, various degrees
> Of substance, and in things that live, of life;
> But more refin'd, more spiritous, and pure,
> As neerer to him plac't or neerer tending
> Each in thir several active Sphears assignd,
> Till body up to spirit work, in bounds
> Proportiond to each kind.   (V, 469–79)

Raphel's poetic method also resembles Lucretius' practice of couching philosophical and scientific precepts in vibrant imagery and relating them directly to the experience and observation of his addressee—as when Lucretius refers Memnius to the phenomenon of plant nourishment and growth as a proof that void spaces must exist between atomic particles in all substances:

> crescunt arbusta et fetus in tempore fundunt,
> quod cibus in totas usque ab radicibus imis
> per truncos ac per ramos diffunditur omnis;
> inter saepta meant voces et clausa domorum
> transvolitant; rigidum permanat frigus ad ossa.
> quod, nisi inania sint qua possent corpora quaeque
> transire, haud ulla fieri ratione videres.[24]

Raphael's act of eating the Edenic fruit displays before Adam's eyes the great principle of "one first matter" comprising all things and capable of various degrees of refinement as it nourishes progressively higher forms of life. The angel also draws an example from plant growth:

> So from the root
> Springs lighter the green stalk, from thence the leaves
> More aerie, last the bright consummate floure
> Spirits odorous breathes: flours and thir fruit
> Mans nourishment, by gradual scale sublim'd
> To vital Spirits aspire, to animal,
> To intellectual, give both life and sense,
> Fansie and understanding, whence the Soule
> Reason receives, and reason is her being,
> Discursive, or Intuitive; discourse

Is oftest yours, the latter most is ours,
Differing but in degree, of kind the same.
Wonder not then, what God for you saw good
If I refuse not, but convert, as you,
To proper substance, time may come when men
With Angels may participate, and find
No inconvenient Diet, nor too light Fare:
And from these corporal nutriments perhaps
Your bodies may at last turn all to Spirit,
Improv'd by tract of time, and wingd ascend
Ethereal, as wee, or may at choice
Here or in Heav'nly Paradises dwell;
If ye be found obedient.   (V, 479–501)

The source is probably not Lucretius, for the plant topos had become a commonplace in philosophical-scientific discourse, in both prose and poetry. But we are meant to note that Raphael "invents" this topos— brilliantly suited to Adam in his garden—and uses it to better purpose than later philosophers will in his prototypical philosophical poem on the nature of things.

Raphael next invents the genre of the classical epic. Adam, responding to Raphael's apparently casual remark about disobedient angels, asks for a "full relation" of that story (V, 556). This request causes Raphael to confront a difficult problem of literary accommodation. The subject is "High matter" involving "th'invisible exploits / Of warring Spirits," while the audience is limited to "human sense." Moreover, his own emotions may prove difficult to control: "how shall I relate / . . . without remorse / The ruin of so many glorious once." Finally, these "secrets of another world" are perhaps not lawful to reveal. The last problem is solved by a dispensation allowing the revelation for Adam's good, and Raphael proposes to deal with the limitations of his audience "by lik'ning spiritual to corporal forms"—leaving open the question of whether such corporeal forms are in fact Platonic shadows of spiritual reality or not (V, 563–76).

Acting upon this decision, Raphael presents the war in heaven as a miniature *Iliad*, based upon a true history yet with large scope for invention. Raphael's epic, like Homer's, begins with a ceremony (the elevation of the Son) at which an Achillean hero feels his honor affronted and withdraws with his forces to his own regions. From the reader's comparatist perspective, Satan is seen to be a debased Achilles, as Francis Blessington observes[25]: his claims of equality with his ruler are without any basis whatsoever, his council of war is in fact a temptation, and

his withdrawal of allegiance escalates to open warfare against his erst-
while comrades. We recognize also that the warfare in heaven is Homeric, complete with single combats, epic boasts, mockery of foes, flyt-
ings, chariot clashes, and legions attacking legions with spears and
shields. But the hill-hurlings from Hesiod's *Theogony* and the diabolical
cannon and gunpowder from later epics such as Erasmo di Valvasone's
Angeleida and Spenser's *Faerie Queene*[26] identify this celestial battle as
the source of the epic-warfare topos in literature wherever it is used.

While the bard's audience must learn by comparing later epics with
Raphael's original, Adam is to learn directly from Raphael's epic. If
Homer's epic was widely recognized as the original *paideia*, Raphael
creates the prototype of the Homeric "epic of strife" for Adam and Eve
to learn from, designed to convey a sounder view of heroism, power,
and glory. Since he speaks as an epic narrator who was also a participant
in the struggle, Raphael's tone is in the main heroic, with occasional
mock-epic overtones as he (infrequently) associates himself with the
perspective of the omnipotent God who has his foes in derision. Raphael
accords certain of his companions in arms—Gabriel, Michael, and especially Abdiel—their moments of *aristeia* during the first day's fighting,
which begins with a blow from Abdiel that brings Satan to his knees and
ends with Michael inflicting a painful wound upon Satan during their
single combat. Raphael insists, however, that the Homeric ideals of
martial prowess and battle glory have little real importance:

> I might relate of thousands, and thir names
> Eternize here on Earth; but those elect
> Angels contented with thir fame in Heav'n
> Seek not the praise of men: the other sort
> In might though wondrous and in Acts of Warr,
> Nor of Renown less eager, yet by doome
> Canceld from Heav'n and sacred memorie,
> Nameless in dark oblivion let them dwell.
> For strength from Truth divided and from Just,
> Illaudable, naught merits but dispraise
> And ignominie.   (VI, 373–83).

In Raphael's epic, the angelic warriors are severely tested during
the celestial battle, as Stella Revard has shown, [27] but they heroically
maintain their loyalty, obedience, and faith; in its essence, though not in
its martial manifestation, this heroism is a fitting model for Adam and
Eve. Though sent forth by God as an invincible army charged to cast the
rebels from heaven, they find on the first day that their fiercest combat
can gain them only a temporary advantage, since the wounds they inflict

upon the enemy promptly heal. On the second day they are felled by the Satanic cannon and gunpowder and are humiliated by the rebels' taunts and jeers as they tumble about in their armor. And though they retaliate by hurling the hills of heaven upon their opponents, they soon receive these missives hurled back upon themselves. Moreover, in this regression from sophisticated to primitive weaponry they experience the near destruction of heaven itself: "Warr seem'd a civil Game / To this uproar; horrid confusion heapt / Upon confusion rose: and now all Heav'n / Had gon to wrack, with ruin overspred, / Had not th' Almightie Father . . . advis'd" (VI,667–74). Yet while the angels do not gain individual glory by winning decisive victories through martial prowess, they are all accorded true honor by the Son of God for their faithful and fearless warfare in God's cause, at his behest, and in loving accord with his design: "Faithful hath been your warfare, and of God / Accepted, fearless in his righteous Cause, / And as ye have receivd, so have ye don / Invincibly" (VI,803–06).

In addition to these loyal angels whose obedience and faith were tested in battle and found heroic, Raphael's epic focuses upon two heroes whose deeds flank and thereby provide a touchstone for the military actions. One is Abdiel, the moral hero, who alone defended the right in the camp of the enemy and who attempted by heroic argument to persuade his fellows from their evil course. The other is the Son, the agent of God's omnipotence, who engaged the entire Satanic army in single combat but derided his enemies, even as he conquered them, for measuring all worth by physical strength:

> they may have thir wish, to trie with mee
> In Battel which the stronger proves, they all,
> Or I alone against them, since by strength
> They measure all, of other excellence
> Not emulous, nor care who them excells.   (VI, 818–22)

Moreover, before the battle the Son displayed his own preferred use of power in restoring the heavenly landscape. By its conception and design Raphael's prototypical epic (rather like Milton's own) undertakes to display to its audience, Adam and Eve, the dangerous lure of evil, the deceptive rhetoric of temptation, the danger of power severed from right, the chaos attendant upon sin, and the nature of true moral heroism and true epic glory.

Adam's next query concerns the origin of heaven and earth, and it elicits additional "revealed" knowledge—the Creation story from Genesis. Though Adam assures Raphael that he does not ask in order to explore God's secrets but only to magnify his works, the form of Adam's question—"what cause / Mov'd the Creator in his holy Rest / Through all Eternitie so late to build / In *Chaos*" (VII, 90–93)—shows Adam making a precarious beginning in theological speculation. Besides the implication of divine mutability and laziness in Adam's words, his curiosity about God's activity before the Creation has long been seen as the very hallmark of presumptive inquiry into God's secret ways.[28] The genre Raphael chooses for his response is nicely calculated to lead Adam from such fruitless and dangerous inquiries into hidden mysteries by underscoring the necessarily radical accommodation of all knowledge of God to human understanding. Accordingly, Raphael does not merely summarize or paraphrase the first two chapters of Genesis: he creates a poetic hexameron, a brief biblical epic which we should recognize as a prototype of Tasso's *Il Mondo Creato* and especially Du Bartas' *La Semaine ou creation du monde*.

Du Bartas' *Semaine*, as Susan Synder observes, is set forth as an encyclopedic epic—"an epic of the divine plan in the physical universe, with God the Maker as its epic hero"—and contemporaries acclaimed it as such both in the original and in Sylvester's extremely popular translation, which had been published in nine editions by 1641.[29] Scattering his superlatives broadcast, Gabriel Harvey compares Du Bartas with Homer, Virgil, Dante, and the Holy Spirit itself: "Bartas [is] . . . for the highnesse of his subject and the majesty of his verse nothing inferiour unto Dante (whome some Italians preferre before Virgil or Homer), a right inspired and enravished Poet, full of chosen, grave, profound, venerable, and stately matter, even in the next Degree to the sacred and reverend stile of heavenly Divinity it selfe."[30] And in a dedicatory poem Robert Nicholson lauds both poet and translator for epic accomplishment: the loss we would have suffered had "golden *Homer*" and "great *Maro*" kept silence would have been great, "But O, what rich incomparable treasures / Had the world wanted, had this modern glory, / Divine du BARTAS hid his heavenly ceasures, / Singing the mightie *Worlds* immortall story." Moreover, England's debts to Chapman and Phaer for their translations of Homer and Virgil are outweighed by her debt to Sylvester for unfolding "These holy wonders."[31]

The terms of Adam's petition—"Deign to descend now lower" (VII, 84)—indicate that he thinks he has proposed a topic less exalted than the epic exploits of the angels and the Messianic King; in this judgment Adam locates himself with some Renaissance neoclassicists and indeed with Du Bartas himself, who claimed for his muse the "middle Region" between heaven and earth.[32] But Raphael declares the creating work of God to be the highest of all subjects, far exceeding Adam's limited capacity and straining (for the first time) the angel's own adequacy as narrator: "To recount Almightie works / What words or tongue of Seraph can suffice, / Or heart of man suffice to comprehend?" (VII, 112–14). His subject, like that of the Miltonic bard, seems to require him to soar "with no middle flight" (I, 14) and at the same time to achieve a radical theological and literary accommodation to the audience.

Raphael's prototypical hexameral epic meets this formidable challenge with a design and style vastly superior to what we find in the poems we are to recognize as its literary progeny, and it is precisely suited to Adam and Eve's situation. In the first place, Raphael eschews the lengthy catalogs and the encyclopedic lore so characteristic of the genre for a sharply focused description of the wonders and processes of creation. Second, while scholars have identified echoes from passages in Sylvester's *DuBartas* and in Lucretius, Ovid, and others describing nature's luxuriant creativity, Raphael's prototypical *Semaine* presents as it were the original from which such passages were derived—a magnificently unified vision of the divine creative power and energy, rendered through pervasive and vibrant imagery of procreation and generation.[33] The Spirit broods and infuses his vital virtue and vital warmth into the fluid mass; the earth is first an embryon in the womb of waters and then itself the womb which brings forth the "tumid Hills," the "tender grass," and all manner of vegetation, bursting with life and seeds of new life:

> Forth flourish't thick the clustring Vine, forth crept
> The smelling Gourd, up stood the cornie Reed
> Embattell'd in her field: and the humble Shrub,
> And Bush with frizl'd hair implicit: last
> Rose as in Dance the stately Trees, and spred
> Thir branches hung with copious Fruit, or gemm'd
> Thir blossoms.   (VII, 320–26).

The sea generates "Frie innumerable," the caves and fens hatch from an egg "Bursting with kindly rupture" a numerous brood of birds, and then the Earth "Op'ning her fertil Woomb teem'd at a Birth / Innumerous living Creatures" (VII, 400, 419, 454–5):

> The grassie Clods now Calv'd, now half appeer'd
> The Tawnie Lion, pawing to get free
> His hinder parts, then springs as broke from Bonds,
> And Rampant shakes his Brinded main; the Ounce,
> The Libbard, and the Tyger, as the Moale

Rising, the crumbl'd Earth above them threw
In Hillocks; the swift Stag from under ground
Bore up his branching head: scarse from his mould
Behemoth biggest born of Earth upheav'd
His vastness: Fleec't the Flocks and bleating rose,
As Plants.   (VII, 463–73).

By couching his poetic hexameron in the imagery of sexual generation, Raphael accommodates it brilliantly to Adam and Eve: besides making the subject comprehensible to them, he reinforces their awareness of their own dignity and happiness by inviting them to recognize their own mode of creation by sexual generation as an imitation of and participation in the divine act.

Finally, Raphael's ideal hexameral epic avoids the biblical literalism and strident apologetics that often characterize Du Bartas[34] by its clearly acknowledged status as an accommodated poem. Raphael underscores this at the outset by his sharp distinction between the immediacy of God's creating act, "more swift / Then time or motion," and his own narrative of a six-days' Creation, unfolded by "process of speech . . . / So told as earthly notion can receave" (VII, 176–79). We are made yet more conscious of this accommodation by genre and imagery when we compare Uriel's very different account of the Creation to Satan disguised as a cherub (III, 694–735). Uriel's account is not conceived as a hexameron and is entirely devoid of imagery of generation, focusing rather upon the features most apparent and most important from the angelic perspective—the elements, the place and course of the stars and planets, and "this Ethereal quintessence of Heav'n" (III, 716).

The final genre Raphael invents is the speculative scientific treatise, a prototype in verse of Galileo's *Dialogue Concerning the Two Chief World Systems—Ptolemaic & Copernican*.[35] Prompted perhaps by Raphael's description of the angelic creation hymn with its reference to "Starrs / Numerous, and every Starr perhaps a World / Of destind habitation" (VII, 620–22), Adam poses to Raphael a question concerning the design of the cosmos and its motion, "Which onely thy solution can resolve" (VIII, 14). Raphael, however, presents his response in a genre which will not resolve the question but will instead provide a model for scientific speculation, then and later. Just how deliberate and significant Raphael's genre choice is will be apparent when we recall that this question was commonly treated in the hexameral literature (and by Du Bartas) as an aspect of the fourth day's creation of the planets and in that context resolved in biblical literalist terms, on divine authority. Raphael, by refusing to resolve the issue on his angelic authority and by inventing a distinct genre for scientific discourse, removes such inquiry from the province of revelation and places it squarely in the realm of human speculation. Raphael's genre choice provides the underpinning for his "Benevolent and facil" opening words to Adam, "To ask or search I blame thee not, for Heav'n / Is as the Book of God before thee set, / Wherein to read his wondrous Works" (VIII, 65–68).

Galileo's dialogue has as interlocutors three friends met together to discuss the Ptolemaic and Copernican systems in a spirit of friendly inquiry. Salviati, who undertakes to "act the part of Copernicus in our arguments and wear his mask,"[36] supports the Copernican system with cogent reasoning, careful astronomical observation (aided by the telescope), and elaborate mathematical calculations. Simplicio, stout defender of Aristotelian physics and Ptolemaic astronomy, grounds his arguments chiefly upon ancient authority and piety. Sagredo is an urbane, open-minded, intelligent layman who desires to be informed about the two systems so that he may decide rationally which to credit. Galileo's dialogue leaves no question whatsoever that Salviati's arguments carry the day: the inconclusiveness of the ending and Simplicio's final appeal to the unsearchable way of God (along with a few other disclaimers) were a transparent, and in the event futile, attempt to satisfy the censors.

In Raphael's prototypical dialogue, these positions are all represented, but with large differences. Adam occupies the position of Sagredo, the intelligent layman striving to make sense of the cosmos and fully conscious of the irrationality of the planetary system as the naked eye (and Ptolemy) perceive it: "Has Nature, then, produced and directed all these enormous, perfect, and most noble celestial bodies, invariant, eternal, and divine, for no other purpose than to serve the changeable, transitory, and mortal earth? . . . Take away this purpose of serving the earth, and the innumerable host of celestial bodies is left useless and superfluous."[37] As he initiates the discussion with Raphael, Adam voices in similar terms his sense of irrationality and absurdity in the geocentric cosmos he perceives. The entire firmament seems to move with incorporeal speed through incomprehensible space,

> meerly to officiate light
> Round this opacous Earth, this punctual spot,
> One day and night; in all thir vast survey
> Useless besides, reasoning I oft admire,
> How Nature wise and frugal could commit
> Such disproportions, with superfluous hand
> So many nobler Bodies to create,

Greater so manifold to this one use,
For aught appeers, and on thir Orbs impose
Such restless revolution day by day
Repeated, while the sedentarie Earth,
That better might with farr less compass move,
Serv'd by more noble than her self, attaines
Her end without least motion.   (VIII, 22–35)

To explore Adam's inquiry, Raphael develops what is formally an evenhanded dialogue in which he plays both the Ptolemaic and the Copernican roles, though his perspective is as clearly Copernican as Galileo's. He begins by defining sharply for Adam the issue to be discussed, "Whether Heav'n move or Earth"—though Adam has not actually supposed that the earth might move—and he proceeds to indicate that the resolution of this question "Imports not" to the recognition that God's works are indeed wonderful. He then sets aside other questions as beyond the ken of man or angel: "the rest / From Man or Angel the great Architect / Did wisely to conceal" (VIII, 70–73). Such matters are, presumably, God's secret reasons for disposing as he does in the cosmos, and as Raphael later specifies (VIII, 169–70, 175–76), God's ways toward other worlds and other creatures in the universe.

Raphael's Ptolemaic argument is a far cry from Simplicio's. There are no appeals to authority, or to the need for higher illumination, or to Aristotelian physics; indeed, from the sample of Adam's reasoning he has just heard, Raphael associates with Adam's progeny the specific follies of the Ptolemaic apologists, guessing "how they will . . . /build, unbuild, contrive / To save appeerances, how gird the Sphear / With Centric and Eccentric scribbl'd o're, / Cycle and Epicycle, Orb in Orb" (VIII, 81–84). Raphael simply offers a critique of the false values implicit in Adam's complaint of disproportion in a geocentric universe (and the aspersions Adam thereby, albeit unintentionally, casts upon its Maker). Raphael's critique makes these points: the greatness and brightness of the other planets do not make them superior to the fertile earth; the noble planets at any rate do not serve the earth itself but man, who is more noble still; and (contrary to Simplicio's notions)[38] man is not the focus of the cosmic system but is rather "Lodg'd in a small partition, and the rest / Ordain'd for uses to his Lord best known" (VIII, 105–06).

As he prepares to shift to his Copernican argument, Raphael suggests that the cosmic system one credits depends on one's vantage point. To Adam on earth the universe seems Ptolemaic and thereby irrational: Raphael states that he developed his previous Ptolemaic argument "to shew / Invalid that which thee to doubt it mov'd; / Not that I so affirm, though so it seem / To thee who hast thy dwelling here on Earth" (VIII, 115–16). To angels who move among the planets the cosmos evidently seems Copernican, for Raphael proceeds to describe such a cosmos through a series of provocative suggestions, highlighting several topics explored at length by Salviati: that the sun may be a stationary center to the world; that the seemingly steadfast earth might move "Insensibly three different Motions," fetching day and night by her travels; that the earth might enlighten the moon by day as the moon enlightens earth by night; that the spots on the moon might be atmospheric clouds, possibly producing food for moon-dwellers, if any. Then, moving considerably beyond the topics addressed by Salviati, Raphael introduces Adam to advanced scientific speculations about life on other planets and unknown galaxies throughout the universe—dizzying speculations which are quite beyond Adam's wildest imaginings, though couched in the animistic, sexual imagery so precisely suited to Adam's comprehension:

> and other Suns perhaps
> With thir attendant Moons thou wilt descrie
> Communicating Male and Femal Light,
> Which two great Sexes animate the World,
> Stor'd in each Orb perhaps with some that live. (VIII, 148–52)

Raphael's prototypical Galilean dialogue is not designed (like Galileo's) to demonstrate and argue for a theory, but rather to help Adam discover, as no other genre could, the appropriate terms and attitudes which should govern scientific inquiry into the cosmos. Raphael's sudden shift from human to angelic perspective should encourage Adam to distrust naive sense impressions and to abandon the notion that human concerns must be the focus and end of the entire cosmos—attitudes which Salviati also urged upon his friends as essential to scientific discourse.[39] Raphael's dialogue of one, in which he plays the roles both of Ptolemaic apologist and daring modern theorist, makes Adam confront his inevitable limitations in the study of astronomical science. Adam's sons must wait some centuries before the telescope—or space probes and moon landings—bring them somewhat closer to Raphael's angle of vision (itself limited), and they will then be thinking in terms of the relativity of space and time, and black holes. In preparation for all this, Adam is to learn from Raphael's dialogue that he should not rashly conclude nature defective and God's ways imperfect on the basis of his earthbound and necessarily inadequate understanding of God's purpose in the cosmos, nor yet assume that the scientific orthodoxy of the moment—Ptolemaic or otherwise—can explain the whole order of things for all time. Finally, Raphael's choice of genre reinforces the scale of human values. By at once indulging and refusing to satisfy Adam's scientific curiosity, while at the same time demonstrating the limitations pertaining to the human condition, Raphael underscores his advice that Adam's primary attention, care, and joy should be directed to human things: "thy being," "this Paradise / And thy fair *Eve*" (VIII, 170–74). Adam and his progeny are to learn from Raphael's dialogue that scientific speculation or activity must not displace or violate the human person, the human environment, and human society.

The other subordinate narrator, the archangel Michael, is charged to reveal the course of biblical history to fallen Adam. Like Raphael, Michael has his mission and manner prescribed by God in very general terms, but unlike Raphael he is to derive his subject matter from God by direct illumination: God charges him to drive Adam and Eve from Paradise "not disconsolate" and to "reveale / To *Adam* what shall come in future dayes, / As I shall thee enlighten, intermix / My Cov'nant in the womans seed renewd" (XI, 113–16). In that Michael receives this subject matter by means of visionary scenes and then mediates it to Adam, he is a prophet in the strict, technical sense of the term, whereas Raphael is a prophet only in the broad sense that he is authorized by God to reveal divine truth. Summarizing the tradition of Hebrew exegesis to explain the stricter kind of prophecy, John Smith declares:

In all proper *Prophesie* . . . they [the Hebrew prophets] supposed the *Imaginative* power to be set forth as a *Stage* upon which certain *Visa* and *Simulacra* were represented to their Understandings, just indeed as they are to us in our common Dreams; only that the Understandings of the Prophets were alwaies kept awake and strongly acted by God in the midst of these apparitions, to see the intelligible Mysteries in them, and so in these Types and Shadows, which were Symbols of some spiritual things, to behold the Antitypes themselves.[40]

Michael enacts quite precisely the role of prophets such as Isaiah, Elijah, Ezekiel, and especially John of Patmos, whose Book of Revelation was described in the Geneva Bible as "a summe of those prophecies, which were writen before, but shulde be fulfilled after the comming of Christ."[41] Adam, accordingly, addresses Michael as "Seer blest" (XII, 553). It is worth noting, however, that the mode which both Michael and Adam experience as prophecy the Miltonic bard and his audience perceive as history—the biblical record of all our woe and of the course of providential history through the ages.

Like Raphael, Michael is a poet as well as a prophet: though he draws his subject matter from visionary scenes—present rather than past experience—he too must choose the appropriate literary genres to accommodate that subject matter to his audience. From one perspective, Michael's entire narrative may be seen as a prototype of the Book of Revelation, incorporating the mixture of literary genres—epic, tragedy, history—commonly associated with that book in Milton's day. The Book of Revelation was understood to present the epic conflict of Christ and Antichrist, God and Satan throughout history and at the end of time; in this conflict the elect are portrayed "fighting or a warfaring" in spiritual combat against the forces of evil.[42] The Book of Revelation was also taken to be a "most long and doleful Tragedy, which shall overflow with scourges, slaughters, and destructions," as well as "an ecclesiastical history of the troubles and persecutions of the Church."[43] In similar terms, Michael introduces his narrative with an epic statement of theme identifying that narrative as the counterpoint in the fallen human world to Raphael's Homeric brief epic, and as an illustration of the "better fortitude / Of Patience and Heroic Martyrdom" (IX, 31–32) which the Miltonic bard has claimed as the true heroic subject: "Expect to hear, supernal Grace contending / With sinfulness of Men; thereby to learn / True patience" (XI, 359–61). Michael's narrative is also history and tragedy—the history of the few just and the many wicked from the first age to the last, presented as tragic scenes and stories of sin and suffering.

Within this apocalyptic, mixed-genre narrative, Michael disposes his material into two segments, comprising two distinct genres which are differentiated by conception of subject and manner of presentation in accordance with Adam's needs. The first segment is a series of tragic masques or pageants, interpreted as emblems.[44] Because Adam has been blind to sin and its effects, Michael first purges his eyes and then points out to him from the Hill of Speculation several scenes from antediluvian history: the murder of Abel; a lazar house full of loathsome diseases; the deceptively attractive but actually sinful society of the sons of God and the daughters of Cain; the wholesale destruction wrought by the giant offspring of that union; the luxurious riot of the ensuing generation; and finally, God's destruction of the entire world by flood, saving only Noah and his family.

In their manner of presentation these tragic masques closely resemble those in the Book of Revelation, described by David Pareus (among others) as "a *Propheticall drama*, show, or representation" presented by several angels to John of Patmos, setting forth "by diverse *shewes* and *apparitions* . . . diverse, or rather (as we shall see) the same things touching the Church, not past, but to come."[45] Milton, we recall, twice cited Pareus as his authority for describing the Book of Revelation

as a "high and stately Tragedy, shutting up and intermingling her solemn Scenes and Acts with a sevenfold *Chorus* of haleluja's and harping
symphonies."[46] We ought to note, however, that in *Paradise Lost* Michael is the true prophet enlightened by God as to the meaning of the
pageants. Adam, by contrast, sees the visions but understands little of
what he sees: in this he seems to enact what John Smith designates as
the lowest order of prophecy, wherein "we have first the outward frame
of things *Dramatically* set forth so potently in the Prophet's phansie, as
that his Mind was not at the same time capable of the mystical meaning,
yet that was afterward made known to him, but yet with much obscuri-
tie still attending it."[47]

Moreover, there are important differences between the tragic
masques Michael presents and those of the Book of Revelation. For one
thing, Michael's masques (except for the lazar house) are historical pageants, not symbolic shows. For another, unlike the angels who presented visions to John of Patmos, Michael also undertakes the task of
interpretation. He does so by further generic accommodation, presenting these historical scenes to Adam as emblems requiring interpretation,
and taking occasion from Adam's mistakes to interpret them rightly.
Michael gives the several tragic scenes thematic unity by interpreting
them all as moral emblems which manifest the ravages of sin throughout
history, beginning with the murder of Abel and ending climactically
with the near destruction of the entire human race in the great Flood;
he also points to notable emblems of the new heroism in Enoch and
Noah. In this first segment, Michael's comments are not overtly typological: though the bard's audience understands the world's destruction
by flood and its subsequent renovation to be a type of the Apocalypse
and Millennium, Adam merely laments the world's wickedness and re-
joices over the just Noah from whom God will raise another world.
Michael's interpretations are, however, apocalyptic: he presents the
tragic pageants as manifestations of a world given over to sin and evil
and subject to divine justice and judgment. The four horsemen ranging
at large through these pageants are Death, War, Pestilence (the lazar
house filled with the diseases of intemperance), and in place of Famine,
Flood.

Michael's masques are not, then, modeled directly on the visions of
the Apocalypse, and Adam does not understand them by prophetic illumination. Rather, Michael orders his tragic scenes into a biblical poem
which teaches Adam to view historical events from an apocalyptic perspective. A suggestive generic analogue is Agrippa D'Aubigné's epic-
tragedy *Les Tragiques* (1616), in which the events of the French reli-

gious wars, the persecutions of Protestants throughout Europe, and the trials of the biblical Children of Israel are viewed as aspects of a single story, the apocalyptic conflict of Christ and Antichrist.[48] The fifth book of *Les Tragiques*, "Fers," offers a particularly interesting parallel to the mode of vision here experienced by Adam. D'Aubigné's speaker views (in heaven) a series of tableaux painted by the angels which record scenes of suffering and persecution in the contemporary religious wars; these emblemlike tableaux are then interpreted to him *sub specie aeternitatis* by means of commentaries affixed to them. Michael, in the first segment of his narrative, invents a biblical brief epic which is in some ways a prototype of D'Aubigné's poem, an epic-tragic-emblematic work in which history (in this case antediluvian biblical history foreseen) is presented as apocalypse.

The second segment of Michael's discourse is a narrative of biblical history from Abraham to the end of time set forth as the providential design of God. Michael changes his manner of presentation in response to a change in Adam's condition—"I perceave / Thy mortal sight to faile; objects divine / Must needs impaire and wearie human sense" (XII, 8–10)—and also to the demands of his new subject, providential history. Michael himself continues to receive his subject from God in the visionary mode of prophecy—"I see him, but thou canst not" (XII, 128)—but he now mediates these visions to Adam in the common mode of revealed Scripture. In substance, Michael's narrative is an expansion of Hebrews, chapter xi, presenting a résumé and interpretation of the typological progression of exemplary Old Testament heroes of faith, culminating in and fulfilled by Christ's redemptive sacrifice. Paul's chief examples are also Michael's: Abel, Enoch, Noah (in Book XI), and Abraham, Moses, the warring judges and kings, and the multitudes who suffer for their faith (in Book XII). Such a biblical-historical narrative is suited to Michael's Pauline purpose of teaching Adam the new heroism by example and leading him to comprehend the typological pattern of history by faith: Paul in Romans x, 7 declares that "Faith commeth by hearing" the Word of God, and in Hebrews xi, 1 he defines faith as "the substance of things hoped for, the evidence of things not seen."[49] Adam now stands before Michael as any Christian stands before the interpreters of the Word of God in Scripture: he hears an account of biblical history, he often responds to it inappropriately, he advances, under constant correction, "From shadowie Types to Truth" (XII, 303), and he learns thereby to understand and praise God's Providence.

But again, Michael does not simply offer a verse paraphrase of or a commentary upon Hebrews, chapter xi. His accommodation is literary as well as theological, as once again he invents a literary genre appropriate to his material and his audience. In conceptual terms, Michael's second narrative may be seen as a prototype of that classic of Christian historiography, Augustine's *City of God*. Augustine traces the perpetual opposition and conflict between the earthly and the heavenly city, tracing their respective origins to the companies of rebel and loyal angels in heaven, and on earth to Cain and Abel. But there is warrant in Augustine for the choice of Nimrod and Abraham as the starting point of Michael's prophesied history: Augustine observes that with Abraham the City of God "begins to be more conspicuous, and the divine promises which are now fulfilled in Christ are more fully revealed"; he also identifies Nimrod as both the builder of Babel and the founder of Babylon, that quintessential historical manifestation of the earthly city.[50] Michael's prototypical *City of God* presents Nimrod and Abraham at the outset as the founders of the two cities considered as historical and political entities. Nimrod, the "mightie Hunter," instituted tyrannical government on earth, and Abraham, the man of faith, founded the elect nation convenanted to God and saved by faith in the Promises. Michael's narrative, like Augustine's, culminates in an account of the Apocalypse and Millennium, but in both narratives the terms are essentially typological rather than apocalyptic. By means of his prophetic-historical narrative Michael leads Adam by stages to understand the covenant of grace and to read in the Old Testament types their Christic and apocalyptic fulfillments. Moreover, Michael's account renders the values of the two cities very much as Augustine articulates them:

Two cities have been formed by two loves: the earthly by the love of self, even to the contempt of God; the heavenly by the love of God, even to the contempt of self. . . . The one seeks glory from men; but the greatest glory of the other is God, the witness of conscience. . . . In the one, the princes and the nations it subdues are ruled by the love of ruling; in the other, the princes and the subjects serve one another in love. . . . The one delights in its own strength, represented in the persons of its rulers; the other says to its God, "I will love Thee, O Lord, my strength." And therefore the wise men of the one city [are vain], . . . glorying in their own wisdom, and being possessed by pride. . . . But in the other city there is no human wisdom, but only godliness, which offers due worship to the true God, and looks for its reward in the society of the saints.[51]

At the close of Michael's narrative, Adam's affirmation makes clear that he now understands and accepts the values of the city of God:

> Henceforth I learne, that to obey is best,
> And love with fear the onely God, to walk

As in his presence, ever to observe
His providence, and on him sole depend,
Mercifull over all his works, with good
Still overcoming evil, and by small
Accomplishing great things, by things deemd weak
Subverting worldly strong, and worldly wise
By simply meek; that suffering for Truths sake
Is fortitude to highest victorie,
And to the faithful Death the Gate of Life;
Taught this by his example whom I now
Acknowledge my Redeemer ever blest.   (XII, 561–73)

In formal terms, the second segment of Michael's discourse is a prototype of the brief epic based on biblical history—a miniature and completed version of Du Bartas' incomplete *Seconde Semaine*. Du Bartas proposed to trace the Providence of God as it shaped the history of the Church from Paradise to the Last Judgment: his new hexameron, complementing the seven days of Creation, is based upon the scheme of the seven historical eras as outlined by Augustine. Du Bartas' epic conception of his subject is indicated by his combined thematic statement and invocation:

Grant me the story of thy Church to sing,
And gests of kinges: Let me this Totall bring
From thy first Sabaoth to his fatall toombe,
My stile extending to the day of doombe.[52]

But the intended unity and teleological direction are not realized in the poem. Du Bartas lived to complete only four of his projected seven days; his use of typology, though considerable, is sporadic; and his diffuseness and digressions blur the pattern he would define. Also, Du Bartas attempts to assimilate his biblical narratives to epic by pervasive use of epic and romance topoi and conventions: the numerous Old Testament battles and skirmishes are elaborated into epic warfare with heroes and heroines, challenges, vaunts, addresses to troops, councils of war; there are also allegorical interludes, councils in heaven, soliloquies, ecphrases, passionate declarations of love, apostrophes, catalogues, epic similes. By contrast, Michael's prototypical *Seconde Semaine* achieves conceptual rigor and structural cohesion from its Pauline and Augustinian models, and it wholly eliminates conventional epic apparatus. Michael's poem in Book XII of *Paradise Lost* is accordingly a true counterpoint to Raphael's Homeric brief epic in Book VI: it is a fully achieved epic of providential history in which all the elect are called upon, in tragic circumstances, to display some version of the new Christian heroism—unwavering faith and love, moral courage, "the better fortitude / Of Patience and Heroic Martyrdom."

As we have seen, the suordinate narrators Milton creates in *Paradise Lost* are imagined as poets inventing literary forms—chiefly varieties of epic—as a means to accommodate particular subjects to a specific audience, Adam and Eve. They present, as it were, the ideal forms of these genres in miniature: the "Lucretian" philosophical poem, the Homeric epic, the hexameron, the scientific treatise in verse, the apocalyptic epic comprised of tragic pageants, the epic of biblical history. In so doing, the angelic poets may be presumed to realize the highest potential of the various genres, to teach, move, and delight Adam and Eve; at another level, these angelic poems provide a standard against which the bard's audience is expected to measure the values conveyed by other noteworthy poems in the several genres. If Milton's subordinate narrators use such literary strategies, I think we may fairly expect to find that the Miltonic bard—the all-encompassing narrative voice of the poem—employs generic choices and changes in similar ways. Unlike Raphael and Michael, who have to invent literary forms as yet unknown to their audience, the bard addresses an audience knowledgeable about the literary tradition and the values exhibited in particular kinds and works. He can therefore use genre changes and permutations to provide multiple perspectives upon the personages and incidents of the poem and to engage the reader continually in a process of comparison and evaluation, thereby developing and exercising the reader's moral sense. The poetics exhibited by Milton's angelic poets lends support to a hypothesis which I am exploring elsewhere: that it is by humanistic and literary means (notably, genre), rather than primarily by prophetic authority or verbal entrapment, that Milton leads his readers from partial to more complete, from simple to more complex, understanding of the human condition.

Harvard University

NOTES

1. See especially C. M. Bowra, *From Virgil to Milton* (London, 1944); Davis P. Harding, *The Club of Hercules: Studies in the Classical Background of Paradise Lost*, Illinois Studies in Language and Literature, L (Urbana, 1962); John M. Steadman, *Milton and the Renaissance Hero* (Oxford, 1967); K. W. Gransden, "*Paradise Lost* and the Ae-

neid," *Essays in Criticism*, XVII (1967), 281–303; Mario A. Di Cesare, *"Paradise Lost* and Epic Tradition," in *Milton Studies*, I, ed. James D. Simmonds (Pittsburgh, 1969), pp. 31–50; Francis C. Blessington, *"Paradise Lost" and the Classical Epic* (Boston, 1979).

2. See, e.g., Martin Mueller, *"Paradise Lost* and the *Iliad*," *Comparative Literature Studies*, VI (1969), 292–316; John M. Steadman, *Milton and the Renaissance Hero*, and *Milton's Epic Characters: Image and Idol* (Chapel Hill, 1968); Manoocher Aryanpur, *"Paradise Lost* and the *Odyssey*," *TSLL*, IX (1967), 151–66; Blessington, *"Paradise Lost" and the Classical Epic*.

3. See, e.g., Merritt Y. Hughes, "Milton's Celestial Battles and the Theogonies," in his *Ten Perspectives on Milton* (New Haven, 1965), pp. 196–219; Stella Purce Revard, *The War in Heaven: "Paradise Lost" and the Tradition of Satan's Rebellion* (Ithaca, 1980); Davis P. Harding, *Milton and the Renaissance Ovid* (Urbana, 1946); Louis L. Martz, *"Paradise Lost:* Figurations of Ovid," in his *Poet of Exile: A Study of Milton's Poetry* (New Haven, 1980), pp. 203–44; A. Bartlett Giamatti, *The Earthly Paradise and the Renaissance Epic* (Princeton, 1966); Merritt Y. Hughes, "Milton's Limbo of Vanities," and Wayne Shumacher, *"Paradise Lost* and the Italian Epic Tradition," in *Th'Upright Heart and Pure*, ed. Amadeus P. Fiore (Pittsburgh, 1967), pp. 7–24, 87–100; Irene Samuel, *Dante and Milton: "The Commedia" and "Paradise Lost"* (Ithaca, 1966); Edwin Greenlaw, "Spenser's Influence on *Paradise Lost*," XVII (1920), 320–59; A. Kent Hieatt, *Chaucer, Spenser, Milton: Mythopoeic Continuities and Transformations"* (Montreal, 1975), pp. 153–270; Kathleen Williams, "Milton, Greatest Spenserian," in *Milton and the Line of Vision*, ed. Joseph A. Wittreich, Jr. (Madison, 1975), pp. 25–55; George C. Taylor, *Milton's Use of Du Bartas* (Cambridge, Mass., 1967); J. M. Evans, *"Paradise Lost" and the Genesis Tradition* (Oxford, 1968).

4. See, e.g., John Steadman, "The Epic as Pseudomorph: Methodology in Milton Studies," in *Milton Studies*, VII, ed. Albert C. Labriola and Michael Leib (Pittsburgh, 1973), pp. 3–25; Joseph A. Wittreich, "A Poet Amongst Poets: Milton and the Tradition of Prophecy," in *Milton and the Line of Vision*, pp. 97–142; Michael Fixler, "The Apocalypse Within *Paradise Lost*," in *New Essays on "Paradise Lost"*, ed. Thomas Kranidas (Berkeley and Los Angeles, 1969), pp. 131–78; T. J. B. Spencer, *"Paradise Lost:* The Anti-Epic," in *Approaches to "Paradise Lost": The York Tercentenary Lectures*, ed. C. A. Patrides (Toronto, 1968); Harold E. Toliver, "Milton's Household Epic," in *Milton Studies*, IX, ed. James D. Simmonds (Pittsburgh, 1976), pp. 105–20; Joan Webber, *Milton and His Epic Tradition* (Seattle, 1979).

5. See, e.g., James Holly Hanford, "The Dramatic Element in *Paradise Lost*," *SP*, XIV (1917), 178–95; Arthur E. Barker, Structural Pattern in *Paradise Lost*," *PQ*, XXVIII (1949), 16–36; Ernest Sirluck, *"Paradise Lost":* A *Deliberate Epic* (Cambridge, 1967); Roger E. Rollin, *"Paradise Lost:* 'Tragical-Comical-Historical-Pastoral,' " in *Milton Studies*, V, ed. James D. Simmonds (Pittsburgh, 1973), pp. 3–37; John M. Steadman, *Epic and Tragic Structure in "Paradise Lost"* (Chicago, 1976); F. T. Prince, "Milton and the Theatrical Sublime," in *Approaches to "Paradise Lost*," ed. Patrides, pp. 53–63; John G. Demaray, *Milton's Theatrical Epic: The Invention and Design of "Paradise Lost"* (Cambridge, Mass., 1980); Thomas Kranidas, "Adam and Eve in the Garden: A Study of *Paradise Lost*, Book V," *SEL*, IV (1964), 71–83; Irene Samuel, "The Dialogue in Heaven: A Reconsideration of *Paradise Lost* III.1–417," *PMLA*, LXXII (1957), 601–11; Alwin Thaler, "Shakespearean Recollections in Milton: A Summing Up," in his *Shakespeare and Our World* (Knoxville, 1966), 139–227.

6. The major study is John R. Knott, *Milton's Pastoral Vision: An Approach to "Paradise Lost"* (Chicago, 1971). See also Joseph E. Duncan, *Milton's Earthly Paradise: A*

Historical Study of Eden (Minneapolis, 1972); William Empson, "Milton and Bentley: The Pastoral of the Innocence of Man and Nature," in his *Some Versions of Pastoral* (London, 1935), pp. 149–94; Northrop Frye, *The Return of Eden* (Toronto, 1965); Roy Daniells, "A Happy Rural Seat of Various View," in *"Paradise Lost": A Tercentenary Tribute*, ed. B. Rajan (Toronto, 1967), pp. 3–17; G. Stanley Koehler, "Milton and the Art of Landscape," in *Milton Studies*, VIII, ed. James D. Simmonds (Pittsburgh, 1975), pp. 3–40; Barbara K. Lewalski, "Innocence and Experience in Milton's Eden," in *New Essays on "Paradise Lost*," ed. Kranidas, pp. 86–117; Rollin, "*Paradise Lost*: 'Tragical-Comical-Historical-Pastoral'."

7. See, e.g., Joseph Summers, "Grateful Vicissitude," in his *The Muse's Method: An Introduction to "Paradise Lost*," (Cambridge, Mass., 1962), pp. 71–86; Donald Davie, "Syntax and Music in *Paradise Lost*," in *The Living Milton*, ed. Frank Kermode (London, 1960), pp. 70–84; William Haller, "Hail Wedded Love," *ELH*, XIII (1946), 79–97; Gary M. McCown, "Milton and the Epic Epithalamium," in *Milton Studies*, V, pp. 39–66; John Demaray, "Love's Epic Revel in *Paradise Lost*: A Theatrical Vision of Marriage," *MLQ*, XXXVIII (1977), 3–20; Lee M. Johnson, "Milton's Blank Verse Sonnets," in *Milton Studies*, V, pp. 129–53; Anna K. Nardo, "The Submerged Sonnet as Lyric Moment in Miltonic Epic," *Genre*, IX (1976), 21–35; Richard M. Bridges, "Milton's Original Psalm," *Milton Quarterly*, XIV (1980), 12–21; Judy L. Van Sickle, "Song as Structure and Symbol in Four Poems of John Milton," Ph.D. diss., Brown University, 1980, pp. 190–267.

8. See, e.g., J. B. Broadbent, *Some Graver Subject: An Essay on "Paradise Lost"* (London, 1960), pp. 110–20; and "Milton's Rhetoric," *MP*, LVI (1958–59), 224–42; John M. Steadman, " 'Semblance of Worth': Pandaemonium and Deliberative Oratory," *Neophilologus*, XLVIII (1964), 159–76, rpt. in Steadman, *Milton's Epic Characters: Image and Idol* (Chapel Hill, 1968), pp. 241–62; Steadman, "Ethos and Dianoia: Character and Rhetoric in *Paradise Lost*," in *Language and Style in Milton*, ed. R. D. Emma and J. T. Shawcross (New York, 1967), 193–232; Dennis Burden, *The Logical Epic: A Study of the Argument of "Paradise Lost"* (London, 1967); Samuel, "Dialogue in Heaven," pp. 601–11; Stanley E. Fish, *Surprised by Sin: The Reader in "Paradise Lost"* (Berkeley and Los Angeles, 1967), pp. 57–157; H. R. MacCallum, "Milton and Sacred History, Books XI–XII of *Paradise Lost*," in *Essays in English Literature from the Renaissance to the Victorian Age, Presented to A. S. P. Woodhouse*, ed. M. Maclure and F. W. Watt (Toronto, 1964), pp. 149–68.

9. Rosalie L. Colie, *The Resources of Kind: Genre-Theory in the Renaissance*, ed. Barbara K. Lewalski (Berkeley and Los Angeles, 1973), pp. 22–23.

10. Chapman, "The Preface to the Reader," *Homer's Iliad*, in *Chapman's Homer*, ed. Allardyce Nicoll, 2 vols. (Princeton, 1957), I, 14; "To the Understander," *Achilles Shield*, in *Chapman's Homer*, I, 549.

11. Julius-Caesar Scaliger, *Poetices libri septem* (I, 3; III, 25), trans. E. M. Padelford, in *Select Translations from Scaliger's Poetics* (New York, 1905), pp. 20, 52, 54.

12. For a survey of this "biblical poetics" tradition see Barbara K. Lewalski, *Milton's Brief Epic: The Genre, Meaning, and Art of "Paradise Regained"* (Providence, 1966), pp. 10–36, and *Protestant Poetics and the Seventeenth-Century Religious Lyric* (Princeton, 1979), pp. 31–71; Joseph Wittreich, *Visionary Poetics: Milton's Tradition and His Legacy* (San Marino, Calif., 1979), pp. 9–26.

13. *Discourses on the Heroic Poem*, trans. Mariella Cavalchini and Irene Samuel (Oxford, 1973), p. 78. See also pp. 76–77, 191–95.

14. Aristotle, *Poetics* (XXIII–XXIV), in *Aristotle's Theory of Poetry and Fine Art*, 4th ed., ed. and trans. S. H. Butcher (New York, 1951), pp. 89–97; William Webbe, *A*

Discourse of English Poetrie (1586), in *Elizabethan Critical Essays*, ed. G. G. Smith, 2 vols. (Oxford, 1971), I, 249; Giraldi Cinthio, *On Romances* [*Discorso intorno al comporre dei romanzi* (1554)], ed. and trans. Henry L. Snuggs (Lexington, Ky., 1968), pp. 53, 57; Jacopo Mazzoni, *Della difesa della Comedia di Dante* (1587), cited in Bernard Weinberg, *A History of Literary Criticism of the Italian Renaissance*, 2 vols. (Chicago, 1961), II, 877–83; Puttenham, *The Arte of English Poesie* (London, 1589), pp. 31–4; Scaliger, *Poetices libri septem* (I, 2), pp. 16–17.

15. *The Defence of Poesie* (London, 1595), sig. E3.

16. John Smith, "Of Prophesie," in his *Select Discourses* (London, 1660), pp. 169–71.

17. Ibid., p. 173.

18. For discussion of some intellectual sources for these ideas, see Denis Saurat, *Milton: Man and Thinker* (New York, 1925), pp. 301–09; W. C. Curry, *Milton's Ontology, Cosmogony and Physics* (Lexington, Ky., 1966), pp. 114–43, 158–82; Kester Svendsen, *Milton and Science* (Cambridge, Mass., 1956), pp. 9–42, 114–36; Lee A. Jacobus, *Sudden Apprehension: Aspects of Knowledge in "Paradise Lost"* (The Hague, 1976), pp. 45–88.

19. See, e.g., Antonio Sebastiano Minturno, *De Poeta* (Venice, 1559), p. 417; Scaliger, *Poetices libri septem* (I, 2), pp. 16–17.

20. *Arte of English Poesie*, p. 35.

21. *Defence of Poesie*, sig. C2.

22. *De rerum natura* (I, 54–61), trans. W. H. D. Rouse, ed. M. F. Smith, Loeb Classical Library (Cambridge, Mass., 1975), p. 6: "For I shall begin to discourse to you upon the most high system of heaven and of the gods, and I shall disclose the first-beginnings of things [the atoms], from which nature makes all things and increases and nourishes them, and into which the same nature again reduces them when dissolved— which, in discussing philosophy, we are accustomed to call matter, and bodies that generate things, and seeds of things, and to entitle the same first bodies, because from them as first elements all things are."

23. Ibid. (II, 991–1006), p. 172: "Lastly, we are all sprung from celestial seed; all have that same father, from whom our fostering mother earth receives liquid drops of water, and then teeming brings forth bright corn and luxuriant trees and the race of mankind, brings forth all the generations of wild beasts, providing food with which all nourish their bodies and lead a sweet life and beget their offspring; therefore she has with reason obtained the name of mother. that also which once came from earth, to earth returns back again, and what fell from the borders of ether, that is again brought back, and the regions of heaven again receive it. Nor does death so destroy things as to annihilate the bodies of matter, but it disperses their combination abroad; then it conjoins others with others, and brings it about that thus all things alter their shapes and change their colours and receive sensation and in a moment of time yield it up again."

24. Ibid. (I, 351–57), p. 30: "Trees grow and at their time put forth their fruits, because their food is distributed all over them from the lowest roots through trunks and through branches. Sounds pass through walls and fly through closed houses, stiffening cold permeates to the bones. But, if there were no void there which bodies might pass through in each case, you could not see this happen in any way."

25. *"Paradise Lost" and the Classical Epic*, esp, pp. 8–14.

26. *Angeleida* (Venice, 1590), (II, 20), trans. Watson Kirkconnell, in his *The Celestial Cycle* (Toronto, 1952), p. 81; *Faerie Queene* (I,vii,13), ed. J. C. Smith and E. De Selincourt (Oxford, 1970), p. 35. See the discussion in Revard, *War in Heaven*, pp. 186–90.

27. Revard, in *War in Heaven*, points out that Milton's account in *PL* is unique among Renaissance treatments of the subject in denying the angels a decisive victory and Michael

the central role in achieving that victory (pp. 129–97). She notes that the first day's combat in *PL* bears some resemblance to the treatment of the entire war in Valvasone, Murtola, Vondel, and others, but in *PL* the day ends with an inconclusive rather than a decisive encounter between Satan and Michael. She notes further that there are no precedents for the angels' humiliation and confusion at the hands of the rebels. See also Summers, *Muse's Method*, pp. 122–37.

28. See, e.g., Augustine, *Confessions*, in *Basic Writings of Saint Augustine*, ed. Whitney J. Oates, 2 vols. (New York, 1948), I, 202; Calvin, *Institutes* (I, xiv), ed. John T. McNeill, Library of Christian Classics XX (Philadelphia, 1960), p. 160. Milton, in *CD* (I,vii) declared that "Anyone who asks what God did before the creation of the world is a fool; and anyone who answers him is not much wiser (YP, VI, 299). For further discussion of the interplay between Raphael and Adam on this point, see Lewalski, "Innocence and Experience," pp. 106–08.

29. Susan Snyder, ed., *The Divine Weeks and Works of Guillaume De Saluste, Sieur Du Bartas, translated by Josuah Sylvester*, 2 vols. (Oxford, 1979), I, 2, 5. *La Semaine* was published in 1578; the unfinished sequel, *La Seconde Semaine*, dealing with the seven ages of biblical history, was first published in 1584. The standard edition of Du Bartas is *The Works of Guillaume de Salluste, Sieur du Bartas*, ed. U. T. Holmes, J. C. Lyons, and R. W. Linker, 3 vols. (Chapel Hill, 1953–40).

30. *Pierce's Superrogation*, in Smith, *Elizabethan Critical Essays*, I, 265.

31. In Snyder, ed., Sylvester's *Du Bartas*, Appendix, II, 916.

32. Ibid., "First Week, First Day," 136.

33. See esp. Sylvester's *Du Bartas*, "First Week, First Day," 285–90, and *PL* VIII, 276–80; Sylvester's *Du Bartas*, "Third Day," 533–44, and *PL* VII, 313–19; Sylvester's *Du Bartas*, "Fifth Day," 879–88, and *PL* VII, 442–46. See also Lucretius, *De rerum natura* V, 783–825. For an extended discussion of echoes from Sylvester's *Du Bartas*, see Taylor, *Milton's Use of Du Bartas*; Grant McColley, *Paradise Lost: An Account of its Growth and Major Origins, with a Discussion of Milton's Use of Sources and Literary Patterns* (Chicago, 1940). For suggestive discussions of the imagery of *PL* VII, see Summers, *Muse's Method*, pp. 137–46, and Michael Lieb, *The Dialectics of Creation* (Amherst, Mass., 1969), pp. 56–63.

34. See, for example, "First Week, First Day," 51–118, 373–416, and "Fourth Day," 81–180.

35. [*Dialogo . . . soprai due massime sistemi del mondo, Tolemaico, e Copernicano*], trans. Stillman Drake, 2d ed. (Berkeley and Los Angeles, 1967).

36. Ibid., p. 131.

37. Ibid., pp. 59–60.

38. Ibid., p. 61: "In brief, if we proceed to examine and weigh carefully all these things, we shall find that the goal to which all are directed is the need, the use, the comfort and the delight of men."

39. Ibid., pp. 256, 367–71.

40. Smith, "Of Prophets," pp. 178–79.

41. *The Bible and Holy Scriptures Conteyned in the Olde and Newe Testament* (Geneva, 1560), Argument to the Book of Revelation, fol. 114ᵛ. For discussion from various perspectives of Milton's use of the Book of Revelation and development of a poetics of prophecy, see, e.g., William Kerrigan, *The Prophetic Milton* (Charlottesville, Va., 1974); Wittreich, *Visionary Poetics;* Fixler, "Apocalypse within *Paradise Lost*" and *Milton and the Kingdoms of God* (Evanston, Ill., 1964).

42. See, e.g., Franciscus Junius, *The Apocalypse, or Revelation of St. John*, trans. T. Barbar (Cambridge, 1596), p. 247.

43. See, e.g., Thomas Brightman, *A Revelation of the Apocalypse*, in *Works* (London, 1644), p. 234; Henry Bullinger, *A Hundred Sermons upon the Apocalypse* (London, 1573), sig. Aiiiˇ. See also Barbara K. Lewalski, "*Samson Agonistes* and the 'Tragedy' of the Apocalypse," *PMLA*, LXXXV (1970), 1050–62.

44. Demaray, *Milton's Theatrical Epic*, pp. 102–15, explores the masque dimension and backgrounds of Michael's prophecy.

45. Pareus, *A Commentary upon the Divine Revelation of the Apostle and Evangelist John*, trans. Elias Arnold (Amsterdam, 1644), p. 20.

46. In the preface to *SA*, Milton observed that "*Paraeus*, commenting on the Revelation, divides the whole Book as a Tragedy, into Acts distinguisht each by a Chorus of Heavenly Harpings and Song between."

47. "Of Prophesie," p. 179.

48. Ed. A. Garnier and J. Plattard, 4 vols., (Paris, 1932). See Richard L. Regosin, *The Poetry of Inspiration: Agrippa D'Aubigné's "Les Tragiques"* (Chapel Hill, 1970).

49. For further discussion of these Pauline terms as they shape Milton's poetic strategy in these passages, see Barbara K. Lewalski, "Structure and the Symbolism of Vision in Michael's Prophecy, *Paradise Lost*, Books XI–XII," *PQ*, XLII (1963), 25–35.

50. *City of God*, trans. Marcus Dods (New York, 1950), pp. 526–27, 537.

51. Ibid., p. 477.

52. Sylvester's *Du Bartas*, "Second Week, First Day," 9–12, (Snyder, I, 316).

PARADISE LOST:
THE UNCERTAIN EPIC

Balachandra Rajan

THE PROBLEM of the genre of *Paradise Lost* seems to have been a problem from the day the poem was published. Dryden may have said that "this man . . . cuts us all out and the ancients too,"[1] but it did not take long for the caution of the critic to make its inroads on the generosity of the poet. In the preface to *Sylvae* (1685) the objections are stylistic—to the "flats" among Milton's elevations, to his "antiquated words," and to the "perpetual harshness" of their sound. But eight years later, in the *Discourse Concerning the Original and Progress of Satire*, the qualifications become more substantial. The earlier objections are repeated, and Milton's lack of talent in rhyming is added to them. But we are also told that Milton's subject "is not that of an heroic poem properly so called. His design is the losing of our happiness: his event is not prosperous like that of all other epic works; his heavenly machines are many and his human persons are but two."[2] In the dedication to his translation of the *Aeneid* (1697) Dryden begins by saying that "a heroic poem, truly such, is undoubtedly the greatest work which the soul of man is capable to perform."[3] Homer and Virgil are sovereign in the genre. "The next, but the next with a long interval between was the *Jerusalem*."[4] Spenser would have had a better case than some continental claimants to the succession "had his action been finished, or had been one." Milton's title would have been less suspect "if the devil had not been his hero, instead of Adam; if the giant had not failed the knight, and driven him out of his stronghold, to wander through the world with his lady errant; and if there had not been more machining persons than human in his poem."[5] Dryden, it will be observed, gives his objections force by both repeating and extending them. To earlier statements about the unfortunate outcome and the excess of heavenly machinery in *Paradise Lost* he now adds the suggestion that the action, the epic propriety of which may be dubious, is in any case centered on the wrong hero. The persistence of crucial objections and the adding of related ones thus come to constitute a platform from which the genre of the poem can be interrogated.

105

Much can be discerned from Dryden's platform. The unfortunate outcome exposes Milton's poem to consideration as tragic rather than epic. If Satan is the hero, he is the hero within an antiquest that invites us to view *Paradise Lost* as anti-epic or parodic epic. Addison's response to Dryden argues that no hero was intended but suggests Christ, if need be, as the hero. This defense of the poem converts it into a providential epic, but one which engages the human only at its periphery.[6] It thus undermines one of Dryden's objections but only at the cost of underlining another. The Romantic reinstatement of Satan as the hero is, of course, not an endorsement of Dryden. It attacks the question of what the poem is by suggesting that there is a poem other than the official poem in which the real nature of Milton's accomplishment is to be found. Generic uncertainty is compounded by viewing *Paradise Lost* as an act of creative subversion in which the true poem overthrows the establishment exercise.

The two-poem theory, in turn, has ramifications which continue into the present. We can simply reverse the Romantic valuation and regard the true poem as the official one. The true poem can then stand in relation to the false as icon does to idol, or as reality to parody within an antithetical universe.[7] We can regard the two poems as confronting each other creatively or as A. J. A. Waldock would have it, locked in destructive conflict.[8] It can be argued that the two poems only appear to be two and that it is the purpose of reader education to bring them into concurrence.[9] Finally, like A. S. P. Woodhouse, we can think of the two poems as engaged with each other through a double protagonist, each functioning within a different genre.[10]

It may be that the course of criticism after Dryden is misguided and that, as John M. Steadman proposes, Milton is writing an "illustrious" epic fully compatible with Italian Neo-Aristotelianism, while Dryden's criticisms are made from the vantage point of a Neo-Aristotelianism that is distinctly French.[11] Certainly neither Aristotle nor the Italians prescribe a fortunate outcome for the epic. But Milton published *Paradise Lost* in 1667, when Italian Neo-Aristotelianism was hardly representative of current critical trends. We are accustomed to these gestures of obsolescence in Milton, which include the imaginative adoption of a slightly antiquated model of the universe. The voice of the outsider is also a voice from the past, a voice disowning if not excoriating the triviality of the present. Nevertheless, the history of reading *Paradise Lost* points to real difficulties which are not disposed of by a more accurate generic assignation. A poem which may be two poems initially or finally, in which there are three possible heroes and even the possibility of two heroes rather than one, is not a poem about which one can be certain.

Some of the problems of placing *Paradise Lost* are interestingly suggested by William Willkie in a preface (1757) to a heroic poem of his own. Willkie is writing about the difficulties of reconciling the untrue with the true, or historical, in an epic poem. Spenser accomplishes this reconciliation through the evasions of allegory. Willkie then notes (remembering Dryden) that in *Paradise Lost* "persons in machinery overshadow the human characters" and adds (remembering Addison) that "the heroes of the poem are all of them immortal." *Paradise Lost* escapes a requirement that looms over epic poetry by being "a work altogether irregular. . . . The subject of it is not epic, but tragic. . . . Adam and Eve are not designed to be objects of admiration, but of pity. . . . It is tragic in its plot but epic in its dress and machinery."[12]

Willkie may be the first critic to recognize that *Paradise Lost* is not only a mixed-genre poem but a mixed-genre poem with a different protagonist for each of its primary genres. It is true that given Aristotle's views of the importance of plot, the identification of the epic with "dress and machinery" relegates it to a status in *Paradise Lost* which is peripheral rather than central. It is also true that Willkie describes *Paradise Lost* as "altogether irregular," though he does so in an age which was beginning to admire irregularity; the observation does not mean that the poem is to be reproached for its generic lawlessness. Nevertheless, Willkie's remarks do broach the question of whether it is necessary or even desirable to locate *Paradise Lost* unambiguously within any single genre.

It may be argued that the difficulties surrounding the generic assignation of *Paradise Lost* are difficulties encountered by the reader rather than difficulties to which the author admits. That does not make the difficulties any less real, but it may be instructive to look at some of the ways in which the poem announces itself and at the related proposition that the poem always knows what kind of a poem it is. *Paradise Lost* treats itself as "adventurous Song" in the first book (13), as "sacred Song" in the third book (29), as "Song" of which the "copious matter" is the Son's name and arts (III, 412–13), as "Song" related to "celestial song" in the seventh book (12, 30), and as "Heroic Song" in the ninth book, but only after the audience has been advised that the forthcoming notes of the song will be "Tragic" (6, 25). These descriptions are not so divergent as to render reconciliation difficult, but they certainly do not suggest resolute consistency in the poem's classification of itself. They suggest rather the desire to have the best of several worlds, which is characteristic of a mixed-genre poet.

In the poems that precede *Paradise Lost,* Milton's attitude to inherited genres is powerfully revisionary. We console ourselves by describing it as a strong case of tradition and the individual talent or by saying, as John Reesing does, that Milton strains the mold but does not break it.[13] The *Ode on the Morning of Christ's Nativity,* in describing itself as both a hymn and an ode, may be initiating Milton's career with a mixed-genre announcement.[14] In *Comus* the poet makes use of the antithetical dispositions of a genre new enough to be open to experiment in order to construct a staging ground for issues and confrontations which we have come to call Miltonic. *Lycidas* directs the capacity of the pastoral for protest into a protest against the pastoral genre itself. In each case Milton identifies certain propensities of the genre as giving the genre its way of achieving understanding and then reorganizes the form around those propensities. In each case the ordering power of the genre is made to compass a higher degree of inclusiveness than the genre has hitherto accommodated. We can expect these creative habits to continue as Milton comes to his most inclusive undertaking.

A primary characteristic of the epic is inclusiveness. When Aristotle differentiates tragedy from epic, he does not do so on the basis of the outcome, the agent, or the emotion excited by the literary work. His concern is with the manner of presentation and the magnitude of the action.[15] The tragic action should confine itself as far as possible to a single circuit of the sun. The epic action can be longer, and a month is extended to a year by Italian critics. While the longer action can sustain itself by an adequate proliferation of incident, the epic, as it graduates from the tale of a tribe to the statement of a civilization, tends increasingly to sustain itself by cultural omnivorousness as much as by narrative complication. The epic and the encyclopedic are thus brought into convergence. In a late epic the encyclopedic interest will involve consideration of the uses of the past, including the past of the epic genre itself. When the generic inheritance is codified to the extent of seeming petrified, the consideration can be revisionary and can extend—as is arguable in Milton's case—into a revisionary treatment of the whole past. A genre can also be enlarged and thus freed from impending exhaustion of possibilities by incorporating into it the possibilities of another genre not hitherto digested. Mixed genres are thus a natural deliverance from the constraints of a genre which it is necessary to use and which has already been used too heavily. In an epic, such absorptiveness can be particularly felicitous since it is clearly the literary application of a principle on which the epic has increasingly been based. An encyclopedic epic should include a generic compendium.

Studies by Rosalie Colie and more recently by Barbara Lewalski have drawn attention tellingly to the generic inclusiveness of *Paradise Lost*.[16] Lewalski's suggestion that the various genres in the epic are means of accommodation to the reader, or of the narrator within the poem to the auditor, also responds to a problem that arises when we think of the epic as a generic compendium. The encyclopedic substance of an epic is a matter of what it contains; the generic variety is a matter of how what is contained is conveyed. Multeity of genres is most convincingly called for when the area of exploration is sufficiently inclusive to require more than one style of mediation or access. God's creation, as a fully comprehensive poem, is also a poem that engages us in an adequate variety of relationships. Any mimesis of the perfect original should be similarly rich in means of accommodation or opportunities for engagement.[17]

Nevertheless, it should not be assumed that the purpose, or even the designed purpose, of generic multeity is always to contribute to the overall harmony, to show how many styles of discourse lead us to the one Word, or to the unifying capability that is the "one word" of the poem. Multiple genres can provide the ingredients for subversion as well as for synthesis. Their purpose may be to show not the overall concord but the fragmentation of any single style of understanding that unavoidably comes about when the fictive is brought into engagement with the actual. I am not suggesting that Milton's use of mixed genres was governed by this principle or that it proceeded to this point irrespective of the original principle by which it was governed. But on the other hand it is not easy to argue that his poem is the unperturbed implementation of a "great idea" or "fore-conceit," as the Creation is in the seventh book of *Paradise Lost*. A blueprint for the epic must have existed in the author's mind, particularly if, as Allan H. Gilbert long ago argued,[18] the poem was not written in the order in which it unfolds. But the blueprint cannot have been unaffected by the stresses and strains within the poem and by the poem's reconsideration of itself during the deeply frustrating decade of its formation.

If many genres are to be fitted together harmoniously in a poem, they must be subject to a primary genre which is unambiguously proclaimed and clearly dominant. When a primary genre is subject to revisionary treatment and when its status is further undermined by another genre asserting a claim to primacy, the subordinate genres are as likely to reflect this central confrontation as to soothe it.

In *The Reason of Church-Government* (1642), Milton was asking himself "whether those dramatic constitutions wherein Sophocles and

Euripides raigne" were not "more doctrinal and exemplary to a nation" (YP, I, 812–15) than the epic undertaking by which he was fascinated.[19] We know from Edward Phillips that *Paradise Lost* began as a tragedy and that Milton showed Phillips the first ten lines of Satan's address to the sun as the planned beginning of the drama he intended to write.[20] The draft of "Adam unparadiz'd" in the Trinity manuscript shows us the dramatic nucleus in which *Paradise Lost* began. Even though the poem moved away from the nucleus it continued to remain engaged to its origins.

The ten books of the first edition of *Paradise Lost*, read as five acts of two books each, are tragic in several of their dispositons. In the fourth act the Creation is undone by the Fall. The fifth act gives us the tragic aftermath of the fourth, the expansion of evil into space and its extension into history. The repentance of Adam and Eve, sandwiched between two huge movements of destructiveness, simply does not have the importance which the twelve-book version succeeds in winning from it. It is true that Christ's victory is the climax of the third act, but this matters less when Satan's victory is so effectively dominant in the fifth.

If this reading of the tragic weight of the ten-book structure is not erroneous, we can regard the twelve-book version as designed, among other things, to take corrective action. The creative forces are underlined slightly in the poems contest of energies. Christ's presence in the poem is strengthened by the division of the poem into three parts, each consisting of four books, with Christ the protagonist of the four central books. Two victories of light—the Battle in Heaven, and the Creation—are juxtaposed at the center of this central part. The repentance of Adam and Eve is given greater weight. Having said this much, it becomes important to add that the degree of corrective action is slight. It may be that no more could be done, since the poem had been in print for seven years. It may also be that Milton did not wish to do more.

Arthur E. Barker rightly observes that the twelve-book version does not supersede the ten-book one, that one must read both poems and be aware of both patterns, and that the poem is suspended "between the horns of a paradox."[21] For such a paradox to exist, the poem's primary genres must be in contest with, rather than concordant with, each other. The poem does not seek the assimilation of one genre by another or even, to quote Coleridge's famous phrase, "the balance or reconciliation of opposite or discordant qualities."[22] Rather it seeks to navigate between genres, remaining responsive to the current of each without surrendering to the pull of either.

Such a hypothesis seems natural when we remind ourselves of the poem's antithetical world, the embattled contraries between which the choosing center is suspended, as the poem itself is suspended creatively between competing claims on its identity. It is not simply a mixed-genre poem but a poem of which generic uncertainty may be a keynote. Critics may be understandably reluctant to admit uncertainty at the heart of a poem. A work of art thus divided is considered to be in a state of civil war. But creative indeterminacy can also be read as a sign of the authentic rather than the chaotic. Two powerful patterns of possibility contest with each other, as they do in reality. The outcome will shift from moment to moment. The poem's obligation is to draw the field of force and not to delineate the local and interim settlement.

Against this hypothesis it can be argued that Aristotle treats tragedy and epic as concordant genres.[23] The manner of presentation and the magnitude of the action are important but not fundamental differences and certainly not differences that might place either genre in potential conflict with the other. When Thomas Hobbes tells us that "the heroic poem, dramatic, is tragedy," he is carrying convergence a step further. He does so in proceeding to the masterfully sterile conclusion that "there can be no more or less than six kinds of poetry."[24] The Italian critics avoid Hobbes's overwhelming simplicity, but, as Steadman shows, they do not on the whole regard tragedy and epic as divergent.[25]

This objection has force. It can be partially countered by arguing that even though the Italian critics may not have seen tragedy and epic as divergent, they did recognize the creative potentiality of divergent genres. If God's creation is the perfect poem, its mimesis may consist not only of simulating its variety (which includes generic variety) but also of simulating the manner in which the first poem triumphed over its own divisiveness. Creation, we must not forget, was won out of chaos, from equal energies implacably opposed. The best poem may be that in which the center succeeds in holding against the maximum of centrifugal force. Like Milton's universe, such a poem is continually threatened by its contents. Tasso seems to be advocating a poetics of contrariety on this model when he argues that "the art of composing a poem resembles the plan of the Universe which is composed of contraries." He goes on to maintain that "such a variety will be so much the more marvellous as it brings with it a measure of difficulty and almost impossibility."[26] Guarini is less given to the tour de force than Tasso. In defending tragicomedy, Guarini considers it as a third genre arising from two genres which are divergent, but not so divergent that they cannot be creatively mingled. Each genre tempers the other so that the overall composition corresponds more fully "to the mixture of the human body which consists entirely in the tempering of the four humors."[27]

There is thus some sanction in Renaissance criticism for divergent genres curbing each other's excesses, or divergent genres being made to submit to the cohesive force of the poem. Milton's poem can be viewed from both prospects, but like any deeply creative achievement it has to go beyond the gestures towards it that are made by critical theory.

As has been indicated, Milton equivocates mildly about the kind of song he is singing when he links *Paradise Lost* to that particular word. The varying epithets are not difficult to bring together, but the variations remind us to be cautious in our classification of the poem. No more than a reminder is needed, since the poem at its very outset, in announcing the compass of its subject, is also conveying that announcement through a vivid drama of contesting genres. The opening lines of *Paradise Lost* have been commented on in great detail and from what may seem every possible perspective,[28] but their status as a generic manifesto still remains to be examined. In attempting the unattempted Milton may have been attempting an unattempted mixture.

Milton's virtuosity in stating the subject of the whole poem before the predicate of its initial sentence isolates the first five lines spectacularly from the narrative flow. The minidrama of these lines is therefore all the more effective in counselling us not only on what the poem is to be about but also on how it is to be experienced. From the beginning the tragic weight accumulates, reinforced by the alliterative joinings and by the alternative scansions of the first line. If the dominant stress falls on "Mans," we are reading a poem somberly homocentric in its allocation of destructiveness. If it falls on "First" we are reading a poem of the gestation of evil, with the alliterative movement through "First," "Fruit," and "Forbidden" compounding the inexorable growth.[29] "Tree," "tast," and "mortal" are the origin of this growth, though dramatically they are arrived at as its climax, the tragic center of the darkening song. "World" and "woe" sound the dimensions of a universe of tragedy. Nothing so far has restrained the onward movement, the accumulation of sorrow. The prospective genre of the poem—tragedy—has been uncomprisingly and, it would seem, irrevocably stated. Yet on the basis of a text from the Book of Romans (v, 19) a countermovement launches itself, generating itself from the previous movements by virtue of the coupling between man and "greater Man." There is even a counter-alliteration, responding to the massed alliterative linkages of destructiveness, affirming the victory of the light in "Restore" and "regain." This is what one might say on a superficial reading. A reading more open to the poem's reality would recognize that the relationship between human tragedy and providential epic is more complex than the simple overcoming of one genre by another. It is possible to say, by adjusting one's mind slightly to the impact of the opening, that the epic retrieval stands at the horizon of the poem, while the tragic gestation (to which the bulk of the first five lines are given) unavoidably dominates its stage. It is possible to reflect on the distancing force of "till" and ask if the deliverance at the horizon is more than potential. How far does the tragic actuality frustrate and even nullify the epic promise? It is certainly true, as the mind moves with the poem in its unfolding, that we cannot avoid passing through the tragic proliferation before arriving at the genre that might contain it. The two genres are, in fact, inexorably entangled by the powerfully staged drama of the poem's syntax. The poem does not choose between affiliations. It forms itself out of the contest between them.

Paradise Lost presents itself not only as a mixed-genre poem but as a mixed-genre poem of deep generic uncertainty. It has to be uncertain because the very history that it seeks to understand has, perhaps fortunately, not yet found its genre. The poem seeks its identity between contesting possibilities, as does that human community which is both the poem's subject and its audience.

Though the contest of primary genres in the opening lines of *Paradise Lost* has been examined, not every genre in those first five lines has been identified. Between the accumulating onslaught of the tragic, "Under her own waight groaning" as the twelfth book says of history (539), and the restorative encirclement of the providential, there is the muted phrase "With loss of *Eden*." The residual alliteration with "World" and "woe" attaches this part of the line to the tragic momentum. The loss can be taken as the sum of our sadness, the distillation of everything that has gone before it in the sentence. But the half-line is also an entry into a possible triumphant future, that Ithaca which the highest of heroes may regain. The phrase stands between two worlds, distanced from itself by the poem's initial onslaught of destructiveness and distanced again from itself by the postponing force of "till." The curiously nondescript language suggests the absence, or rather the residual and unavoidably veiled presence, of what the phrase invokes. It can no longer be known in its own right but only through the genres of loss and seeking.

In the days when it was fashionable to distinguish between the real and the nominal subjects of *Paradise Lost*, Paul Elmer More observed that the real subject of the poem was Paradise.[30] The remark is neither naive nor tautological. The strong affinities of Eden with Arcadia, the Golden Age, and the pastoral strain in the Bible not only establish it in the landscape of memory, including literary memory, but also affiliate it to a third genre, the pastoral. The three genres, in turn, affiliate themselves to the three main locales of the poem, so that we can think with caution but without injustice of a tragic Hell (including human fallenness), an epic Heaven, and a pastoral Paradise. Since the forces in the universe of *Paradise Lost* converge so powerfully upon its choosing center, one can argue that the pastoral understanding plays a crucial part in the poem's declaration of itself.

John R. Knott, Jr., skillfully underlines the *otium* of Paradise, its "grateful vicissitude," the harmony of man with nature, and the harmony of nature with itself.[31] Cities in *Paradise Lost* are not statements of civilization. Babel and Pandemonium tell of their pride. The world is likened once to a metropolis "With glistering Spires and Pinnacles adorn'd" (III, 550), but it is viewed thus by Satan in the image of the desirable. Little is said of the metropolitan amenities of Heaven except that its shape is "undetermined," that it is adorned with opal towers and battlements of sapphire (II, 1047–50), and that the dust of its main road is gold (VII, 577). It is Satan, not God, who lives in what might metaphorically be called a palace, a superstructure built on a structure of pyramids and towers "From Diamond Quarries hew'n, and Rocks of Gold" (V, 754–61). Heaven is most frequently spoken of in pastoral language, possibly as an accommodation to Adam, who is unfamiliar with city life, but more probably to indicate the continuity between the celestial and the unfallen.

Yet though the ideal order of *Paradise Lost* has extensive pastoral elements and though the poem can be poignantly pastoral in its nostalgia, the "happy rural seat of various view" (IV, 247) does not always open out into pastoral prospects. The weeping trees that are spoken of in the next line suggest a place haunted by tragedy as well as by creative plenitude. There is much foreboding in the language of Paradise—in the wantonness of its energies, the "mazy error" of its brooks, and in its surpassing of that "fair field" where the "fairer flower," Proserpina, was gathered (V, 294–97; IV, 268–72; IV, 237–40). More important, Paradise is not a place of tranquility, of fragile but deep peace before the gathering storm. In its nature it is free from the burden of the past, but in its nature it is also singularly subject to the anxieties of the unprecedented. Nearly everything that happens in Paradise happens for the first time, so if one's response to life is not the result of a pre-existent, celestially implanted program, it can only come together and manifest a pattern through a series of related improvisations. Baffling dreams, angelic visitations, and discussions with the author of one's being on the need of the self for an otherness seem part of the normalities of Paradise.

"Is there no change of death in Paradise?" Wallace Stevens asks. "Does ripe fruit never fall? Or do the boughs / Hang always heavy in that perfect sky."[32] In the stasis of perfection, all change is the death of perfection. Yet not to change is to perpetuate the permanence of life-lessness. Milton provides for change in Paradise that is quite other than the "change of death," thereby adroitly satisfying the second of Stevens's desiderata for a supreme fiction: "It must change."[33] In his repeated use of the figure of the dance in describing ideal order, he advises us of a perfection consummated in motion rather than memorialized in still-ness.[34] Motion must include alteration in one's state of being as well as alteration in one's place, and this alteration takes place, as Raphael suggests, by the working of a body up to spirit, "in bounds / Propor-tioned to each kind" (V, 478–79). Such evolution cannot take place by standing still on an ontological escalator. In a world in which the perfec-tion of the human species includes the power of free choice—a power the importance of which is underlined by the enormous cosmic price which the divine is prepared to pay to keep it in being—there must be a steady succession of opportunities for self-formative choosing. It is hard to believe that Adam and Eve, if they had not eaten of the apple, would have lived happily ever after as creative gardeners.[35] The Appleton es-tate in Marvell's poem subversively mimeticizes the world from which it withdraws. Milton's Garden, in its crises, makes itself continuous with that future which is to become its tragic legacy. It is no accident that the images Michael uses to characterize progress in history correspond to the images Raphael uses to characterize upward evolution on the onto-logical scale (V, 996–98; V, 575–77; XII, 300–304). In the first place, the equivalence makes evident the restoration of the *status quo ante*. By making himself eligible for the continuing intervention of "supernal grace," man is able to stand as he once did "On even ground against his mortal foe" (III, 179). In the second place, the statement of equivalence, made through figures of progress with which we are not unfamiliar, joins the prelapsarian and postlapsarian worlds. The status of man is radically different, and his commitment to destructiveness requires the steady application of a counterforce that no longer lies within his natural capac-ity. But if the conditions for that counterforce are brought into being, the two worlds can reflect each other in their opportunities and chal-lenges. The pastoral idyll never quite existed. The Garden was fully itself only in creative dependence on a shaping principle beyond itself. It was not a place of withdrawal but of change and growth built on evolving interrelationships with the entire structure of reality which surrounded it. What was lost was not the Garden but that creative possibility which the Garden embodied and promised.

This excursion into the poem suggests how it responds to those stresses and balances which the first five lines urge so compellingly on our reading of what follows. The pastoral statement does not exist by itself. It is annexed in the first place to a tragic unfolding through which we are obliged to make our way in order to measure what is meant by "loss of *Eden.*" It is attached in the second place to a providential counter-poem through which the lost possibilities can be recovered and fulfilled. In fact, its location and attachments are suggestive of the created world in *Paradise Lost*, suspended from Heaven by a golden chain and connected to Hell by a causeway. What the pastoral center comes to mean depends on how it is oriented. As a generic claim, it must yield to those more powerful claimants which seek possession of the structure of things.[36] The drama of genres which the first five lines enact is thus singularly accurate in prefiguring not only the generic character of the poem but the disposition of real forces which that character represents.

One of the unusual strengths of *Paradise Lost* is the poem's capacity to reconsider itself. It can indulge in "tedious havoc" and then excoriate it (IX, 27–33). It can describe the fall of Mulciber in language of limpid beauty and then pull us back from our involvement with a "Thus they relate / Erring" (I, 738–48), leaving us to wonder whether the event is being questioned or whether language itself is being rebuked as falsification. It propounds huge structures of elaboration and ornament to arrive at the "upright heart" in its unadorned authenticity. It uses the past with lavish erudition and overgoes it with competitive zest, largely to underline the obsolescence of what it invokes. It appoints Michael, the leader of the angelic battalions, to preach the politics of nonviolence and the primacy of the interior victory. Some of these dismissals are designed to educate the reader and to instruct him in discriminating truth from its cunning resemblance (see YP, II, 154). Others arise because the poem, in charting the progress from shadowy types to truth, endows itself with a history that to some degree mirrors the history it interprets. But we are also looking at a poem that is endeavoring to achieve its identity and which, as the opening lines have promised, will form itself among contesting generic possibilities. It must not only make itself but justify what it makes against the challenges of an era of deep change. Since its attitude to the inheritance is so powerfully revisionary, honesty demands that it also be self-revising.

In the fifth book of *Paradise Lost* Adam and Eve, after a troubled night, do not simply address the Almighty in prayer. Rather they participate in a prayer which the whole creation offers to its maker out of the way in which it moves and lives. The prayer is Vaughan's "great hymn / And Symphony of nature," the ardent music of "the world in tune." It is also Herbert's "something understood," a structure of relationships which the mind experiences as the ground of its being.[37] "Firm peace" and "wonted calm" are its consequences (V, 209–10). We are told that Adam and Eve have previously made their "unisons" in "various style" (145–46). The plentitude of innocence offers more than one way of access and relationship. The "unmediated" art of the person praying (148–49)[38] may even find the opportunity to invent a genre.

At the end of the tenth book, Adam and Eve pray again. The first prayer preceded the descent of Raphael. The second precedes the descent of Michael. The world has changed, and a lost structure of possibility, borne away as in the real world on the flood of history's disappointments, has also taken with it its proper language. The new desolation calls for the unadorned, the concentration on what is primary. Many poems have an energy of destitution within them, waving their leaves and flowers in the sun so that they may wither into the truth of themselves.[39] In *Paradise Lost* that destitutive energy is launched by an immense act of original destructiveness. From the moment that Adam and Eve eat the apple, much in the poem is rendered obsolete, including some of its literary genres. In these stern dismissals lies a great deal of the poem's authenticity as well as its weight of sadness. But the world remains before us and remains capable of yielding us its language. If *Paradise Lost* is an uncertain epic, it is uncertain not because it is confused or vacillating, but because it is clear about how it must form itself.

University of Western Ontario

NOTES

1. *Early Lives of Milton*, ed. Helen Darbishire (London, 1932), p. 296.
2. *Of Dramatic Poetry and Other Critical Essays*, ed. George Watson (London, 1962), II, 32, 84–85.
3. Ibid., II, 223.
4. Ibid., II, 232. For futher statements on the sovereignty of Virgil and Homer in the genre, see II, 167; II, 195. Spenser (II, 150; II, 83–84) is Virgilian. But Milton, though Spenser's "poetical son" (II, 270), is Homeric rather than Virgilian (II, 150).

5. Ibid., II, 233.

6. *Milton, The Critical Heritage*, ed. John T. Shawcross (London, 1970), p. 166.

7. John M. Steadman, *Milton and the Renaissance Hero* (Oxford, 1967); Balachandra Rajan, "The Cunning Resemblance," in *Milton Studies*, VII, ed. Albert C. Labriola and Michael Lieb (Pittsburgh, 1975), pp. 29–48.

8. *"Paradise Lost" and Its Critics* (Cambridge, 1947).

9. Stanley Fish, *Surprised by Sin* (Berkeley and Los Angeles, 1971).

10. *The Heavenly Muse*, ed. Hugh MacCallum (Toronto, 1972), pp. 176–94.

11. *Epic and Tragic Structure in "Paradise Lost"* (Chicago, 1976).

12. William Willkie, "Preface to the *Epigoniad*," in *Milton 1732–1801, the Critical Heritage*, ed. John T. Shawcross (London, 1972), p. 240.

13. *Milton's Poetic Art* (Cambridge, Mass., 1969), p. 49. See also p. 135.

14. For the poem as a hymn see Philip Rollinson, "Milton's Nativity Poem and the Decorum of Genre," in *Milton Studies*, VII, pp. 165–88. For the poem as an ode, see David B. Morris, "Drama and Stasis in Milton's *Ode on the Morning of Christ's Nativity*," SP, LVII (1971), 207–22. For the poem as both, see Hugh MacCallum, "The Narrator of Milton's *On the Morning of Christ's Nativity*," in *Familiar Colloquy: Essays Presented to Arthur Edward Barker*, ed. Patricia Bruckmann (Salzburg, 1976), pp. 179–95. Milton's reference in *The Reason of Church-Government* to "magnifick Odes and Hymns" (YP, I, 815), suggests that he may have thought of the two genres as strongly related to each other. The relationship may well be in the manner envisaged by Nehemiah Rogers, who writes of hymns as "special songs of praise and thanksgiving" and of odes as containing "doctrine of the chiefe good, or mans eternall felicitie" and as being made "after a more majesticall forme, than ordinary" (*A Strange Vineyard in Palaestina: in an Exposition of Isaiahs Parabolical Song of the Beloved* [London, 1623], pp. 8–9).

15. *Poetics*, 1449b, 1459b.

16. Rosalie Colie, *The Resources of Kind: Genre Theory in the Renaissance*, ed. Barbara K. Lewalski (Berkeley and Los Angeles, 1973); Lewalski, "The Genres of *Paradise Lost*," paper read at the Modern Language Association Meeting, San Francisco, Dec. 28, 1979; cf. Lewalski's essay in this volume.

17. Tasso describes the writing of a poem as "a work almost godlike that seems to imitate the First Maker" (*Discourses on the Heroic Poem*, trans. Mariella Cavalchini and Irene Samuel [Oxford, 1971], p. 97). For the creation as the perfect poem see also S. K. Heninger, Jr., *Touches of Sweet Harmony* (San Marino, Calif., 1976), pp. 290–94.

18. *On the Composition of "Paradise Lost"* (Chapel Hill, N.C., 1947).

19. "Milton's "whether" reflects the continuous controversy about the status of epic and tragedy relative to each other. The Renaissance and, more emphatically, Dryden found epic the higher of the two genres. But Aristotle (*Poetics*, 1402a) had declared in favor of tragedy.

20. "The Life of Mr. John Milton," in *Early Lives of Milton*, pp. 72–73.

21. "Structural Pattern in *Paradise Lost*," rpt. in *Milton: Modern Essays in Criticism*, ed. Arthur E. Barker (New York, 1965), p. 154.

22. *Biographia Literaria*, XIV.

23. *Poetics*, loc. cit.

24. "The Answer of Mr. Hobbes to Sr. Will. D'Avenant's Preface before *Gondibert*," in *Critical Essays of the Seventeenth Century*, ed. J. E. Spingarn, 3 vols. (Oxford, 1908), II, 54–55.

25. *Epic and Tragic Structure in "Paradise Lost."*

26. *Discourses on the Heroic Poem*, p. 78.

27. "The Compendium of Tragicomic Poetry," in *Literary Criticism: Plato to Dryden*, ed. Allan H. Gilbert (New York, 1940), p. 512.

28. Among the examinations are David Daiches, "The Opening of *Paradise Lost*," in *The Living Milton*, ed. Frank Kermode (London, 1960), pp. 55–69, and Joseph Summers, *The Muse's Method* (London, 1962), pp. 11–31. Book-length studies of the invocations include Anne D. Ferry, *Milton's Epic Voice* (Cambridge, Mass., 1963), and William Riggs, *The Christian Poet in "Paradise Lost"* (Berkeley and Los Angeles, 1972).

29. In asking some seventy students to read this line, I have found that 45 percent put the dominant stress on "Mans" and 45 percent put it on "First." The remainder put it on the third syllable of "disobedience." Of those stressing "Mans," the great majority were men. Of those stressing "First" the great majority were women.

30. *Shelburne Essays*, quoted by E. M. W. Tillyard, *Milton* (London, 1930), p. 283.

31. *Milton's Pastoral Vision* (Chicago, 1971). The phrase from PL "grateful vicissitude" (VI, 8), describes the alternation of light and darkness issuing from a cave within the mount of God. It is used by Summers (*Muse's Method*, pp. 71–86) as emblematic of Paradise.

32. "Sunday Morning," in *Harmonium* (New York, 1923), p. 92.

33. *Notes Toward a Supreme Fiction* (Cummington, Mass., 1942), p. 21.

34. Summers, *Muse's Method*, pp. 85–86.

35. See, for example, Barbara K. Lewalski, "Innocence and Experience in Milton's Eden," in *New Essays on "Paradise Lost*," ed. Thomas Kranidas (Berkeley and Los Angeles, 1969), pp. 86–117.

36. Knott observes (*Milton's Pastoral Vision*, p. xiv) that "the very conflict of modes, epic against pastoral, seems to doom Eden in advance."

37. Vaughan, "The Morning-watch," in *The Complete Poetry of Henry Vaughan*, ed. French Fogle (New York, 1964), pp. 176–77. Herbert, "Prayer" (1), in *The Works of George Herbert*, ed. F. E. Hutchinson (Oxford, 1941), p. 51.

38. Since the poet cannot attain a prelapsarian oneness with creation, his verse in *PL*, IX, 24 is "unpremeditated" rather than "unmeditated." The word has specific and intriguing echoes in the "unpremeditated art" of Shelley's skylark and in the "unpremeditated, joyous energy" which Yeats finds in the statues of Mausolus and Artemisia at the British Museum (*Autobiographies* [London, 1955], p. 150).

39. The thought is from Yeats, "The Coming of Wisdom with Times," in *Collected Poems* (London, 1950), p. 105.

ON THE USES OF ELIZABETHAN DRAMA: THE REVALUATION OF EPIC IN *PARADISE LOST*

Richard S. Ide

MILTON'S DISPARAGEMENT of English 'play-writes," whose dramas he judges to be indecorous and formally deficient by neoclassical rules,[1] should not obscure the fact that his conception of tragedy is distinctly Elizabethan. "High and excellent Tragedy," writes Sidney, "maketh Kinges feare to be Tyrants" and "teacheth the uncertainety of this world, and upon how weake foundations guilden roofes are builded."[2] For Puttenham, the function of tragedy is to reprehend those men of high estate given over to "all maner of lusts and licentiousnes of life"; in tragedy, "their infamous life and tyrannies" are exposed and reproached and "their miserable ends painted out . . . to shew the mutabilitie of fortune, and the just punishment of God in revenge of a vicious and evill life."[3] Tragedy teaches that the sinner will reap what he sows; for the Elizabethan theorist, the castigation of vice is a terrifying testimony to God's vengeance. Fulke Greville stresses the point when he states that according to the "Moderne" theory, the function of tragedy is "to point out Gods revenging aspect upon every particular sin, to the despaire, or confusion of mortality."[4] Sin on the part of man, just punishment on the part of heaven—this is precisely the tragic note Milton strikes in *Paradise Lost*.

Happily, this staunchly moral theory of tragedy, deriving from the late morality play and the literary tradition of *The Mirror for Magistrates*,[5] was more often honored in the breach than the observance by mature Elizabethan dramatists. But one should nevertheless recall the direct, twofold legacy of native tragic theory and practice: the Elizabethan revenge play and the tragedy of damnation. Plays in the mainstream of the Elizabethan revenge tradition, from Kyd's *The Spanish Tragedy* (c. 1587–88) to Shakespeare's *Hamlet* (c. 1601) to Tourneur's *The Atheist's Tragedy* (c. 1610–11), are "consistent demonstrations of the pattern of moral law"[6] on which Elizabethan tragic theory is based. Dominated by thematic concerns about God's government of the world,

121

about the relationship between earthly and heavenly justice, and about the morality of wreaking the vengeance that is God's alone, the Elizabethan revenge play typically concludes with an awesome exhibition of divine vengeance. One by one, scheming villains and (usually) revengers alike are hoisted on their own petards—this extraordinary network of ironic judgments designed to "terrifie men from the like abhorred practises"[7] by demonstrating that this world is, to borrow Thomas Beard's title, *The Theatre of Gods Judgements*.[8]

In *Paradise Lost*, although Satan strikes the pose of villain revenger when setting out to deceive man, it is Adam and Eve and all of mankind who—through the Son, the seed destined to bruise the head of the serpent—will have revenge against Satan's villainy at the Resurrection and at the end of time. That, says Adam of the protevangelical promise, "Would be revenge indeed" (X, 1036). But it is a revenge to be exacted by God in God's due time. Meanwhile, as Heywood's Frankford and Tourneur's Charlemont and a few other minor figures of the tradition well know, the true "revenger" suffers patiently and leaves vengeance to God. God's revenge on Satan is foreshadowed on the third day of the war in heaven, when the Son assumes his role as duly appointed minister of God's vengeance (VI, 808). Not content to remind his readers of this promised triumph, however, Milton underscores the idea that God will have final revenge on Satan by creating the "cartoon" scene of Book X.[9] Milton subjects Satan to ridicule and several precise ironies in making him reenact his triumph in the garden as punishment. The derisive tone, the ironic deflation of expectations, the awesome demonstration of divine vengeance, and (though not exactly a play-within-a-play) the *spectacle* of this scene—all of which elements are also present in *Samson Agonistes* when the Philistines suffer their ironic fate at the moment of their triumph—should be related to the numerous ironic catastrophes of the Elizabethan revenge tradition.[10] It may be said of Satan in *Paradise Lost* and the Philistines in *Samson Agonistes*, as it is of D'Amville in Tourneur's *The Atheist's Tragedy* (who, in lifting the axe to kill the innocent Charlemont and thus to crown his villainy, "*strikes out his own brains*"): "The power of that eternal providence / . . . overthrew his projects in their pride" (V, ii, 235 S.d., 264–65).[11]

The influence of the Elizabethan tragedy of damnation on Milton's portrayal of Satan is even more evident. For the most part, the Satan who arrives in Eden is a malcontent, an immoral politician, and a vicelike tempter, who, with his numerous disguises and scheming soliloquies, acts and sounds the role of the Elizabethan stage villain. At other times he is protrayed as a rebel of towering stature, a Marlovian overreacher. He is, most importantly, however, a tragic hero in a tragedy of damnation. In the well-known soliloquy given to Satan at the beginning of Book IV, in which James Holly Hanford and Dame Helen Gardner perceive that he is made to sound like Faustus, Claudius, or Macbeth,[12] one can be relatively certain that Milton's intention is not only to show that the damned sinner is his own nemesis but to provide a tragic example of impenitence. In that soliloquy Satan faces his sin and acknowledges the justice of God's punishment; what Milton terms "natural regeneration" is at work in him (see *Of Christian Doctrine* I, xvii). But Satan will not humble himself, submit to his punishment, turn from evil, and pledge himself to good. He has heard God's call, His invitation to salvation, but he will not harken to it. As a result, having scorned and neglected God's "offered grace" (III, 187), he will heap on himself damnation, becoming the prototype of all damned sinners:

> But hard be hard'nd, blind be blinded more,
> That they may stumble on, and deeper fall.   (III, 200–01)

Milton's description of Adam and Eve's sin and the ironic deflation of their expectations immediately thereafter reinforce the point of Milton's prologue to Book IX; potentially, theirs is a tragedy of damnation like Satan's:

> I now must change
> Those Notes to Tragic; foul distrust, and breach
> Disloyal on the part of Man, revolt,
> And disobedience: On the part of Heav'n
> Now alienated, distance and distaste,
> Anger and just rebuke, and judgement giv'n,
> That brought into this World a world of woe,
> Sinne and her shadow Death, and Miserie
> Deaths Harbinger.   (IX, 5–13)

Paradoxically, however, Milton goes on to assert that this tragic argument of individual sin and divine retribution constitutes a heroic argument:

> Sad task, yet argument
> Not less but more Heroic than the wrauth
> Of stern *Achilles* on his Foe pursu'd
> Thrice Fugitive about *Troy* Wall; or rage
> Of *Turnus* for *Lavinia* disespous'd,
> Or *Neptun's* ire or *Juno's*, that so long
> Perplex'd the *Greek* and *Cytherea's* Son.   (IX, 13–19)

This fascinating passage distinguishes the heroism celebrated in *Paradise Lost* from that in the *Iliad*, the *Odyssey*, and the *Aeneid* in four crucial respects. First, God's wrath is a just, rational passion, an *ira per zelum*, compared to which the bloody, vengeful motives of Achilles and Turnus are perverse imitations. This implied criticism of epic heroism, however, is not strictly antimilitaristic; the issue is true heroism versus false heroism. Even as the motives for Achilles' and Turnus's extraordinary martial prowess are criticized and we are made to relate them to Satan, the Achillean hero of Book VI, the reader might properly recall God's just wrath and glorious display of martial omnipotence in that same Iliadic book.

The second distinguishing aspect of the passage relates to the suffering and trials God inflicts on sinful man. God's punishment might better be celebrated in a heroic poem than the adversity stemming from the ire of Neptune and Juno, because it is just and purposeful rather than partial and perplexing. This assurance of providential justice, in turn, fosters a response to adversity on the part of man which is superior to that of Odysseus and Aeneas—Milton's third distinction between true heroism and the inferior heroism of the classical epic. When Milton states pointedly that the "better fortitude / Of Patience and Heroic Martyrdom" had been heretofore "Unsung" (IX, 31–33), he refuses the invitation of allegorical interpreters of the *Odyssey* and the *Aeneid*, for whom Odysseus and Aeneas were exemplars of Stoic-Christian virtue.[13] From Milton's point of view, it would seem, the inadequate, unenlightened version of providential justice in the classical epic nurtures a self-centered conception of patience—one tending toward Stoic pride, toward an unwarranted confidence in human ability to determine one's own destiny, perhaps even toward defiance of heaven. True patience, on the other hand, Milton would define in this context—quite precisely—as humble submission to divine justice. (Christ, who "submitted himself voluntarily, both in life and in death, to the divine justice" [YP, VI, 438], is the exemplar of this "better fortitude.") Implicit in the sinner's acceptance of suffering and death as just punishment for sin, of course, is an acknowledgement of one's own sinfulness and sincere penitence.

Milton's approach to the classical epic is thus radically subversive. Though he retains the form, style, and conventions of classical epic, he effectively empties the genre of its traditional subject matter, going so far as to suggest that the classical arguments hitherto deemed heroic are, in fact, tragic. If the Elizabethan moral critic like Puttenham was disposed to think of epic and tragedy as counter-genres treating similar subject matter in similar styles but with different modes of presentation and with different intentions—epic being a narrative genre of approbation, tragedy a dramatic genre of reprobation—Milton collapses the distinctions by consigning the values of classical epic and their "heroic" exemplars to hell. Satan's singular epic grandeur in Books I and II, we should remember, proclaims his defiance of God's just punishment; this defiant, impenitent, epic hero is, in reality, a tragic sinner heaping on himself damnation.[14]

Conversely, the new heroism celebrated by Milton's epic is predicated on the penitent sinner's submitting to God's just punishment, as Adam and Eve do in Book X. By traditional standards, of course, such a heroism would be judged nonheroic, and, as C. A. Patrides points out, it could never have been manifested "had not the God-man volunteered his 'unexampl'd love,' which enabled the Godhead to send to man the speediest of its winged messengers, 'Prevenient Grace' (III, 410; IX, 3)."[15] Man, justly condemned under God's tragic curse, "Attonement for himself or offering meet, / Indebted and undon, hath none to bring" (III, 234–35). Even as Christ's voluntary submission to God's justice merits his exaltation, beginning with the Resurrecton, the satisfaction of God's justice bought by Christ's suffering and death redeems the penitent sinner from the punishment to which he himself has humbly submitted. This "unexampl'd love," which is incomparably superior to the loving intercession of Athena for the *"Greek"* or *"Cytheria"* for her "Son" (IX, 19)—Milton's fourth distinction between *Paradise Lost* and the classical epic—enables God to fulfill His gracious purpose toward man. Consequently, in the very pronouncement of Adam and Eve's tragic doom, the Son, in whom are reconciled justice and mercy, prophesies that the seed of the woman will bruise the serpent's head, thus joining the merciful promise of redemption to the administration of divine justice.[16]

From the beginning, when Milton first thought of *Paradise Lost* as a "tragedy," the sinners' *heroic* recovery was essential to his conception. In "Adam unparadiz'd," the fourth and fullest draft in the Trinity manuscript, the actual Temptation and Fall occur offstage after the second act and are related by Lucifer at the beginning of the third: "heer again may appear Lucifer relating, & insulting in what he had don to the destruction of man" (CM, XVIII, 231). The rest of the third act is concerned with punishment, depicting the torments of Adam's conscience, and with what appears to be a formal arraignment in which Justice "cites him to the place whither Jehova call'd for him" (CM, XVIII, 231). The entire fourth act dramatizes Adam and Eve's mutual recrimination and the appeal of Justice; the principle issue in Act IV is elucidated by the concluding chorus which "admonisheth Adam, & bids him beware by Lucifers example of impenitence" (CM, XVIII, 231–32)—an "example," as we saw, that Milton retains for his epic. In the fifth act, Adam, comforted by Mercy's promise of the Messiah, "repents gives god the glory, submitts to his penalty" (CM, XVIII, 232).

We are fortunate, of course, that Milton recast this dramatic conception in a narrative form, which enabled him not only to provide a full description of the temptation and sin but in many other ways to fulfill his original dramatic purpose.[17] However, two crucial points about "Adam unparadiz'd" in relation to Paradise Lost should not be overlooked. First, the material of Book X (the administration of divine justice and Adam's response to it) was initially more prominent than that of Book IX (the actual sin). And second, Adam's exemplary, penitent submission to his penalty in "Adam unparadiz'd" would seem to have suggested to Milton the idea of recasting his dramatic material in the form of a heroic poem. "Adam unparadiz'd" was never strictly a tragedy; although it has a tragic movement of human sin and divine punishment, the final movement of spiritual recovery transforms the drama into a tragicomedy. Knowing that in the fallen world the only truly "heroic" stance possible to man is to acknowledge his sinful nature, to repent his sins, and humbly to submit to God's justice, Milton appears to have decided at some unknown moment in the planning of Paradise Lost to celebrate the exemplary virtue exhibited by Adam in the second half of the drama in the form of epic, thus transvaluing the genre and, by doing so, validating anew the theory that epic was the literary kind most appropriate to the expression of exemplary behavior.[18]

As early as "Adam unparadiz'd," then, the heroic recovery now depicted in Books X through XII of Paradise Lost was fundamental to Milton's artistic intention. Just as early, Satan's example of impenitence was associated with tragedy, and Adam's exemplary behavior with tragicomedy. Satan fell and kept falling; Adam fell and subsequently recovered. Just so, in Paradise Lost, while Milton uses Elizabethan tragic theory and practice to compromise, indeed condemn, Satanic heroism, for the depiction of the new heroism exhibited by Adam and Eve in Book X he exploits the resources of Elizabethan tragicomedy. More specifically, Milton adapts to his epic purpose a species of Elizabethan tragicomedy known as "the comedy of forgiveness," the precise countergenre to the tragedy of damnation.

Paradise Lost has a double peripeteia—of tragic fall and tragicomic restoration[19]—and the second turn, the happy reversal of tragic expectations, is of special concern to us. Two strains of Elizabethan tragicomedy may be distinguished according to their handling of this crucial peripeteia.[20] In the romantic or sentimental strain, which Beaumont and Fletcher perfected and bequeathed to Caroline and Restoration drama, the tragicomic reversal results from a happy coincidence or discovery which unravels the carefully tied knot of complications, or it sometimes results from a sudden change of heart on the part of the villain, who is then forgiven.[21] But in the second, religious strain of tragicomedy, the comedy of forgiveness, which derives from the miracle and morality plays by way of the academic drama referred to as "Christian Terence," the reversal is effected more or less explicitly by the intervention of Providence.[22] Prominent in this second kind of tragicomedy is the sense that divine intervention is *earned* by patience in adversity and repentance for sin. The tragicomic reversal from evil to good, death to life, or loss to recovery thus comes to symbolize a transformation of character, which is what Jackson I. Cope means when he says that tragicomedy "achieves substance through inner reversal, the metamorphosis of character, and transcendent rebirth through that metamorphosis."[23]

The spiritual rebirth attending one's patience and repentance is usually presided over by an intercessory figure. Sometimes the intercessor, much like Dorothea in Greene's *James IV* or Helena in *All's Well That Ends Well*, seems to fulfill the function of the Blessed Virgin or Christ in the miracle play tradition. At other times the figure who effects the repentance and conversion process on behalf of Providence is a scourge, someone like Malevole in *The Malcontent* or Paulina in *The Winter's Tale*. At still other times, the intercessory figure is an active plotter who seems to embody Providence or, at the least, to become the instrument of a providential design—a figure like the duke in *Measure for Measure* or Prospero in *The Tempest*. But the actual change of mind, the conversion itself, is not easily dramatized, and, as Robert G. Hunter has remarked, this problem of characterization "is obviously made a good deal simpler if [the conversion] can be effected by a god from the machine."[24] Nevertheless, one must distinguish the trite use of the deus ex machina like that in *The Rare Triumphs of Love and Fortune* or *Sir Clyomon and Sir Clamydes*, where a happy reversal or sudden change of mind is "effected," from the symbolic theophany of *Cymbeline*, for example, where the descent of Jupiter signifies that a metamorphosis of character has occurred and the divine intervention has been earned. The former is fundamentally a plot device; the latter is principally a device of characterization, symbolizing an inner reversal, a spiritual conversion.

The theophany in *Cymbeline* takes place in a prison scene (V, iv). Initially, Posthumus' only thoughts are of attaining liberty through death; having betrayed Imogen, he has nothing for which to live. His physical enfetterment thus reflects on his spiritual bondage:

> POST.:   My conscience, thou art fetter'd
> More than my shanks and wrists. You good gods, give me
> The penitent instrument to pick that bolt,
> Then free for ever! Is't enough I am sorry?
> So children temporal fathers do appease;
> Gods are more full of mercy. Must I repent,
> I cannot do it better than in gyves,
> Desir'd more than constrain'd. To satisfy,
> If of my freedom 'tis the main part, take
> No stricter render of me than my all. . . .
> If you will take this audit, take this life,
> And cancel these cold bonds.[25]   (V, iv, 8–28)

Posthumus then falls asleep and, to the accompaniment of solemn music, the spirits of his dead family—father, mother, two brothers—intercede on his behalf, asking the gods to ease Posthumus' pain. Interestingly, they pray in fourteeners as they circle the sleeping Posthumus, Shakespeare self-consciously calling attention to the fact that in this "mouldy tale" he is using a device from an older dramatic tradition—that of the miracle play and its early Elizabethan legacy—to dramatize a pattern of repentance, intercession, and the deity's merciful response. The prayers are heard, Jupiter descends from the machine, and, in quatrains, explains his providence:

> JUP.: Whom best I love, I cross; to make my gift,
> The more delay'd, delighted. Be content,
> Your low-laid son our godhead will uplift.
> His comforts thrive, his trials well are spent. . . .
> He shall be lord of Lady Imogen,
> And happier much by his affliction made.   (V, iv, 101–08)

Like the duke in *Measure for Measure*, who will not tell Isabella that her brother Claudio is alive, in order "To make her heavenly comforts of despair, / When it is least expected" (IV, iii, 110–11), Jupiter apparently takes a gratuitous pleasure in effecting an unexpected tragicomic reversal, a merciful *coup de théâtre*. In fact, however, Jupiter's delay is purposeful, allowing Posthumus to purify himself through suffering and sorrow so that he is worthy of the comic reversal.

Acceptance of sorrow and affliction prepares one for the miraculous intervention of divine grace. Patience is a restorative agent. After Strozza has explained the miraculous nature of his recovery in Chapman's *The Gentleman Usher*, his physician observes that true patience is a "most sacred medcine" (V, ii, 10).[26] That lesson is one that Paulina in *The Winter's Tale* has learned well. She announces herself as Leontes' physician (II, iii, 37–38, 54), and for sixteen years she administers the bitter physic of sorrow, humiliation, and repentance so that he is prepared for the intervention of divine grace. Before the miracle occurs, however, Leontes must also "awake [his] faith" (V, iii, 95). Similarly, in *The Tempest*, Prospero impresses upon Alonzo that faith is as necessary an attribute of patience as is repentance:

> ALON.:   Irreparable is the loss, and patience
> Says, it is past her cure.
> PROS.:   I rather think
> You have not sought her help, of whose soft grace
> For the like loss I have her sovereign aid,
> And rest myself content.   (V, i, 140–44)

One submits to patience's "cure" with faith that it will lead to eventual recovery. So, too, in *Paradise Lost*, even though Milton reserves the term *saving faith* for its precise operation subsequent to repentance, Adam and Eve's acknowledgment of their sin and their acceptance of God's judgment are followed immediately by an awareness of how mercifully the Judge has treated them. Trust in God's mercy is as much a part of the heroic patience Milton celebrates as is sincere penitence.

In *Cymbeline*, Jupiter also relates that not only is Posthumus going to be "uplifted" by "our godhead," but he shall be "happier much by his affliction made." His fall will be fortunate. Arthur C. Kirsch has discussed the doctrine of the Fortunate Fall in relation to Battista Guarini's *Il Pastor Fido*, and Jackson Cope has related it to *The Gentleman Usher* and *The Tempest*.[27] The point is not simply that the providential pattern for human time provides a paradigm for the tragicomic form in which things are better in Act V than they were in Act I. Rather, in the religious strain of tragicomedy, the doctrine of the Fortunate Fall describes the individual's spiritual progress of fall and recovery. The tragicomic reversal signals a spiritual redemption from the mortal effects of sin and a restoration to a state of innocence—much, indeed, as Milton defines it in *Of Christian Doctrine:* "MAN'S RESTORATION is the act by which man, freed from sin and death by God the Father through Jesus Christ, is raised to a far more excellent state of grace and glory than that from which he fell" (YP, VI, 415). This new spiritual status may be symbolized by concrete, external rewards, be they riches or position or marriage (as with Posthumus) or even new life (e.g., Hermione's "resurrection" is symbolic of Leontes' spiritual regeneration); but the rewards themselves are less important that the inner reality they signify: the virtuous man's spiritual wealth, or, of more immediate concern, the sinner's deliverance into a "far more excellent state of grace and glory than that from which he fell." Through repentance and faith on the part of man and the intervention of redemptive grace on the part of heaven, the sinner attains "A paradise within . . . happier farr" (XII, 587).

The relevance of these fundamental conceptions of the comedy of forgiveness to *Paradise Lost* needs no lengthly demonstration. The stress on patience (both repentance and faith), God's mercy, the intervention of grace, the doctrine of the Fortunate Fall, the inner paradise, and other concepts is found in both this religious strain of Elizabethan tragicomedy and in Milton's Christian epic, and not simply because they share and exploit a common doctrinal fund. *Paradise Lost* was originally conceived as a drama of loss and recovery, and though Milton finally writes it as an epic, he retains tragicomic values and the double peripeteia of a tragicomic action to inform Adam and Eve's spiritual progress. In this regard, the tradition of Elizabethan tragicomedy provides special access to a crucial episode in *Paradise Lost:* the intercession of the Son at the beginning of Book XI, the moment of tragicomic peripeteia.

The genesis of this pivotal moment in Milton's justification of God's ways to man lies in the debates between Justice and Mercy in the Trinity manuscript. Traditionally, we recall, the debate between the four daughters of God (sometimes a fifth sister, Sapientia, is brought into the debate as a kind of arbitrator between Truth and Justice on the one side and Mercy and Peace on the other) might occur at any point in human history from the Creation to the Last Judgment.[28] Most often, as in the Coventry mystery play cycle, it is associated with the Incarnation. In the mystery cycle, the allegory is essentially theological. The debate's purpose is to explain the necessity of the Redemption and—because justice and mercy are reconciled by the Redemption—to promise the possibility of salvation for sinful man. This function explains the placement of the debate just prior to Christ's coming to redeem man. Of course, Adam and Eve's Fall is in the background of the debate (it is the reason there must be a Redemption), but the allegory's primary purpose is to explain and promote God's plan for man's salvation, not to dramatize God's merciful judgment of Adam and Eve per se. In *The Castle of Perseverance*, on the other hand, the debate occurs after the protagonist's death and focuses on the final disposition of the individual sinner. The difference is important: if the debate in the mystery cycle addresses the Redemption as theological doctrine, in the morality play the debate illustrates the Redemption as it applies to the individual soul.[29] The debate in the *Ludus Coventriae*, by placing the Redemption at the center of time, redeeming the Fall and anticipating the rewards for the faithful at the Last Judgment, emphasizes the importance of the Redemption in terms of God's providential plan for all time; the debate in the morality play stresses the importance of the Redemption to the individual's spiritual drama of loss and recovery.

Milton's third dramatic sketch of the Fall in the Trinity manuscript, entitled "Paradise Lost," perfects the two earlier sketches. Its most significant element (aside from the fact that the Fall itself is reported, not dramatized) is the placement of the debate between Justice and Mercy at the beginning of the tragedy, *before* the actual Fall; the sisters debate "what should become of man if he fall" (CM, XVIII, 229). This placement suggests that Milton wishes to provide a broad providential context for the Fall, anticipating the actual event itself with a prophecy of God's plan for salvation. Milton adds the figure of "Wisdom" to the debate, and clearly she has the last word; her daughters—Faith, Hope, and Charity—come to Adam at the end of the drama to "comfort him and instruct him" (CM, XVIII, 230). About what? Most certainly about the substance of the initial debate, about the Redemption and the salvation it earns for man at the end of time. After this glimpse into the future, the chorus "breifly concludes" (CM, XVIII, 230). There is no hint in the sketch to suggest that Adam and Eve's spiritual recovery is dramatized; rather, the effect of the Redemption on them as individuals is incorporated into the larger tragicomic pattern shaping human time.

Milton's fourth dramatic sketch, however, "Adam unparadiz'd," is more clearly a morality play. Strictly speaking, there is no debate between Justice and Mercy, but the two figures do come to Adam *after* the Fall, in sequential order. First comes Justice to arraign Adam before Jehovah, then to "reason with him" and convince him of God's justice (CM, XVIII, 231), after which, as we saw, the chorus bids Adam "beware by Lucifers example of impenitence." Adam "is humbl'd relents, dispaires," but "at last appeares Mercy comforts him promises the Messiah" (CM, XVIII, 231). Adam then is instructed by Faith, Hope, and Charity, and the result is that "he repents gives god the glory, submitts to his penalty the chorus breifly concludes" (CM, XVIII, 232). The theological attributes of justice and mercy are directly related to Adam's spiritual progress; he must first acknowledge that his punishment is just and, after awaking his faith in God's mercy, repent and patiently submit to this penalty. Significantly, in this dramatic draft stressing individual regeneration rather than providential design, the promise of the Redemption ("promises the Messiah") precedes the final repentance and patient submission to God's justice. If the Redemption is principally related to the tragicomic shape of human history in "Paradise Lost," in "Adam unparadiz'd" it is suggested to be an instrument of individual regeneration.

It is but a small step from Milton's third dramatic sketch, with the implications of its debate between Justice and Mercy before the Fall (the doctrinal stress on the Redemption, the reconciliation between Justice and Mercy, and the salvation of man), to the dialogue in heaven in Book III of *Paradise Lost*. It is not much more of a step from "Adam unparadiz'd," with its application of the Redemption to individual regeneration, to the beginnng of Book XI where one learns that the grace won by the Redemption is the external cause of Adam and Eve's spiritual recovery and one witnesses the Redeemer's intercession on behalf of the penitent sinners. Book III celebrates the Redemption as a divinely ordained peripeteia in the providential tragicomedy extending from the Fall to the Last Judgment; the Son's intercession on behalf of Adam and Eve constitutes a Christian deus ex machina in the tragicomic drama of the regenerate soul.

The dialogue in heaven is not simply an adaptation of the heavenly councils in the classical epic; it is a prologue or induction to Adam and Eve's tragicomedy (as was the debate between Justice and Mercy in "Paradise Lost"). At once a celestial spectator and dramatic "presenter," the Father looks down on Adam and Eve in Paradise and then on the approaching Satan; speaking to the Son, He then ascribes a villainous motive to Satan and anticipates the action that is about to unfold in Eden, the Fall of man. The heavenly perspective encourages one to regard the events that will take place in Eden as a drama on the world stage; more specifically, one soon learns from the "Silvan Scene" of Eden's "woodie Theatre" (IV, 140–41) that the drama will be a pastoral tragicomedy in which Adam and Eve are the protagonists and Satan is the satyr-villain.[30] As the dialogue continues, however, the pastoral tragicomedy is perceived to be part of a more expansive providential drama, becoming the first episode in something like a mystery play cycle.[31] This grand drama Michael will flesh out in historical detail and apocalyptic vision in Books XI and XII, but in Book III Milton wants to reveal only its essential outline of tragedy—peripeteia—comedy and the three events from which this tragicomic pattern takes definition: the Fall, the Redemption (including the Incarnation, Crucifixion, and Resurrection), and the Last Judgment.

Milton's God the Father exhibits both justice and mercy in Book III, and there is only the semblance of "debate" between the divine attributes. It is the Father who asserts that because of the difference between the sins of the fallen angels and of man—a distinction typically put in the mouth of Mercy—"Man therefore shall find grace" (III, 131). To be sure, other arguments typically given to Mercy are raised by the Son in the speech that follows immediately (III, 144–66), but they are couched as rhetorical questions emphasizing the inevitability of the merciful decision the Father has already made. The initial stress in the dialogue, therefore, falls not on whether there will be grace, but on the restorative operation of grace if it is accepted by man (III, 167–202). Only then, almost halfway into the dialogue, is the conventional complaint of Justice introduced—"Die hee or Justice must" (III, 210)—and the need to satisfy Justice decreed. Since one knows already that man shall find grace, however, the key issue is not whether Justice will be satisfied, but how it will be satisfied. The answer, of course, is by the Redemption:

> Father, thy word is past, man shall find grace;
> And shall grace not find means, that finds her way,
> The speediest of thy winged messengers,
> To visit all thy creatures, and to all
> Comes unprevented, unimplor'd, unsought,
> Happie for man, so coming; he her aide
> Can never seek, once dead in sins and lost;
> Attonement for himself or offering meet,
> Indebted and undon, hath non to bring:
> Behold mee then, mee for him, life for life
> I offer, on mee let thine anger fall.   (III, 227–37)

The dialogue in heaven pivots at this moment, emphasis shifting from grace in the first half of the dialogue to the Redemption in the second. At this rhetorical nexus, however, the two emphases are related as effect and cause. The "Happie" arrival of grace—here personified and described in such a way as to suggest its miraculous, restorative role in the tragicomedy of individual regeneration—is soon redefined as the advent of the Redeemer, and its restorative effects on man as the life-giving efficacy of the Redemption (III, 281–302). In this way Milton's "debate" in heaven provides the theological underpinnings for the intercession episode at the beginning of Book XI, where the Redemption will be related to the spiritual life of the individual sinner.

At the end of Book X, Adam and Eve harken to God's invitation to

salvation, responding with "Prayer, repentance, and obedience due . . .
endevord with sincere intent" (III, 191–92). Like Posthumus, Leontes,
or Alonzo, they assume the posture typical of protagonists in a comedy
of forgiveness. As "Adam unparadiz'd" has led us to expect, moreover,
Milton's rare use of epic repetition suggests that this tragicomic posture
is truly heroic. Attaining this heroic stature has been a long and difficult
process, and it is important to note that Milton renders that process
dramatically: Adam's tortured soliloquy in Book X leads directly into an
extended, variously paced dialogue with Eve that for intensity and range
of emotions is unequalled in the entire epic. There follows, however,
the intercession episode at the beginning of Book XI, which, though
continuous with the action, is set apart from it by the break between
books and by a markedly different mode of narration:

> Thus they in lowliest plight repentant stood
> Praying, for from the Mercie-seat above
> Prevenient Grace descending had remov'd
> The stonie from thir hearts, & made new flesh
> Regenerate grow instead, that sighs now breath'd
> Unutterable, which the Spirit of prayer
> Inspir'd, and wing'd for Heav'n with speedier flight
> Then loudest Oratorie: yet thir port
> Not of mean suiters, nor important less
> Seem'd thir Petition, then when th' ancient Pair
> In Fables old, less ancient yet then these,
> *Deucalion* and chaste *Pyrrha* to restore
> The Race of Mankind drownd, before the Shrine
> Of *Themis* stood devout. To Heav'n thir prayers
> Flew up, nor missed the way, by envious windes
> Blow'n vagabond or frustrate: in they passd
> Dimentionless through Heav'nly dores; then clad
> With incense, where the Golden Altar fum'd,
> By thir great Intercessor, came in sight
> Before the Fathers Throne: Them the glad Son
> Presenting, thus to intercede began.
>   See Father, what first fruits on Earth are sprung
> From thy implanted Grace in Man, these Sighs
> And Prayers, which in this Golden Censer, mixt
> With Incense, I thy Priest before thee bring,
> Fruits of more pleasing savour from thy seed
> Sow'n with contrition in his heart, then those
> Which his own hand manuring all the Trees
> Of Paradise could have produc't, ere fall'n
> From innocence.   (XI, 1–30)

This is the moment of tragicomic peripeteia earned by Adam and Eve's heroic patience. In this first comedy of forgiveness, the intercessor himself, not a surrogate, interprets the prayers of the repentant sinners; God responds mercifully (XI, 45–47), and Adam and Eve are restored. In *Cymbeline* Shakespeare calls attention to the miraculous moment of divine intervention by using music and anachronistic fourteeners, by embodying spirits and setting them in ritualistic motion, and by actually having Jupiter descend from the machine. In *Paradise Lost* Milton stresses the miracle of redemption by using the break between books to separate human effort from divine response and by eschewing the heavily dramatic mode of narration at the end of Book X in favor of paradox and commonplace tropes, literary and biblical allusions, and the consciously old-fashioned use of allegory and personification. If Shakespeare's miracle is presented as a dramatic inset, Milton's is presented as a narrative inset. What is extraordinary (if predictable) about Milton's adaptation of the tragicomic reversal is his effort to articulate the doctrinal complexity of Christian restoration, beginning with the double paradox inherent in the better fortitude of Christian patience.

Adam and Eve are prostrate at the close of Book X, having humbly submitted themselves to God's justice, but as Book XI begins, their posture is re-evaluated in terms of Christian heroism: "Thus they in lowliest plight repentant *stood* / Praying" (my emphasis).[32] John E. Parish has accounted for the paradox of being prostrate and standing at the same time by referring the latter to Adam and Eve's spiritual uprightness,[33] but the further paradox is that this spiritual stance is itself attributable to the efficacy of divine grace:

> Prevenient Grace descending had remov'd
> The stonie from thir hearts, & made new flesh
> Regenerate grow instead.   (XI, 3–5)

The "stony heart" trope, commonly employed in conjunction with the doctrine of prevenient grace, signifies an unrepentant soul hardened by sin and pride.[34] Claudius, in *Hamlet*, has such a "stony heart" (III, iii, 70–71) and so does Satan, and both neglect God's invitation to salvation:

> This my long sufferance and my day of grace
> They who neglect and scorn, shall never taste;
> But hard be hard'nd, blind be blinded more.   (III, 198–200)

But Adam and Eve accept the "offerd grace" that will "soft'n stonie hearts" (III, 187, 189) and so transform their tragedy of damnation into a Christian tragicomedy. Their hearts are turned to new flesh, with a georgic implication: their hearts have been made fertile gardens where the first fruits of regenerate faith are sown.[35]

In *Of Christian Doctrine* we are told that the two effects of regeneration are repentance and saving faith, the latter sown or "implanted" (Milton's term) in the "new heart" of the regenerate individual after repentance.[36] Although Adam will not be able fully to articulate his faith until after he learns about the Redemption from Michael, the operation of faith begins in one's will (not the intellect),[37] and this is the moment when Adam first feels the saving faith in his heart. We know this because Adam will soon state that even as he was praying he was persuaded that their prayers of repentance were being heard and, having been reminded of the "seed" that will bruise their foe, now believes that they have been mercifully redeemed from death (XI, 141–61). In the intercession episode itself, the certainty of redemption Adam feels in his heart is conveyed by Milton's allusion to the "first fruits."

While it is true that the "first fruits" of regenerate grace or the "first fruits of the Spirit" (Romans viii, 23) are sown in the heart of Adam and Eve by the Father, this divine grace comes to man, as we have seen, because the Son himself furnishes the "means," the "Attonement," or the "offering meet" on behalf of man. This is precisely the function that the Son is fulfilling in this episode: he intercedes for Adam and Eve *as Redeemer:*

> Now therefore bend thine eare
> To supplicaton, heare his sighs though mute;
> Unskilful with what words to pray, let mee
> Interpret for him, mee his Advocate
> And propitiation, all his works on mee
> Good and not good ingraft, my Merit those
> Shall perfet, and for these my Death shall pay.
> Accept me.   (XI, 30–37)

The Son's "office of intercession and redemption are ioyned together" (Geneva gloss, 1 John ii, 1–2),[38] and, just as the heavenly debate in Book III has suggested, God's regenerative grace and Christ himself are indistinguishable. This is the reason that the "seed" of saving faith implanted in the hearts of Adam and Eve by God's grace can be offered to the Father as already mature, that is, as the "first fruits" of spiritual resurrection; for Christ has ingrafted the sinners in himself, and what the Son offers the Father is himself ("Accept me"), the Redeemer, the "first fruits of them that sleep" (1 Corinthians XV, 20).

Adam and Eve have been *restored* by the "greater man"; they have been "freed from sin and death by God the Father through Jesus Christ, [and are] raised to a far more excellent state of grace and glory that that from which [they] fell." Because saving faith has been sown in the garden of their hearts and they, in turn, have been transplanted in the Redeemer, the "first fruits" of spiritual regeneration offered to God are "more pleasing" than anything Adam and Eve might have offered while still in the state of innocence. Their fall is fortunate.

At the end of Book XII, after Michael has instructed Adam about the Redemption in human history, and the saving faith that began in Adam's will and was first felt at the beginning of Book XI comes to maturity in his intellect, Adam is able to articulate the paradox of Christian tragicomedy that informs his own spiritual history:

> O goodness infinite, goodness immense!
> That all this good of evil shall produce,
> And evil turn to good; more wonderful
> Then that which by creation first brought forth
> Light out of darkness! full of doubt I stand,
> Whether I should repent me now of sin
> By mee done and occasiond, or rejoyce
> Much more, that much more good thereof shall spring,
> To God more glory, more good will to Men
> From God, and over wrauth grace shall abound.   (XII, 469–78)

Repent or rejoice? For Milton's fit reader, aware of the uses to which the poet has appropriated the Elizabethan counter-genres of the tragedy of damnation and the comedy of forgiveness, Adam's doubt might be understood as an injunction: beware the impenitence of Lucifer, repent so that you may rejoice.

University of Southern California

NOTES

1. See, for example, *Of Education* (YP, VI, 404–05) and the preface to *SA*.

2. "An Apology for Poetry," quoted from *Elizabethan Critical Essays*, ed. G. Gregory Smith, 2 vols. (Oxford, 1904), I, 177. *u*'s and *j*'s have been modernized.

3. "The Arte of English Poesie," in Smith, *Elizabethan Critical Essays*, II, 35.

4. *Life of Sir Philip Sidney* (1652), ed. Nowell Smith (Oxford, 1907), p. 221. For similar evaluations of this Elizabethan moral conception of tragedy, see Fredson T. Bowers, *Elizabethan Revenge Tragedy, 1589–1642* (1940; rpt. Gloucester, Mass., 1959), esp. pp. 259–63; L. G. Salingar, "Tourneur and the Tragedy of Revenge," in *The Age of*

Shakespeare, Pelican Guide to English Literature, XI, ed. Boris Ford (Baltimore, 1955), pp. 334–35; and G. F. Waller, "Time, Providence and Tragedy in *The Atheist's Tragedy* and *King Lear*," *English Miscellany*, XXIII (1972), 55–74.

5. See Willard Farnham, *The Medieval Heritage of Elizabethan Tragedy* (1936; rpt. Oxford, 1956).

6. Salingar, "Tourneur and the Tragedy of Revenge," p. 335.

7. Thomas Heywood's description of the function of tragedy, quoted from *An Apology for Actors* (1612), sig. F3ᵛ, intro. by Richard H. Perkinson (New York, 1941).

8. London, 1612.

9. A. J. A. Waldock, *"Paradise Lost" and Its Critics* (Cambridge, 1947), p. 91; the term is used to complain that Milton is too obvious and heavy-handed in turning Satan into a negative exemplum.

10. John F. Andrews, "'Dearly Bought Revenge': *Samson Agonistes, Hamlet*, and Elizabethan Revenge Tragedy," in *Milton Studies*, XIII, ed. James D. Simmonds (Pittsburgh, 1979), pp. 81–107, does not relate the Philistines' ironic punishment to the revenge convention of the play-within-a-play. See Richard S. Ide, "Elizabethan Revenge Tragedy and the Providential Play-within-a-Play," *Iowa State Journal of Research*, LVI (1981), 91–96.

11. Citations are to *The Plays of Cyril Tourneur*, ed. George Parfitt (Cambridge, 1978).

12. Hanford, "The Dramatic Element in *Paradise Lost*," *SP*, XIV (1917), esp. 185; Gardner, "Milton's Satan and the Theme of Damnation in Elizabethan Tragedy," *Essays and Studies*, N.S. I (1948), 46–66, rpt. in Gardner, *A Reading of "Paradise Lost"* (Oxford, 1965), App. A. Gardner also singles out a second soliloquy, that of IX, 99–178.

13. See Don Cameron Allen, *Mysteriously Meant: The Rediscovery of Pagan Symbolism and Allegorical Interpretation in the Renaissance* (Baltimore, 1970), IV, VI.

14. For a similar evaluation of Satanic heroism, see Dennis H. Burden, *The Logical Epic: A Study of the Argument of "Paradise Lost"* (London, 1967), pp. 10–12, 57–75.

15. *Milton and the Christian Tradition* (Oxford, 1966), p. 152.

16. On the reconciliation of justice with mercy in Christ, see esp. Roland Mushat Frye, *God, Man and Satan: Patterns of Christian Thought in "Paradise Lost," "Pilgrim's Progress," and the Great Theologians* (Princeton, 1960), pp. 74–81; and Patrides, *Milton and the Christian Tradition*, pp. 136–39.

17. On this point see esp. Hanford, "Dramatic Element," pp. 186–89.

18. This speculation places special emphasis on the segments of *Paradise Lost* that Allan H. Gilbert labels group 3, including Adam and Eve's reconciliation and penitence as well as Satan's impenitent soliloquy; see Gilbert, *On the Composition of "Paradise Lost"* (1947; rpt. New York, 1966).

19. But see John Steadman, *Epic and Tragic Structure in "Paradise Lost"* (Chicago, 1976), pp. 9–12, who contends that the subject of *PL* is the Fall and that other episodes are extraneous to it.

20. On the importance of the tragicomic reversal, see Frank Humphrey Ristine, *English Tragicomedy: Its Origin and History* (1910; rpt. New York, 1963), pp. xii–xiii; Madeleine Doran, *Endeavors of Art: A Study of Form in Elizabethan Drama* (Madison, 1954), pp. 186–87; and Marvin T. Herrick, *Tragicomedy* (Urbana, 1955), esp. pp. 27–31.

21. On Fletcher's achievement, see Eugene M. Waith, *The Pattern of Tragicomedy in Beaumont and Fletcher* (New Haven, 1952). A recent discussion of the pattern of intrigue in Restoration tragicomedy is Laura S. Brown, "The Divided Plot: Tragicomic Form in the Restoration," *ELH*, XLVI (1980), 67–79.

22. The formative influence of the miracle plays, morality plays, and Christian Terence on Elizabethan tragicomedy has been discussed by Ristine, *English Tragicomedy*, esp. pp. 12–17; Herrick, *Tragicomedy*, II; and Robert G. Hunter, *Shakespeare and the Comedy of Forgiveness* (New York, 1965), II, III, though Hunter scrupulously avoids using the term *tragicomedy*.

23. *The Theater and the Dream: From Metaphor to Form in Renaissance Drama* (Baltimore, 1973), p. 265.

24. *Shakespeare and the Comedy of Forgiveness*, p. 68.

25. Citations are to *The Riverside Shakespeare*, ed. G. Blakemore Evans, et. al. (Boston, 1974).

26. See Cope's important discussion of *The Gentleman Usher*, in *The Theater and the Dream*, pp. 32–52.

27. Kirsch, *Jacobean Dramatic Perspectives* (Charlottesville, 1972), pp. 10–12; Cope, *The Theater and the Dream*, pp. 236–44 passim, 261–66.

28. On the tradition of "The Parliament of Heaven," see Hope Traver, *The Four Daughters of God* (Philadelphia, 1907), and Samuel C. Chew, *The Virtues Reconciled* (Toronto, 1947). Of special relevance to Milton are Robert L. Ramsay, "Morality Themes in Milton's Poetry," *SP*, XV (1918), esp. 132–40, and Patrides, *Milton and the Christian Tradition*, pp. 130–31.

29. For this distinction I am indebted to Hunter, *Shakespeare and the Comedy of Forgiveness*, pp. 13–19.

30. For discussions of the relationship between the satyr play and tragicomedy, see Waith, *Tragicomedy in Beaumont and Fletcher*, II; Doran, *Endeavors of Art*, pp. 201–30; and G. K. Hunter's introduction to Marston's *The Malcontent*, ed. George K. Hunter, The Revels Plays (London, 1975), esp. pp. lxi–lxiv. On the *scena satyrica* in *PL*, see Steadman, *Epic and Tragic Structure*, pp. 25–26, and the general discussion of pastoral tragicomedy in Roger B. Rollin, "*Paradise Lost:* 'Tragical-Comical-Historical-Pastoral,'" in *Milton Studies*, V, ed. James D. Simmonds (Pittsburgh, 1973), pp. 20–23.

31. Not only the scope of the drama about to unfold but the emblem of God's eye and the inevitable pun on "foreseeing" (i.e., *providens*) suggest that Milton's God looks down on the world stage and speaks as the figure of Providence. Raymond B. Waddington, "Here Comes the Son: Providential Theme and Symbolic Pattern in *Paradise Lost*, Book III," *MP*, LXXIX (1982), 256–66, discusses the "eye of Providence" emblem.

32. On "standing" as the posture of Christian heroism in *PL*, see esp. Stanley Fish, *Surprised by Sin: The Reader in "Paradise Lost"* (Berkeley and Los Angeles, 1967), IV; Nicholas R. Jones, "'Stand' and 'Fall' as Images of Posture in *Paradise Lost*," in *Milton Studies*, VIII, ed. James D. Simmonds (Pittsburgh, 1975), pp. 221–46; and Boyd M. Berry, *Process of Speech: Puritan Religious Writing and "Paradise Lost"* (Baltimore, 1976), XII.

33. "Standing Prostrate: The Paradox in *Paradise Lost*, X, 1099 and XI, 1," *English Miscellany*, XV (1964), 89–101.

34. Sometimes God must force entry into the "stony heart"; the sinner's pride must be smashed, his heart broken (*corda contrita*), and so made "contrite." In the contrite heart, Christ's altar can be reconstructed, God's temple built anew. Herbert's Latin epigram, *Petrae scissae*, turns on the pun of *corda contrita;* his *The Altar* begins with a variation of the trope: "A broken altar," we understand, is a contrite heart.

35. Kathleen M. Swaim, "Flower, Fruit, and Seed: A Reading of *Paradise Lost*," in *Milton Studies*, V, ed. James D. Simmonds (Pittsburgh, 1973), pp. 155–76, comments extensively on the complex of metaphors generally related to fruition in Book XI. Also of

general relevance is Barbara Lewalski, "Innocence and Experience in Milton's Eden," in *New Essays on Paradise Lost*, ed. Thomas Kranidas (Berkeley and Los Angeles, 1969), pp. 86–117, and Albert Labriola, "The Aesthetics of Self-Diminution: Christian Iconography and *Paradise Lost*," in *Milton Studies*, VII, ed. Albert C. Labriola and Michael Lieb (Pittsburgh, 1975), esp. pp. 269–82.

36. In the *Christian Doctrine*, Milton defines "saving faith" as "THE FIRM PERSUASION IMPLANTED IN US BY THE GIFT OF GOD, BY VIRTUE OF WHICH WE BELIEVE, ON THE AUTHORITY OF GOD'S PROMISE, THAT ALL THOSE THINGS WHICH GOD HAS PROMISED US IN CHRIST ARE OURS, AND ESPECIALLY THE GRACE OF ETERNAL LIFE" (YP, VI, 471). "New heart" is a scriptural phrase Milton quotes in relation to the regeneration of one's whole mind (YP, VI, 462). On repentance preceding faith, see YP, VI, 469.

37. On the relationship of knowledge to faith, Milton writes: "It follows that we must have a right knowledge of God before we can receive him or approach him. Thus faith springs from a true knowledge of God, though this may at first be imperfect. Then faith progresses towards good from this beginning. It may be deduced from this that the seat of faith is not really the intellect but the will" (YP, VI, 476). Knowledge will perfect the faith, but its operation begins in the will, and the Son's intercession on behalf of Adam and Eve suggests that even an inarticulate, unknowledgeable expression of repentance and faith is acceptable to him. But see George Muldrow, *Milton and the Drama of the Soul* (Paris, 1970), p. 78, and Boyd Berry, *Process of Speech*, pp. 258–60.

38. Quoted from *The Geneva Bible, A Facsimile of the 1560 Edition*, intro. Lloyd E. Berry (Madison, 1969).

MILTON THE APOCALYPTIC HISTORIAN: COMPETING GENRES IN *PARADISE LOST*, BOOKS XI–XII

Thomas Amorose

---

*P*ARADISE LOST ends with a beginning; it is not the work of a poet disappointed with his world. And yet the history of humanity that precedes Adam and Eve's departure from Eden is hardly full of optimism about the fallen human condition. The ususal explanation for the copresence in Books XI and XII of so much expectation for the future with so much suffering and error is that the former somehow derives from the latter. Such a paradoxical relationship is then construed by many readers as evidence for God's miraculous intervention in history to correct man's mistakes and render good from evil. But this relationship can also be conceived of, perhaps more importantly, as an indication of God's process in history for leading man back to him: the last two books of *Paradise Lost* show God producing his desired results through the annihilation of patterns of behavior that obstruct his freeing mankind from fallen history. Christopher Hill has said that "liberty for Milton was always largely negative. It involved criticism, destruction, iconoclasm, as means for establishing freedom."[1] The object of this part of *Paradise Lost* is to subvert belief in imprisoning forms of action. For this and other reasons, Books XI and XII should be considered an apocalyptic, indeed a millenarian, presentation of history.

Katherine Firth, in outlining what she refers to as an "apocalyptic tradition" that used scriptural prophecy to interpret the meaning of historical events, claims that Milton's "patriotic millenarianism" vanishes in his later career. Having lived to see his belief in national election and a guaranteed historical progression toward the Second Coming shattered, Milton refused to entertain any historical pattern "save the endless recurrence of moral judgment" of mankind by God—"the providential history of a disillusioned and disappointed man."[2] It is as though, according to Firth, Milton had given up hope for human participation in the shaping of history: he had placed responsibility for history solely in the hands of a God who suspends man in time, which is portrayed as an endlessly repeating alternation of human act and divine judgment; no discernible plan had been established for man's participation in the final resolution of fallen history. But it is a mistake, as has been pointed out increasingly in recent years, to separate Milton the apologist for the cause of reformation from Milton the epic poet.[3] And, indeed, we see that Milton turns to history in *Paradise Lost* primarily in order to show the means of avoiding an "endless recurrence of moral judgment." He does so by rejecting the Greco-Roman conception of history as a series of cycles.

But neither does he accept unquestioningly the other historical model available to Renaissance thinkers, the Judaeo-Christian, which presents historical events as elements in a linear progression from the Fall to the Last Judgment, although this is what most readings of Books XI and XII seem to suggest.[4] Instead, Milton creates out of this straightforward progression a three-part dialectic, a variation on the Judaeo-Christian scheme that emphasizes God's complex innovation in bringing man back to him, the active participation of mankind in achieving such a goal, and the struggle between opposing forces that results in a new way of existence. All of these are characteristic themes in the apocalyptic tradition. The arrangement of these books is such that they consistently point to the future, to a time beyond even the period that witnesses the benefits of the supposed fulfillment of history through the Crucifixion. But for Milton the process of moving in that direction, as he shows in this review of history, had always been and continues to be a process subverting those two conservative views of history and the behavior that those views praise and, by praising, encourage.

I

The notion of "history" is, of course, a complex one in the Renaissance, and it undergoes enormous change over the course of the period. What concerns us here is a necessarily broad sketch of the differences between the characteristic northern and southern European conceptions of "history," so that we may understand the implications of Milton's historiography as it is manifested in Books XI and XII of *Paradise Lost*. Milton's apocalyptic view of history can be attributed to his choice between these two essentially competing conceptions and to his experience in the English Revolution.

From the modern standpoint, the study and writing of history in the Renaissance was hardly an objective enterprise. Sixteenth-century Italian humanists sought to create an accurate form of history-writing that could be distinguished from the mere keeping of annals and chronicles, on the one hand, and from the mere recapitulation of classical sources for the sake of teaching students rhetoric or hollow moral aphorisms on the other. But no sooner did they do so than the writing of history was pressed into the service of political and religious causes. Its very virtue could be turned into a weapon for any cause wishing to establish and defend its legitimacy. History supposedly dealt in the truthful presentation of the past.[5] So if it could be shown that one's cause had genuine historical precedent, then that cause gained in credibility.

Two distinct historiographic models emerged from two distinct sets of reasons for writing history. In southern Europe, the growth of national consciousness was mainly responsible for the development of secular, political histories. God's Providence, the center of medieval chronicles, was deemphasized. Past deeds of famous or infamous men were stressed, with the stated or unstated belief that the study of history leads to success and therefore is most profitable when those alive today can learn from the successes and failures of those who came before them.[6] In northern Europe, however, the outbreak of religious reformation created the need for a form of history that justified severance from the Church of Rome. Although northern history-writing has been defined as "a narrowing and intensification of the medieval theocentric *weltanschauung*, the absolute subordination of history to theological and pedagogical ends,"[7] in reality it is the result of writers appropriating Italian humanist historiographic techniques for the purpose of defending reformation. In part, the defense was an offense, an attack on the Roman Church's historical foundations.[8]

Related to this distinction in purpose for writing history is a distinction in the pattern given to history in the two different cultures of the North and the South. In the South, where history was expected to provide examples of past solutions to problems so that these solutions could be applied to present exigencies, the course of human events was conceived of necessarily as cyclical; for only if some portion of the past were repeated in the present could former actions serve as models of conduct in the contemporary world. In the North, where history was developed to provide precedent for the reform movement, the pattern given to history was linear. Protestants claimed that the traditions of the Church of Rome had seriously deviated from the beliefs held by the original Church. Histories were then written to show that some remnant of that original Church's spirit had survived over the ages, despite suppression at the hands of the Roman Church. This remnant was portrayed as inspiring a counter-tradition, submerged in the mainstream of history, and present reformation was portrayed as a continuation of that counter-tradition. The charge of innovation could then be turned back on the accuser: change was necessary in order to return to a natural faith free from the unwarranted elaborations on doctrine and church practice introduced by the Roman Church. The emphasis was placed on a straightforward line of sucession from the original church.[9]

Different sources were cited for both models of history. Southerners discovered a cyclical patterning of history in classical authors; Northerners based their linear conception of history on the age-old typological interpretation of that document which they relied on in almost all matters, the Bible.[10]

Yet some apologists for reform went further and sought to defend their cause by demonstrating that history ought to be read specifically in light of the prophetic parts of Scripture. The two—history and prophecy—seemed to them interrelated and served to explain and verify one another. *Carion's Chronicle* (London, 1532), the "first Protestant work of history in the apocalyptic tradition" according to Firth, attempted to demonstrate the validity of prophecy by citing history. It divided history into three periods, each two thousand years in length, in accordance with numerical interpretations of the prophetic books of the Bible. The first age was one without law, the second, one with law, and the third, the period of Christ's Incarnation. This tripartite division is characteristic of histories in this tradition.[11] Writers of these historical accounts also showed how in the last period—also frequently divided into three parts—the struggle between Rome and the North could be read as the struggle between Christ and the Antichrist described in Revelation. Thus, once it was shown that prophecy described and predicted an entire history of dispute between Rome and reformers, Scripture itself could be said to justify the Protestant cause.

Seventeenth-century apocalyptic histories became increasingly millenarian, especially in England; influenced by utopian writers from the Continent, English historians no longer attempted to justify the present by reference to the past, as had sixteenth-century apocalyptic historians. Instead, they looked to a future based on expectations derived from reading history as a fulfillment of prophecy. The relationship between prophecy and history in earlier reformist histories is reversed: history is no longer a test of prophecy; prophecy dictates a pattern by which history is to be read.[12] Prophecy instilled in reformers' minds the desire to create a new consciousness oriented toward the future and the urge to renovate individuals in order to transform mankind as a whole into a race of visionaries.[13] Once this transformation is accomplished, they felt, history will be consummated and can end. In the eyes of its authors, the true object of prophetic history-writing is to move mankind beyond history, and those involved in working toward this end could easily conceive of themselves as being there already, in that they could see the overarching, transcendental form external to time that would someday subsume time. To one viewing history as the execution of a plan that is already outlined by God in prophetic writings, the outcome seemed inevitable, predestined.[14]

Milton's views on history, like his views on all matters, are eclectic and individualistic. They are also, again as elsewhere in his thinking, revisionist. Milton recognizes the dangers implicit in both the Greco-Roman cyclical conception of history and the Judaeo-Christian linear conception of history as merely a sequential series of events leading to the Second Coming. Because Milton subscribes to an apocalyptic vision of history as the unfolding of events "under the vigilant eye of God" within "a sacred framework," he denies the ultimate validity of the cyclical view of history, since it implies that the cycles are controlled by their own dynamic; they seem to be purposeless and to lead nowhere.[15] But because he also has lived through a failed millenarian revolution, he likewise condemns any notion of providential history that presents the Apocalypse as being inevitable, when such inevitability would imply that individual effort toward that end need no longer be the center of each person's concern. History for Milton is not merely about "the outcome of generations of men"; it is about "the human means efficacious toward a providential outcome."[16] There are real choices for characters who serve in *Paradise Lost* as agents of God's Will, and Milton's *History of Britain* shows what happens to a nation in any period of history when it fails to seize forcefully an opportunity for its own improvement offered by God.[17]

Nevertheless, while Milton cannot accept in later life the millenarian belief that ultimate reform is imminent, he still maintains the orientation toward the future rather than the past that is prevalent in the millenarian perception of history. He merely places that ultimate reform in the unforeseeable future. He also keeps the tripartite division typical in apocalyptic versions of history, but he will not give a period to the struggle of progressive reform against intransigent institutions. He looks to scriptural prophecy to guide him in viewing historical events, while recognizing that God's plans are beyond mortal comprehension.

There is therefore great danger in concluding—as Firth apparently does—that, because individual actors are highlighted in Books XI and XII of *Paradise Lost*, Milton regards an isolated, ahistorical existence as the only condition under which virtue is possible. For, in fact, what

Milton shows through this emphasis on individual figures is that only on the individual level can anyone participate fully in a larger, eternal pattern; only on this level can one be informed about how history can be brought into conformity with that pattern. Rosalie Colie writes that Milton uses multiple devices to blend time and eternity in *Paradise Lost* and that Adam enters the fallen world at the end of Book XII "with as much as he can of God's point of view on history."[18] No less is expected from any of us.

Such a metaphysical role for the actors in Books XI and XII creates for them a peculiar relationship to the world and a peculiar pattern of action, when compared to those of characters in standard Renaissance histories and in epics previous to *Paradise Lost*. A perfect gloss on the role is the similar role of Christ in the *Ode on the Morning of Christ's Nativity* and in *Paradise Regained*. In the former, according to Rosamond Tuve, Christ's Incarnation is "an event both in and not within created nature, a peace both in and not within time."[19] And in the latter, as Barbara Lewalski points out, Christ shows an openness about God's future plans for him that allows Christ "to build upon, but yet not be bound by, historical precedents and types."[20] So these figures act in history but find meaning and special purpose in attempting to work when possible within history in order to make history conform to a plan external to it, a plan dictated from eternity. Very often, however, their "action" takes the typical Miltonic form of waiting, with attention always focused on possible providential directives that may emanate either from within or from the outside world.

II

The subversion in Books XI and XII of ultimately inaccurate views of historical events is achieved through the interplay of the three genres that are invoked in the vision-narrative: epic, history, and prophecy. According to Rosalie Colie, genres in the Renaissance represented "fixes" on reality, and therefore specific ways of viewing the world. Combining genres usually created a larger collective vision.[21] For Milton, according to Wittreich, perfect literary form "is attendant upon [the] discovery that individual forms, because they are pliable, submit to new combinations, new relationships, allowing for the creation of more complex orders."[22] It seems possible that combinations could produce, rather than concord or perfection, intentional dissonance between ways of viewing the world. Genres could be used to force versions of reality to compete with one another. A writer could then argue that one way of being and of viewing the world is superior to any other by showing a preference for one genre's conventions over those of others. Such seems to be the case in this history of the world. The prophetic mode wins out as the valid way of viewing human events, while the epic perspective and that presented in history-writing uninfluenced by prophecy are consciously subverted. Prophecy performs its usual task: it forces us to read the text in order to go beyond it.[23] In this case, Milton as poet-prophet asks us to read of cosmically significant, epic actions in eternity only to show how that kind of action in Books XI and XII proves to be a foolishly disastrous way of engaging the fallen world. At the same time, he requires that we read of traditional subjects of history—the Creation and, more important for the discussion here, the events of the Old and New Testament, as well as more recent ecclesiastical history—so that he may then trace a pattern of visionary figures who seem to rise above the historical narrative and participate as effective actors with God in shaping mankind's destiny. History and epic by themselves seem to be portrayals of superficial events shaped into patterns that can be deceiving.

That the biblical narrative could be conceived of as composed of several "kinds" should not surprise us, for the Bible was considered in the Renaissance to be the repository, indeed the summary, of all genres.[24] What needs to be pointed out here is that each of the three genres being discussed strives in *Paradise Lost* to represent the events contained in that summary document; each could do so because epic, history, and prophecy were themselves considered summary forms. So the rivalling of these three "fixes" on reality amounts to nothing less than a questioning of the very scheme of all things. Because prophecy finally emerges in the last two—and for us fallen readers, the most important—books as the dominant form, the proper mental set for observing human events, we can say that Milton in his final years lost none of his visionary historian's impulse: he judges events by whether they participate in some transcendent movement or exist only as mundane occurrences. And the fact that the traditional epic code of heroism is made extinct in this poem by the Son's victory in the War in Heaven over Satan (the old-style epic hero) even before history begins suggests that also emerging from Books XI and XII is a new mode of heroism. The prophet is hero, and his peculiar form of heroic action is based on adherence to a transcendent code.

The method for subverting epic and history seems clear. Milton presents on the surface of these last books both the linear and the cyclical models of history: those men chosen by God or favored by him seem to participate in a simple linear movement back to oneness, while those inattentive to his wishes are definitely caught up in a pattern of endlessly recurring cycles of peace and disruption. In the cyclical configuration, thesis and antithesis clash and yet produce no resolution: unstable peace gives way to some disruptive force, usually war, which instead of settling any particular dispute leads to unstable peace again when war has wearied itself. What should be a dialectic, in other words, becomes a cycle of destruction.

But both linear and cyclical are only the apparent patterns. Underneath, or perhaps above them, God is acting as a guiding force in history, at first distant from man, then known through signs, and finally known directly through Christ. What at first seems to be a simple linear progression is in fact a dialectic, one with much larger movements than those of peace and disruption, one directing man out of history and back to God. To be more specific, those chosen or favored by God participate in a progressive, three-part historical dialectic controlled by moral and political directives from God to man. Milton's division of the history into two books assists in making this dialectic clear. Each of the three parts represents an age, the first of which, occupying all of Book XI, is an age of conscience during which chosen men rely on an inward, and partial, source for those directives. The second, which begins Book XII, is represented by an age of law, a time when the chosen people come to rely on an external and, as recognized by the select nation itself, incomplete set of guidelines. And the third part of the dialectic, the synthesis, is represented by an age of inward law initiated by Christ's sacrifice, during which outward Law and inward conscience are combined, in effect internalizing the Law so that the individual soul becomes the most reliable source for knowledge of God's directives.[25]

The refinement of the linear conception of history into the form of a three-part dialectic, recalling the tripartite schemes common in works of the apocalyptic tradition, and the denigration of the cyclical conception combine to subvert the value of any reading of history that is bound to history. At the same time, they subvert simple historical readings that do not take into account a God who creates unity through struggle. In this case, the struggle is between inward and outward relationships with God. The outcome produces within man all the knowledge he needs to serve as God's agent on earth. That which is of most importance for the progress of mankind lies outside history. History as a genre is thus involved in a self-contradiction: it concentrates on characters and events that will not have any ultimate historical significance.

In a similar fashion, epic standards are used to undermine epic. Milton is devising in these last books of *Paradise Lost* an anti-epic in which general mankind's fallen imitation of the vastly significant actions related in the earlier books of the poem produces decidedly insignificant and ineffective results. The outcome is irony: the distance between the results actors intend to produce by their actions and the true effects of those actions is enormous; most often, acts produce results exactly the opposite of those desired, with mankind as a whole apparently never comprehending its qwn ineffectiveness. It is as if Milton is using a change from an age characterized by straightforward relationships among things—in Eden—to an age of irony, in order to turn epic back on itself and demonstrate that those grand "epic" movements seen in the earlier books cannot serve as guidelines for action in a fallen world. As we shall see, those whose actions indeed seem grand by previous epic standards are thwarted in Books XI and XII by the cycles in which they involve themselves. Even Israel, a "select nation"—that entity celebrated in epics previous to Milton's—must be destroyed in order for history to be consummated.[26]

III

It would be a mistake, however, to conceive of Books XI and XII as being only negative and undermining. For while this subversion of misguided ways of perceiving the fallen world is proceeding, a valid vision of history, the prophetic vision, begins to emerge. It is as though Michael is sent to Adam in order to expurgate error so that a rebuilding of vision can occur, a form of purifying not uncommon in prophetic literature. Specifically, Michael presents Adam with the two alternatives available to mankind. Every individual has a choice between overinvolvement with the world and one's position in it and attentiveness to God's Will. History receives its earlier-mentioned dual configuration from the fact that one element of mankind pursues the first option while another element pursues the second. When some choose overinvolvement, the result is enslavement to a system of ironies which creates in history endless repetitive cycles comprised of a type of war which, ironically, never results in lasting stability, followed by a "peace" which, again ironically, only foments instability and future conflict. But when others, a select few, choose vigilance to God's Will, the result is relief from the irony-producing cycles and participation in an effective dialectic that allows transcendence of history and leads man back to God. There is no better way of discussing the subversion of epic and of conventional historiography, and the simultaneous emergence of an apocalyptic vision of history, than to separate the two and examine each by itself, beginning with the subversion process.

Michael's task is to destroy in Adam the temptation to regard the cycles as anything more than the most superficial configuration of history, replete with false epic heroes and leading nowhere. His presentation of the cycles begins with an attempt to expose Adam to the most basic of ironies to which those overinvolved with the world are subjected: that what is natural is not always good. Michael's method at first is to allow Adam to draw conclusions about man's proper relation to nature, only so that the angel may subvert those conclusions by offering further evidence that invalidates them. In the beginning of the first cycle, Cain slays Abel, even though Abel's sacrifice is "sincere" and, as Michael tells Adam, Abel is "approv'd" by Heaven (XI, 443, 458). Adam's response is outrage: "Is Pietie thus and pure Devotion paid?" (XI, 452). It seems that the next episode, that of the lazar house, is a response to Adam's concern. It shows that attentiveness to God and to that which is natural for man is indeed rewarded, if only in the form of a less painful death than would otherwise await him. Michael seems to suggest that there is still extant in the world some just relation of action and outcome, based on man's responsibility for himself:

> Thir Makers Image, answerd *Michael*, then
> Forsook them, when themselves they villifi'd
> To serve ungovern'd appetite. . . .
> Therefore so abject is thir punishment,
> Disfiguring not Gods likeness, but thir own,
> Or if his likeness, by themselves defac't
> While they pervert pure Natures healthful rules
> To loathsom sickness, worthily, since they
> Gods Image did not reverence in themselves.   (XI, 515–25)

The next episode, however, destroys any easy equation of a natural life with a wholesome and godly life, and Adam is to feel the pain of existence in a world where God and nature may dictate opposing directives. When Adam sees the sons of Lamech with their practiced artisanship apparently working in harmony with nature's materials, and when he sees the sons of Seth and these artisans' daughters amid "Songs, Garlands, Flours, / And charming Symphonies," he correspondingly admits to feelings of "delight, / The bent of Nature" (XI, 594–96). He sees in the first scene of this episode an improvement on nature through craft, in the second, the consummation of nature in the marriage of man and woman: "Here Nature seems fulfilld in all her ends" (XI, 602). But Michael chastises Adam for giving in to natural pleasure, reminding him that man is created "to nobler end / Holie and pure, conformitie divine" (XI, 605–06). The points Michael is making through use of this method become clear at the end of this cycle of reversals: that a stong involve-ment with nature after the Fall constitutes overinvolvement with the world, that nature by itself can be no source of hope, and that therefore the correct viewer of events must seek something beyond nature and somehow participate in the divine. The schism between the surface features of the world—including the apparent process of history—and God becomes painfully evident.

The warring between two cities in the next episode begins a new, second cycle of upheaval followed by a questionable peace, not by some resolution brought about through the struggle. This disturbance in an age of giants is parallel to the disturbance in the first cycle, only here matters have reached epic proportion, and Michael demonstrates that in this cycle, too, mankind seems condemned to a life of ironies. The effect produced is an undermining of epic heroes' two chief characteristics: physical prowess proven in battle and wisdom demonstrated in council. On both sides in this war are men seeking "to be styl'd great Conquer-ours" triumphing over others, striving to be called "Patrons of Mankind, Gods, and Sons of Gods" through tournaments (XI, 695–96). Mean-while, "what most merits fame" remains hidden while these self-styled heroes seek to become patrons of mankind by destroying it (XI, 699). This crazy distance between intention and means to the intended end continues as men choose to ignore Enoch, who offers the only real resolution to a seemingly endless massacre: the establishment of justice, decisions on what is right and wrong between groups, and the discovery of the truth so that peace may prevail (XI, 666–68). There is a higher authority, he argues, than any determined on the battlefield, and men are to be held accountable for their acts in a context broader than that of the immediate quest for fame and glory. Because the council will not listen to Enoch, its members can reach no agreement on a plan of action and fall finally into "factious opposton" (XI, 664).[27] This degeneration of peaceful meeting into internecine struggle—a sort of miniature of the larger cycles of peace and disruption operating in history—stems from the failure of these "heroes" to accept the only resolution possible here, deference to the law of God. Thus, heroic action is made to seem foolish because it proves ineffective; the "heroes" seem to miss the point of action and appear out of control when they deliberate in council.

Epic is further undermined by a denigration of its other major motif besides action: the motif of leisure, ease, respite from war. Once again, irony is the tool of subversion. When "calm" is apparently restored, what emerges is more a period of dissolution and carelessness than a time of constructive and directed peace:

> All now was turn'd to jollitie and game,
> To luxurie and riot, feast and dance,
> Marrying or prostituting, as befell,
> Rape or Adulterie, where passing faire
> Allurd them.   (XI, 714–18)

This course of purposeless pleasure and ease, Michael tells Adam, bears within it the seeds of disruption, small "civil Broiles" and "hostil deeds in Peace" that show how unstable and unsatisfying this kind of "peace" can be (XI, 718, 796). A further disjunction between what appears to be true and the actual state of affairs has to do with the status of the supposed conquerors who dominate this scene of temporary, and shaky, cessation of war. Noah, says Michael, preaches to them "as to Souls / In Prison under Judgements imminent" (XI, 724–25). The metaphor is fitting, since these supposed victors are in fact imprisoned—by overinvolvement with their own moment in time. Indeed, Michael invites the comparison between this group and their captives, who refusing to live in a fashion that will guarantee them freedom,

> practice how to live secure,
> Worldlie or dissolute, on what thir Lords
> Shall leave them to enjoy.   (XI, 802–04)

Captor and captive alike serve a single master: the events that surround them. Those who seem in charge of the situation are as helpless as those whom they rule, who, to compound the system of ironies, are captives only to their own unwillingness to overcome circumstances. In such a world, turning one's back on events as Noah does ironically proves to be safer and more peaceful than either supposedly secure obsequiousness or slothful victory. For the Flood is imminent, and those entangled in concern for how best to survive without discomfort will be those who will suffer the greatest of all devastations.

Book XII continues in the same vein, proving ineffective the cyclical and epic versions of history. The quiet side of this particular cycle is seen first. While "the dread of judgement past remains / Fresh in thir mindes, fearing the Deitie," people manage an unexceptional peace, more out of fear than from a sense of purposeful progress or attention to God's Will (XII, 14–15). Here once again is peace without meaning, resulting only from fear of punishment and producing little basis for further stability. It is no surprise, then, when a self-announced hero, Nimrod, disrupts this dubious calm. As they are first presented, however, Nimrod's desires seem remarkably senseless and without particular cause: it is he who,

not content
With fair equalitie, fraternal state,
Will arrogate Dominion undeserv'd
Over his brethren, and quite dispossess
Concord and law of Nature from the Earth.   (XII, 25–29)

Nevertheless, Michael points out that the presence of a Nimrod in history makes perfect sense. "Since thy original lapse," he says to Adam,

true Libertie
Is lost, which alwayes with right Reason dwells
Twinn'd, and from her hath no dividual being.   (XII, 83–85)

When reason is lost, passion strips the individual of internal freedom; this state invites tyrants such as Nimrod to rob fellow humans of outward liberty. Such is "Justice" and the "fatal curse annext" to the fallen state (XII, 99). The implication here is that until the cycles produce a true peace—which they cannot do—humanity will be susceptible to such figures who inadvertently work man's misery. And the epic hero, who believes that his discontent and the superhuman feat of constructing the Tower of Babel that such discontent motivates distinguish him in some way, is in reality only an insignificant part of the cruel and pointless machinery of the cycles.

Beginning with Abraham, the "one peculiar Nation" is the focal point of the vision-narrative, and its presentation also highlights the shortcomings of any viewing of history as merely a series of cycles, on the one hand, or as an epic on the other (XII, 111). It is true in these books that peace becomes an opportunity for constructive development toward a lasting connection to God rather than a cause for further instability, and that war becomes a means of guarding God's Covenant with man by protecting the agents of that Covenant, the select nation. Nevertheless, the cycle of disruption and peace continues, still without resolution. The prosperity deriving from the peaceful sojourn of the chosen nation in Egypt, narrated next, is the very basis for the end of that peace: Pharaoh's successor, becoming suspicious of the select people's growth into a nation, seeks to stop that growth by holding them captive. Michael's terms demonstrate the irony. Joseph dies, he explains,

and leaves his Race
Growing into a Nation, and now grown
Suspected to a sequent King, who seeks
To stop thir overgrowth, as inmate guests
Too numerous.   (XII, 163–67)

The positive growth of a nation causes the potentially damaging growth of suspicion in the king, who views such expansion as "overgrowth": development in one direction causes an equal but opposite development in another.

And rather than celebrating the geographical expansiveness and psychological "directedness" of a particular, special nation, as conventional epic would do, Michael's "song" emphasizes the spiritual confinement and physical aimlessness of Israel—a sort of converse epic. The peace in the desert that follows the Egyptian plague and military pursuit is seemingly both accidental—not a peace based on victory over or settlement with Pharaoh's successor—and restrictive, the result of worry that

> Least entring on the *Canaanite* allarmd
> Warr terrifie them inexpert, and feare
> Return them back to *Egypt*.   (XII, 217–19)

Granted, during this wandering God hands down his civil and religious laws, and rites are arranged that bring man closer to God. Yet when Adam comments that "So many Laws argue so many sins," Michael points out that, even in this time of peace between God and man, God's chosen ones live under the "imposition of strict Laws" which comprise a system of bondage productive of "servil fear" (XII, 283, 304–05). The disruptions that break this peace can be viewed as coming about because of the difficulties inherent in such an arrangement, where law is imposed on a group from outside it; and imposed only in order to show the inadequacy of the Israelites: to "discover sin" and "evince / Thir natural pravitie" so that they realize some future expiation for sin is required (XII, 290, 287–88). Also, even though God may save the chosen people from their attacking foes when the Israelites are penitent for their sins, such rescue is merely a continuation of the purposeless cyclical pattern that is being traced here, not a resolution of it. For the pattern will continue with peaceful times and promising signs from God alternating with periods when Israel's faults

> will so incense
> God, as to leave them, and expose thir Land,
> Thir Citie, his Temple, and his holy Ark
> With all his sacred things, a scorn and prey.   (XII, 338–41)

Surely the concept of such a "select" nation—incapable of maintaining spiritual direction and confined physically by its vulnerability—is a serious departure from that found in most previous epics.

With the coming of Christ, the chosen people, now not just a select nation but a body composed of all those who believe in Christ, seem to transcend the cycles of history. Yet two features of Michael's narrative seem to suggest differently, and serve to point out still that existence within the cyclical pattern leads nowhere, and thus subvert the worth of a reading of history that concentrates on the cycles.[28] These two features also cast doubt on the epic conception of "action." First, it is not by their own acts that Christians can hope to be delivered from this seemingly endless series of oppositions without resolution. It is solely through Christ and "his merits / To save them, not thir own, though legal works," as well as his obedience, which his followers can share in only by faith (XII, 409–10). Second, since that faith is "not void of workes" which the Christian is required to perform and yet those works cannot produce ultimate resolutions to earthly conflict, man is subjected to the greatest of all ironies: he must act, even though he knows his action will not guarantee any particular progress or relief from persecution (XII, 427). Even the Apostles' "race well run" fails to establish a line of successors who can guide and improve mankind (XII, 505).

It may seem that history has returned to where it began, with the "just" few being persecuted or ignored by the many. But that is not the case. Even though few in number, these true "worshippers" possess a knowledge of God that their predecessors in Book XI lacked; God has made himself more evident to his followers externally through the coming of Christ and internally through "His Spirit within them, and the Law of Faith / Working through love" written upon their hearts (XII, 488–89). So we must assume that change has occurred, that the endless cycles of irresolvable disruption and false peace are not the ultimate configuration of history. Nor can we say that a simple linear progression is responsible for the change, for there is no sense given in these books of a steady, cumulative process of reunification with God. The pattern seems more complicated, more agonistic: as mentioned earlier, it takes the form of a dialectic of conscience and external law that is resolved by the advent of Christ. An apocalyptic vision of history is emerging in the midst of the subversion process, and we can discern its outline by noting similarities between Michael's vision-narrative and characteristics of the prophetic tradition of history writing sketched above.

The most obvious similarity is, of course, the tripartite division. This feature not only emphasizes the struggle of the few of God's agents against the intransigent majority of humanity, but also, and more importantly, it highlights the struggle that is internal to the select group, which takes the form of a three-part dialectic. The first part of the dialectic is repesented in Book XI, in which the "one just Man" knows God through his sense of what is right and just; it is through conscience formed naturally within man that he knows what goes with God's Will, what against, and applies his standards to the outside world. Yet even though God's laws are held within conscience, conscience itself is damaged and performs only half its function, merely pointing out man's inadequacies. Those characters in touch with conscience in Book XI can only observe rites or preach justice and morality and, when they are not heeded, withdraw from the sinful world and await the repair of man's corruption at some later, unspecified date.

From the beginning of Michael's presentation, then, there is an orientation of the figures toward the future and some unforseen development that is typical in the tradition of prophetic literature. In this light, the important characters of Book XI are Abel, Enoch, and Noah, examples of the type of the "one just Man," who emerges as a new, anti-epic hero, the prophet-hero. His actions take the recognizable Miltonic form of waiting, here for directives from a God outside of history. He also displays a natural, innate sense of what is right in dealing with this distant God and with other men. Abel is the first whom Adam sees, and what Michael stresses about Abel is his sincerity and his recognition that "Pietie" and "pure Devotion" are the proper responses to a God who is the source of his well-being (XI, 452). And yet the only direct knowledge of God that Abel possesses comes through God's signal, the ascending smoke which shows that the sacrifice is acceptable. That is not much, and it is conscience, we can presume, that apprises Abel of his relationship to God and of the necessity for piety and devotion. But the purpose for showing piety and devotion, other than only to appease God through sacrifices, apparently goes unknown. As a result, conscience can only tell Abel that he must offer expiation for sin. It cannot tell him how he may get out from under that sin. For such information, humanity must wait.

That there is some movement toward a better future is evident in the developments within this type of the "one just Man" in its next manifestation. Enoch's conscience seems to dictate more specifically than did Abel's what God wishes, and the times seem to call for more specific articulation of God's Will. Still, God is not with Enoch in the way he was with Adam and in the way that he will be with every believer after Christ. At the council during the age of giants, discussed earlier, Enoch speaks

much of Right and Wrong,
Of Justice, of Religion, Truth and Peace,
And Judgment from above.   (XI, 666–68)

Like Abel, Enoch knows "of Religion"—of how to worship God correctly. But he also knows how one person should treat another; conscience, in addition to telling man how to relate to God, is also telling
him how to relate to others. When the external code is mere 'Sword-
Law," the internal code, articulated by Enoch, dictates "Justice," which
would guarantee "Peace" (XI, 672, 667). Enoch is the conscience of his
people but goes unheeded. And, although Michael shows Enoch being
whisked away from the threatening group, enveloped in "a balmie
Cloud," the angel gives no indication that Enoch has knowledge of
God's plans for man or of his role in those plans (XI, 706). Conscience
once again tells only of sin and makes the "one just Man" aware that
mankind cannot reform itself.

By the time in the narrative when Noah is presented, we begin to
perceive that the line of these "just" men constitutes a tradition of true
believers submerged in the chronicle of a world hostile to God's Word,
and this tradition seems analogous to the counter-tradition of true Christians which northern European historiographers detail in their accounts
of the Church. Noah is the epitome of the figure in this line: iconoclastic,
suspicious of custom, rising above mundane history as a prophet of things
to come—the clearest manifestation yet of the new-style hero emerging in
the narrative. He, like Enoch, has internal standards, which are in strong
opposition to the indiscriminate riot that surrounds him. Mankind is
closer to destruction in this stage of history than it had been in the last,
and so Noah is more strenuous in declaring the need for "Repentance"
and "Conversion" (XI, 724). He urges, in effect, a life based on principles,
so that man may become the master of history rather than its victim
through overinvolvement. Noah resists and warns against two forces: the
"allurement" of worldly excess, and "custom" (XI, 810). Both distract man
from the long-term historical process directed by God. The "one just
Man" rises above the moment, and Noah's seemingly passive decision to
remove "his Tents far off" from others is a metaphor for withdrawal from
distractions. Such is the nature of the new heroic "action" that these
figures display. And yet Michael still gives no sign that Noah is aware of
the historical significance of his actions. It is as though Noah rises above
the cycles of history but is unable to assist humanity in freeing itself from
those cycles. Conscience thus informs him of man's inadequacies but does
not suggest any plan for overcoming those inadequacies.

Beginning with Abraham in Book XII, God directs mankind with signs and indications of his Will in the external world.[29] His direction culminates in the Law, and the second part of the dialectic comes into being. But, as Michael tells Adam, "the Law by Ceremonies / Cannot appease" conscience (XII, 297–98). Conscience and the Law—external and internal directives—are in opposition to one another. So humanity must patiently wait in this period of history also, reading in the Law some future event that will provide a way out of its sinful dilemma. Nevertheless, with Abraham, the "one just Man" assumes a more active role as instrument of God. He is called by God from a land of idolaters— the conscientious man again drawn away from distraction:

> him God the most High voutsafes
> To call by Vision from his Fathers house,
> His kindred and false Gods, into a Land
> Which he will shew him.   (XII, 120–23)

But Abraham is, more importantly, the faithful man,

> trusting all his wealth
> With God, who call'd him, in a land unknown.   (XII, 133–34)

What Michael praises about this just man is this faith, which carries Abraham along even though he does not know the purposes of his mission: he

> straight obeys,
> Not knowing to what Land, yet firm believes.   (XII, 126–27)

Rather than a conscience of his people, then, Abraham seems to be more the agent of a God who forcefully directs history and seeks through external signs to move his people into a separate land. God's role in history has decidedly changed from that of a force for reminding man of what he is not to that of telling man of what he can be. Besides increasing the orientation toward the future, this shift changes the select individual's reliance on conscience to a reliance on faith in external signs. The two fail to come together, however, and there is tension within the spiritual life of God's agents. It is as if the characteristic themes of histories in the apocalyptic tradition play against one another here in order to make clear the insufficiencies of this part of the dialectic: God is present in history as an active force, but as an active force for pointing out inadequacy and pointing toward a better future; his external signs give consolation, yet cannot appease conscience; certain figures become instruments of God, but they cannot fully understand the purposes of his directives. As mentioned earlier, Milton is altering to suit his own purposes the tradition with which he is working. He wishes to show that complacent belief in the inevitable historical triumph of good is an unrealistic position for any individual actor to maintain.

The tensions increase as God draws closer to his select nation. Moses is to act explicitly as the "Minister / Of Law" and is privileged to receive many indications of God's new relationship through covenant with man (XII, 308–09). Yet struggle between the opposing forces of the Law and lawlessness still occur. Pharaoh, "the lawless Tyrant," refuses to acknowledge the chosen nation's God or his message and must be opposed by "Signs and Judgements dire," the Egyptian plagues (XII, 173, 175). Granted, signs of God's Covenant are many: an angel who goes in a cloud before the chosen people, a pillar of fire, and others. But, again, the chief purpose of the Law is not to assure man but to instruct him about his "natural pravitie, by stirring up / Sin against Law to fight" (XII, 288–89). Thus, the Law appears to men

> imperfet, and but giv'nc
> With purpose to resign them in full time
> Up to a better Cov'nant.   (XII, 300–02)

That "better Cov'nant" arrives in the form of Christ, who finally "God with man unites," thereby producing a synthesis of the previously antagonistic forces operating in the dialectic (XII, 382). This unification takes the form of an interiorization of God's presence. What enlightens the believer is God's "Spirit within" him and the "Law of Faith" which God will write upon his heart (XII, 488–89). The Spirit within repairs conscience, so that believers are motivated to perform outward works of goodness not only out of a sense of what is right toward others or appropriate as worship of God—the case with figures in Book XI—but out of love, which is based on an awareness of God's presence within. The law of faith grants assurance and guidance so that faith is not directed outward to a God seen only through signs; faith dwells inside, where God dwells, and like the Spirit expresses itself through love. Moreover, this inner sense of God provides the "inward consolations" that strengthen believers against persecution from their opposition (XII, 495). The resultant "paradise within" provides the only reliable guide in a fallen world:

> for on Earth
> Who against Faith and Conscience can be heard
> Infallible?   (XII, 587, 528–30)

And, in line with other apocalyptic readings of history, Michael's presentation emphasizes reliance on the Bible and visionary understanding, often working in tandem: the "truth" is "Left onely in those written Records pure" which are "not but by the Spirit understood"—that "Spirit within" granted to true believers (XII, 511, 513–14). What has evolved is self-reliance based on inward faith and repaired conscience.

Adam recites the essential lessons of Books XI and XII at the end of the narrative, and they serve as the best summary of what the reader is also to learn about history: God dwells with man and also works in the historical process. It is this presence that allows the special heroes of these books to stay in touch with the transcendental plan. Even after Christ, these special figures must be attentive, and active in the Miltonic sense of the word; the synthesis rendered by Christ's coming does not cause passivity, complacence, or resignation. And it is the "paradise within" that permits God's agents to work in history for the purpose of bringing history in line with divine guidance. Adam has learned "ever to observe / His providence," ever to contemplate history and see that it is ultimately controlled by God, and not by those men whose actions apparently lead it only into a series of cycles without resolution (XII, 563–64). Adam learns how God works in history and summarizes concisely the broader, apocalyptic pattern of the historical process in which God acts through agents who seem, by the traditional standards of history and epic, unimportant. Their method, however, like Michael's, is one involving quiet destruction that will create conditions from which a new order may emerge:

> with good
> Still overcoming evil, and by small
> Accomplishing great things, by things deemd weak
> Subverting worldly strong, ānd worldly wise
> By simply meek.   (XII, 565–69)

State University of New York, Potsdam

NOTES

1. *Milton and the English Revolution* (New York, 1977), p. 178.
2. *The Apocalyptic Tradition in Reformation England, 1530–1645* (Oxford, 1979), p. 235.
3. Three prominent explicators of Milton's consistency over the course of his career in urging reformation are Hill, *Milton and the English Revolution;* Joan Malory Webber,

Milton and His Epic Tradition (Seattle, 1978); and Joseph Wittreich, *Visionary Poetics: Milton's Tradition and His Legacy* (San Marino, Calif., 1979).

4. Readings of this sort abound. For an intelligent example from the last decade, see Raymond B. Waddington's "The Death of Adam: Vision and Voice in Books XI and XII of *Paradise Lost*," *MP*, LXX (1972), 9–21. For readings that describe, on the other hand, greater complexity of arrangement of Books XI and XII, see Hill's *Milton and the English Revolution*, p. 347, Wittreich's "A Poet Amongst Poets': Milton and the Tradition of Prophecy," in *Milton and the Line of Vision*, ed. Joseph Wittreich (Madison, 1975), pp. 131–40, and Mary Wilson Carpenter's "Milton's Secret Garden: Structural Correspondences Between Michael's Prophecy and *Paradise Regained*," in *Milton Studies*, XIV, ed. James D. Simmonds (Pittsburgh, 1980), pp. 153–82. For reviews of earlier scholarship see C. A. Moore, "The Conclusion of *Paradise Lost*," *PMLA*, XXXVI (1921), 1–34; Mary Ann Radzinowicz, " 'Man as Probationer of Immortality': *Paradise Lost*, XI–XII," in *Approaches to Paradise Lost*, ed. C. A. Patrides (Toronto, 1968), pp. 31–52; and Barbara K. Lewalski, "Structure and the Symbolism of Vision in Michael's Prophecy: *Paradise Lost*, Books XI–XII," *PQ*, XLIII (1964), 25–35.

5. Herschel Baker, *The Race of Time: Three Lectures on Renaissance Historiography* (Toronto, 1967), p. 16.

6. F. J. Levy, *Tudor Historical Thought* (San Marino, Calif., 1967), p. 35.

7. John L. Brown, *The "Methodus ad facilem historiarum cognitionem" of Jean Bodin: A Critical Study* (Washington, D. C., 1939), p. 68.

8. Levy, *Tudor Historical Thought*, p. 41.

9. Ibid., pp. 41, 79–80, and elsewhere.

10. For a thorough discussion of these two conceptions of history, see C. A. Patrides, *The Phoenix and the Ladder* (Berkeley and Los Angeles, 1964). The same argument is contained in Chap. VIII of his *Milton and the Christian Tradition* (Oxford, 1966) and Chap. I of his *Grand Design of God* (London, 1972).

11. Firth, *Apocalyptic Tradition*, p. 16.

12. Ibid., p. 17.

13. Wittreich, *Visionary Poetics*, p. 26.

14. Levy, *Tudor Historical Thought*, p. 100.

15. Patrides, *The Phoenix and the Ladder*, p. 3. French Fogle reports that once Milton was free from the Cambridge curriculum and cloistered at Horton, almost all of his reading in history was in works pertaining to postclassical, ecclesiastical, medieval, or "modern" subjects. This would seem to indicate that Milton's primary interest was in providential accounts of history. See Fogle's introduction to Milton's *History of Britain* (YP, V, xxiv).

16. Mary Ann Radzinowicz, *Toward "Samson Agonistes": The Growth of Milton's Mind* (Princeton, 1978), p. 88.

17. See the "Digression" to the *History* (YP, V, 441).

18. "Time and Eternity: Paradox and Structure in *Paradise Lost*," *Journal of the Warburg and Courtauld Institutes*, XXIII (1960), 136, 133.

19. *Images and Themes in Five Poems by Milton* (Cambridge, Mass. 1957), p. 39.

20. "Time and Eternity in *Paradise Regained*," in *The Prison and the Pinnacle*, ed. B. Rajan (Toronto, 1973), p. 74.

21. *The Resources of Kind: Genre-Theory in the Renaissance*, ed. Barbara K. Lewalski (Berkeley and Los Angeles, 1973), pp. 8–9, 20.

22. *Visionary Poetics*, p. 9.

23. For a discussion of this peculiarity of prophetic literature, see Wittreich, *Vision-*

ary Poetics, p. 31. On Milton as prophet, his politics as apocalyptic, and his poetry as visionary, see among others Wittreich, *Visionary Poetics;* Austin C. Dobbins, *Milton and the Book of Revelation: The Heavenly Cycle* (University, Ala., 1975); Michael Fixler, *Milton and the Kingdoms of God* (London, 1964), and "The Apocalypse Within Paradise Lost," in *New Essays on Paradise Lost*, ed. Thomas Kranidas (Berkeley and Los Angeles, 1971); and William Kerrigan, *The Prophetic Milton* (Charlottesville, 1974).

24. See Radzinowicz, *Toward "Samson Agonistes,"* p. 89; Wittreich, *Visionary Poetics*, p. 7; Barbara K. Lewalski, *Protestant Poetics and the Seventeenth-Century Religious Lyric* (Princeton, 1979), pp. 8–9, 13.

25. But see the argument by Stanley Fish, *Surprised by Sin: The Reader in Paradise Lost* (Berkeley and Los Angeles, 1971), that the experience of these books requires "the surrender of the reflective intellect, the opening of the mind to a flood of undifferentiated associations" (p. 327), and the claim by Michael Cavanagh, "A Meeting of Epic and History: Books XI and XII of *Paradise Lost,*" *ELH*, XXXVIII [1971], 220, that the cycles of history are controlled by God, who uses them to set off the virtues of those capable of standing aside from the cycles and to eliminate "the grosser sort" of people and send them to damnation. On the relation of God and man in history, see also Radzinowicz, " 'Man as Probationer of Immortality'," pp. 36–37, and Colie, "Time and Eternity," p. 128.

26. Louis Martz, *Poet of Exile* (New Haven, 1980), IX, X, also observes that Books XI and XII are presented in an ironic mode, though he does not treat specifically of their structure. Northrop Frye describes Books XI and XII as a "contrast epic, where one pole is the ironic human situation and the other the origin or continuation of a divine society"; see *The Anatomy of Criticism: Four Essays* (Princeton, 1957), pp. 317, 324. For a thorough treatment of the tendency of all epics to subvert their own premises, see Webber's *Milton and His Epic Tradition*.

27. Lawrence A. Sasek, "The Drama of *Paradise Lost:* Books XI–XII," in *Milton: Modern Essays in Criticism*, ed. Arthur E. Barker (New York, 1965), pp. 342–56, discusses how "the just man has little chance to sway the world by his own eloquence or virtue" (p. 351).

28. Such a view contradicts that of Fish, who sees the cycles of history as being broken at the time of the Crucifixion "by the victory over sin and death" (*Surprised by Sin*, p. 329).

29. H. R. MacCallum, "Milton and Sacred History: Books XI and XII of *Paradise Lost,*" in *Essays in English Literature from the Renaissance to the Victorian Age*, ed. Millar MacClure and F. W. Watt (Toronto, 1966), pp. 149–68, cites the Puritan Samuel Mather's *The Figures or Types of the Old Testament* (1620) in relation to these books. On the basis of this text, MacCallum discerns a two-part dialectic in the last two books of the poem. I see a fuller, three-part dialectic.

THINGS AND ACTIONS INDIFFERENT: THE TEMPTATION OF PLOT IN *PARADISE REGAINED*

Stanley Fish

I T H A S for some time been obvious to me (although perhaps not to many others) that the paradigmatic moment in Milton's poetry occurs in *Paradise Lost*, Book XII, when Adam asks Michael to specify the time and place when Christ and Satan will meet in a final battle:

> Needs must the Serpent now his capital bruise
> Expect with mortal paine: say where and when
> Thir fight, what stroke shall bruise the Victors heel. (XII, 383–85)

Michael's reply is, as his replies so often are, a rebuke:

> To whom thus *Michael*. Dream not of thir fight,
> As of a Duel, or the local wounds
> Of head or heel: not therefore joynes the Son
> Manhood to God-head, with more strength to foil
> Thy enemie; nor so is overcome
> *Satan*, whose fall from Heav'n, a deadlier bruise,
> Disabl'd not to give thee thy deaths wound:
> Which hee, who comes thy Saviour, shall recure,
> Not by destroying *Satan*, but his works
> In thee and in thy Seed.   (XII, 386–95)

These lines challenge the assumptions underlying Adam's question in several ways. First of all, when Michael says, "Dream not of thir fight, / as of a Duel, or the local wounds / Of head or heel," he means that Adam is wrong to think of it as a fight in which a single blow (much like the blow Michael had once thought to inflict on Satan and so end intestine war in heaven) will forever settle the issue between them. The whole point of the Incarnation and Crucifixion will have been lost if they are only to be preliminary to a battle that might have been fought without going to all that trouble: "not therefore joynes the Son / Manhood to God-head." Why then? The answer to the question alerts us to another and central aspect of Adam's error. Godhead has joined itself to

163

manhood in order to destroy not Satan—who has already in the essential sense destroyed himself—but "his works / In thee." The contest, insofar as there is one, is not so much *between* the mighty antagonists as it is *for* the soul of man. Nor can the prize be won simply by claiming it as the victor's spoil; for it is only when the soul inclines to one or the other of the combatants that the victory will have occurred. Thus the fight is not only for the soul; it is in the soul, and while Adam is in some sense what the fight is about, he is also an active agent in its resolution. Resolution is of course too strong a word; for whichever way Adam inclines, that will not be the end of the matter. As Michael points out, the works of Satan must be destroyed not simply in thee, but in thy seed. Just as Adam earlier learned that death is no single stroke but a long day's dying, so must he now learn that the redemption of man will be a long day's living, in the course of which there will be innumerable reenactments of the fight—not really a fight—of which Adam here dreams. The effect of line 395—"In thee and in thy Seed"—is at once to insist on the interiority of Satan's works—they manifest themselves in tendencies of human behavior—and to emphasize the time, no less than all of time, that will be required to extirpate them.

Adam, then, is wrong on three related counts: (1) to conceive of the moral life as climaxing in a single decisive encounter; (2) to see himself in relation to that encounter as an outsider; and (3) to think of that encounter as an event in the world of circumstances rather than as a process that is continually occurring in the interior world of the spirit. He is entirely mistaken as to the nature of moral action, which he tends to identify with something that is measurable by the changes it effects in the external world. True moral action is internal and always has the form specified by Michael in the very next lines:

> nor can this be,
> But by fulfiling that which thou didst want,
> Obedience to the Law of God.   (XII, 395–97)

Obedience. This is the only rule of action Michael delivers, and it is followed immediately by a perfect and exemplary illustration, the Passion. As an act, the Passion is distinguished by the immobility of the actor. It would seem from one point of view—the point of view from which Adam calls for the heroics of a duel—that Christ doesn't *do* anything, but in fact he does everything—that is, he performs the only act that merits the name; he obeys, and it is "this God-like act" that, Michael declares, "Shall bruise the head of *Satan*" (XII, 430). What is remarkable about this bruising is that it will occur without contact.

Satan's wound is inflicted at long distance and is incurred not because of something that is done to him (in the crude physical sense expected by Adam) but because of something that is shown to him, a mode of being whose very presence in the world brings about his defeat. The moment of the Passion (which is here of course only anticipated) is characteristic of the "victories" enjoyed by Milton's heroes, who never clash with their great opposites but repulse them merely by declaring and holding fast to a vision of the world in which Satanic power is an illusion. This is what the Lady in *Comus* does when she declares, "Thou canst not touch the freedom of my minde" (662), thereby denying the relevance of the (bodily) sphere over which the sorcerer has apparent power, and it is what Christ will do, again and again, in *Paradise Regained*. The declaration (whether in word or deed) is always received in the same way by the antihero, who reels as if struck by a blow, even though no blow has been landed. The pattern for this encounter (hardly an encounter at all) is set in the *Ode on the Morning of Christ's Nativity* when the fleeing of the pagan deities is attributed to the force of a recumbent babe who exerts his control without moving from his cradle and who, at the moment when his power is most felt, is in the act (if that is the word) of falling asleep (237–44).

The moral in all of these poems is the same moral Michael points to here: the true form of action is not something one does (a wound inflicted, a battle waged), but something one is. Or, to put the matter more precisely, for Milton being *is* an action, which therefore cannot be identified with any particular gesture or set of gestures but with an orientation or allegiance of which any gesture can be the expression.

By thus interiorizing the notion of action, Milton commits himself to a series of positions that finally have consequences for his poetry. First of all, if the form of action is interior, then any external form action happens to take is accidental and, in some sense, beside the point; and it follows that one cannot in advance make a list of actions that will always be either virtuous or evil. By the same reasoning, if all outward acts are equally the manifestation of some inner state, no one act can be said to be more important than any other; and, conversely, no act can be said to be inconsequential. Indeed, nothing is ever inconsequential. If, even in the smallest things, one is bearing witness to some kind of inner allegiance, then action is continual and admits of no respite; since obedience is not a matter of following directions but of having a direction, one has it not at particular times or in response to extraordinary circumstances, but at all times and in response to any and every circumstance. And since every circumstance presents the possibility of either keeping to or straying from the way, there is finally no meaningful distinction to be made between them. That is, one cannot speak meaningfully of moments when more is at stake than at other moments or of choices that are more or less difficult or significant than other choices; although life will present you with what appears to be a variety of situations, your obligation is to see through that variety and discern in each situation the challenge it offers to your continuing obedience; your obligation, in short, is to remember that, despite appearance to the contrary, the issues are always the same, as are the dangers. Those dangers can be enumerated simply by reversing the account of obligation. Any attempt to persuade you that one moment is more important than another, or that one action is absolutely crucial (in the sense that having performed it you can now relax), or that a change in scene means a change in what is at stake is an attempt to distract you from your commitment to obedience and substitute for that commitment the commitments that seem urged on you by empirical circumstances. One can only resist such an attempt by resisting the appeal located in words like *crisis, climax, change, development, denouement,* and *suspense.* It is in this list of things that are to be denied that one finds both the subject and the extraordinary difficulty of Milton's mature poetry. The subject is the tension between obedience, as a continuing obligation, and narrative; the difficulty, for both Milton and his reader, is the writing of poetry, and of narrative poetry, that in no way relies on crisis, climax, change, development, and suspense but instead makes them the vehicles of temptation.

I have called that temptation the temptation of plot, and it informs the strategy of Milton's villains, the most brilliant and diabolical of whom is the Satan of *Paradise Regained.* It is Satan's continual effort in *Paradise Regained* to persuade the Son of God that the Son himself is a character in a plot, in a narrative where every change of scene brings new opportunities and new risks. What defeats Satan finally is the Son's inability or unwillingness (they amount to the same thing) to recognize the fact that there is a plot at all, for as Satan discovers to his repeated frustration, the Son sees no difference at all between the various objects and actions that are offered to him and urged on him in the course of four books. The series of adverbs and adjectives that introduce the Son's replies—"unalter'd," "temperately," "patiently," "calmly," "Unmov'd," "unmov'd," "with disdain," "sagely," "In brief"—not only demonstrate the strength of his resolve but indicate that the affirmation of that resolve is made in exactly the same way—with equal ease—no matter what form the temptation takes. In no case is the Son unmoved or unaltered *after* a period in which alteration or movement seems possible, nor does his firmness require more of an exertion at one point than at any other. Where Satan's rhetoric continually suggests that he is ascending a scale of progressive lures, Christ's responses have the effect of leveling that scale by refusing to recognize it. It is no wonder then that Satan exclaims in exasperation, "What dost thou in this World?", for as far as he can see the possibilities of action in response to circumstances have been exhausted by the appeals he has already made:

> Since neither wealth, nor honor, arms nor arts,
> Kingdom nor Empire pleases thee, nor aught
> By me propos'd in life contemplative,
> Or active, tended on by glory, or fame,
> What dost thou in this World?   (IV, 368–72)

Or, in other words, "Since you refuse to act in the name of any one of these things, and since there are not other things in the name of which you might act, you finally are not acting at all." But in fact the Son has been acting precisely by refusing to act in the name of any of these things, for by doing so he refuses to make any one of them his God. In each of the plots Satan constructs, one or more of these things has been put forward as the highest possible value; and therefore to resist the appeal to act in its name is to resist the temptation to substitute that value for the value of obedience to God. *Paradise Regained* is sometimes characterized as a poem of rejection, but in fact the Son never rejects anything because it is evil in and of itself but because, in the circumstances as Satan has arranged them, it is presented as crucial, uniquely compelling, and, in a word, necessary.

The terms of this rejection that is not a rejection are most explicitly stated in the Son's response to the claims made by Satan for Greek philosophy:

> These rules will render thee a King compleat
> Within thy self, much more with Empire joyn'd.
>   To whom our Savior sagely thus repli'd.
> Think not but that I know these things; or think
> I know them not; not therefore am I short
> Of knowing what I aught: he who receives
> Light from above, from the fountain of light,
> No other doctrine needs, though granted true.   (IV, 283–90)

The Son goes on to say, "But these are false" (291), but their falsity is, as it were, an extratheoretical point and is not the reason for their being rejected. They would be rejected, as the Son is careful to point out,

even if they were true, because they have been offered as indispensable
to his spiritual goal ("These rules will render thee a King compleat /
Within thy self") and therefore as a substitute for "light from above."
The metaphor of the fountain is quite precise here: if one is fed by the
fountain, one has no need for the tributaries, although in circumstances
where the confusion of the two is not an issue one can drink from them
or not as expedience or charity may dictate. In short, this rejection is
not a judgment, and indeed the Son goes to remarkable lengths in order
to avoid, and even to evade, a judgment. First of all, he refuses to
identify himself either as one who knows these things or as one who is
ignorant of them (although he teases Satan and the reader with these
alternate possibilities), and as a result the "therefore" in "not therefore
am I short" follows from either of these conditions. That is, the
knowledge he *is* claiming ("knowing what I aught") depends neither on
his partaking of these things nor on his abstaining from them. He therefore will neither affirm them as necessary nor condemn them as evil or
forbidden, because to do either would be to make them the repository of
value, whereas for the Son their value at any one moment inheres in
their relationship to the obligation he has already identified as primary:
"me hungering to do my father's will" (II, 259). Offered as an alternative
to that obligation ("you absolutely must avail yourself to these rules")
they are evil because idolatrous (one is being asked to worship them);
but offered in the absence of such claims they may be embraced or not
as the occasion seems to dictate. To give them a fixed value, even a
negative one, would be to make them the touchstone of moral judgment; embracing them or disdaining them would in and of itself make
you either a good or a bad person; and for the Son, the touchstone of
moral judgment is always and unvaryingly the relationship of any alternative to his determination to serve. In short, "these things," and indeed all things, are neither good nor bad in themselves but may at
different times be one or the other depending on whether their use in
particular circumstances advances or subverts God's glory.

The previous sentence is a textbook definition of the doctrine of
"things indifferent," or *adiaphora*, a doctrine frequently invoked by
Milton and one that holds the key to the structure (if that is the word) of
Paradise Regained. Generally speaking, the doctrine of things indifferent comes in two versions, although they are not always precisely differentiated. The first, and stronger, version originates with the Stoics, who
identify virtue with the self and believe that self to be sufficient. Consequently all things external to the self are lacking in intrinsic value or
disvalue and acquire value only in relation to an inner disposition or

intention. Thus the entire external world for the Stoics is a mass of *adiaphora*, which, depending on the circumstances "could become either good or evil."[1] The second and more restricted version of the doctrine is theological and depends on a distinction between that which the Scripture explicitly commands or forbids and that concerning which it is silent. Francis Mason's definition is both typical and succinct:

Necessarie I call that which the eternall God hath in his word precisely and determinately commanded or forbidden, either expresly or by infallible consequence. Indifferent, which the Lord hath not so commanded nor forbidden, but is contained in the holy Scripture, rather potentially then actually, comprehended in generall directions, not precisely defined by particular determinations.

Mason goes on to assert that in the absence of an explicit command or prohibition a thing indifferent falls under the jurisdiction of the civil magistrates, "the Lords viceregents upon earth, who according to the exigence of the state, may by their discretion command it to be done."[2] This is the conservative or Anglican position, which is countered by the Puritan insistence that decisions concerning things indifferent should be left to the consciences of individual believers. Otherwise, they contend, the liberty that men enjoy under the New Dispensation is unlawfully infringed:

All such humaine lawes therefore, that . . . upon any penalties, binde men to those things that are confessed indifferent, which are such things as God hath left to the free libertie of man to doe or not to . . . doe: is a deprivying of men of that libertie that God hath graunted unto them, & therfore such a lawe is neither good nor indifferent.[3]

One sees immediately that the dispute over things indifferent is an aspect of the more general dispute over the authority of the ecclesiastical hierarchy in relation to the inner light of the individual. Nor is it difficult to anticipate the strategies each party pursues. The right, citing over and over again 1 Corinthians xiv, 40, "Let all things be done honestly and by order," attempts to restrict the area in which the individual has competence, and Anglican apologists point regularly to the dire consequences of allowing every man "to doe what he list." In Mason's words, "He that denieth this [i.e., Church authority over things indifferent], taketh away the Sunne out of the world, dissolveth universally the fabricke of government, overthroweth families, corporations, Churches, and kingdoms, and wrappeth all things in the dismall darknesse of Anarchie and confusion."[4] To this antinomian fear the Puritan left opposes the doctrine of Christian liberty, which in its extreme form, as embraced by Milton, so expands the scope of individual conscience as to make even the commands and interdictions of the Decalogue non-binding and things indifferent. Indeed the larger the claim made for the authority of the inner light, the larger the category of things indifferent, so that finally the left-wing definition is, like the Stoic definition, more philosophical than theological and tends toward the inclusion of every-thing:

There is nothing so good of it selfe, but it may be made Evill by accident, nothing so evill of it self but it may become good by accident. Nothing so good or Evil but it may become Indifferent by accident, nothing so Indifferent of it selfe but it may become Good or Evill by accident.[5]

By "accident," Bradshaw means "in a particular circumstance"; in his vision, therefore, good, evil, and indifferent are ever-present and ever-operative categories, but they are not attached to any stipulated list of actions or objects. What this means is that the expansion of Christian liberty is also the expansion of Christian responsibility; for if, on the one hand, no action or object is intrinsically good or evil but, on the other hand, every action is either good or evil as it "doth either glorifie or dishonor God" in a particular circumstance, then the determination of the value of an object or action must be made again and again, and one cannot look for help to the enjoinings and forbiddings of any fixed for-mula, even if that formula is the Decalogue. The result is a moral life that is fraught with anxiety and danger, for in a world where every action, however small or large, is equally the potential vehicle of good or evil, no action can be taken without risk, and, indeed, "a man may by takynge up a straw or a rush commit a Moral vice. For example if he shoulde use to doe it in the time of prayer."[6] Paradoxically, then, the strong version of the doctrine of things indifferent ends by declaring, as does Lord Brooke in A Discourse Opening the Nature of Episcopacy, that nothing is indifferent.[7] The indifference of things obtains only in their existence apart from circumstances; but since our involvement with things is always circumstantial, they are never, for us at any one time, indifferent. As Milton says in a passage of the Areopagitica, "great care and wisdom is requir'd to the right managing of this point" (YP, II, 535). Care is required because the pitfalls are so many and so intimately related. On the one hand one must be wary lest one embrace something (an object, an action, a person) as good in and of itself and therefore as necessary, for that would be to make it one's God. This is exactly what Adam does when he decides that Eve is everything to him, and he receives a precise rebuke: "Was shee thy God, that her thou didst obey /

Before his voice" (*PL* X, 145–46). On the other hand, one must be wary of declaring something (an object, an action, or a person) intrinsically evil, for that would be to shift the responsibility for evil from the intention or disposition of the agent to something external to and independent of him. This is what, in *Samson Agonistes*, Dalila does or tries to do in a number of directions as she argues in a variety of ways that the Devil made her do it. But on the third hand (that there is one is what makes the "right managing" so difficult), one must not conclude that because things (and actions and persons) are neither good nor bad in themselves, it doesn't matter very much whether one rejects them or embraces them. It always matters; it's just that the way in which it matters is not fixed once and for all in a list of intrinsically good and bad things, but must be determined, and then determined again, in the innumerable situations that make up the moral life.

Being faithful, then, to the doctrine of things indifferent (in its strong or philosophical version) requires the withstanding of three temptations: (1) the temptation of idolatry, or the temptation to label something absolutely and intrinsically good; (2) the temptation to judgment (which is at once an evasion of responsibility and an arrogation of responsibility), or the temptation to label something absolutely and intrinsically evil; and (3) the temptation to relaxation, or the temptation to think that because things are neither good nor evil in themselves they are neither good nor evil in practice. The relationship between these temptations is such that to withstand any one of them is to run the risk of courting another. In the very act of rejecting something as idolatrous, one may fall into the error of condemning it as inherently evil, and one may be so wary of the danger of either extreme that he will hazard no judgment at all and thereby abdicate his moral responsibility.

In *Paradise Regained* these are the errors that Christ is invited to make in every one of the temptations to which Satan exposes him. Thus, as we have seen, the temptation of Athens is not the temptation to accept the rules of Greek philosophy (and art and literature) but the temptation (1) to accept them as necessary, or (2) to reject them as absolutely forbidden, or (3) to say that one's relationship to them doesn't matter, for in this case, when they are being offered as necessary, it matters very much, and they must be rejected *for the time being*. The same formula (with slight variations) will do for all of the temptations. The banquet in Book II is presented to Christ as something he must eat, or alternatively as something from which he must abstain either because, (despite Satan's assertion to the contrary), the food includes "Meats by the Law unclean" (II, 328) or because the meats may have been offered first to idols. Christ's response is striking for what it does not say—for its evasiveness:

> Said'st thou not that to all things I had right?
> And who withholds my pow'r that right to use?
> Shall I receive by gift what of my own,
> When and where likes me best, I can command?
> I can at will, doubt not, as soon as thou,
> Command a Table in this Wilderness,
> And call swift flights of Angels ministrant
> Array'd in Glory on my cup to attend.   (II, 379–86)

These lines have sometimes been read as an admission (or declaration) by Christ of his divinity, but they are nothing of the sort. Indeed, they admit, or declare, nothing. Rather, everything Christ says he says in the context of Satan's assertions, which he entertains as hypotheses; that is, Christ in effect argues, "Didn't you say (although I never claimed it and am not claiming it now) that everything belonged by right to me? And if what you say is true (although I am by no means affirming it), then, by your own words, there is no need for me to accept anything from you." In the second part of Christ's reply, the evasive work performed earlier by "Said'st thou not" (381) is done by "as soon as thou" (385). The boast Christ appears to make is no boast at all because the power he seems to claim—the power to command a table in the wilderness—he claims only insofar as it is also Satan's; not "I can do this," but "I can do this as well as you can." We, however, along with the two protagonists, know that Satan's power is not his own—he himself makes the point in Book I (377)—and therefore what looks like that assumption (and presumption) of Godhead is actually a refusal to claim it. The statement Christ is making is finally as complex and intricate as the doctrine (of things indifferent) he is affirming: "I don't need you, since I can do it myself just as well as you can; but since you can't in fact do it yourself, neither can I, and the only difference between us is that I know it, and glory in that knowledge." It is a remarkable linguistic performance, in which an assertion of radical dependence (on God, light from above, and so forth) is at the same time an assertion of radical independence (of Satan and his gifts). Moreover, all of this is managed, and necessarily so, without saying anything about the offered gifts (here the food) at all. The whole point of Satan's stage setting had been to get Christ to pronounce on the food one way or the other, but Christ neither embraces the food nor rejects it; instead he positions himself in such a way as to make no judgment on it at all. The strategy is available to him because the food does not correspond to a pressing need; he feels hunger but fears no harm, since he feels it "Without this bodies wasting" (II, 256). In another situation, when the need was in fact pressing, his decision about the food—which is here to make no decision—might take another form, but here he can treat it as a thing indifferent and reject it on grounds of convenience and expediency ("as I like / The giver" [II, 321–22]).

Christ's performance here underlines a point that must be made with respect to each of the temptations: they are always more complicated than they seem at first because the terms in which they are posed are not explicitly stated. As Satan presents the issue, a temptation inheres in the embracing of a thing or action, and therefore it would seem that the proper response would be simply to reject the thing or action in question. But, as we have seen, this way of presenting the issue is as much of a trap as the proffered lure, because it makes externals rather than one's attitude towards them crucial. Christ therefore is always in the position of responding not to the overt but to the hidden terms of a temptation, and that is why his replies often seem oblique and beside the point. In fact they are reformulations of the point, in the course of which the true danger lurking in a Satanic appeal is exposed and thereby avoided. In one exchange that danger is so well hidden that only Christ and a single literary critic seem to have noticed it.[8] As Satan prepares to leave the Son at the end of the first day he makes what is apparently an almost casual request:

> Thy Father, who is holy, wise and pure,
> Suffers the Hypocrite or Atheous Priest
> To tread his Sacred Courts, and minister
> About his Altar, handling holy things,
> Praying or vowing, and vouchsaf'd his voice
> To *Balaam* Reprobate, a Prophet yet
> Inspir'd; disdain not such access to me.
>   To whom our Saviour with unalter'd brow.
> Thy coming hither, though I know thy scope,
> I bid not or forbid; do as thou find'st
> Permission from above; thou canst not more.
> He added not.   (I, 486–97)

It would seem that the Son is here being tempted to accept the example of Balaam as an argument for permitting Satan to stay, but the real temptation is to assume that the permission is his either to grant or deny. Balaam is brought in by Satan largely as a diversionary tactic designed to draw attention away from the presumption inherent in the alternative actions the situation would seem to demand. If the Son welcomes Satan he will seem to be accepting him, if only on a social level (one of the things the Son is never guity of in this poem is civility), and if the Son sends Satan away he will seem to claim a prerogative that belongs only to God. He of course does neither, and instead speaks in the precise and evasive language appropriate to the doctrine of things indifferent: "I bid not or forbid." It is not that he is indifferent to Satan's presence (he tells him more than once that he doesn't like him), but he knows that a power greater than his controls that presence: "do as thou find'st / Permission from above." In thus declaring the limits on Satan's freedom, the Son (characteristically) admits the limits on his own and steps out of the trap that has been set for him, a trap in which Satan himself is the bait. Later, in Book IV, Satan makes a quite different appeal, one that renders his presence far from indifferent, and Christ responds by saying what he declines to say here: "Get thee behind me" (IV, 193). The difference between this unequivocal rejection and the earlier refusal to reject is that in Book IV Satan offers himself as an idol—"On this condition, if thou wilt fall down, / And worship me as thy superior Lord" (IV, 166–67); as an idol Satan must be personally repudiated, whereas as a mere presence in the world he can be left to higher dispensation.

Again we see how nice the discriminations are that must be made and how easy it is to blur them or override them. When the narrative voice comments that the Son "added not" (497), he is paying tribute to the precision of Christ's performance; despite the opportunity to go too far in one direction or the other (by either embracing or judging Satan), the Son says just enough to establish his dependence, *and no more*. More would have almost certainly been self-assertion in some way or another, and Christ is in the business not of asserting the self but of giving it no scope—including linguistic scope—beyond that necessary to affirm his obedience. To obey or not to obey is the only issue ever at stake in *Paradise Regained*, although Satan is always trying to divert the Son's attention to other issues or, even more diabolically, to tempt him with a course of action that seems on its face to be the very manifestation of obedience. That is, the tempter urges the wrong thing but in a form that looks very much like the right one (a "false resemblance"), and in the first encounter that form is no less than charity.

> But if thou be the Son of God, Command
> That out of these hard stones be made thee bread;
> So shalt thou save thyself and us relieve.   (I, 342–44)

While it is easy to see what is wrong with working a miracle at the Devil's bidding, it is not so easy to see what is wrong with relieving the misery of others. The temptation to turn stones into bread is deliberately obvious and serves as a stalking horse for the real temptation, which is to do good works or, more precisely, to identify the doing of good works not as Milton identifies them in *Of Christian Doctrine*—as works informed by faith—but as works that answer to an empirically observable need. True works of faith may or may not redress social conditions, but when the redressing of social conditions is placed in the position of the highest obligation—as the action one *must* perform—then it becomes an action no less idolatrous than the action of falling down and worshipping a false God. Indeed, it *is* a false God, because it has been identified as the one indispensable thing to do and therefore as necessary to salvation. All of this is comprehended in Christ's cryptic reply: "Think'st thou such force in Bread?" (I, 347). The force that Satan attributes to bread resides only with God, who of course may, if he chooses, use bread as his vehicle. As always the Son is careful not to err in either direction by making too much or too little of a thing indifferent. "Think'st thou *such* force in bread" does not deny that there is some force in bread, and "Man lives not by Bread only" (I, 349) silently insists that bread is one of the things—although not the necessary and sufficient thing—that man lives by. Again we see how great the care is that must go into the right managing of this point: if the Son had left out the word "only" he would have committed an error as fatal as the error he is explicitly tempted to commit, the error of making bread all.

The question "Think'st thou such force in _____?" identifies the danger and the way of avoiding it in every one of the scenes Satan constructs. Thinks thou such force in riches? in kingdoms? in arms? in manners? in civility? in literature? in philosophy? Satan continually offers these things as indispensable and necessary, and Christ continually rejects them *as they are offered,* while being very careful not to condemn them altogether and thus make them, rather than an interior disposition, the source of evil. My argument is not simply that the doctrine of things indifferent is to be found everywhere in *Paradise Regained,* but that *Paradise Regained* is a working out of the doctrine, and that because it is a working out of the doctrine every moment in it is necessarily the same: everything is *always* at stake. The consequences of this sameness for what one can say about the poem are far-reaching and in large part take the form of what one cannot say. One cannot say, for example, that there is any significance to the order of temptations or to the fact that more lines are devoted to some than others. I do not mean that one could not find reasons for the differences in proportion; the Athens temptation may be more elaborate than the tempation of riches because Milton felt that his readers were more likely to be literary than material idolaters. But this would not be a reason tied to the unfolding of a plot, to the gradual emergence of crisis, to a succession of choices, some of which are more important than others because they take the central figure further and further down a particular path until his destiny (for good or ill) is irreversible. In *Paradise Regained* one cannot say that this or that moment is crucial, because every moment is crucial (every moment offers an opportunity to be either faithful or idolatrous); one cannot say that *here* is where victory or defeat occurs, because the possibility of their occurrence is ever-present and ever-renewed; one cannot say that *this* decision makes all the difference, because it is a decision that will have to be made again in the very next moment; one cannot say "from this point it is all downhill," because the poem has neither steep inclines nor easy descents but is always pitched at the same level of tension that makes reading it so strenuous. Like the Son, *you* can never relax.

The fact remains, however, that these things that one cannot say about *Paradise Regained* are what critics are always saying, although they are not always saying them in the same way. To a great extent the history of *Paradise Regained* criticism is a history of attempts to establish just those kinds of distinctions (between one episode and another, between degrees of danger and risk, between the ease and difficulty of diverse temptations) that are subversive of the poem's lesson. Whether it is the triple temptation, or the three offices of Christ, or the neoplatonic tripartite soul, or the scale of ethical goods, or the responsibilities of the Church, or the recovery by the hero of his divine knowledge, the models that have been proposed as providing the structure of the poem always have the effect of dividing it up, of foregrounding some moments at the expense of others, of identifying climaxes, resolutions, and denouements, of declaring some scenes integral and others preliminary or ceremonial—the effect, in short, of giving the poem a plot. The disagreement as to exactly what the plot is has led to differing characterizations of its shape and to a host of questions and debates. Is the gluttony temptation an extension of the bread-into-stones temptation, or does it belong to another episode? If the first temptation is the temptation of distrust, what do you say about the temptation of the tower? Is the answer to this question to be found in Milton's following of Luke's sequence rather than Matthew's? Since the storm scene is not found in any of the biblical accounts, is it a temptation at all, or simply a "dra-

matic interlude"? In fact how many temptations are there? Every number from three to nine has been given as an answer, and with each
answer one or more of the temptations is divided into two, three, four,
five, . . . parts. As Edward Tayler has recently observed, "The arith-
metical gymnastics in this arena do not inspire confidence in our
profession."[9]

There is an even severer judgment to be made: the critics who are
busy debating the kinds of schematizations and formal organizations that
should be kept in mind when reading *Paradise Regained* are, in effect,
doing the Devil's work. It is Satan's effort in the poem to persuade Jesus
to those differences and distinctions, hierarchies of values, that will
obscure the singleness of his obligation and get him to abandon what he
knows to be the most important thing (obedience to God) for the thing
(or action) that seems to be the most important in the light of some
partial (that is, empirical) perspective. It is Satan's effort, in short, to
divert the Son's attention from his chosen allegiance ("me hungering to
do the Father's will") by urging on him the allegiances (to social reform,
the arts, charitable works) that seem to be demanded by changing circumstances. That is why plot is so crucial to Satan's strategy (a strategy
in which he himself believes): plot is always saying, "The situation has
changed, and you must now rethink what it is that you have to do"; the
Son is always saying (even when he doesn't say it), "The situation cannot
have changed because there is only one situation, and what you have to
do is what you have always had to do, affirm your loyalty to God." Satan
builds plots (like mousetraps) by presenting inessential differences as if
they were constitutive, and the Son unbuilds them by seeing through
those differences to the eternal choice (between God and idols) they
really present. But what the Son unbuilds, the critics build up again,
multiplying distinctions, insisting on progressions, labelling beginnings,
middles, and ends, and in general acting as extensions of the Satanic
effort.

They are, of course, encouraged in their activities by the poem,
which after all does have four books, frequent changes of scene, varying styles, temporal signatures, announced shifts of topic, shorter and
longer speeches—everything, in short, that would support the assumption that different things are at stake at different times. While it is
true, as I have been asserting, that the poem is everywhere the same,
it is not obviously so, and it is the task of the reader to penetrate to
that sameness amidst so many signs of difference. It is a task made
more difficult by the performance of the Son, who sees the signs of
difference *immediately* for what they are (camouflage and distractions)

and therefore does not need to go through the effort of setting them aside. As a result he presents a difficult model, one who as often as not leaves out the steps that would enable someone to follow him and therefore contributes to the possibility of misunderstanding the nature of what he does.

This possibility is perhaps greatest in the tower or pinnacle scene, which has a critical literature of its own. The two points at issue are (1) whether or not this scene is a part of the temptation proper or is a "climactic epilogue" to an action already complete, and (2) whether this confrontation is decisive in a way that its predecessors were not. Those who would detach the episode from the main body of the poem take their cue partly from the narrator, who says of Satan at the conclusion of the Athens temptation, "for all his darts were spent" (IV, 366), and partly from Satan himself when he announces "Another method I must now begin" (IV, 540). To the extent that a reader takes Satan at his word (surely a questionable procedure), he will be prepared to find this scene unlike the others, but to the extent that he remains undistracted by this final stage direction (for so it is) he will be able to discern with Christ (who says at line 497, "desist, thou are discern'd") the same old trap with its attendant and familiar dangers.

That trap takes the form (as it has before) of presenting the Son with two alternative courses of actions, either of which would constitute presumption. He can "stand upright" (IV, 551) or he can cast himself down. The first would be an assertion of his divinity (an "I can command a table in the wilderness" without the saving qualification of "as soon as thou"), and the second would be to make a trial of God by commanding him to a particular performance ("See, I am putting my trust in you; now save me!"). The strategy is once again to position the Son in such a way that anything he does will be to Satan's advantage; at the very least he will finally know who his adversary is: if the Son stands upright, he is divine; if he falls, he is mere man; if he casts himself down, he will invite God to save him, and, whether God or man, he will be violating the discipline of faith and obedience. If this were all, the temptation would be subtle enough, but Satan adds another turn to its screw by offering as a *reason* for the Son's casting himself down the testimony of Scripture:

> Cast thy self down; safely if Son of God:
> For it is written, He will give command
> Concerning thee to his Angels, in thir hands
> They shall up lift thee, lest at any time
> Thou chance to dash thy foot against a stone.   (IV, 555–59)

The brilliance of this last move inheres in its apparent fidelity to Christ's own principle of action as he has often invoked it. Man does not live by bread alone but by the Word of God, he declares at the first encounter, and in every subsequent encounter the Word of God is preferred to the various words spoken by the world. As recently as line 175, the Son has turned away a temptation with the formula "It is written," and when Satan appropriates the same formula here he seems to be inviting the Son to reaffirm an allegiance he has himself repeatedly proclaimed. This is not simply the temptation to presumption (although it is surely that), but the temptation of Scripture.

That is, in addition to the choice of standing or casting himself down Satan gives Christ the choice of either embracing the Scripture (and with it Satan's urgings) or rejecting it. He of course does neither; instead he adds it to the ever-growing and finally all-inclusive list of things indifferent. Satan presents the Scripture as if its value were independent of its use, as if it were good in and of itself, but the value of the Scripture, no less than the value of riches or learning, depends on the spirit with which it is appropriated. Like anything else the Scripture can be perverted; the Devil can quote it. What Satan offers is not the Scripture pure and simple (there is no such thing) but a reading of it which makes it an extension of the presumption he urges. The Son rejects that reading (just as earlier he rejects the signs and portents of the storm: "not sent from God, but thee" [IV, 491]), and then, in order to show that it is the interpreter and not the Scripture he rejects, he attaches himself to another verse, one that names the impiety with which a thing indifferent has been polluted: "Tempt not the Lord thy God; he said and stood" (IV, 561). It is a brilliantly compressed moment that not only illustrates in the most rigorous way the doctrine of things indifferent (by extending it to include even Scripture) but also gives definitive form to the analogous doctrine of false resemblances:

> Who therefore seeks in these
> True wisdom, finds her not, or by delusion
> Far worse, her false resemblance only meets,
> An empty cloud.   (IV, 318–21)

The distinction between true and false resemblances is not a distinction between different things (one of which is superficially like the other), but between different attitudes or intentional dispositions toward the same thing, which is therefore no longer the same. Thus, in this case, the Scriptures, when they are quoted by the Devil or for diabolic purposes, are not true resemblances of themselves but are hollow forms, or, as the Son puts it, "empty clouds," just as when bread is made into an idol it does not nourish but wastes, and when poetry is detached from the praising of God, it is "As varnish on a Harlots cheek" (IV, 344). Nowhere is Milton's relentless interiorization of value more dramatically on display than it is here, when his hero looks at the Bible itself and finds it no more intrinsically valuable than the things—bread, riches, kingdom, learning—that he has earlier rejected in its name.[10]

It is by resisting the temptation to make an idol of the Scriptures that the Son can be said to stand in line 561: "Tempt not the Lord thy God; he said and stood." The correct way to read this line, and a way that will seem inevitable if one understands what the Son has done by answering Scripture with Scripture, is to read "and stood" as "and in so doing (that is, in saying that) stood firm, remained unaltered and unmoved." This reading has the advantage of deemphasizing the physical or punctual sense of "stood," which if allowed to be heard too strongly presents this as a decisive and climactic gesture: he stood up in triumph, he stood revealed as God, and so forth. But this is precisely what Satan (and some readers) want and what the Son refuses to do—that is, treat this moment as something different, as one in which *more* is at stake, in which everything is settled; as, in fact, a fight or a local duel. Instead the Son treats this moment as he has every other, not by making some definitive declaration or taking some action that would amount to the "single stroke" for which so many of Milton's heroes and villains and readers long, but by being, as he has been so many times before, creatively evasive. He does not stand up in a grand flourish of assertion, nor does he cast himself down in an impetuous hazarding of all. He does the only thing that Satan could not imagine him doing; he does nothing, or as Barbara Lewalski puts it in what remains the single best account of the moment, he calmly maintains "the impossible posture into which Satan has thrust him."[11] Just how impossible that posture is one cannot finally say; Satan is not himself sure of the matter: he only says "to stand upright / Will ask thee skill" (IV, 551–52). This comment suggests that there is a level of skill— short of miracle—that would suffice, but that Satan does not expect the Son or any other mere man to have it. That he does have it, and that it is not a skill dependent on divine intervention (whether of the Son or the Father), is evidenced by the phrase "uneasy station" (IV, 584), which suggests not a revealed God standing gloriously at front and center stage but a man who is doing the best that he can in a difficult situation to be true to the best that he knows.

The station is uneasy because it is precarious; it requires balance. It is thus a perfect visual emblem of what has been required of the Son all along, a keeping to a path so straight and narrow that the deviation of a single step to the right or left would prove disastrous. What the Son does not do here—swerve in one direction or another—is the physical equivalent of what he does not say in Book I: "he added not." In both cases the discipline of obedience is perfect, but it is a discipline, and one that must be exercised continually, rather than during a single and final moment after which all trial and struggle cease.

There is no final moment in *Paradise Regained*. In this last scene, which ends nothing, the Son does no more or less than he does before and will have to do again: he refuses to locate value in a thing indifferent, even though that thing is the Scripture, and he refuses to reduce the moral life to a single climactic action in which everything is settled once and for all. Indeed these two temptations— the temptation to either embrace or reject and the temptation to dream of a fight or a duel—are finally one and the same, for they are both invitations to externalize the moral life, either by making good and evil the property of things or by making the struggle between good and evil an event in the world of circumstances rather than a succession of events in the inner world of spiritual choice; and, by the same reasoning, they are both temptations that find their perfect expression in the dynamics of plot, which, by substituting the curve and arc of greater and lesser moments for the straight line of a moment endlessly repeated, relieves us of the obligation to be per-petually alert.

It is of course always Milton's way to present his readers with the most compelling form of the temptation he would have them resist. And in *Paradise Regained* we are certainly invited to assume that *this* is the local duel of which Adam is to dream not. For this assumption we have no less an authority than the angels of heaven, who sing "Victory and Triumph to the Son of God / Now entring his great duel" (I, 173–74). But then the qualification follows immediately: "his great duel, not of arms, / But to vanquish by wisdom hellish wiles" (I, 174–75). And when the "vanquishing" finally does occur it is like every other noncontest in Milton's poetry and prose. First of all, there is no contact; Satan falls not because he has been hit but because he has *not* been hit, because he has failed once again to draw from Christ that frontal assault, that deliberate single stroke, that would at least tell Satan where he is and with whom he is dealing ("For Son of God to me is yet in doubt" [IV, 501]). What amazes Satan is not a new revelation but the ability of his antagonist (whoever he is) to evade the demand for a revelation without resorting to easy quietism (to do something at the same time that he declines to do anything). What amazes him is the Son's perfect balance despite an "uneasy station" and, totally unbalanced himself (as he always has been), he falls.

But then he doesn't; or doesn't fall in any sense that allows us to say, "Well, that's over" or even to point to *that* fall as opposed to any other. Rather he falls and rises again and again, and for seventy-five lines. First he falls in a comparison with Anteus, who in his own career mirrors the Satanic ability to rise again ("and oft foil'd still rose, / Receiving from his mother Earth new strength, / Fresh from his fall" [IV, 565–69]); then he falls in a comparison with the Sphinx (the answer to whose riddle is like the answer to Satan's question: man [IV, 572–76]), but he falls not to the ground but into a seminar: "And to his crew, that sat consulting, brought / Joyless triumphals of his hop't success" (IV, 577–78). But this has happened before, and although we aren't told so, the diabolic consulting will no doubt produce new resolves and new plans; meanwhile Satan is not better or worse off than when Belial asked in Book II of *Paradise Lost*, "is this then worst, / Thus sitting, thus consulting?" (II, 163–64). The refrain "So Satan fell" (580) already sounds much less climactic than the first report of his "fall" (562). There are, however, other and severer falls in store for Satan, and they are rehearsed by the angelic choir beginning at line 596. They recall Satan's first fall ("and down from Heav'n cast / With all his Army" [IV, 605–06]) and speak of this new fall as if it were an act of completion ("now thou hast . . . / . . . regain'd lost Paradise" [IV, 606–08]). But then they look forward to another fall that sounds just like the first ("thou shalt fall from Heav'n trod down" [IV, 620]), and this present fall is demoted to a preliminary status: "thou feel'st / Thy wound, yet not thy last and deadliest wound / By this repulse receiv'd, and hold'st in Hell / No triumph" (IV, 621–24). But he still holds something in Hell, and he will no doubt venture forth again, if only so that again the Son "Shall chase thee with the terror of his voice / From thy Demoniac holds" (IV, 627–28). When at line 634 the Son receives the epithet "Queller of Satan," one can only read it as referring not to an action already performed and done with but to an action that will have to be performed again and again. "Queller of Satan" is not a title you have by right after only one encounter but a title that must be earned repeatedly.

The effect of what Joan Webber has called "these remarkable lines" is to diminish the dramatic impact of any one of these falls by removing them from the story line of a plot into a timeless realm where they are eternally occurring. It is, as Webber goes on to say, a story "which is without beginning or end, and yet begins and ends at every point." I can do no better than reproduce her summary statement:

Both space and time are of infinite importance and of no importance at all. The Son is everywhere. He has warred, and has yet to war down Satan. Paradise is regained and Satan's power ended as if it had never been; Satan still rules and is yet to be cast out. His snares are broken, but Jesus has not yet begun to save mankind. The Son is everyone and the battle is within.[12]

This is of course the lesson of Michael's rebuke—"Not by destroying Satan, but his works / In thee and in thy Seed"—but it is a lesson that one can never learn too often. In the closing lines of the poem Milton gives us an opportunity to learn it again as he instructs us for the last time as to how not to read his poem. The moment is, as it should be, at once small and large; its pressure barely perceptible yet as great as anything we feel in the course of four books. It is, quite characteristically, a moment *between* lines:

> now thou hast aveng'd
> Supplanted *Adam,* and by vanquishing
> Temptation, hast regain'd lost Paradise.   (IV, 606–08)

There are several surprises here. First there is the slight surprise of hearing that it is Adam and not the Father who is avenged, a surprise that reminds us that this was done for our sake, and not as a matter of family honor. And then there is the complicated ambiguity of "supplanted," which means both "overthrown" or "pushed off balance," as Adam certainly was by Satan, and "superseded" or "ousted," as Adam is now by Christ, who, as George Herbert never tires of reminding us, in saving us disables us to perform in any way that he has not already made possible. But the biggest (although in presentation very small) surprise is the one that awaits us in line 608 when we discover that the object of "vanquishing" is not Satan, as the military language and the scene just past would seem to dictate, but temptation. "Temptation" is not only the word we get; it correctly names our desire for the word we didn't get. That is, it is a temptation to expect something other than (the word) *temptation,* to expect an *external* object of "vanquishing," and insofar as we succumb to it we prove again on our pulse the power and appeal of that dream to which Adam falls when he asks, "say where and when / Thir fight."[13]

Johns Hopkins University

NOTES

1. Bernard J. Verkamp, *The Indifferent Mean* (Detroit, 1978), p. 21.

2. *The Authoritie of the Church in making Canons and Constitutions concerning things Indifferent* (London, 1607), p. 4. *S*'s and *u*'s have been modernized.

3. William Bradshaw, *A Treatise of the Nature and Use of Things Indifferent* (London, 1605), pp. 25–26. *S*'s and *u*'s have been modernized.

4. *Authoritie of the Church*, pp. 9, 13–14.

5. Bradshaw, *Treatise*, pp. 16–17.

6. Ibid., p. 20.

7. See Lord Brooke, *A Discourse Opening the Nature of Episcopacy* (London, 1642), p. 26.

8. See Burton Jasper Webber, *Wedges and Wings: The Patterning of "Paradise Regained"* (Carbondale, Ill., 1975), pp. 19–20.

9. *Milton's Poetry: Its Development in Time* (Pittsburgh, 1979), p. 254.

10. See *CD*, I, xxx, where Milton makes a distinction between Scripture which is simply external, i.e., the written word, and the internal Scripture which is written on our hearts by the spirit:

Under the gospel we possess, as it were, a two-fold Scripture; one external, which is the written word, and the other internal, which is the Holy Spirit, written in the hearts of believers, according to the promise of God, and with the intent that it should by no means be neglected; as was shown above, chap. xxvii. on the gospel. Hence, although the external ground which we possess for our belief at the present day in the written word is highly important, and, in most instances at least, prior in point of reception, that which is internal, and the peculiar possession of each believer, is far superior to all, namely, the Spirit itself. (*The Student's Milton*, ed. Frank Allen Patterson [New York, 1930], p. 1041)

11. *Milton's Brief Epic: The Genre, Meaning, and Art of "Paradise Regained"* (Providence, 1966), p. 316.

12. See *Milton and His Epic Tradition* (Seattle, 1979), pp. 206–08.

13. Any student of Milton criticism will know that the present interpretation builds on the work of far more predecessors than have been cited in these notes. Northrop Frye neatly articulated the doctrine of things indifferent (although he did not use that phrase) when he explained that "the moral status of the instrumental depends on the mental attitude toward; if the initial attitude is one of dependence, the instrument will become an illusory end in itself" ("The Typology of *Paradise Regained*," in *Milton: Modern Essays in Criticism*, ed. A. E. Barker [New York, 1965], p. 435). And at about the same time, A. S. P. Woodhouse *did* name the doctrine (which of course had already been extensively discussed by Barker in his brilliant and still authoritative study *Milton and the Puritan Dilemma* [Toronto, 1942]) and specify its relationship to Satan's temptations: "One must remember of course that all Satan's gifts and suggestions are offered with evil intent, to betray Christ, in one way or other, into disobedience to God. Even though what was offered were in itself a thing indifferent, like the apple in Eden, it would become evil in the circumstances as it came into competition with obedience to God" ("Theme and Pattern in *Paradise Regained*," *University of Toronto Quarterly*, XXV [1955–56], 178). Many have characterized *Paradise Regained* as static rather than as dramatic, sometimes in complaint, sometimes in praise. For the latter, see especially Jackson I. Cope, "*Paradise Regained:* Inner Ritual" (*Milton Studies*, I, ed. James D. Simmonds [Pittsburgh, 1969], pp. 51–65), and Tayler, *Milton's Poetry*, passim. Ralph Condee has commented well on

the extent to which Milton in this poem "rejects the normal devices of suspense in a plot," allowing a moment of suspense occasionally only in order to "dismiss it" (*Structure in Milton's Poetry* [University Park, 1974], pp. 167, 168). This rejection of course also entails the rejection of those psychological readings in which the point of the poem is the hero's development or growing self-awareness. Here I stand with Irene Samuel when she writes that "to read [*Paradise Regained*] as a 'Who Am I?' poem is to limit it to a mimesis of the particular, a matter for the historian-chronicler-biographer-theologian; to read it as a 'How am I to live?' poem is to see its availability as the mimesis of a universal action, a program for every man" ("The Regaining of Paradise," in *The Prison and the Pinnacle* [Toronto, 1973], p. 126). It seems to me (as it does to Samuel) equally limiting to read the poem as an attempt by Satan to discover the identity of his adversary, at least if one assumes in such a reading that discovery is possible. Given Milton's radical identification of perception with moral status, it would be impossible for Satan to know who the Son is unless he himself were "a composition and patterne" of the same "best and honourablest things" (YP, I, 890). Sameness, in short, is a condition of recognition, so that for Satan to recognize the Son, he would first have to be like him, and then he would no longer be Satan. Finally, for a reading that appeared after this one was already in press, but which is supporting and confirming, see Alan Fisher, "Why is *Paradise Regained* So Cold?" (*Milton Studies*, XIV, ed. James D. Simmonds [Pittsburgh, 1980], pp. 195–217). Fisher's essay is preceded in that same volume by two pieces—Mary Wilson Carpenter, "Milton's Secret Garden," and William B. Hunter, Jr., "The Double Set of Temptations in *Paradise Regained*"—which demonstrate that the impulse to understand the poem by distinguishing and arranging its episodes into some structure or plot is still very much alive.

PARADISE REGAINED:
A LAST CHANCE AT TRUE ROMANCE

Annabel M. Patterson

I

WHEN BEN JONSON's library was burned out in 1623 he wittily recalled the burning of another famous library and complained of injustice to the god of fire. Being neither an obsessive reader of romances like Don Quixote, nor a writer of them, he had not deserved such punishment. The conflagration would have been intelligible, Jonson complained

> Had [he] compil'd from *Amadis de Gaule*,
> Th' *Esplandians*, *Arthurs*, *Palmerins*, and all
> The learned Librarie of *Don Quixote*.
>
> . . . .
> The whole summe
> Of errant Knight-hood, with their Dames, and Dwarfes,
> Their charmed Boates, and their inchanted Wharfes;
> The *Tristrams*, *Lanc'lots*, *Turpins*, and the *Peers*,
> All the madde *Rolands*, and sweet *Oliveers*;
> To *Merlins* Marvailes, and his *Caballs* losse.
>
> . . . .
> Their Seales, their Characters, Hermetique rings,
> Their Jemme of Riches, and bright Stone, that brings
> Invisibilitie, and strength, and tongues:[1]

This poem gives direct entrance into romance tradition as perceived by a writer not very distant in time, training, or temperament from Milton. Like Jonson, Milton was profoundly ambivalent about that problematical mixture of texts and concepts covered by the term *romance*. He too had read *Don Quixote* and would have certainly understood why the priest and the housekeeper, the Church and commonsense, had disposed of the old knight's library. He too knew that mad Rolands and sweet Olivers had always been inseparable companions and that the gifts of the Spirit must compete with powers ("Invisibilitie, and strength, and tongues") that a writer might find still more marvellous.

The subject of this essay is the story of Milton's attitudes to romance tradition and their culmination in *Paradise Regained*. Recent criticism has given us at least two versions of that story: in one, Milton is seen as moving from a youthful enthusiasm for romance to outright rejection; in the other, as saving the genre from rejection by reforming it to Christian specifications, a project continuous from *Comus* through *Paradise Lost* and *Paradise Regained*. On both sides, also, very different causes or motives have been proposed. Milton became an antiromantic because he was unable to reconcile his ideal of *castitas* with the often salacious content of romance,[2] or because Arthurian legend became discredited during the civil wars, when good Parliamentarians relied on Saxon history.[3] Alternatively, he remained a romantic, a believer in ideal and moral fictions, under the influence of Spenser and Sidney or Italian seicento criticism.[4] All of these proposals have persuasive force when read independently, but to bring them together into a coherent theory of motivation requires effort. Formalist and contextualist explanations, politics and aesthetics, need to be made compatible. We need to look more closely at the sequence, chronology, and lexical detail of Milton's recorded responses to romance tradition, and we particularly need to distinguish, as in Milton criticism is seldom done, between different branches of the genre. If Milton recognized a range of romance possibilities and assigned them different values, the question of what he rejected, what he retained, and when becomes more complicated.

When Ben Jonson described the contents of Don Quixote's library as "the whole summe / Of errant Knight-hood," he was overtly declining distinctions made by Cervantes himself. For Cervantes, or rather for his self-appointed censors, the priest and the housekeeper, the most dangerous type of romance was that descended from *Amadis de Gaule*, chivalric tales with a high fantasy content. Although style played some part in the priest's judgments, the principal criterion by which the romances were sorted was that of verisimilitude. The original *Amadis* (1508) was saved, possibly because of its antichivalric humor,[5] but its fantastic or "mendacious" (*mentiroso*) offspring, *Amadis of Greece, Esplandian, Palmerin de Oliva*, were burned. When he came to *The Mirror of Chivalries (Espejo de principes y cavalleros)* the priest, however, hesitated:

Therein are Lord Reynald of Montalban with his friends and companions, worse thieves than Cacus; and the Twelve Peers, and that faithful historian Turpin. But I am for condemning them to nothing worse than perpetual banishment, if only because they had a share in inspiring the famous Mateo Boiardo, from whom the Christian poet Ludovico Ariosto also spun his web. . . . In short, I say that this book and every one we find that deals with these affairs of France, shall be thrown out and deposited in a dry well till we see, after further deliberation, what is to be done with them.[6]

Implied in this passage is a theory of romance to which Milton would surely have had equal access. It refers to the medieval recognition of three types of romance: (1) the *romans d'antiquité—de Thèbes, d'Enéas,* and *de Troie;* (2) the Matter of Britain, Arthurian legends made significant in Geoffrey of Monmouth's *Historia regum Britanniae;* and (3) the Matter of France, Carolingian or crusader stories as exemplified by the *Chanson de Roland* (1100). By medieval convention, the Matter of France took precedence over the others in point of veracity or historicity,[7] and its authenticity was supposed to derive from an eye-witness source, Archbishop Turpin of Rheims.[8] This distinction survived into the sixteenth century. In his essay *I Romanzi* (1554), Pigna contrasted Arthurian with Carolingian knights on the grounds that the latter were "del palagio reale, I era titolo come e diquei che sono della camera del Re Christianissimo. I su nel vero Carlo Magno facitore de Paladini"; that is, they derived their name "from a real, not an enchanted palace, the dwelling of the most Christian king, the true Charlemagne, maker of Paladins."[9] In the same year Giraldi Cinthio repeated the false etymology of "romance" as deriving from "Remense," Turpin of Rheims.[10] At the beginning of the seventeenth century Cervantes still indicated a vestigial respect for the Matter of France, even if his reference to "that faithful historian Turpin" was loaded with irony.

In the great age of chivalric romance in Europe, however, the old distinctions became submerged. In the late twelfth century Chretien de Troyes transformed parts of the Matter of Britain into elegant French fictions. Chretien's *Lancelot* and *Perceval* initiated the two most important developments in Arthurian story—the tragic tale of sexual complexity and betrayal leading to the collapse of the Round Table fellowship, and the spiritualized version of chivalric quest focused on the Grail. Linked in the thirteenth-century vulgate cycle of romances but contrasted absolutely in their moral direction, these two great centers of British legend were repatriated in the late fifteenth century by Malory. Meanwhile the Matter of France was evolving in similar directions. From the twelfth-century *Historia Karoli Magni et Rotholandi*, where a love element was first introduced, Roland was gradually transformed into an amorous hero, culminating in Boiardo's *Orlando Innamorato* (1483), while Renard of Montalban, one of the four sons of Aymon who rebelled against Charlemagne, acquired wonderful adventures of his own, a sorcerer friend to rival Merlin, and a marvellous magic horse.[11] By the late fifteenth century, then, the Matters of Britain and France had become indistinguishable in ethical or epistemological terms and both were competing in the realm of the fantastic or the Marvellous. If one sees the Spanish Amadis cycle as another rival development, Jonson's merging of them all into a conglomerate "errant Knight-hood," with the emphasis on magic, is no less reasonable an evaluation than that of Cervantes, from whom he chose to differ slightly.

Perhaps the most important difference between them, however, is in their opinions, expressed or implied, of Ariosto. For Cervantes, he was "the Christian poet" who had redeemed the Matter of France; for Jonson, the author of Roland's amorous madness. In the contrast between these two attitudes to Ariosto lies the problematical heart of romance theory, as Milton would have perceived it. Was the *Orlando Furioso,* published in 1516, merely the most extravagant and hence successful example of its kind; or did it, on the contrary, subject romance to examination and reform from a moral and Christian perspective? On the one hand, Ariosto picked up the stories of Roland and Renard (Orlando and Rinaldo) where others had left them, producing a web of fictions more sophisticated than anything the genre had seen before, especially in its mixture of eroticism with irony; on the other hand, what appears to be merely a continuation of Boiardo's poem becomes, on inspection, a critique of its own origins. Opening among the intricacies of the forest of the Ardennes, where pagan and Christian knights compete for magical objects and for Angelica, the poem moves in its second half into a simpler, more brutal world in which both lives and stories can come to an end.[12] Orlando *innamorato* is first recognized as *furioso*—literally mad with love—and then cured. When Astolfo returns from the Earthly Paradise with Orlando's wits in a bottle, Ariosto offers us a simile that extends the significance of the recovery:

> Come chi da noioso e grave sonno
> Ove o vedere abominevol forme
> Di mostri che non son, né ch'esser ponno,
> Ogli par cosa far strana et enorme,
> Ancor si maraviglia poi che donno
> È fatto de' suoi sensi, e che non dorme;
> Così, poiche fu Orlando d'error tratto
> Restò maraviglioso e stupefatto.   (XXXIX, 58)

[As one who, in a deep and unpleasant sleep, has been seeing horrible forms of monsters who do not and cannot exist, or has dreamt of committing some enormity, lingers in amazement, when he is once more in control of his senses, and sleeps no more: so Orlando, recoverd from his error, remained amazed and stupefied.][13]

Awaking from the nightmare of error—knight-errantry in its darkest state of punning—Orlando discovers the wonders of rationality; it is surely no coincidence that Ariosto builds into this passage a lexical rejection of the Marvellous (*maravigliose*), even as his poem gradually rejects or collapses the enchantments of romance tradition.[14]

Ariosto's contemporaries seem to have divided into at least two schools of criticism. Some, taking the lead from the *Furioso*'s patches of overt allegory, wrote elaborate moral interpretations of the poem. Among these, of course, was Sir John Harington, whose translation and commentary (1591) Milton owned and extensively annotated. Others perceived the poem as a challenge to Neo-Aristotelian notions of form and seriousness, and applauded it or censured it accordingly. While often this argument took the form of regretting that the *Furioso* was not a classical epic, it also generated the first real theory of romance as a separate genre. The essays of Pigna and Giraldi Cinthio were among the products of this controversy.[15] More significantly, at least for Milton, Torquato Tasso was spurred into action. As poet, he produced the *Gerusalemme Liberata;* as critic, he developed a compromise genre theory in which, on every issue thought to distinguish romance from epic, he came down squarely in the middle. If unity of narrative structure, a single action with beginning, middle, and end, were opposed to the romance web of interlaced narrative strands and multiple heroes, Tasso argued for variety *within* unity, and portrayed several heroes converging in a single cause. If epic historicity or Aristotelian verisimilitude were contrasted with the blatant fictionality of romance, Tasso argued for history—preferably Christian history—at beginning and end but allowed his kind of heroic poem a fabulous soft center. And on the issue of the Marvellous, "those wonders that move not only the unlearned but the judicious as well . . . , enchanted rings, flying steeds, ships turned into nymphs . . . and other inventions that please even in prose,"[16] Tasso was too prudent either to condone them or to do without them. A Christian poet, he argued, might still introduce such attractions into his poem, provided he invoked the principle of divine permission:

The poet ought to attribute actions that far exceed human power to God, to his angels or to those granted power by God or by demons, for example, saints, wizards, and fairies. Such actions, if considered in themselves, will seem marvelous; nay, they are commonly called miracles. But if regarded in terms of their agents' efficacy and power, they will seem verisimilar. (Pp. 37–38)

Tasso's theory, in other words, made explicit his program to reform romance from within, whereas Ariosto's similar intention was merely implicit in the structure of his poem. In fact, the *Gerusalemme Liberata* disposed the history of the First Crusade around a highly romantic core, including an earthly paradise, a seductive witch, an enchanted forest with talking trees, and sexually fallen but ultimately regenerate heroes on whose recovery that of the Holy City depends.

These, then, were the main lines of romance tradition as inherited by Cervantes, Jonson, and Milton. It was almost entirely chivalric, but we should not forget as a context for Milton's genre theory the existence of a pastoral romance tradition, sometimes closely affiliated with the chivalric, as in Sir Philip Sidney's *Arcadia*,[17] and sometimes distinguished from it. In *Don Quixote*, the priest was originally for sparing all the pastoral romances "because they do not and will not do the mischief those books of chivalry have done"; and when Don Quixote's niece protests that they may do another kind of mischief by persuading her uncle to play shepherd or "even worse, turn poet," he still insists on sparing Montemayor's *Diana* and Gil Polo's continuation (p. 61). Almost every text that I have mentioned will reappear in the story of Milton's attitude to the romances, and while Malory, Ariosto, and Tasso (and, of course, Spenser, who tried to combine all three) were unquestionably crucial to Milton's genre theory throughout, Montemayor's *Diana* and Sidney's *Arcadia* had the distinction, perhaps, of being featured in his most violent *volte-face*.

II

It is customary to document Milton's early allegiance to the romances from two texts. In *Il Penseroso* (1631?), the permissible entertainment for the thoughtful man includes whatever "great Bards"

> In sage and solemn tunes have sung,
> Of Turneys and of Trophies hung;
> Of Forests, and inchantments drear,
> Where more is meant then meets the ear.   (116–20)

Preceded by an allusion to Chaucer's *Squire's Tale*, the account of chivalric romance is otherwise remarkably nonspecific. What is specified is the moral control that Il Penseroso requires in his reading matter. The marvels of the *Squire's Tale* are perfectly balanced, "the *wondrous* Hors of Brass" against "the *vertuous* Ring and Glass" (113–14); the chivalric poems are "sage and solemn" by virtue, presumably, of their allegorical strategies, "where more is meant then meets the ear." This conventional defense, which could cover Ariosto, Tasso, and Spenser, is recognizably part of an anti-Puritan poetics. Sir John Harington prefaced his translation of the *Furioso* with a very Sidneian "Apologie of Poetrie," encouraging his readers to look in the *Furioso* for "divers and sundry meanings . . . sences or mysteries" and citing Plutarch's definition of allegory: "when one thing is told, and by that another is understood" (¶iuj).

It is interesting that this defense does not appear in the other, more often quoted statement, in the *Apology for Smectymnuus*, of Milton's early devotion to the romances. This passage, too, describes a "solemne" man's program of reading; it is perhaps not always remembered that the program is an ideal hierarchy of texts rather than an account of actual reading experience. It is, moreover, a retrospective account, written in 1642 in the heat of controversy, with the avowed purpose of defending Milton's own character and hence undoubtedly to be suspected of revisionism. At any rate, Milton claims to have proceeded, in his youth, from the lyric poems of Dante and Petrarch to

those lofty Fables and Romances, which recount in solemne cantos the deeds of Knighthood founded by our victorious Kings; & from hence had in renowne all over Christendome. (YP, I, 813)

The defense of the romances is here, first, in terms of a national, Christian ideal integral to the story, rather than hidden meaning; and second, in terms of a personal ideal of behavior expressed, but not necessarily exemplified, in the romances. Milton describes how he learned; probably from Malory, "what a noble virtue chastity sure must be, to the defense of which so many worthies, by such a dear adventure of themselves, had sworn." But when he "found in the story afterward any of them, by word or deed, breaking that oath," his response was that of Sidney in the *Apology for Poetry;* it was an abuse of the genre, the "fault of the poet," rather than anything unmanageable in the chivalric ideal itself.

Although the differences between the statement in *Il Penseroso* and that in the *Apology for Smectymnuus* may seem smaller than their aesthetic affinities, in that both of them imply a Sidneian rationale for imaginative literature, between them lie a series of events, simultaneously literary and political, that explain the apologetic context and tone of 1642. It is important to realize that not only Arthurian legend but romance generally, both chivalric and pastoral, had become during the 1630s increasingly associated with Charles I and Henrietta Maria. Charles's personal iconography brought a new political significance to the figure of St. George, already identified in Spenser's *Faerie Queene* as the leading figure in a specifically English chivalric romance. In 1628, Rubens painted a "St. George and the Dragon," featuring Charles as the warrior-saint and Henrietta Maria as the rescued maiden. Peter Heylyn's *Historie of St. George of Cappadoccia* (1631, "corrected and enlarged" in 1633) was commissioned by Charles, and its frontispiece carried portraits of him and Edward III, relating both to St. George and the Order of the Garter. In 1642 this ideology was repeated, with awkward tact, by Sir John Denham, in the context of Charles's failed campaign against the Scots, when the fusion of martyr and soldier in the king's personality had become all too apparent. In his "Heroicke face," wrote Denham in *Cooper's Hill*, "I see the Saint [George] / Better exprest then in the liveliest paint."[18] In Henrietta Maria's personal circle, however, the pastoral romance was dominant. Sidney's *Arcadia* was republished in 1627, 1628, 1629, 1633, and 1638 and dramatized by James Shirley in 1632 and by Henry Glapthorne in 1634. Fletcher's *Faithful Shepherdess*, which had been a failure in James's London in 1609, was published in new quartos in 1629 and 1634 and performed "with applause" before the king and queen in 1633. At Christmas, 1625, John Donne wrote to his friend Sir Henry Goodyere:

They continue at Court, in the resolution of the Queen[s] pastorall; . . . perchance you may doubt whether you be a thorough Courtier, if you come not up to see this, The Queen a Sheperdesse.[19]

In 1633, also, the queen performed in Walter Montague's interminable *Shepherd's Paradise*, and William Prynne's *Histriomastix* was published, initiating the most violent and far-reaching literary-political dispute of the century. Despite his disclaimers at his trial, it was clear that Prynne had extended his attack on stage plays to cover every important form of Caroline culture—masques, pastorals, romances ("Arcadias" were specifically mentioned); and he even attacked the reading and writing of any form of fiction. In Prynne's antipoetics the central, informing principle was that there could never be a truly moral fiction, that it was impossible to reform imaginative literature from within.[20]

Milton's first response to *Histriomastix* was, predictably, to assert a moderate aesthetics. In *Comus* (1634), he produced, in a form particularly associated with the court, a heavily moralized fiction; it was surely no coincidence that the masque also constituted a defense of the Bridgewater family, whose reputation had been tarnished by the Castlehaven scandal,[21] that symptom of aristocratic decadence to which Prynne himself had referred.[22] But by 1639–1640, when the disastrous effects of the Caroline romance were beginning to be obvious, Milton was clearly rethinking the nature of romance as a genre, and not from a reader's but a writer's point of view. In his 1639 Latin verse epistle to Mansus, Tasso's friend, Milton wrote of his own literary ambitions:

> If ever I shall summon back our native kings into our songs, and Arthur, waging his wars beneath the earth, or if ever I shall proclaim the magnanimous heroes of the Table which their mutual fidelity made invincible, and (if only the Spirit be with me) shall shatter the Saxon phalanxes under the British Mars.

And a year later, he concluded the *Epitaphium Damonis* with a promise to move beyond pastoral to a more demanding narrative mode. The subject is to be British legend from its origins, but its focus will be Malory's *Morte D'Arthur:* "Then I shall tell of Igraine pregnant with Arthur by fatal deception, the counterfeiting of Gorlois' features and arms by Merlin's treachery."[23]

Based on these two statements, the belief that Milton intended to write an *Arthuriad* has grown into a commonplace, and it certainly seems possible that he hoped to produce a poem in a compromise genre, as authorized by Tasso, and one that would reclaim ("Summon back"). the Matter of Britain from the European romancers who had destroyed its credibility. What has not been emphasized, however, are the signs of anxiety inhering in the project. In *Manso,* the proposal is mooted hypothetically and conditionally: "If ever . . . , if ever . . . , if only the spirit be with me"; in *Damon's Epitaph,* the problem of credibility or truthfulness seems to have seeped into the Arthurian story in its origins ("fatali fraude . . . mendaces"). The possibility that Milton had real doubts is increased by another, little-known statement from the same period. Among Milton's sketches for literary projects jotted into the Trinity manuscript in 1639–1640, "Cupids funeral pile: Sodom Burning" would seem, by its title and content, to bear on this problem.

In this sketch for a play, the moral dynamic is between Lot and his shepherds, on one side, and the aristocracy and priests of Sodom, on the other. The latter are suspiciously Cavalier in behavior, "the Gallantry of the town pass[ing] by in Procession with musick and song to the temple of Venus Urania . . . everyone with his mistresse, or Ganymed, glittering along the streets" (CM, XVIII, 233–34). Visitors from Salem—in fact the angels who come to warn Lot of Sodom's imminent destruction—provoke a debate about the "strict raigne of Melchizideck" in their own terrain. Lot is provoked into speaking "thwartly" against the Sodomites, who "taxe him of praesumption, singularity, breach of city custome, in fine, offer violence":

In the last scene, to the king & nobles, when the firie thunders begin aloft, the Angel appears all girt with flames, which he saith are the flames of true love, & tells the K., who falls down with terror, his just suffering. . . . Then calling to the thunders, lightning & fires, he bids them . . . to come & destroy a godlesse nation. (CM, XVIII, 234)

For this account, Milton selectively combined Genesis, Chapters xiv and xix, but the emphasis on the "strict raigne of Melchizideck," on Lot's role as an unpopular spokesman for moral probity, and the "dispute[ing] of love & how it differs from lust" are all, of course, Milton's own. It seems clear that while the very conception of the play is within the scope of a moderate aesthetic, its emphases are decidedly Puritan, and its implied topicality, its critique of a "godlesse" culture that has abused romance as a mode of behavior, must surely have some connection with Milton's hesitancies about the genre.

Generic hesitancy is perhaps dominant in *The Reason of Church-Government* (1642), despite its apparent boastfulness. Having determined to "be an interpreter & relater of the best and sagest things . . . in the mother dialect," Milton is still in search of the most appropriate genre and subject matter. Ariosto features as a model for cultural nationalism[24] and Tasso for heroic poetry, but with the emphasis on neoclassical tradition and historicity. "Tasso gave to a Prince of Italy his chois" of heroic subject, "Godfreys expedition against the infidels, or Belisarius against the Gothes, or Charlemain against the Lombards." So Milton would have to decide, significantly, for himself, "what K. or Knight before the conquest might be chosen in whom to lay the pattern of a Christian Heroe" (YP, I, 811, 813–14). Once again, caution and conditions are lexically everywhere. A British subject "might" be chosen; if art or instinct "may be trusted" it "haply would be no rashnesse." It is odd, also, that neither Malory nor Spenser is included among the possible models.

If there is a decreased emphasis on romance in Milton's literary plans by 1642, there is an increased emphasis on it, at least at the metaphorical level, in his political program. In both *The Reason of Church-Government* and the preceding *Of Reformation* he used chivalric metaphor honorifically, to dignify the early stages of the revolution. He praised the refusal of Parliament to fight the Scots over the prayer book, to "ingage the unattainted Honour of English Knighthood, to unfurle the streaming Red Crosse . . . for so unworthy a purpose" (YP, I, 597), and he urged them instead to take on the dragon of episcopacy: "And if our Princes and Knights will imitate the fame of that old champion [St. George], as by their order of Knighthood solemnly taken, they vow, farre be it that they should uphold and side with this English Dragon; but rather to doe as indeed their oath binds them, they should make it their Knightly adventure to pursue & vanquish this mighty sailewing'd monster" (YP, I, 857). Conditionally, Milton still reserved a place for Charles in the chivalry of reformation, but his use of the St. George legend contrasts dramatically with Denham's in *Cooper's Hill*, also published in 1642 and referring to the same events. Instead of the Arthurian legends that had featured in his early plans for a national epic, Milton was now attempting to reclaim for his nation its patron saint, as a safer repository of the chivalric ideal than the knights of the Round Table, and one that the king had no right to monopolize.

The belief that the chivalric or crusading ideal could be reconstituted politically was a heady one. It carried Milton through the antiprelatical pamphlets, into the divorce tracts, and there it gave him a rude surprise. Discovering that not everyone admires a crusader, Milton also discovered a sudden antipathy for the Presbyterians, whose cause he had been supporting but who had proved to be so much less adventurous than he had hoped. *Areopagitica* (November, 1644) consequently sounded, for all its trumpet calls to intellectual freedom, something of a retreat—a step backward to *Il Penseroso's* genre theory; by 1644 the romance model is "sage and serious" and *allegorical* Spenser, and Milton rebukes the Presbyterians for seeking absurdly to banish the "countryman's Arcadias, and his Montemayors" (YP, II, 324–25). Like Prynne and like his own Lot in "Sodom Burning," Milton had now experienced what it felt like to be accused "of praesumption, singularity, breach of citty custome." His response, ironically, was not to suffer violence but to offer it. His irregular sonnet *On the New Forcers of Consicence* threated the Presbyterians with the revenge of a more liberated Parliament, one that would (presumably inflamed by his oratory) "Clip ye as close as marginal P[rynne's] ears" (17). This brutal jeer would be revised out of the published text of 1673; by that time Milton would have moved considerably close to Prynne's position.

After the retreat, the rebound. In *Eikonoklastes* (1649) Milton unleashed, in a fury of disappointment, his sense that the romantic mode, cultural or political, was irretrievably spoiled. It has been argued that his exploitation of Pamela's prayer, the famous piece of plagiarism from Sidney's *Arcadia* in *Eikon Basilike*, was just a local and occasional issue not affecting his attitude to romance overall, but it is remarkable how deliberately Milton broadens that issue to include in one scathing critique the morals, politics, and aesthetics of the king *and* the romance tradition, since the two have become inseparable. Milton accuses Charles of "so little care of truth"

. . . as immediatly before his death to popp into the hand of that grave Bishop who attended him . . . a Prayer stol'n word for word from the mouth of a heathen fiction praying to a heathen God; & that in no serious Book, but the vain amatorious Poem of Sir Philip Sidney's *Arcadia,*—a Book in that kind full of worth and witt, but among religious thoughts and duties not worthy to be nam'd; nor to be read at any time without good caution; much less in time of trouble and affliction to be a Christian's Prayer-Book. (YP, III, 362)

One by one the phrases of the indictment mount; even the minor concession of "worth and witt" is qualified by the damning generic dismissal "in that kind." In the 1650 edition of the tract, Milton expanded this passage to take in, at one fell swoop, most of European romance:

For he certainly whose mind could serve him to seek a Christian prayer out of a Pagan Legend, and assume it for his own, might gather up the rest God knowes from whence; one perhaps out of the French *Astraea,* another out of the Spanish *Diana; Amadis* and *Palmerin* could hardly scape him . . . so long as such sweet rapsodies of Heathenism and Knight-errantry could yield him prayers. (YP, III, 366–67)

Charles is associated both with "heathen" (Roman Catholic) cultures and with the negative epistemology of antiromantic thought. Fiction has indeed become fraud. "How dishonorable then, and how unworthy of a Christian King, were these ignoble shifts, . . . this deception . . . [of] the cheated People" (YP, III, 367).

At approximately the same time (1648–1649), when researching his *History of Britain,* Milton came definitively to the conclusion that there was no historical basis for Arthurian story. As Barbara Lewalski cogently put it, he proceeded in the *History* to disavow Arthur "with all the truculence of one who has been deceived on a matter of importance."[25] Arthur, he now asserted, was "more renown'd in Songs and Romances then in true stories" (YP, X, 128). And in *The First Defense* there is a highly ambiguous remark about the truth-content of the Matter of France. Replying to Salmasius' contention that a king has no peer, Milton demanded, "what then are these twelve most ancient peers of France? Are they empty dreams of Turpin? Are they so called in vain mockery?" (YP, IV, i, 463). Ostensibly an assertion of the truth of Carolingian story, the passage seems ironic both in its questioning syntax and in its language; "an Turpini fabulae sunt et nugae?" "Fabulae et nugae" was a commonplace in the lexicon of those who disapproved of imaginative literature. In any other context the question would more naturally provoke a positive answer.

III

By the end of his career as a polemicist Milton appears to have lost confidence in most of romance tradition, though not in the possibility of heroism, especially his own. In *Paradise Lost* and *Paradise Regained* he seems to have made two last attempts to reform and reconstitute the genre according to higher standards than his predecessors. In *Paradise Lost*, however, the attempt was both an incomplete compromise and subordinated to other generic pressures, especially epic. In *Paradise Regained* he finished the job.

Paradise Lost in fact privileges one type of romance—the pastoral romance—as being capable of authenticity. Adam and Eve's story is presented as the original pastoral romance ("Hesperian fables true, if true, here only" (IV, 250–51) from which all other decadent forms derive. The Paradisal romance is, as we would now expect, significantly constrasted to "Court Amours / Mixt Dance, or wanton Mask" (IV, 767–68). On the chivalric romance Milton appears to be still indecisive. On the one hand, his opening lines promise "Things unattempted yet in Prose or Rhyme," an echo of Ariosto's "cosa non detta in prosa mai ne in rima" (I, ii, 2) that permits us to posit Ariosto as a model, perhaps even as "the Christian poet" of Cervantes. On the other, Milton offers a general condemnation of what *all* the chivalric romances have achieved. Satan's forces, gathered on the burning lake, are compared in number to all reports

> In *Fable or Romance* of Uther's Son
> Begirt with British and Armoric Knights;
> And all who since, *Baptiz'd or Infidel*
> Jousted in Aspramont or Montalban,
> Damasco, or Marocco, or Trebisond,
> Or whom Biserta sent from Afric shore
> When Charlemain with all his Peerage fell
> By Fontarabbia.   (I, 579–86; my italics)

By implication, both the Matter of Britain and the Matter of France are rejected as demonic. The choices italicized here are no choices; quest and crusade are equally false and lead equally to disaster, the Morte D'Arthure or the fall of Charlemagne. The latter cadence Milton himself invented, since even in the tragic *Chanson de Roland* Charlemagne survives to avenge the champion's death. The unqualified, unexcepting enclosure of "*all* who since . . . with *all* his Peerage fell" is final in another way. The metrical and rhetorical closure of "fell" announces Milton's conclusive disposition of all such stories. And yet it is also clear that much of what Milton condemned he also managed to retain in one way or another. The contrast between his rejection of "fabled knights in battles feigned" (IX, 30–31) and the totally imagined War in Heaven is a case in point.

In *Paradise Regained,* there are no such difficulties. The poem appears to be constructed on rigorously antiromantic lines, or at least on lines that would have been perceived as antiromantic according to the available genre theory. If we recall the outlines of Tasso's theory, for example, Milton appears to have gone well beyond the *Discorsi del poema eroico* in strictness. Instead of multiple heroes (Satan, Christ, Adam, and Eve) competing for our attention, the focus is narrowed to a single hero facing a single adversary, in a narrative with a simple chronology. One might easily assume that Milton had deliberately replaced the interweavings of romance and his own earlier poem by a Neo-Aristotelian structure, unless, of course, one preferred to assume that such a choice was never made, that romance structure was not one of the possibilities he declined.

Narrative structure does in fact seem to be a concern in *Paradise Regained,* and at a more interesting level of conception than in Tasso's or other seicento criticism. The poem's lexical patterns seem constantly to suggest what Tasso terms the "quantitative parts" of narrative, "the beginning, the middle, and the end, as Aristotle calls them, in defining the whole."[26] When *Paradise Regained* opens, we hear God's announcement to Gabriel that he will now "begin to verify that solemn message late" delivered by the dove (I, 132–33). Yet the "beginning" is constantly redefined or deferred. At I, 186, the Son considers "How best the mighty work he might begin," and at I, 287–88, he interprets the dove's message as a sign that he should "openly begin," although what is now unstated. At II, 113–14, the Son is still inquiring of himself "How to begin, how to accomplish best / His end of being on Earth." The object of "begin" is now stated but immediately confused by the ambiguous presence of "end." To begin is, somehow, also to end. In Book III, the concern for beginning is transferred to Satan, who tries to persuade the Son that his reign will be the "happier . . . the sooner it begins" (179), and in a crucial speech almost immediately afterwards the Son reveals how far his sense of the structure of things has changed:

> All things are best fulfilled in their due time,
> And time there is for all things, Truth hath said:
> If of my reign Prophetic Writ hath told
> That it shall never end, so when begin
> The Father in purpose hath decreed.   (III, 182–86)

When the Son demands of Satan, "what concerns it thee when I begin," Satan in turn reveals that his desire for an unequivocal beginning is really a need for the inevitable end:

> I would be at the worst; worst is my Port,
> My harbour and my ultimate repose.
> The end I would attain.   (II, 209–11)

Similarly, it is Satan who begins to insist that the Son's story must also have a middle, that is, a means to its end. At III, 89, Christ proposes "means far different"; at III, 355–56, Satan asserts that "prediction supposes means, / Without means us'd, what it predicts revokes," and Christ rejects this argument. Most significantly, at IV, 152, Christ reveals his most mature understanding of the problem in a statement that reveals nothing:

> of my Kingdom there shall be no end;
> Means there shall be to this, but what the means
> Is not for thee to know, nor me to tell.

A story that has not yet begun and has an unknowable middle will lead, by witty paradox, to "no end." It should be no surprise, therefore, that after the third temptation has been successfully resisted, angels halt the poem by invoking the true beginning: "Now enter, and begin to save mankind" (IV, 634). It appears that Milton rejected both the errant narrative structures of romance and the rule-governed neoclassical alternative.[27] Pressure for structuring the narrative comes, after Book I, entirely from Satan. The Son, on the other hand, learns to be an intelligent reader of his own experience, "quietly expecting / Without distrust or doubt" (III, 192–93) the process of the new Christian narrative whose rules are yet to be revealed.

If Milton's response to the problem of structure was, one might almost say, Christian deconstruction,[28] his approach to that of veracity in *Paradise Regained* was equally complex. Again, it might appear at first to be a simple, rigorous antiromanticism. A strict adherence to biblical history—the texts of Matthew and Luke relating to the temptations—is supported by an accurate secular chronology locating the poem's action, as Malcolm Kelsall pointed out, late in the reign of Tiberius, at "about the autumn of A.D. 29 [when] the aged ruler was guttering in the last decade of his life"[29] and Rome was in fact controlled by Sejanus. Milton's Jerusalem is therefore at least as historically grounded as Tasso's and considerably more so than his earlier Salem, moral symbol of "the strict raigne of Melchizidek," in "Cupid's Burning." Yet Milton invokes the

historical criterion only to subvert it. When the Son rejects the Kingdoms of the World he does so in apocalyptic language that denies historical perception and effort. His Kingdom will be "as a stone that shall
to pieces dash / All Monarchies besides throughout the world" (IV, 148–
49), and his refusal to intervene in the history of either Rome or Jerusalem implies rebuke to any political interpretation of his messianic role—
that is, any ideal of a religious or national crusade.

Milton also constantly invokes in *Paradise Regained* the dichotomy
between truth and fiction that we have traced as a concern in his poetics. It might seem that he had finally found a solution by simply dividing
these rival modes between his two protagonists and elaborating the
contrast between the divine Word and the Father of Lies. This program
is articulated in its baldest form at the end of Book III: "So fares it when
with truth falshood contends." More interesting is the debate on truth
that concludes Book I, where Satan is accused of exactly that epistemological compromise on which the defenders of romance had relied.
Whereas Tasso argued that "poets intermingle fictions among true
things and fables among true thoughts; like a man who fuses gold with
silver,"[30] Christ declares, in anger:

> That hath been thy craft,
> By mixing somewhat true to vent more lies.   (I, 432–33)

To complicate the issue still further, it is Christ, of course, who accuses
Satan of originating misinterpretation:

> what have been thy answers, what but dark,
> Ambiguous, and with double sense deluding,
> Which they who asked have seldom understood,
> And not well understood, as good not known.   (I, 432–37)

But it is Satan who is driven by the need to know the truth and who is
tormented by ambiguity—not in the language of which he is author,
"the persuasive Rhetoric / that sleek't his tongue" (IV, 5), but in the
divine Word itself. The entire temptation is motivated by Satan's need
to understand what he has heard directly from "the Sov'reign voice" as
the poem opens: "In what degree or meaning thou art call'd / The Son of
God, which bears no single sence" (IV, 515–16). Comparing the Old
Testament prophecies with what he has been able to "read" or "spell" in
the starry "characters" of Heaven, Satan complains, "A Kingdom they
portend thee, but what Kingdom, / Real or Allegoric I discern not" (IV,
389–90).

The answer, apparently, is neither. Somewhere between literal and allegorical conceptions of truth, between determinacy and indeterminacy, Christ takes his impossible stand on the pinnacle of the temple, and in a new epistemological compromise that is not Tasso's. "Tempt not the Lord thy God" may also, in this context, bear "no single sence" but to insist on determining what sense it bears aligns the reader with Satan. And Satan is aligned, not with the heroic interpreter of the Sphinx's riddle but with the Sphinx herself, who "once found out and solv'd," fell "headlong." Dare one still suggest, at this antihermeneutical moment, that the syntax of "found out and solv'd" is ambiguous, or that "headlong" may be a double entendre?

We are justified, I think, in relating these metaliterary procedures to romance theory by the presence of three otherwise gratuitous allusions to Milton's romantic predecessors. The first appears as a comment on the status in this poem of eroticism, which can no longer, of course, outside of Eden, be authentic. Eroticism appears in *Paradise Regained* only as the fantasy of demons, who think to "Set women in his eye" (II, 153), and it is explicitly linked with deceit, illusion, and the Arthurian romance. The ill spirits who attend Satan's banquet of the senses are

> Fairer then feignd of old, or fabl'd since
> Of Fairy damsels met in Forest wide
> By Knights of Logres, or of Lyones,
> Lancelot or Pelleas, or Pellenore.   (II, 358–61)

Later in the second temptation the Matter of France suffers a similar fate when it appears as a metaphor of power abused and confused. Like the Satanic forces in Book I of *Paradise Lost*, the Parthians are compared to the great romance musters:

> Such forces met not, nor so wide a camp
> When Agrican with all his Northern powers
> Beseigd Albracca, as Romances tell;
> The City of Gallaphrone, from thence to win
> The fairest of her Sex Angelica
> His daughter, sought by many Prowest Knights,
> Both Paynim, and the Peers of Charlemane.   (III, 337–43)

Ostensibly a figure of scale, the figure proves to be really a sharp analysis of what went wrong in the world of Boiardo's poem. "Both Paynim . . . and the Peers of Charlemane" pursue Angelica, symbol of a mistaken ideal. So in the Italian romanticization of the Carolingian story, Christian and pagan theories of literature have become confused.

But the most gratuitous and the most central of Milton's allusions to romance occurs in connection with the third temptation. When Satan catches Christ up to carry him to the pinnacle of the temple, Milton observes that he did so "without wing / Of Hippogrif" (IV, 541–42). The allusion is to Ariosto's famous flying steed, half horse, half griffin, by which Astolfo reached the Earthly Paradise and returned with Orlando's wits. Milton's early editor Thomas Newton remarked: "Here Milton design'd a reflection upon the Italian poets, and particularly upon Ariosto . . . [who] frequently makes use of this creature . . . : but Milton would insinuate that he employ'd no such machinery."[31] More precisely, Barbara Lewalski saw that Satan "effects a marvel surpassing Astolfo's flight."[32] These insights perhaps do not go far enough. The allusion alerts us to the presence in *Paradise Regained* of the third major issue in romance theory—the status of the Marvellous—which is where this paper began.

The hippogriff has, in fact, a tradition of its own, a small but intriguing note in the history of poetics and genre. It is best to work backward here, starting with Wordsworth's *Peter Bell*, finally published in 1819[33] with an introduction defining the Marvellous for the new Romantics: "The dragon's wing, the magic ring," wrote Wordsworth, "I shall not covet for my dower." Their substitute, in the realm of mysterious support systems, is to be the "sympathetic heart" and "soul of power":

> These given, what more need I desire
> To stir, to soothe, or elevate?
> What nobler marvels than the mind
> May in life's daily prospect find,
> May find or there create?
>
> .   .   .   .
>
> But grant my wishes,—let us now
> Descend from this ethereal height;
> Then take thy way, adventurous Skiff,
> More daring far than Hippogriff,
> And be thy own delight!

Wordsworth's "adventurous Skiff" is the symbol of an imagination that can do without the supernatural because it finds "nobler marvels" in daily life and ordinary human responses. Five years earlier Sir Walter Scott had built a similar credo into his generic specifications for *Waverley* (1814): "I do not invite my fair readers, whose sex and impatience give them the greatest right to complain of these circumstances, into a flying chariot drawn by hippogriffs, or moved by enchantment. Mine is a humble English post-chaise, drawn upon four wheels, and keeping his majesty's highway."[34] Though somewhat skewed by its special and condescending address to a female audience, Scott's statement was an important part of his plan for *Waverley* as a new kind of historical antiromance.

As compared to these nineteenth-century perceptions, Renaissance comments on the hippogriff seem banal. For Pigna, it was no different in status from the enchanted palace or the horn that made the palace disintegrate. Each was a marvel, and each was to be interpreted allegorically. He concluded that the hippogriff was "l'emblema della Gloria."[35] For Sir John Harington, Ruggiero's flight on the hippogriff signified his being "overcome . . . of this passion of love."[36] For Tasso, the hippogriff had "no moral meaning, but was merely one of those wonders . . . that move not only the unlearned but the judicious as well." The Christian poet should therefore try to accommodate such fantastic elements to his theological system, as miracles performed by God, angels, or demons.[37] But to Ariosto himself, the hippogriff was unique:

> Non è finto il destrier, ma naturale,
>
> . . . .
>
> Non finzion d'incanto, come il resto,
> Ma vero e natural si vedea questo.
>
> (Canto IV, 18, 1; 19, 7–8)

[The steed was no fiction, but natural; . . . not fashioned by enchantment, like everything else, but true and natural.]

Unless we are to disregard this statement as pure irony, Ariosto's concepton of the hippogriff was that it was the only "true" marvel in his poem. It is tempting to explain this paradox in fully Romantic, Wordsworthian terms: that the flight on the hippogriff signifies the imaginative flight that will restore the world of romance to its senses.

Could Milton have read the hippogriff in this way? If so, "without wing / Of Hippogrif" connotes more than the desire to outdo Ariosto, more than a Tassonian principle of marvels by divine permission. It implies, rather, the final rejection of that Renaissance compromise ideal, the reform of romance from within, differently attempted by Ariosto, Tasso, Spenser, and Milton himself in *Paradise-Lost*. Here too, as with the questions of structure and truth-content, Milton resists generic classification. His attitude to the Marvellous in *Paradise Regained* is neither romantic nor antiromantic. It is Satan who desires a miracle and who urges the Son to perform one, in both the first and the third temptations. It is Satan, also, who constantly invokes the sense of wonder, whose "words impression left / Of much amazement to th'infernal Crew" (I, 106–07) when he tells them of the Son, Satan who "wonder[s] that the Son of God / In this wild solitude so long should bide" (II, 303–04) and who urges Christ not to "deprive / All Earth her wonder at [his] acts" (III, 23–24). Most significantly, it is Satan who, "smitten with amazement," falls from the pinnacle, defeated by his own, now obsolete, generic expectations. But we cannot simply say that *Paradise Regained* equates the Marvellous with the power and mental set of demons. In the first temptation the Son refuses to satisfy the hunger for miracles for the sake of his own hunger. That seems a reasonable disappointment. In the third temptation he alters our very sense of what a miracle is. Merely by maintaining his "uneasy station" on the pinnacle, a point conceptually somewhere between natural and supernatural, Christ sublimates the problem of the Marvellous, preempting all subsequent scepticism in the history of Christian thought. Was it really a miracle? The answer is neither yes nor no, but so typically Miltonic that is satisfies: to understand the stand on the pinnacle "Will ask thee skill."

University of Maryland

NOTES

1. "An Execration upon Vulcan," 29–31, 66–71, 73–75, quoted from *Ben Jonson*, ed. C. H. Herford, Percy Simpson, and Evelyn Simpson, 13 vols. (Oxford, 1947), VIII, 203–06.

2. George Williamson, "Milton the Anti-Romantic," *MP*, XL (1962), 13–21.

3. Roberta Brinkley, *Arthurian Legend in the Seventeenth Century* (Baltimore, 1932), pp. 126–61.

4. W. Nicholas Knight,"'To enter Lists with God': Transformation of Spenserian Chivalric Tradition," *Costerus* II, (1973), 83–108; Barbara K. Lewalski, "Milton: Revaluations of Romance," in *Four Essays on Romance*, ed. Herschel Baker (Cambridge, Mass., 1971), pp. 57–70.

5. For an account of the *Amadis* and its successors, see John J. O'Connor, *Amadis de Gaule and Its Influence on Elizabethan Literature* (Rahway, N.J., 1970).

6. M. de Cervantes Saavedra, *The Adventures of Don Quixote* (1604), trans. J. M. Cohen (Penguin, 1950), p. 59.

7. In his *Chanson de Saisnes* (c. 1260), Jean Bodel wrote:

> Li conte de Bretaigne s'il sont vain et plaisant,
> Et cil de Romme sage et de sens aprendant.
> Cil de France sont voir chascun jour aparant.　　　(v, 9–11)

The legends of Britain are so vain and pleasing; those of Rome are wise and of moral import. Those of France are true and proven every day.

8. See Willem de Briane's translation of the *Historia Turpini* (1189–1218) in *Chronique de Turpin*, ed. André de Mandach (Geneva, 1963), p. 53:

Ici commence la veraye estoyre si cum li fort roys Charlemain . . . e sachunt certeynement tous ceus ke le orrunt ke l'estoyre est veraie . . . e cruée de clers et de lais. Ly bons archesweke Turpyn de Reyns, ke fu compagnoun Charles en Espayne . . . escrist a Vienne.

[Here begins the true history of the brave King Charlemagne . . . and everyone who hears it knows for certain that the story is true . . . and believed by clerics and laymen. The good archbishop Turpin of Rheims, who was Charles's companion in Spain, wrote it in Vienna.]

9. Giovanni Battista Pigna, *I Romanzi* (Venice, 1554), pp. 48–49.

10. Giovannbattista Giraldi Cinthio, *Discorso intorno al comporre dei romanzi* (1554), trans. H. L. Snuggs (Lexington, Ky., 1968), p. 6.

11. W. C. Calin, *The Old French Epic of Revolt* (Paris, 1962), provides an account of the *Doon de Mayence*, or rebel cycle of Carolingian tales, including *The Four Sons of Aymon*.

12. My reading of Ariosto coincides with Patricia Parker's in *Inescapable Romance* (Princeton, 1979), pp. 16–53. This important Derridean discussion of romance theory foregrounds Ariosto's own pun on error/errantry and sees the poem as rejecting Boiardo's world halfway through. See also D. S. Carne-Ross' pioneering essay "The One and the Many: A Reading of *Orlando Furioso*, Cantos 1 and 8," *Arion*, V (1966), 195–234.

13. *Orlando Furioso*, ed. G. Nencioni (Florence, 1957), p. 536, (my translation).

14. E.g., *Orlando Furioso* XXII, 17 (the collapse of the magic dome); XXII (Ruggiero drowns his magic shield, determined to manage without supernatural aid); and VII, 73, the use of the ring of reason to unmask Alcina's false beauty, "che gia' molti anni avean celato il vero" (which for many years had hidden the truth.).

15. For the literary arguments generated by the *Furioso*, see Bernard Weinberg, *A History of Literary Criticism in the Italian Renaissance*, 2 vols. (Chicago, 1961), II.

16. *Discourses on the Heroic Poem*, trans. Mariella Cavalchini and Irene Samuel (Oxford, 1973), p. 35.

17. Milton, of course, read the *Arcadia* in its partly revised form in the countess of Pembroke's composite edition. Sidney's revisions, as far as they went, actually moved the genre of the *Arcadia* from pastoral to chivalric romance.

18. *Expansed Hieroglyphicks: A Study of Sir John Denham's Cooper's Hill*, ed. Brendan O'Hehir (Berkeley and Los Angeles, 1969), pp. 118–19.

19. Donne, *Letters To Severall Persons of Honour* (1651), ed. M. Thomas Hester. (Delmar, N.Y., 1977), pp. 235–36.

20. In the "Second Part" of *Histriomastix* (1633; Garland facsimile, ed. A. Freeman [New York 1974]) Prynne dealt at length with the reformist or Sidneian arguments for an ideal literature. See, for example, p. 918: "amorous Playes and Poems though intermixed with grave Sentences and Morals, are dangerous to be read or penned, because more will be corrupted by their amorousnesse, then instructed or edified by their Morals."

21. See Barbara Breasted, "*Comus* and the Castlehaven Scandal," in *Milton Studies*, III, ed. James D. Simmonds (Pittsburgh, 1971), pp. 201–24; Rosemary Mundhenk, "Dark Scandal and the Sun-Clad Power of Chastity," *SEL*, XV (1975), 141–52.

22. *Histriomastix*, pp. 212–14: theatricals lead, among other vices, "even to the most abominable unnaturall sinne of Sodom, to which mens inbred corruption . . . is over-

prone . . . [as] our English Statutes, (which have made it capitall, as a late example of a memorable act of justice on an English Peere can witness) doe more then testifie."

23. Here, because the translation is superior, I cite *Complete Poetry and Major Prose,* ed. Merritt Y. Hughes (New York, 1957), pp. 130, 168.

24. Milton wrote of "that resolution which Ariosto follow'd against the perswasions of Bembo" to write in the vernacular, a story derived either from Pigna's *I Romanzi* (pp. 74–75) or Sir John Harington's "Life of Ariosto" appended to his translation.

25. "Revaluations of Romance," p. 64.

26. *Discourses,* p. 17.

27. Romance structure had early been given a vaguely symbolic dimension. Patricia Parker, *Inescapable Romance,* cites Minturno's rebuke to the romancers (*Arte poetica,* 1564): "because such a composition includes the deeds of errant knights, they obstinately affirm . . . that it is necessary for poetry to be errant as well" (pp. 18–19). Pigna (*I Romanzi*) combined the same insight, put more postively, with a recognition that romance structure causes intense narrative suspense: "un certo ardore e causato, che e di dover la fine della cosa sentire" (a certain passion is generated to learn the way things end) (pp. 44–45). This sounds oddly like Satan's state of mind.

28. Used equally loosely, the same term might be invoked in connection with Milton's inexplicably asymmetrical use of the four-book structure.

29. See Malcolm Kelsall, "The Historicity of *Paradise Regained,*" in *Milton Studies,* XII, ed. James D. Simmonds (Pittsburgh, 1978), p. 237.

30. *Discourses,* p. 58.

31. *Paradise Regain'd* (London, 1785), pp. 192–93.

32. "Revaluations of Romance," p. 68.

33. Wordsworth, *The Poems,* ed. John Hayden, 2 vols. (Penguin, 1977), I, 320. *Peter Bell* was begun in 1798, presumably for inclusion in the *Lyrical Ballads* and as part of the plan by which Wordsworth would deal with natural experience, Coleridge with the supernatural.

34. *Waverley* (New York, 1906), p. 89.

35. *I Romanzi,* p. 90.

36. *Orlando Furioso* (London, 1591), p. 406.

37. *Discourses,* pp. 37–38.

PARADISE REGAINED:
IMPLICATIONS OF EPIC

Stuart Curran

I N 1797 James Ogden, a Manchester reed-maker whose obscurity contrasted sharply with his poetic pretensions, anonymously published
the third and last of his epic poems, *Emanuel; or, Paradise Regained: An
Epic Poem in Nine Books*.[1] Although the byways of English literary
history reveal innumerable attempts to rewrite, extend, or simply steal
from *Paradise Lost*, Ogden's poem is unique in its tribute to Milton's
second epic.[2] "Paradise Regain'd" is the running head throughout the
volume, and so close is the poem to the original in language and plot,
even in pacifism, that one wonders what Ogden thought his purpose
was. Part of it clearly was to enlist Milton, against his own ideology and
that of his principal celebrants at this time, on the side of monarchy,
church, and William Pitt. In this incarnation Satan is apparelled in the
latest French fashion: "Shield, Lord, our CHURCH and KING from this
foul fiend, / In his worst form, by DEMOCRATS now looss'd."[3] But
even in his less topical concerns, Ogden seems compelled to bring
Milton within the fold of orthodox piety and epopee. Expanding *Paradise Regained* by five books and many pages, Ogden adds surprisingly
little by way of episode. Rather, he labors through description and
machinery to load the exposition with typology. In Book I, for instance,
Mary is discovered elaborating the story of Ruth and Naomi in a coat she
devotedly knits for her son, and when Jesus enters the house with John
and Andrew he sits on a couch whose carvings represent Jacob and his
sons. On a grander scale of action, Ogden imports Moses and Elias, who
descend to converse with Jesus some ten days into his desert travail and
return in the climactic scene, after the feast at Cana, to signal his transfiguration before his disciples into the true Emanuel. Along with such
precursors Ogden introduces the central persons and events of the New
Testament, at least to this point, and finds irresistible Jesus' ability to
render miracles. If the focus is still on the central conflict of Jesus and
Satan, *Emanuel* is enlarged almost to the state of a Christiad. It is a
more conventional poem than *Paradise Regained*, more faithful to its
biblical sources and larger in narrative circumference; yet it is sentimen-

tal in execution and far more limited in substance. Ogden misreads his original in poetics as well as politics, dissipating Milton's slow accumulation of import. The certain value to be gained from reading *Emanuel* is a sharpened awareness of what *Paradise Regained* is not, or of what it might have been had Milton attempted to write a conventional Christian epic. By contrast, Ogden's poem illuminates not merely the compression of Milton's second epic but the power of its implicitness.

That *Paradise Regained* stands squarely within an epic mode is no longer in dispute. The rich heritage of biblical epic literature that sustains its aesthetic has been amply and admirably demonstrated by Barbara K. Lewalski. More recently, Joan Malory Webber has enlarged the perimeters of discussion with her eloquent analysis of the poem as focusing the largest concerns of the Western epic tradition—the victory of human consciousness over mortality in an effort to create an integral psyche, an integral civilization.[4] With such large schemes of human and literary history at issue, it should not surprise us that comparatively less attention has been paid to how *Paradise Regained* qualifies as epic, the ways it asserts its epic claims. As generations of head-shaking, and sometimes (like Tillyard) nay-saying, commentators will testify, it does not do so in the same way as *Paradise Lost*.[5]

It is not that *Paradise Regained* lacks recognizable epic conventions. It begins by overtly establishing its claims as an epic sequel to *Paradise Lost* (and in such a way as to invoke *The Aeneid* in passing), continues with multiple council scenes, a panoramic vision of the earth and a catalog of its kingdoms; there is some filling in of Old Testament history, with a nod here and there at figures from the classical past, all rounded out by six epic similes. That one should be moved to count the latter and to note that they all occur toward the end of the work is a reflection of Milton's poetic strategy in *Paradise Regained*.[6] Not only is it not, like its predecessor, to be comprehended by the term *diffuse epic*; it is positively, deliberately, spare. Epic devices are certainly made organic to the nature and meaning of Jesus' temptation in the wilderness, but they are not present for their own sake as ornament nor are they ever in themselves allowed to detract from the central spiritual conflict of Jesus and Satan. The conflict is intense, undiminished, logically inexorable: its claims may be "Above Heroic" (I, 15), but the manner is purposely unheroic.

Throughout his career Milton has excelled in the use of allusions as a kind of compressed shorthand. In *Paradise Regained*, far more than in *Paradise Lost*, the epic form itself is transformed to this end. Although we all share in the central conflict—are intended through its stress to see our inner lives exposed—the wilderness is neither the arena where we live nor a place where epic poems are written and read. The devices and conventions of epic link the austere, lonely, private ritual of Jesus' self-definition and self-creation to the normative world of our public and literary expectations. Almost invariably, Milton subtly shifts epic conventions so as to reverberate against these expectations, testing them and, through them, us. If, as Webber suggests, the issues of *Paradise Regained* draw us naturally to place the poem against the backdrop of Milton's major poems, no less does his spare but pointed use of epic device and epic reference draw into context the line of major poems in this genre.[7]

The essential context is, perhaps, obvious, often discussed but certainly worth renewed emphasis: Jesus resists all of Satan's efforts to deflect him into customary epic heroism. Retired like Achilles in his tent or like the wounded Aeneas, Jesus will not reenter the world zealous to conquer it or to enthrone himself. As in *Paradise Lost*, the candidate for supreme hero is Satan, who blusters like a *miles gloriosus*, plans campaigns, and, though constrained through several days to matching wits, at last resorts to enraged violence. It is Satan, indeed, who in this last act of imperiling Jesus' life recalls the way climactic violence in the classical epic—Achilles or Aeneas returning to the battle-field, Odysseus bursting forth in his palace—drives those in whom it resides to a superhuman fury that destroys everything in its path. Traditionally, such fury is the ultimate seal of fearless heroism, but in *Paradise Regained* this rage, born of baffled frustration, testifies instead to Satan's impotence. No less significant is the willed control of Jesus, whose refusal to react physically is symbolic of the divinity he thus assumes. Satan is as reactive in *Paradise Regained* as he is in *Paradise Lost*, and he falls at last because Jesus stands in his absolute integrity, independent of his adversary.

Yet if in *Paradise Lost* martial heroism is explicitly associated with the Satanic mission—so accentuated as to make the conventionally heroic an attribute of Satan—in *Paradise Regained* Milton draws back even from a figurative recasting of the heroic mode like that employed in Books V and VI of *Paradise Lost*.[8] The war in heaven, although metaphoric of spiritual conflict, gains its emotional power from being rendered as epic battle. The archangels adopt the role of the Greek princes—Agamemnon, Diomedes, Odysseus, Menelaos—rallying their forces for the battle and ever in its vanguard:

> Go *Michael* of Celestial Armies Prince,
> And thou in Military prowess next

> *Gabriel*, lead forth to Battel these my Sons
> Invincible, lead forth my armed Saints
> By Thousands and by Millions rang'd for fight.   (VI, 44–48)

And, as in the *Iliad*, the absence of the key prince causes a stalemate between the contending armies. Thus, when the Son at last mounts his chariot to lead the angelic host to victory, he reminds us explicitly of the irresistible Achilles, returned to the field in the brilliant armor of the gods to sweep all his opponents before him.

There is none of this in *Paradise Regained*. The battle array of the Parthians is presented from an immense distance, dispassionately, and the troops are denominated by the region they come from, not by name. The mustering of these troops is, we surmise, in preparation for battle, but it is represented as pure spectacle, cut short before any physical conflict can intrude. The absence of such conflict only underscores the intense verbal duel that for a moment centers on the Parthians, then swirls off to another corner of a battlefield as large as the earth itself. There is in *Paradise Regained* only one violent act, isolated as a startling intrusion on the mental duel, itself rudimentary and symbolic, representative of the essential dishonor of the heroic. In so compressed an artistic structure, the singular event contains multitudes.

In *Paradise Regained*, moreover, Milton almost wryly exposes another aspect of Satan's affinity with traditional heroism. It is no small irony that Jesus' adversary consistently thinks within a framework defined by classical epics. He is a diabolic version of the pious René Le Bossu, who would shortly treat the learned of Europe to a catalog of what traits were proper and what not to the epic hero.[9] When, in the council called to plot the downfall of Jesus, Belial proposes a mere undisguised carnal temptation, Satan rebukes him for his lack of sophistication. He credits Jesus with sharing with him a common education in the same books, those epics cited as valuable in the formation of a Renaissance prince:

> with manlier objects we must try
> His constancy, with such as have more shew
> Of worth, of honour, glory, and popular praise.   (II, 225–27)

Satan is genuinely puzzled by Jesus' lack of response to Satan's studied delineation of this program. The irony has a double edge, of course, since Milton predicates this episode on *our* having the customary literary education that Jesus appears to disregard or lack.

If we intensify our perspective on this scene, however, converting the disputants into primary antagonists of a psychomachia, it is clear that

Satan's temptation comes from deep within Jesus' mind. The guiding principle for the logical expansion of issues between Satan and Jesus is that Jesus always first articulates the attraction of the ends to which Satan goes on to tempt him. The very speciousness of the adversary's arguments verifies the intuitive rejection of them that occurs within Jesus before he has unravelled the constituent syllogisms. So with the temptation of epic heroism. As man, Jesus has been raised in a culture, however comparatively untainted by worldly goals, that has elevated traditional heroism as the highest attainment of an ambitious youth. Beginning his spiritual debate in the wilderness before Satan appears, Jesus acknowledges his youthful ardor:

> victorious deeds
> Flam'd in my heart, heroic acts, one while
> To rescue *Israel* from the *Roman* yoke,
> Then to subdue and quell o'er all the earth
> Brute violence and proud Tyrannick pow'r,
> Till truth were freed, and equity restor'd.   (I, 215–20)

Even though he values the power of persuasion in attaining these ends, the ends themselves are intended to strike a responsive chord within Milton's fit audience, whether smarting from the ignominy of the Restoration or, in later times, asserting the primacy of liberty against power and privilege. To reject the emotional call of heroism to such noble ends is to step beyond the precincts of one's culture and into an isolation as potentially dangerous and expansive as the symbolic wilderness into which Jesus has withdrawn to contemplate his destiny. It is not simply Satan who is impatient to "behold [the] God-like deeds" (I, 386) of the ordained hero; Jesus bears within his mind the unequivocal injunction of his mother, "By matchless Deeds express thy matchless Sire" (I, 233).

The issue is thus set long before Satan exposes the distasteful, concealed underpinnings of conventional heroism. From the initial soliloquy of Jesus in Book I, through the rejection of kingdoms in Book IV, to the pinnacle scene where Jesus' refusal to act signifies his ultimate triumph, the essential concern of Milton's second epic is the very nature of epic heroism. The argument may turn on personal glory to begin with, but even after Jesus has firmly, even radically, committed himself to the suppression of individual ego, there is the far thornier problem of duty: "If Kingdom move thee not, let move thee Zeal, / And Duty" (III, 171–72). Satan utters that imperative, but the words are morally neutral. Indeed, by invoking Zeal and Duty, Satan ironically asserts the implicit responsibility assumed in the symbolic baptism with which

Paradise Regained begins. It is one thing to reject the honor of Achilles as a guiding principle of one's life; it is quite another to foresake the model provided in the self-abnegating devotion of the pious Aeneas.

Of the classical epics, the *Aeneid* casts the strongest shadow on *Paradise Regained*. It is the only one to which direct allusion is made, an allusion customarily taken as simply a generic signal.[10] Yet however diverse the voluminous scholarship on Milton in recent years, it finds common ground in the recognition that Milton's learned allusions are seldom imprecise or lacking in layered nuance. Milton's conscious modeling of his opening lines on what in the Renaissance was accepted as the conventional beginning of the *Aeneid* sharply distinguishes his epic purpose from Virgil's. The Latin master, who has previously indulged his imagination within a pastoral retreat, now forces his genius into the turbulent public realm of nation building:

> Ille ego, qui quondam gracili modulatus avena
> carmen, et egressus silvis vicina coegi
> ut quamvis avido parerent arva colono
> gratam opus agricolis; at nunc horrentia Martis
> arma virumque cano.

I am he who on a slender pipe once turned a song, and, having left the woods, forced the nearby fields richly to requite the eager tiller of soil, a work beneficial to the farmer; yet now of the terrible arms of Mars and the man I sing.

Like Virgil, Milton, "who e're while the happy Garden sung" (I, 1), will celebrate "one mans firm obedience" (I, 4), but he does not glorify arms nor seek out the battlefields of distant lands; instead, a "Desert" is "his Victorious Field" (I, 9), his antagonist is "the Spiritual Foe" (I, 10), and, if the "deeds [are] / Above Heroic," they are also "in secret done" (I, 14–15). Milton easily positions Virgil as foil to his epic intent through his initial adoption of an allusive language.

But without further allusion the circumstances of the epic continually reinforce and deepen the context. All epics, at least up to Milton's time, are infused with historical detail (or what, without records and centuries after the fact, passes for such detail). We are so accustomed to the syncretic richness of Milton's biblical allusions that it is easy to ignore the force of other historical contexts. And yet, as is notably illustrated in the twelfth book of *Paradise Lost* by our sudden realization that Charles I is heir to Nimrod and through him to the dictatorship of Satan, Milton's epics are not confined in range to the biblical records that provide central historical support. Especially in *Paradise Regained*, though the force of typology constantly recalls the long durance of Israel awaiting its Messiah, the historical detail looks beyond its borders. Indeed, the poem virtually ignores its local setting, in comparison with the attention it lavishes on those to the east and west of Israel. On the supposition that what Milton refuses as option is as indicative of his larger conceptions as what he adopts, the paucity of local reference is worth our contemplation.

If all that is known—to us, to Jesus, to Satan—is that Jesus has been chosen to regain the throne of David, one might expect to learn what that entails. In fact, however, both participants in the wilderness debate learn what it will not entail. The kingdom of David will be metaphorical: not a worldly enclave, but, "like a tree / Spreading and over-shadowing all the Earth" (IV, 147–48), a spiritual community closed to the power manipulations that Satan alone can understand, and therefore inviolate before his wiles. In coming to this realization, Jesus progressively distances himself from Aeneas as epic model. Although *Paradise Regained* is set within a historical context and assumes a people seeking its identity, it is, significantly, not a nationalistic epic.

Yet insofar as national power and aspiration are continually, even increasingly, before our eyes, it is the context of the *Aeneid* that provides a particular focus. Rome is the only locality described in specific detail in *Paradise Regained*—lavishly so, as Satan devotes some seventy lines (IV, 27–97) to its urban outlines, its geographical setting, and its possessions. Such descriptions are conventional to the epic, but there is, it should be recalled, a specific precedent for this in the vision granted Aeneas of the future empire whose rudiments he is to found in Latium (*Aeneid* VI, 756–886). That empire, as Virgil celebrates its fame, has slowly nurtured the barbarous into civilization, displacing local power struggles, establishing a general, lasting peace. Whether or not one questions the motives of a laureate, Virgil's encomium to Augustan Rome as the pinnacle of a humane community is the ideological demiurge of his entire epic, justifying the ruin of Troy and the bloodbath on the plains of Italy.

In *Paradise Regained*, however, the Roman empire is seen from an opposite perspective. The very first specific historical reference in the poem, for instance, occurs with Jesus' noble impulse "To rescue *Israel* from the *Roman* yoke" (I, 217). The necessity for this rescue is recognized by both disputants, as Satan's bland understatement indicates:

> *Judaea* now and all the promis'd land
> Reduc't a Province under Roman yoke,
> Obeys *Tiberius;* nor is always rul'd
> With temperate sway.   (III, 157–60)

The glowing tribute to Rome offered by Satan intrinsically suggests the decline from Virgil's Augustan paradigm already begun under Octavius' son and successor:

> This Emperour hath no Son, and now is old,
> Old, and lascivious, and from *Rome* retir'd
> To *Capreae* an Island small but strong
> On the Campanian shore, with purpose there
> His horrid lusts in private to enjoy,
> Committing to a wicked Favourite
> All publick cares, and yet of him suspicious,
> Hated of all, and hating.   (IV, 90–97)

This passage contradicts—deliberately, one might assume, given Milton's knowledge of Virgil—Jupiter's promise to the future race of Rome: "His ego nec metas rerum nec tempora pono: / Imperium sine fine dedi" (I set no limits to their fortunes and / no time; I give them empire without end).[11] Lacking direct means of succession, ruled through the standoff of mutual hatred, imperial Rome for all its trappings is an anticivilization. It is the exposed dead-end of Virgil's civic ideal, a monstrous perversion of the life mission of the devout Aeneas—or perhaps, rather, the natural culmination of martial heroism attempting to rear the fragile structures of a civilized community on blood-drenched ground.

Even Satan feels something of this. To his mind at least, the Parthians and their allies, now dominated by Rome, offer Jesus a much stronger power base to work from. They have a primitive vigor no longer to be found in Rome's highly structured and far-flung empire. With them are untested possibilities for the ambitious soldier able to bring their forces within his grasp. Although he does not say it explicitly, Satan, recognizing the eastern origins of Jesus, in effect offers him the unique opportunity of succeeding Aeneas as Asia's epic hero. What could be more logical, if the race of Aeneas, its line expiring with the childless Tiberius, has exhausted its mission, than that a new hero, one of whose parents is likewise divine, should begin the old undertaking once more and from the same eastern lands. But Jesus also recognizes that he is to be the center of a new dispensation. He defines it differently—unepically.

That is not, however, to assert that *Paradise Regained* is anything so simple—or, in actual fact, so nonexistent—as an antiepic. As Joan Webber so incisively remarks, in discussing the tradition of Western epics, "We are trying to define a genre by a series of great poems each of which rejects the assumptions of its predecessors."[12] Jesus' effort in the wilderness is systematically to revise his own conception of the heroic so as to ensure that, unlike his predecessors', "of [his] Kingdom there shall be no end" (IV, 151). In this undertaking he has, or at least Milton has, Aeneas as both prototype and false example: on the one hand, the devout servant of the divine behest, duty-bound, faithful to family, the compassionate shepherd of his people; and on the other hand, a man continually betrayed by his elemental passions, tempted with disastrous consequences by the unearned luxury of Carthage, desirous of peace but unable to attain it save through slaughter. However resonant the *Aeneid* is for the historical context of *Paradise Regained* and for the radical character of its hero, the failure of its vision is manifest.

There are ways, indeed, in which the *Odyssey* is even more suggestive for the focus and movement of Milton's poem. Webber's passing reference to the *Odyssey* is precisely on the mark: "Jesus' temptations are like the experiences of Odysseus. They try, and manifest his spirit."[13] Aeneas is a public man, scarcely ever pictured in isolation, but if the end of Jesus' meditation in the wilderness is the assumption of a public ministry, *Paradise Regained* is nonetheless the most private of all epics. We begin with Milton's assurance of "deeds / Above Heroic, though in secret done, / And unrecorded left through many an Age" (I, 14–16) and end with a like emphasis, now through inversion sharply stressed: "hee unobserv'd / Home to his Mothers house private return'd" (IV, 638–39). Milton thus underscores the interiority of his epic, its continual subordination of act to mental precondition.[14] In this his precursor is Homer. Theoretically, one might claim a structural model in the brooding self-absorption of Achilles, the silent, charged tension poised against the terrifying violence that surrounds and finally engulfs it. But Odysseus is the better model, not, like Aeneas, for what he attempts to achieve but for what he endures. As Jesus understands with an ease that is ironically weighted, "who best / Can suffer, best can do" (III, 194–95).

The *Odyssey* is an epic of trial, self-testing, self-mastery. As artistic structure it has never seemed the equal of the *Iliad*, partly because its famous adventures are contained within a relatively few books: for nearly half the epic little of outward import happens. Yet even when Odysseus has regained Ithaka in Book XIII, the testing of self and others continues. The probing of limits is the true activity of the *Odyssey*. The obsession with naming, with identity, and self-definition is both primitive and mythically sophisticated. The "many-turning" mind of Odysseus (πολύτροπον: I, 1) is the focus for the ancient world's most exhaustive study of human psychology. Odysseus is at once the representation of all human potentiality and "Nobody–'Ουτος," as he names himself to Polyphemus. At times he seems almost an abstraction of human mental power in and of itself. The epithets that attach to him, except for the heroic tribute "sacker of cities," invariably bear the prefix "πολυ-," the mark of his inherent pluralism. Virtually all of them would apply as well to Milton's Jesus.[15] The form that the final address to Odysseus takes would carry equal weight in *Paradise Regained:* Διογενές Λαερτιάδη, πολυμήχαν' 'Οδυσσεῦ (God-sprung son of Laertes, Odysseus of many resources) (XXIV, 542). The simplicity of Milton's purpose in so intensely focusing on the interiority of Jesus is thus expressed by Satan:

> Thenceforth I thought thee worth my nearer view
> And narrower Scrutiny, that I might learn
> In what degree or meaning thou art call'd
> The Son of God, which bears no single sence.   (IV, 514–17)

As it is in "no single sence" that Odysseus represents the human condition, so with Jesus endeavoring to transfigure himself into the divine. That he rigorously cuts off the options offered him by Satan is true enough, but paradoxical in effect. However distinct the forms it takes, there is essentially one temptation in *Paradise Regained*, that of narrowing one's spiritual and psychological range to accord with an already structured and external pattern. Satan's worldliness is neither cheap nor simple: it begins by defining man as physical being, enlarges its conception to honor the human ability for organizing self-contained social entities, and pins its highest aspirations on the connoisseur's will to value multiple systems of thought or codifications of historical epoch. Even at their best, however, these options impose limits on the mind that aspires to the infinite potentiality of godhead.

What seems at first to disqualify Jesus for the position of epic hero—his social condition—is ironically the precondition necessary to that end. Like Odysseus returned to his house, a nameless wanderer accorded the status of beggar and addressed by all as "Stranger," Jesus stands outside the social structure that would define him: the very first adjectives applied to him by Milton are "obscure, / Unmarkt, unknown" (I, 24–25). And Satan taunts him with the disparity between his condition and his pretensions: "Thou art unknown, unfriended, low of birth" (II, 413). Milton's accent is not simply democratic. Jesus is, indeed, the first epic hero not to come from a lofty social caste, but his low origins are the initial mark in the progressive stripping away of the worldly structures supporting the conventional epic hero—or epic poet.

Milton's renunciation of traditional epic values is thus further tied to the renunciations of Jesus, all of which have literary implications. It is not fortuitous that, despite Satan's fascination with the political alignments of the time, *Paradise Regained* is unconcerned with the past and but for the richness of typological reference would be virtually devoid of reference to history of any kind. Jesus briefly recounts his life in search of clues to his destiny, as does Mary, as does Satan. But the compass is too small, the events of little significance. The attempts to recall the past, indeed, are curiously weighted not with the experiences the past contains but with its portents for the future. And yet, compared with the classical epics, there is little stress on the future either. Satan has been told that he will be vanquished but does not know how or where. An obscure sign, the dove's descent at the baptism of Jesus, coincides with God's pronouncement of Jesus as Messiah: this is a conventional epic harbinger, but none of the participants can discern its true meaning (a nicely realistic touch, since classical epics abound with trustworthy readers of portents). And within *Paradise Regained* itself no one—not even Jesus—is ever able to offer a definitive interpretation. The epic events, as traditionally conceived, are still to be experienced, created, when Jesus returns to his mother's house. Within this epic structure Jesus must define himself.

The more it is contemplated, the more the temporal framework of *Paradise Regained* seems deliberately shorn of the structures one expects in an epic. Rather than portraying a central figure who embodies his nation's history and whose satisfaction is in setting the stage for a glorious future, as with Aeneas, or who through suffering and endurance will pay the debt demanded by the gods for past overreaching and will stabilize his society through renewing its sense of order, as with Odysseus, Milton places Jesus in a wilderness with neither past nor future detailed and assured. The wilderness comprises a field defined by what it is not, as Milton's epic is placed against an epic tradition that it will not recreate. The absence of past and future determines a vacuum to be filled by the revealed presence of Jesus as the Christ. That presence exists simply and profoundly in the present tense. And what Jesus learns through his spiritual wrestling there is how to live in the present. His psychic integration strips away one external structure after another until, in mental terms, he lives without time. If, in perceiving all epic as encyclopedic but unenclosed, Webber can justly argue that "*In medias res* . . . is one way to describe the whole of epic, not just its beginning," *Paradise Regained* purifies this notion to its ideal.[16]

The temptation on the pinnacle in this way becomes the symbolic, highly compressed climax of the unfolding drama in the wilderness. To exist apart from worldly and temporal structures is, Milton suggests, on a human scale to have vanquished death. Jesus' faith in God does not depend on reward, let alone the fear of punishment; he acknowledges that he will suffer, but does not foresee the Crucifixion. Jesus has no intention of sitting on the right side of his Father. At the end of *Paradise Regained* Jesus is simply what he is. The paradise to be regained is not a life after death, but a life without bounds. The former was what Dante explored, deriving his immense epic vision from the mythic centering of the sixth book of the *Aeneid*. *Paradise Regained* is the first of the major epics to exclude a traditional underworld: presumably it is the place to which Satan falls as Jesus stands secure on the pinnacle, but it is never seen in the course of this epic. Milton's most radical revision of the epic line is implied through this omission.

For the underworld, the centrifugal core of a theodicy where divine justice is revealed, tested, and exonerated, has in *Paradise Regained* been raised to the earth on which Jesus walks:

> [the] Son tracing the Desert wild,
> Sole but with holiest Meditations fed,
> Into himself descended, and at once
> All his great work to come before him set.   (II, 109–12)

The Incarnation, by which God descends to earth, has—as Milton reforms epic convention to accord with Christian revelation—transfigured the underworld. Jesus descends into himself to realize the prophecy that will end with the redemption of all his people. As that redemption promises that there shall be no death, the transformation of the underworld into a vital mental state, liberated from the constraints of time and history, is perfectly congruent with the goal Jesus seeks. More, it implies that goal, is its symbolic core.

It is not, then, Milton's focus on mental rather than physical action, not the lack of heroics, not the diminution of the meaning of history that mark the extent of his epic vision: it is rather the exclusion of death from the world of his epic. The numerous attempts to define what is wanting in *Paradise Regained* that earlier epics possess have always boldly missed the point. What the poem lacks is not encyclopedic scope, but the immense sadness of the traditional epic, even of *Paradise Lost*. Spare, compressed, restrained—paradoxically, *Paradise Regained* celebrates the simple, absolute value of life.

And yet, is that value not at the core of all epics, however diverse or diversely interpreted, a constant able to withstand the profusion and cultural limitations of formal definitions of epic in a way that more customary generic hallmarks cannot? One epic may not have a properly defined hero (*Paradise Lost* is the notorious example); another may lack the comprehensive sense of history threaded through the fabric of the *Aeneid;* the *Odyssey,* with Homer nodding, lacks the charged intensity of the *Iliad,* which in turn, despite its soporific catalog of ships, never embarks on the seas that buffet Odysseus around the known geography of the world. What ultimately are the marks by which we define a work as epic are a set of arbitrary conventions, often without organic purpose but nonetheless in general use, great authorial pretension, an arching sense of the dimensions of the culture represented, and, at the highest level, a theodicy, however undefined within the body of the work. That "justification of the gods" translates into the valuation of human effort in the face of what would thwart it and in measuring the capacity of human beings to mold their environment to the ends of human happiness.

If such a definition would appear unrestrictive or unduly lax by the standards of a Le Bossu or Tillyard, it does allow us to recognize epic intention for what it is, whether in *Paradise Regained,* or in Blake's *Jerusalem,* Byron's *Don Juan,* the *Cantos* of Ezra Pound, or, contemporary with us, the *Canto General* of Pablo Neruda and *Terra Nostra* of Carlos Fuentes.[17] Moreover, if all the major literary genres may be said in some sense to have been distilled from the Homeric epics, epic poetry not only subsumes other genres but commonly is tinctured with the particular emphasis of one or another. The cast of the *Iliad* is tragic; the future course of romance is charted along with the Mediterranean coast in the *Odyssey.* Perhaps that is only to say that the epic evolves with evolving cultures and that all epics will have different permutations as a result. So obvious a formulation is surprisingly infrequent among commentators on the epic in general and on Milton's epics in particular.

Though we may prefer the cosmic dimensions and grand style of *Paradise Lost,* we should be able easily to surmise why Milton in his last years insisted on the primacy of *Paradise Regained.* It is in every sense the purer poem. As Louis Martz succinctly renders the underlying impulse, *Paradise Regained* represents "an inward combat created by Milton's brilliant manipulation of styles, a contest in which the flights of poetic splendor are consistently drawn back by the prevailing net of a frugal style to the ground of renunciation and temperance."[18] From whatever perspective one views the poem, it is seen to be stripped down to bare but resonant essentials. This is especially, even fundamentally, so in respect to genre.

To say that *Paradise Regained* is either *sui generis* or unepic is

finally to betray Milton's fine, introspective grasp of his craft.[19] That the
poem displays elements we associate with other genres than epic is true
enough: in his usual manner, Milton pointedly brings to our attention
his poem's affinity with the debate and with drama in the unrelenting
exchange of his antagonists, with pastoral in its retired setting, with
romance in its emphasis on self-testing and education.[20] But far from
diverting attention from the epic mode, these elements testify to the
true inclusiveness of this epic conception.

What is itself implied by Milton's reliance on epic implication is a
generic mode distilled to its quintessence. Warfare is endemic to epics
not because they all uphold a heroic code or represent martial cultures,
but because it is a metaphor for the agents that would thwart human
aspiration. Jesus is introduced in *Paradise Regained* not by name, but
through a patronymic—"Son of *Joseph*" (I, 23)—and thus abstracted he
is placed between other, likewise abstracted figures: "the great Pro-
claimer" (I, 18), who, like Athena in the *Odyssey*, fulfills the role of
heavenly messenger, and "the Adversary" (I, 33), whose metaphorical
purpose is thus defined. Within such abstract definitions the poem progressively realizes the unlimited potentiality through which a hero
claims the status of demigod against the conventional forms of the natural and cultural environment that restrict such overreaching. Among
the latter are many of the values conventional to the classical epic, but if
Milton is intent on exploding their claim to any ultimacy, he does so to
establish or reaffirm a higher value that is not merely propitious to
human happiness but in its very openness is conceived to be the only
sure key to it.

Yet, the religiosity of *Paradise Regained* is paradoxical in the extreme. No one questions how devout an epic it is, but few remark on
how insistently humane is its orientation—or shall we say insistently
realistic? Wherever one looks, epic conventions are transformed by
being forced to earth. Like other epic heroes, Jesus has a divine patron
and a mission, but uniquely he is left to his own devices without
recourse to intervention or miracle. He is not even granted a vision of
what he will bring to pass. In the first representation of his character
that we are given, we discover him "Musing and much revolving in his
brest, / How best the mighty work he might begin / Of Saviour to
mankind" (I, 185–87); and his epic achievement is to unravel this
purpose without any assistance, except insofar as Satan's adversarial
role whets his mind to ever sharper clarity. Spurning what would limit
him, Jesus allies himself with epic aspiration. And in at last claiming
godhood through the renunciation of any claim for his individual ego,

Jesus establishes an empire larger and more enduring than that founded by Aeneas.

In *Paradise Lost* Milton elaborated a brief and obscure passage from Genesis into the essential myth of Christianity. The pretension is as grandiose as the result is unparalleled in modern literature. In *Paradise Regained* he turned to the New Testament, seizing on an obscure representation in the Gospels and so drawing forth its details as to explore the exemplary nature of Jesus. As different as the two works are, in both Milton employs a strategy which, through epic claim and allusion, forces his reader to examine the nature of epic and one's expectations of it. Insofar as *Paradise Regained* compresses its means and ends to an extraordinary degree, the finer is Milton's touch and the more he requires of his reader, who, "much revolving" in his mind, must, like his exemplar, extract from his experience the true meaning of heroism and of epic achievement.

University of Pennsylvania

NOTES

Translations, except as noted, are by the author.

1. Manchester, 1797. Odgen's earlier efforts were *The British Lion Rous'd, or Acts of the British Worthies* (1762), written to celebrate the British victory in the French and Indian War, and *The Revolution* (1790), commemorating the events of 1688.

2. The 1790s, a period of intense political stress in England, also appear to mark the high point in the reputation of *PR*. Aside from this recasting by Ogden, there is Charles Dunster's variorum edition of the poem (London, 1795), immediately followed by the strong praise for *PR* in William Hayley's *Life of Milton* (London, 1796), which in turn strongly influenced Blake's epic, *Milton*. The terms of this revaluation of *PR* are explored by Joseph Wittreich in *Angel of Apocalypse: Blake's Idea of Milton* (Madison, 1975).

3. P. 110.

4. Lewalski, *Milton's Brief Epic: The Genre, Meaning, and Art of "Paradise Regained"* (Providence, 1966); Webber, *Milton and His Epic Tradition* (Seattle, 1979).

5. E. M. W. Tillyard, in *The English Epic and Its Background* (New York, 1954), does not accord *PR* epic status.

6. Lewalski, *Milton's Brief Epic*, pp. 335–36.

7. *Milton and His Epic Tradition*, p. 170. Burton Jasper Weber begins *Wedges and Wings: The Patterning of "Paradise Regained"* (Carbondale, Ill., 1975), by locating specific sources for the three extended similes of *PR* IV, 10–24, in, respectively, the *Odyssey*, the *Iliad*, and the *Aeneid* (p. 1). The argument is provocative but perhaps too pat: the "sources" are not as close to Milton's similes as Weber would wish them.

8. Francis C. Blessington, *"Paradise Lost" and the Classical Epic* (London, 1979), especially in the first chapter, traces this identification.

9. *Traité du poéme épique* (1675) was translated into English in 1695: see *Treatise of the Epick Poem*, ed. Stuart Curran (Gainesville, Fla., 1970).

10. The allusion was recognized by the earliest editors of the poem. See Richard Meadowcourt, *A Critique on Milton's "Paradise Regained"* (1732), and Charles Dunster's variorum edition of *PR* (1795), in *Milton's "Paradise Regained": Two Eighteenth-Century Critiques*, ed. Joseph Wittreich (Gainesville, Fla., 1971), p. 3.

11. *Aeneid*, I, 278–79, trans. Allen Mandelbaum (New York, 1972).

12. *Milton and His Epic Tradition*, p. 5.

13. Ibid., p. 199. For arguments in support of the appellation "antiepic," see T. J. B. Spencer, "*Paradise Lost*: The Anti-Epic," in *Approaches to "Paradise Lost*," ed. C. A. Patrides (Toronto, 1968), pp. 81–98, and Ralph W. Condee, "Milton's Dialogue with the Epic: *Paradise Regained* and the Tradition," *Yale Review*, LIX (1969–70), 364. My quibble with Condee's term does not detract from the value of his essay.

14. Thomas Maresca, *Three English Epics* (Lincoln, Neb., 1980), sees this interiorization as part of the development of the genre, but, ignoring *PR*, sees its fullest elaboration in *PL*.

15. Both Burton Weber (*Wedges and Wings*, p. 1) and Francis Blessington ("*Paradise Lost*" and the Classical Epic, p. 16) identify this pluralism with Satan.

16. *Milton and His Epic Tradition*, p. 91.

17. Webber, in the afterword to *Milton and His Epic Tradition* (pp. 211–16), recognizes that the epic impulse survives but suggests that it has not produced literature of sufficient cultural intensity to stand comparison with the classical and Renaissance epics. For a different view, one marking Milton's influence on the development of the genre, see Stuart Curran, "The Mental Pinnacle: *Paradise Regained* and the Romantic Four-Book Epic," in *Calm of Mind: Tercentenary Essays on "Paradise Regained" and "Samson Agonistes*," ed. Joseph Wittreich (Cleveland, 1971), pp. 133–62, and Brian Wilkie, *Romantic Poets and Epic Tradition* (Madison, 1965). As my final examples indicate, the contemporary epic is more likely to be found—and venerated—amid the struggles for cultural identity of the Third World than in the West.

18. *Poet of Exile: A Study of Milton's Poetry* (New Haven, 1980), p. 258.

19. See Walter MacKellar, ed., *Paradise Regained*, volume 4 of *A Variorum Commentary on the Poems of John Milton* (New York, 1975), p. 11, who agrees with Northrop Frye, "The Typology of *Paradise Regained*," *MP*, LIII (1956), 235, in calling the poem "practically *sui generis*."

20. On the affinities with drama, consult Arnold Stein, *Heroic Knowledge: An Interpretation of "Paradise Regained" and "Samson Agonistes"* (Minneapolis, 1947); for the interplay of epic and pastoral, see Stewart A. Baker, "Sannazaro and Milton's Brief Epic," *CL*, XX (1968), 116–32; the significance of romance motifs was analyzed by Annabel M. Patterson in her presentation to the Northeast Milton Seminar at New York University, March 29, 1980; cf. her essay in this volume.

THE GENRES OF *PARADISE REGAIN'D* AND *SAMSON AGONISTES:* THE WISDOM OF THEIR JOINT PUBLICATION

John T. Shawcross

V EXING HAVE been the questions underlying the title of this essay: what is the genre of each of these works by John Milton, and why were they published together in one volume? The usual assumptions are that *Paradise Regain'd* is a brief epic, that *Samson Agonistes* is a tragedy, and that the works complement each other through the example of a man, the Son, who overcomes all temptation and the illustration of one particular, typical man, Samson, who has succumbed to temptation but who learns to conquer himself and to achieve true heroism. I have previously grappled with the question of "true heroism" for Milton in an essay which concludes that "Heroic action is thus patience . . . , sacrifice of self for the love of mankind, and opposition to the forces of evil which surround man and are within man."[1] Studies of the poems have offered further contrastive bases for the addition of *Samson Agonistes* to *Paradise Regain'd,* such as "The relationship . . . between perfection and fallibility, between the pattern possessed and the pattern stumblingly groped for, between clarity of the completed understanding and the darkness through which the design is seen in fragments, illuminated by the lightning of the 'great event.' "[2]

While I do not wish to engage in a discussion of the dates of composition of the works, the question is manifestly pertinent. The first publication of the poems (1671) may have been ready as early as May 1670; it was licensed on July 1670, and other evidence lends corroboration to a 1670 date.[3] Thomas Ellwood's often cited and consistently interpreted statement concerning *Paradise Regain'd* is open to a contrastive reading which allows that it derived from an abortive version already in manuscript when Ellwood returned *Paradise Lost.*[4] Dates of composition before the completion of *Paradise Lost* have previously been suggested for both works on various bases, and it is clear that a period of five years (between 1665 and 1670) for the original composition of both works may be questionable. The respective dates of composition

225

are important in suggesting whether the poems were generally coeval (at either a later or earlier date) or whether one, being later, was consciously influenced by the other, earlier poem to effect comparisons and contrasts, or whether one or both were revised to achieve "wisdom of joint publication."

Difficulties of publication in 1665, 1666, and into early 1667, because of the plague and then the Great Fire, may have caused delays in the appearance of *Paradise Lost* until late 1667. *Paradise Regain'd*, were it completed before mid-1670, might have been published separately. If it existed in different form before 1665 (as a dramatic poem?), it was certainly revised after *Paradise Lost* was completed (including epical form?). The move from Jewin Street (where Milton took up residence in early 1661) during 1669 may have been particularly significant in regard to *Paradise Regain'd* and *Samson Agonistes*. Did it delay publication? Did it disrupt writing or postpone the final printer's text? Did it discover another nearly completed work that needed only a year's further writing to develop as finished dramatic poem and companion piece? The addition of *Samson Agonistes* to the 1671 volume could have been a publisher's strategy, changing an otherwise 166-page volume to 220 pages. The title page allows for whatever sales advantage a comparison with *Paradise Lost* would achieve, whether only the first or both poems were included. The phrase "To which is added" on the title page may have been the printer's. A mere "and" would have looked odd on that particular title page; "together with" is a possibility, placing *Samson Agonistes* on a more equivalent status. "To which is added" has a tone making *Samson Agonistes* a lesser work, and thus sounding like the printer's means of emphasizing *Paradise Regain'd* further. Yet *Samson* is not lost on the title page, and its own title page with separate pagination for the poem implies a twofold, balanced volume, similar to Sir Thomas Browne's 1658 *Hydriotaphia Together With The Garden of Cyrus*. While the title page design and wordage may not be Milton's, the publishing of the two works in one volume can be assigned, I believe, to Milton's decision. That decision was dependent, it will be argued, upon the contrasting genres of the two works and the implications of those genres, as well as the modes (and substance) of the works. One poem comments upon and illuminates the other, once their genres and modes are understood.

I

The definition of genre under which I write and which I firmly contend must be acknowledged to rid us of the critical confusion that so often surrounds generic discussion—such as the confusion concerning

the difference between tragedy and the tragic, or satire and the satiric—
is dependent upon a literary work's form, structure, and characteristics,
and its author's intent toward that work. It emphatically does not indicate anything about the author's intent toward the subject matter. For
example, the designation of Andrew Marvell's poem upon Cromwell's
return from Ireland as an "Horation ode" tells us that the form is to be
four-line stanzas in English meters approximating Horace's Latin meters; that the structure is going to interrelate these stanzas without sharp
breaks; that the tone will be elevated and the treatment serious; that it
will be a "public" poem; and that the poem will deal with a significant
national or political event. The genre has been chosen so that readers
will know what to expect, or what to look for. But Marvell's attitude
toward his subject has been variously interpreted. That attitude would
be no different if this poem were cast as a dialogue or a brief epic or a
series of lyric stanzas. The genre, in other words, has nothing to do with
the author's "philosophy" or "political persuasion" or "critical stance" or
such matter, although some genres are more appropriate to certain matter and attitudes than others. Genre itself implies attitude toward content itself. The choice of the genre ode implies significance for the
nation, and perhaps if critics stepped back and looked at Marvell's poem
without trying to make him an adherent of Cromwell or of Charles, of
the Parliamentarian government or of the monarchy, a more meaningful
understanding of the poem would emerge, not of Marvell the political
being but of Marvell the poet.

The structure, form, and characteristics of epic have been examined
extensively, most evidence of description coming from specific "epics"—
the *Iliad*, the *Odyssey*, the *Aeneid*, to begin with. Later epics are often
ranged against these three classical works, leading to such arguments as
whether *Divina Commedia* is or is not an epic. *Paradise Lost*'s relationship to this kind of epic has, of course, been pursued, but little has been
explored for *Paradise Regain'd*. Generally accepted are the following
epic earmarks: The structure of an epic implies a series of episodes and
adventures of or concern with a central figure over a period of time, thus
producing a lengthy poem. These episodes and adventures intertwine,
usually in a nonchronological order, particularly having begun *in medias
res*, using flashback or accounts of things past or building on the device
of simultaneity of action. The form depends on the antagonistic force set
against the central figure. The episodes and the chronology, the number, type, and treatment of other figures, and the need for contrast,
comparison, or verbal motifs will create a form that is simpler or more
complex, straightforward or integrated by repetition and juxtapositions,

and internalizing or creating expansiveness. The *Iliad* and the *Odyssey*, for the most part, represent these two extremes of form: the *Odyssey* in a sense is simpler and expansive, with at least a surface straightforwardness—man in his social world; the *Iliad* is more complex, integrated by subtle repetitions and psychological contrasts, and concerned with the inner man. Characteristics of the epic are tempered by the form, but there is a vastness in the setting, action drawn from deeds of valor and courage, and a significance for man, whether nation, race, or mankind. In classical epic there are supernatural forces at work, invocation of a muse, catalogs, and high style and decorum; speeches are formalized, the theme is stated explicitly, and verbal tags (repeated similes, for example) abound. In descent from classical epic, certain kinds of episodes persist, such as epic games, a descent into hell, a battle between hero and antagonist. Further, the epic, because of its length, vastness, complexity, and public significance, subsumes other genres, styles, and modes (thus making epic genre *genera mixta* and epic mode *mixed modes*).[5]

Mode, as distinguished from genre, depends on the content of a literary work and the author's attitude toward that content. In the example of Marvell's *Horatian Ode*, the content could be of encomiastic mode, satiric mode, elegiac mode, even tragic or comic mode, depending on how the critic reads it. *Paradise Lost* as epic exhibits *mixed modes*, and the one pertinent to this discussion (and overhanging the whole in perspective) is the comic.[6]

Like *Paradise Lost*, *Paradise Regain'd* is called simply "A Poem" on its title page. A well-known section of *The Reason of Church-Government* (the Preface to Book II) sets up labels for the poems by discussing the "diffuse epic" and the "brief epic," with the Book of Job as example. Barbara K. Lewalski has examined *Paradise Regain'd* as "brief epic" on the model of Job in terms of conception and structure.[7] An insistence on an active "military" hero, a beginning *in medias res*, epic devices and verbal echoes, a declaration of intention, a council in heaven and two "infernal" councils, and prophecy of victory all place the poem as epic. Aside from its shorter length and concentration of materials (story, action, characters, and so forth) so that it does not become "diffuse," the poem exhibits strict rules regarding structure and the unities: basically an episode constitutes the whole subject, and the single combat of the hero and his antagonist, the epitome and climax of the more usual epic, becomes the whole subject. Herein lies the essence of its being a brief epic. The unified action, place, and time are most noteworthy, with basically only one action with multiple parts, various locales but all tied to the developing action, and a short period of time for the total action, apparently three days. What little of the past needs to be known is filled in by two soliloquies, the Son's in Book I and Mary's in Book II; what little is needed to anchor the subject in religious history is given by the narrator at the outset of Books I and II, by the talk in the heavenly and infernal councils, and by the dialogue generated by Satan as he tries to evaluate the Son and the rumors which have whirled about him. The formal recital of history, that is, is transformed, and analogous episodes are eschewed.[8] The whole is not diffuse and is concentrated. Further, there is a deemphasis on typology and the supernatural, with no allegoric personifications of psychomachia. Typological symbolism is not superimposed, but made to function dramatically as part of the temptation dialogue.[9] The single combat which constitutes the subject becomes the symbol of the perpetual battle of the Son (that is, of man) and Satan through all time. The emphasis on unity and concentration within the poem has created a bareness of style (easily recognized by comparison with *Paradise Lost*), which William Riley Parker explained "in terms of dramatic models, in terms of decorum."[10]

Donald L. Guss was not entirely happy with the definition of "brief epic" which Lewalski had culled from the tradition and previous criticism and had so greatly extended and developed. His definition of the genre is: "an historical narrative of great personages and events, evoking marvel by presenting a supreme example of virtue."[11] I take it that his unhappiness lay in the presentation of definition, which is not approached as definition, and in the source of much comment being a parade of relatively short poems on religious themes, not all of which are epical, let alone epics. Guss stresses the difference of *Paradise Regain'd* from the epic and particularly from *Paradise Lost:* the lack of magnificence, the lack of cosmological surveys, the lack of martial episodes, the lack of public oratory, the emphasis on character rather than deed, the eschewing of elaboration and turning away from that which is grand, and the plain form and direct style.[12] It is this latter consideration that he pursues as a positive characteristic of the brief epic. "Such a style is plain and weighty without being Senecan. Its individual figures, though perhaps not its total effect, are Biblical. Ellipses, coordination, and epigrammatic phrasing make for a packed style; short phrases, verbal repetitions, and parallelism add weight; repetition of the same content in a series of short phrases yields a somber majesty."[13] This biblical style is seen thus in the distich and in the rhetoric with its contrasted words arranged antithetically and its repetitive meanings given in different words.

Prior to Lewalski's work, Stewart A. Baker turned his attention to the problem of the genre of *Paradise Regain'd* although his views were not available for consultation when Lewalski was engaged in writing and publishing her study. Baker sees the brief epic as a distinct literary form reaching its apogee in Sannazaro's *De partu virginis* and Milton's poem.[14] The genre arose, Baker concludes, from a desire to reconcile elements of the classical epic to the personal, moral, and didactic interests of the New Testament and hagiological materials. Its style and structure result from the unheroic and disjointed sequence of Gospel narratives, being thus suitable to meditation and moral debate. It is a middle style, lying between the temperate, didactic style of Jesus and the highly colored rhetorical style of Satan. The metaphor of the Christian soldier allows the unmilitary, moral hero the stature of the epic military hero, Baker argues, exalting by contrast and inversion his moral heroism. The brief epic is therefore one employing objective epic motifs in an absolute moral framework, centering around a brief but significant episode from the hero's career. Its aim is to interpret that career and position in universal Christian history; its strategy lies in meditative soliloquies, didactic orations, scenes of debate, and prophecy.

In a revised form of a major article on the meditative dimension of the poem, Louis L. Martz stresses its didactic nature and merges it with the form and style of Vergil's *Georgics*.[15] He cites Charles Dunster's label, "the *brief*, or didactic, epic,"[16] and suggests a kind of parallelism between *Paradise Lost* / *Aeneid* and *Paradise Regain'd* / *Georgics*. "*Paradise Regain'd* shows the Son in his second, his internal function. Through a process of renunciation *Paradise Regain'd* gradually reveals the voice of Truth speaking within the illuminated mind."[17]

The critical analyses of the poem summarized in the foregoing paragraphs (which at times offer more definition than their originals) are certainly correct and instructive of a good understanding of Milton's achievements in *Paradise Regain'd*. The one thing that bothers me is that little attention is paid to the genre brief epic except as *Paradise Regain'd* exhibits what characteristics will then be used to define that genre. Are all brief epics didactic, as Dunster wrote? Are all brief epics concerned with specific moral issues and virtue, and religiously oriented? Are all brief epics necessarily historical? Are all brief epics written in a plain (and biblical) style or a middle style? Stuart A. Curran warns us that no expectation of the diffuse epic is omitted in the brief epic except its diffuseness.

The brief epic is not a scale model but a concentrated form of its grander counterpart; and just as it tends to turn in upon itself in shape, so, too, there is a comparable internalization of idea. The struggle between good and evil, which is the basic component of all epics, becomes centered in a single individual representative of man, and from his internal conflict emerges the scope of human life, its triumphs and limitations.[18]

It is this kind of definition of brief epic that we need: a definition in terms of form, structure, characteristics, and authorial attitude (the external and the internal forms of a genre) which will be useful in discussing, say, the poems of the Romantics which Curran's discussion suggests (like Robert Southey's *Thalaba the Destroyer*) or the narrative poems of Edwin Arlington Robinson (like *Merlin*).

Accordingly I suggest the following definition of the brief epic, building upon the concepts reviewed before: It is a poetic narrative, perhaps divided into a few (three to seven?) sections or books and totaling, perhaps, something like one to three thousand lines. It depicts one episode in the life of a central figure within a circumscribed period of time, presented ostensibly in chronological order; it may seem to begin *in medias res* (though it does not) by being drawn out of the hero's full life, that which is pertinent from the past being filled in by short accounts given by characters or the narrative voice. (It is possible, we should note, that the "central figure" could be a group treated as an individual, the episode being a timed section out of its fuller existence. However, the complexities which could arise make this generally unlikely for the brief epic.) Its meter is not different from that of the long epic and thus may be traditionally hexameter or blank verse, or less traditionally rhymed verse, so-called free verse, or mixed writing (including stanzaic forms, patterned and nonpatterned meters, or prose).[19] Because the subject of the narrative is one episode, intertwining of story or character elements is minimal and simultaneity of action is greatly reduced, but both intertwining and simultaneity will exist clearly and immediately in relationship with the central figure or the episode. The settings (if more than one) are few. While vastness and cosmological significance may exist in the brief epic, the panoramic vision and sense of man's relation to the space of nature are given smaller compass, with the central figure constantly as the focus. Such characteristics as invocations, catalogs, encyclopedic knowledge, explicit statement of theme and intention, verbal tags and epic devices, prophecy in terms of either the afterward or the public significance arising from the deeds of valor and courage—all may appear and probably do in some form. Aside from the length and lessening of complexities of story, characters, place, and time, the brief epic distinguishes itself by constantly foregrounding the central figure and thereby creating internalization of the action. (Those who find Books V through VI and XI through XII generally excrescences on *Paradise Lost* are, of course, looking at that long epic as one that should constantly foreground Adam and Eve, as if the poem were not a "diffuse" epic; for them apparently it is a poem on Adam and Eve and the Fall, rather than a poem on the losing of Paradise.) Internalization may create a greater emphasis on character than on deed, as in *Paradise Regain'd*, but the brief epic as genre does not as a necessity for classification reduce deeds. (In contrast are the internalizations of Samson, which effect a character finally capable of one great deed.) Likewise there may be a greater emphasis on speech than on narration, as in *Paradise Regain'd* (the verbal debate here engaging the "military" and battle of protagonist and antagonist), but the brief epic as genre does not as necessity for classification demand this imbalance. The significance of any epic—long (diffuse) or brief—lies in the struggle between good and evil for a public audience which is represented by the central figure. The antagonist may, of course, be more than one person, just as in *Samson Agonistes* Samson is beset by father, wife, champion, and Philistines. Such comparative and contrastive treatment of the protagonists of these two works of contrastive genres is enhanced by the double publication in one volume and urges a reading of *Samson Agonistes* which almost exclusively stresses Samson's internalizations. We can almost paraphrase Martz and say, "Through a process of renunciation *Samson Agonistes* gradually reveals the voice of Truth speaking within the illuminated mind."

The preceding, I hope, defines brief epic as genre, rejecting as part of that definition certain concepts which commentators have advanced because they are exhibited in *Paradise Regain'd*. The definition fits *Paradise Regain'd* and thus further suggests that all brief epics are not necessarily historical. As epic, the brief epic should offer mixed genres, mixed modes, and mixed styles. As an earmark of genre, the style of *Paradise Regain'd* that has been described variously by critics therefore has no pertinency. *Paradise Regain'd* does indeed show mixed genres— the hymn, the ode, the dramatic dialogue and the soliloquy, the philosophical poem, the pastoral among them; mixed modes—the tragic and the comic (see later); and mixed styles, as Baker's and Guss's discussions suggest. While there is a bareness in comparison with *Paradise Lost* (which exhibits high, middle, and falsely high styles) and *Samson Agonistes* (a high style that is very different from that in most of *Paradise Lost* because it is fully in human speech), the style of *Paradise Regain'd* intermixes high and middle and plain styles (that is, if we look at middle and plain as being different). The concentration of the brief epic and the reduction of those elements making for complexities will alter the tone and feeling from what they would have been in the diffuse epic, but a specific style is not necessarily attached to the brief epic that is any different from the style of the diffuse epic. The differences among the three major poems of Milton in these regards should be attributed to other reasons, not to genre.

II

William Riley Parker demonstrated that *Samson Agonistes* is built on the structure of Greek drama: there are a *prologos*, a *parados* (or choral ode bringing the chorus on stage), followed by five *epeisodia*, each followed by a *stasimon* (or choral ode), and finally an *exodos* in which is contained a *kommos* (or lament).[20] The episodes confront Samson and the Chorus, Samson and Manoa, Samson and Dalila, Samson and Harapha, and Samson and the Officer. The balance of the organization is clear: the triple temptation to alleged necessity with emphasis upon ease of body, to fraudulence with emphasis upon worldly vanities, and to violence with emphasis upon unfaithfulness to and rivalling of God defines the three central episodes. The first episode has Samson abjectly giving information to a group of compatriots, who speak as one voice, while the final episode has him defiantly rejecting the demands of an officer acting for the Philistine lords. While *Prometheus Bound* and *Oedipus at Colonus* offer somewhat similar structures, they are not symmetric or so organized and so do not offer like episodes or ending. This is an important point, underscoring Milton's use of but transcendence of Greek dramatic form. The uncritical labelling of this work which Milton called a "dramatic poem" as a play or a drama or a tragedy unfortunately demands our attention to these negatively comparative matters.

Since *Prometheus Bound* was apparently part of a trilogy which is not extant, it does not contain the whole of the literary concept being fashioned by Aeschylus, as *Samson* does for Milton's. *Prometheus Bound* appears to be the first play in a trilogy, and we come to anticipate *Prometheus Unbound* and *Prometheus the Fire-Bearer*. *Oedipus at Colonus*, on the other hand, assumes knowledge of *Oedipus Rex* and even *Antigone* at times, appearing as what might have been the last play in a trilogy, although it was not. It was written very late in Sophocles' career, and separately. Some of the parallels with *Samson Agonistes* are strong, but Milton's dramatic poem supplies the background material which brings us to understand what has happened to Samson before the work opens and prepares us to understand the characters and action of the work while they are before us and it is occurring. Contrastively *The Trojan Woman* is more of a pageant cut from the full swath of what might have been a long presentation of war; it is not clearly a beginning, a middle, or an end. *Samson Agonistes* combines all of these into one; its middle section, reflecting the pageantlike technique of the Euripidean play, led Samuel Johnson to his well-known quip that *Samson* has no middle. Quite to the contrary, its middle—the Manoa, Dalila, and Harapha episodes—constitutes, as it were, *Samson Unbound*, that is, the movement from *Samson Bound* that we have come to recognize in the retellings in the prologue and first episode, to *Samson the Fire-Bearer* that we are presented with as the type to lead men from bondage. For men to become unbound, like Samson, they must conquer the triple temptation and then proceed to act. In reverse of *The Trojan Women*, whose main characters are about to embark for Greece to "the new long day" which "dawneth to slavery," Samson leaves the people of Dan supposedly to embark on a new long day which dawneth to freedom. It is an ironic ending when compared with that of *Oedipus at Colonus* or that of *The Trojan Women*. In all, Milton's work seems to take on many features, situations, actions, and the accompanying language of numerous extant Greek plays. It is a distillation, one might say, of the prototypical Greek drama. But it is not a drama in the generic meaning of that word.

In none of the extant Greek plays is the structure so balanced as in *Samson Agonistes*, with its clear focus on the three central sections subsuming the temptation motif (the flesh, the world, and the devil) and the increasing alteration in Samson's attitude toward himself through them—he conquers self-pity, dependence on others' opinions, and pride. The balancing of the structure puts greatest focus on the Dalila section as one climax of the work and in view of Samson's fall and uxoriousness in the past we understand why this must be the central point of reversal of past transgression. The contrasts with the Manoa section preceding and the Harapha section following emphasize that this is the reversal of the drama taking place in terms of Samson's character. Yet the developing of Samson's attitude toward himself opposes a pyramidic structure, since it grows steadily from the very beginning of the work to its very end, with its climax coming as the inward eyes are illuminated. Similar development occurs in *Oedipus at Colonus*, and recently Carole Kessner has demonstrated a like pattern in Euripides' *Herakles*.[21] Oedipus moves from hardness to gentleness of person, a kind of purification resulting from a divine grace whereby he becomes vehicle for universal power. And some of the people he meets—Creon, Polyneices—evoke reactions similar to Samson's when he confronts Dalila and Harapha, helping to develop this change. The main difference in the two works—disregarding the obvious differences caused by subject matter and legends—lies in the culmination of that development of self: Oedipus, according to the messenger's report, simply takes leave of his children, delivers them to the charge of Theseus, and dies with only Theseus present. The emphasis throughout is upon Oedipus as person, not as leader of a people; what happens to Oedipus is significant only for Oedipus and his immediate relatives; the reader can identify with him as he can with Lear. What happens to Samson is supposed to have significance for the people of Dan, is supposed to bring to pass his early destiny of beginning to deliver Israel out of the hand of the Philistines. He is not simply the biblical figure wreaking revenge: he is a type of the Son exemplifying what must be done to escape from bondage. Accordingly this literary vehicle is quite different from the Greek play. We are not merely shown action on stage, although the author is external to the work. We are being manipulated by the imagery, the structure, the echoes, all of which contribute to understanding of the main character and his alteration of attitudes and to the denouement and its significance.[22] In Oedipus we see what we might become ourselves; in Samson we see what we should become. The nature of the employment of these elements is closer to a poem than to the usual play, although certainly such plays as Shakespeare's great tragedies illustrate poetic techniques. The point is that *Samson Agonistes* does more than present just dramatic narrative and characterization, with emphasis on story and characters. Like a poem it engages a closer reading rather than only a visual presentation of something that might have happened, even though the stage scene does offer an accumulation of prior elements that impinge on each successive point in the play. The "build" of a play is linear; of a poem, often convoluted. (This, I assume, is what made it never intended to the stage.) *Samson Agonistes* is not a drama but a kind of poem, one that is cast as a drama and that involves dramatic techniques and effects, but it is a work for reading and mulling over.[23]

The genre drama, though impossible to define in absolute terms, takes the form of characters on a stage speaking to themselves individually or in some kind of conversation between or among themselves; its structure implies acts and scenes; its characteristics include "imitated human action" (according to Aristotle) in some kind of story, with a generally external author. The drama takes on the limitations of the dramatis personae speaking in character and performing specific actions:

it must work within the possible, although it may verge on the unconvincing since these characters are not necessarily the viewer and their actions are not necessarily the viewer's. (Even fantasy lies within the realm of the possible once certain premises are accepted; for example, that there are faerie spirits, like Ariel or Peter Pan, or that animals can talk, as assumed for "Mr. Ed" of the former television show.) Drama allows direct experience for the viewer without, seemingly, an authorial filter: the emphasis is on verisimilitude. The action is supposedly occurring as it is viewed, with its pattern being devised organically. It is not recollected, as is a poem, with its pattern being shaped by hindsight.

A poem, on the other hand, unclassified as to subgenre, involves imagination and sense impressions arising from the language, and so forth, with the authorial intent clearly being to involve the reader in exercise of his imagination so as to proceed to the more improbable of thought and action and ultimately the more convincing since the reader has internalized, and not just vicariously. A dramatic poem would obviously partake of both generic positions at once, but "dramatic" would involve more lineaments of drama and "poem" more substance of poetry. As Denis Donoghue distinguishes,

A poem consists of words. Whatever we choose to regard as the unit of poetic composition—the single word, the syntactical unit, the verse-line—is necessarily verbal. But the unit of a play is not encompassed within the verbal realm. If one isolates a moment from the thousands of contiguous moments in a play, one should regard as the unit of theatrical composition everything that is happening in that moment, simultaneously apprehended. Words are being spoken, gestures are being made, the plot is pressing forward, a visual image is being conveyed on the stage itself.[24]

These latter remarks do not define *Samson Agonistes*. While the change in the character Samson presses forward and each moment allows us simultaneously to apprehend that change, plot does not exist and visual image is not significant.

Samson Agonistes takes on the form of characters on a verbal stage speaking to themselves or in conversation; its structure does not imply acts and scenes, resembling instead a kind of pageant,[25] and thus it does not emphasize a story. Legend is recalled, and what happens on this verbal stage is that the main character alters in mood, attitude, and resolve from despair to fortitude and action—not what we consider a "story." It has been called static, and doubts have been raised about its viability on the theatrical stage (despite some apparently successful readings). Of course: we move out of "imitated human action," with limitations in such action, to the realm of potential human action with few limitations placed on that potentiality. We are convinced by Samson's alteration of mood, attitude, and resolve by empathy, devised through the poetry, and we are convinced that some action—the destruction of the Temple in any meaning appropriate to any specific circumstance of the reader—can be achieved to point the way to freedom from bondage by the Philistines of this world. Allegoric mode is not far away.

The author is external, as in a drama, except that one hears in some of the Chorus's words ideas which are supposed to voice the author's beliefs. But one reads in the language and imagery universal meanings, not just autobiographical and temporal concerns. The question of autobiography and temporality has long been an issue in interpreting the work. Since it has traditionally been dated between 1667 and 1670, allusions have been alleged concerned largely with Milton's blindness, his marriage difficulties with Mary Powell, his contention with Salmasius, and his disillusionment with the fall of the Cromwellian government and the return of the monarchy. This view of the work leads to such interpretations of the poem as Radzinowicz's "Milton wanted to show how his own nation had erred and betrayed the light of God within them; he wanted to show the responsibility of the English people for their tragic enslavement; and in giving them an instance of God's renewal of freedom, he wanted to dramatize the possiblity of recovering liberty, of remaking their national life when they saw occasion."[26] The reductionism in that statement almost removes the work from literature to propaganda. Earlier dating alleges that Milton's blindness is not significant, that Dalila in no way relates to Mary, that Harapha in no way equates with Salmasius, and that the poem does not exhibit post-Restoration references or attitudes. This view of the work has led to some suggestion that it is divorced from the author and his life. The major problem with the various interpretations, it seems to me, is that they begin with a concept of dating firmly in mind, most being on the side of the traditional date. Obvious cases in point are Hugh Richmond's discussion (traditional dating) and Parker's comments upon the lack of theological position in the work (early dating).[27]

I do not want to quibble about definitions, particularly these which are so very slippery. My point is simple: *Samson Agonistes* has quite consistently been read as a drama, not as a poem, and this has led to such criticism—some of it important and "correct" in its own way—as Samuel Johnson's and Parker's and Woodhouse's. But it has at the same time led to misunderstanding of what is going on in the poem, why it is structured as it is, and what Milton's intention was. I argue that we should read the poem as a poem—as we would *Lycidas* or Shelley's *Triumph of Life* or Frost's *West-Running Brook*. As poem, *Samson Agonistes* makes clear that Milton's intention was to achieve reader internalization of the substance, or message, or emotions, or attitudes which will be found in the poem. It does not imply what these are, only that it should not be viewed and made ineffectual by the belief that we have seen an "imitation" of human action, where but by the grace of God we might have gone.[28]

Whenever the work itself may have been started, or developed, or finished, the preliminary statement about the dramatic poem must have been written around the time of publication, between 1668 and 1670.[29] At this time the literary world was particularly concerned with generic labels. *Paradise Lost* (1667) as well as *Paradise Regain'd* (1671) is specifically called just "A Poem," and so is Dryden's *Absalom and Achitophel* (1681), the latter a fact to remember when satire is the topic. (*Absalom and Achitophel* is a poem in the satiric mode, not a verse satire.) If genre has any real significance, it is to clue the reader to the expectations of the author in relation to the reader. The author is telling the reader what to expect, how to read the work, what to look for, and what the characteristics and form of the work are. This does not mean that some of the characteristics and form may not be altered from the standard, as in a fifteen-line sonnet. *Samson Agonistes* is both dramatic and a poem, but the emphasis is on its being read as a poem. The preliminary statement discusses "That sort of Dramatic poem which is call'd tragedy," "the most profitable of all other Poems."[30] Milton's examples of tragedies are clearly what we would label plays, but his work does not have acts and scenes because these refer chiefly to the theatrical stage. And Milton begs comparison with plays by talking of verisimilitude and "the circumscription of time wherein the whole Drama begins and ends."

The genre of *Samson Agonistes*, then, is drama by form and characteristics, but poem by execution and structure; drama by authorial attitude toward his material, but poem by authorial intent for his audience. The work has the form and many of the characteristics of drama, but it has some characteristics and the intention of the poem. It is not the drama of *Herakles* or *Philoctetes*. It is not the poetic drama of *Othello* or *Antony and Cleopatra*. It is close to the published *Comus* as genre, a hybrid that I would suggest combines the masque drama of the theatrical *Comus* of 1634 and the altered, more "poetic" version of 1637. *Samson Agonistes* differs from the dramatic sections of the poem *Paradise Lost* by dint of totally different form and ratios of dramatic and poetic characteristics. And it contrasts particularly with *Paradise Regain'd*, that poem consisting largely of speech lines.

III

Repetition is not needed to compare these two companion pieces in genre: one is a poem with much dialogue cast as an epic form; the other is a poem fully in speech cast as a dramatic form.[31] But their modes must be attended to—the first comic, the second tragic. Patrick Cullen, writing of the design of the poems as companion pieces, shows that they provide "a Christian definition of the two great poetic modes, the heroic and the tragic."[32] Heroic (or epic) mode does not necessitate that a work be "comic" or "tragic," and indeed the epical would subsume both effects in some way. In *Paradise Regain'd* that heroic mode subtends both the tragic potentiality which succumbing to temptation would bring and the comic potentiality which the defeat of evil sets up. The overall effect is comic, since nothing potentially tragic (for example, the storm) prevails. By mode, it will be remembered, I mean the authorial attitude toward the subject matter of the literary work or basically what is expected as reader reaction. Comic mode implies futural significance, some form of joy at least, life and continuance, interest in the central character in the future, defeat or nullification of negative forces (even to the point of averting tragic occurrences). I have, surely, just defined *Paradise Regain'd* as Jesus returns to his mother's house, soon to embark on his ministry in the world and do his father's bidding. For Milton this must have been the essence of the comic in life.

No one has doubted the tragic mode of *Samson Agonistes*, regardless of the specific definition employed (although questions have been raised about its being a tragedy). Only the somewhat comic figure of Harapha or his lines, the Chorus's overblown description of Dalila, and some of the poetry (largely the obstreperous rhyme) of a few choruses have raised a question of dismay alongside recognition of "the Poets error of intermixing Comic stuff with Tragic sadness and gravity." Futural significance is not important for the reader of *Samson*, since the reader is concerned only with Samson, now dead, not with Manoa, Dalila, Harapha, or even the people of Dan, despite the irony of their continued subservience. There can be no joy, even if some of the bad guys have got theirs; the negative forces are not nullified. Nor are we involved in life and continuance. The tragic *Samson Agonistes* which arises against the comic *Paradise Regain'd*, with greater focus because of their order, darkens whatever catharsis is felt and underlines the waste that has been endured in achieving a triumph of will over weakness.

Here, as against the comic of the companion poem, is the essence of the tragic. Mere capitulation to weakness, transitory or unremitted, is not the core: the waste in finally achieving the "fairer Paradise" is.

Others' overviews of the three major works have delineated a pattern of *Paradise Regain'd* and *Samson Agonistes* as companion poems and as developments out of *Paradise Lost*. Joseph Wittreich discusses the way in which *Paradise Regain'd* interprets *Paradise Lost,* and then in turn how *Samson Agonistes* interprets *Paradise Regain'd.*[33] Radzinowicz makes the relationship particularly clear in remarking that in the conclusion of *Paradise Lost* "two themes for future treatment are explicit . . . : the example of the 'Redeemer ever blest' and his version of heroic fortitude, and the addition of human deeds to faith, virtue, patience, temperance, and love in proportion to the knowledge of God given to any man."[34] Wittreich parts company with many commentators on *Samson Agonistes* (for example, as he himself notes, with Arnold Stein's view that the hero of each poem "presents a human and individual way to the same truth"[35]) when he calls it a warning or negative example, thus stressing Samson's fall prior to the beginning of the work and the action required to nullify or reverse that negativity.[36] Like others, Wittreich does not see Samson as a type of Christ but rather as ordinary man, Christ's opposite type, who must undergo the internal trials that Samson does in order to be renovated.[37] Samson, contrasting with the Son of *Paradise Regain'd,* is "a hero binding men down to the cycles of history."[38] This accords with my own view of the poem, approached from a totally different angle. I have previously argued that the real tragedy of *Samson Agonistes* lies in our recognition as the poem ends "that Samson's story is constantly played through time and that we are part of another recurrence."[39] The wisdom of putting these two works together in the same volume is the commerce which is thus established between them: we see in Samson what the Son as Man could have become had he succumbed to any of the temptations of Satan, and in the Son we see what Samson as the "great Deliverer"—the ironic earthly counterpart of the true "heavenly" deliverer—should have been. Perhaps we have misread *Samson Agonistes* so ineptly in the past[40] because we have not fully acknowledged the interrelationships of the two works, seeing the second as a kind of *Lear* in which the hero's "fall" has really occurred prior to the opening of the play and is made visible in his incomprehensible division of his kingdom as it begins. Samson is not Lear; he is rather, to appropriate Wittreich's word, a negative Christ.

The order of the poems in the volume is logical on two counts:

Paradise Regain'd links with *Paradise Lost,* directly of course in its opening sections but also in its development of a major theme of the longer epic; and *Samson Agonistes* moves to the real from the ideal, to the common condition of all men, to the world itself. The reality of the world in *Paradise Lost* is only to begin as Adam and Eve leave Paradise (although we have viewed that world in speculation in Books XI and XII): to understand the meaning of the condition of that real world we need to contrast the ideal. The volume does not offer the buoying up that perhaps the reversal of the poems might create, but Milton's message has never been involved in that kind of falseness, a point to be remembered, I think, as we end *Lycidas*. The fresh woods and pastures new are not going to be without the anxieties defined by the gadding vine, the thankless muse, the fatal and perfidious bark, or the blind mouths. *Samson Agonistes* exemplifies the world that one man chose until Providence truly became his guide; *Paradise Regain'd*, by appearing first, has sharpened the reader's understanding of choice and its commitments. Like an early Jonathan Edwards, Milton can be seen to suggest that freedom of will is lessened each time one makes a choice: the Son keeps his freedom of will by choosing not to act; Samson lessens his freedom each time he chooses to act. What men must learn, Milton implies, is that action should maintain a confederacy with God, who will contribute to that action as guide or provider.

In a forthcoming article on Milton and covenant, I have indicated another important contrast between these two poems. In *Paradise Regain'd* the covenant of grace, existent since the protevangelium, is undergoing change into the New Covenant during the time period of the poem. Milton believed that the Mosaic Law as delivered on Mount Sinai was part of the covenant of grace, not a covenant of works, and that the New Covenant, "far more excellent and perfect than the law" (CM, XVI, 113), abolished the Old Covenant. As I comment in my article, "the tension of the poem is that between the Old Covenant, which was represented by the Law and which gave promise of Messiah, and the New Covenant which is represented by inward law and which is in the process of being created by the Messiah who has come." Satan knows none of this, although the Son is certainly aware that he himself is the Messiah. Satan's temptations, thus, try to get the Son to abrogate the Law and thereby, whether man or man-god, fall from grace. But the Son is filled with an inward law which is asserted and reasserted as its maintenance becomes increasingly difficult. In contrast is *Samson Agonistes* in which the central character can operate only under the Law in his maintenance of the covenant of grace. He, as Hebraic hero, conceives of works as his action in asserting covenant—the slaying of the men at Ashkelon, the hundred foxes, the ass's jawbone. He has, in Milton's view, been wrong, for real achievement comes through action of the inward spirit. It is through the temptations of Manoa, Dalila, and Harapha that Samson is able to develop inward law as he retreats from engagement with mere "works" or rejects them. Succumbing to the first temptation offered by Manoa would constitute relief from Mosaic law, which under the covenant of grace would be an abrogation of the covenant by Samson.[41] Such relief denied, Samson has begun a process of renovation,[42] that which all men can undergo, for God "excludes no man from the way of penitence and eternal salvation, unless that man has continued to reject and despise the offer of grace, and of grace sufficient for salvation, until it is too late" (YP, VI, 194).

While the Son has inward law and exhibits it under increasingly distressful circumstances, Samson develops such inward law (his "inward eyes" are illuminated) and proceeds to his one great work of deliverance, not constrained, not knowing what cause draws him, knowing only that he is now able to do something but "Nothing dishonourable, impure, unworthy / Our God, our Law, my Nation, or my self" (1424–25). *Samson Agonistes* complements *Paradise Regain'd*, where the New Covenant is developed through the Son's actions and contrasted with the Old Covenant under which Satan operates, by exemplifying the covenant of grace as operative under the Old Covenant while invalidating the concept of a covenant of works. Read as a dramatic poem (rather than as a play), one of the major questions of interpretation of *Samson Agonistes* may be solved: its dramatic proportion suggests an organic developing pattern, and its poetic proportion emphasizes the internalization within the work and in the reader, as the inward law emerges from within Samson.

The renovation of Samson (his turning back to God) is developed by confirmation of the self and the past (as in the *prologos*, *parados*, and first episode), by conquering the assaults that have triumphed in the past (as in the three central episodes of ease, worldly position, and pride), and by action (as developed in the fifth episode and reported in the *exodos*). The example of the Son (his dedication to God) is observed by his confirmation of self and the uncertain future (in his soliloquy of Book I), by rejection of self-concerns (in the first temptation), by confuting worldly goods—wealth, power, glory (in the second temptation), and by faith (in the third temptation)—rejection, confutation, and faith all equating action of the inward spirit. It should be clear that the "movement" of the middle episodes of *Samson Agonistes*, though these offer dialogue and opposed actions, presents types in Manoa, Dalila, and Harapha who beset Samson's inward being almost as if in a dream vision—one who must be a stalwart, unmoving central character (not unlike the Son in this regard) assailed by externalities that do not penetrate but are buffeted off (not unlike Satan, it is clear).

Problems in interpretation and understanding that have apparently existed in terms of the volume for scholars may be removed, I think, by recognizing the complementarity of the works: together they form a whole for man, depicting life in all its bifurcations. Typical, perhaps, is the following. In commenting on what he considered "the substance and language of [*Paradise Regain'd's*] gratuitous comment on both women and Greek tragedy," Parker wrote, "To move, in the 1671 volume from Book IV of *Paradise Regained* on to the Preface of *Samson Agonistes* is to encounter intellectual confusion."[43] It would seem the works were quite separate in thought for him, *Samson* being earlier, *Paradise Regain'd* at a distance in time and thus encompassing later concepts. There is no intellectual confusion on Milton's part, whatever the dates of the two poems. The so-called gratuitous comment on women is not a comment on "women" but on the supplying of numerous women for sexual purposes only, as Belial implies. Satan rejects such a lure (the "fond desire" of II, 211) for Jesus; he rejects "the bait of Women" (II, 204) and dotage "on womankind, admiring / Thir shape, thir colour, and attractive grace" (II, 175–76). He does not reject marital relationship for Jesus, nor can he, despite the rather obtusely prudish reactions of some readers, who really seem incapable of reading with understanding Milton's classification of the previous items as "toys" (II, 177) which "Fall flat and shrink into a trivial toy" (II, 223) once admiration is gone. The passage provides a clever way by which Milton was able to include sexual temptation for the Son of God without actually including it; he had to make some reference to sexual appetite, for it is such a major influence in man's life (the Son had emptied himself of godhead!), aside from its obvious relationship with the lure of *voluptaria* in the full-scale temptation motif. Milton is putting down promiscuous sex, not sex, and certainly not marital sex. In the Son we have the sexually abstemious; in contrast Samson is able to unite the temptation of sex and marital sex by convincing himself that the woman of Timna and then Dalila are both worthy to be his wife, only to find himself wrong. But he should have known, of course, that their harlotry might involve sexual insincerity. It is clear that he had been led by his sexual appetite and has rationalized his position to make himself (as agent for his God) psychologically acceptable to himself. The comment in *Paradise Regain'd* is neither pertinent to the point Parker was alleging nor gratuitous: it stresses a motif that is contrasted in *Samson Agonistes*. If we cannot read *Paradise Regain'd* adequately, we have the more mundane *Samson Agonistes* to help us. The complementarity of the two poems is evident in even this relatively small point of substance and thought.

The alleged rejection of Greek learning in *Paradise Regain'd* on Milton's part has had a long history of explication, most of it out of context of the temptation motif of which it is a part. This section is part of the second temptation to worldly things and covetousness; it does not involve seeming necessity (as the first does—hunger) but plurality and nonessentiality. (Belial's women are, likewise, part of the second temptation, offering "plural" and "nonessential" sex, as it were.) The second temptation presents lures that impinge on man's relationship with his community (the first being with himself, the third with his God). The Son argues for basic knowledge and wisdom as against pluralities and nonessential matter (because of their being derived from or ancillary to the basic knowledge in the Bible and particularly in the Psalms). Community, however, is impressed by fine and numerous images of possession, by wealth and glory, and by intellectual show. The comment on the tragedians (IV, 261–66), in the midst of the temptation to assert knowledge over one's fellow man, is neither pertinent to what Parker was assigning it (a "later utterance of Milton's spirit") nor gratuitous: the Son rejects Satan's temptation, and in so doing rejects as "plural" and "nonessential" the alleged "doctrine," the "moral prudence," the "sage Philosophy" which the Greek oratory listed subtends. His point is that wisdom lies in the teachings of God as seen in "*Sion's* songs," in the plainness of the prophets, in the rather singular substance of the Bible, which offers essential knowledge. Satan talks of the "lofty grave Tragoedians" who best teach "moral prudence, with delight receiv'd / In brief sentilious precepts, while they treat / Of fate, and chance, and change in human life; / High actions, and high passions best describing" (*PR* IV, 261–66). The Son rejects the necessity of an intervener, an interpreter for him "who receives / Light from above, from the fountain of light"; he "no other doctrine needs, *though granted true*" (*PR*, IV, 288–90; my italics). The implication is clear: there are those who do not receive the light from above which is open to them. The "better teaching" of the prophets is lost on them. For them some intermediary presentation of "moral prudence, with delight" is necessary, and it is for this reason that Spenser was a better teacher than Aquinas, since the "delight" is missing from the latter's work. The concept is made tangible as we move in the 1671 volume to *Samson Agonistes:* for those who need an intermediary presentation of "moral prudence, with delight," we have a dramatic presentation based on the arts of Greece, but the substance praises God aright, rejects "Fortune and Fate" in favor of Providence, and expresses "moral vertue . . . By light of Nature not in all quite lost" (*PR* IV, 351–52). The plainness of *Paradise Regain'd*, the "majestic unaffected stile," is consciously adhered to as contrast with the "swelling Epithetes" of this Greek form which takes its substance from the "Law and Story" of God's accommodated fountain of light.

We have in these two works published together complementary forces which contrast forms and structures, genres and modes, poetic styles and tone, characters and narrative, treatment of the subject matter, the forms of heroic action, the suprahuman and the distressingly human. But also present is the duplication of message, covenantal concerns, the substance of the subject matter, and means "to imbreed and cherish in a great people the seeds of vertu" (*Reason of Church-Government*, YP, I, 816). *Paradise Lost* had failed, or so it seemed: witness its disrepute between 1667 and 1669 and its apparent lack of importance until the fourth edition of 1688; witness that question which Ellwood had put to him at Chalfont St. Giles. Both works were needed in order for Milton to achieve "those intentions which [had] liv'd within [him] ever since [he] could conceiv [himself] any thing worth to [his] Countrie" (*Reason of Church-Government*, YP, I, 820). *Paradise Regain'd* offered truth to the intellect; *Samson Agonistes*, to the heart. Wisdom cries out from all places, both the tops thereof and in the streets.

University of Kentucky

NOTES

1. "The Hero of *Paradise Lost* One More Time," in *Milton and the Art of Sacred Song*, ed. Roger D. Sundell and J. Max Patrick (Madison, 1979), p. 146.

2. The words are Balachandra Rajan's in " 'To Which is Added *Samson Agonistes*—'," in *The Prison and the Pinnacle*, ed. Rajan (Toronto, 1973), p. 98.

3. I refer to book and library catalogs, early biographical reports, and the title pages of the volume itself, the dates of which seem to have been originally MDCLX, with a second X and I added separately, slightly out of line with the rest of the date and creating a noncentering. The second X is from a different font.

4. See *The History of the Life of Thomas Ellwood* (London, 1714), pp. 233–34. It is incomprehensible to me that critics read Ellwood's remark to mean, essentially, that Ellwood put the substance of *PR* into Milton's mind rather than the need for *PR*. The

poem was surely needed for anyone who could read *PL* and wonder what Milton had to say about "Paradise *found*" rather than *regained*.

5. See Roger Rollin's discussion of *"Paradise Lost:* 'Tragical-Comical-Historical-Pastoral'," in *Milton Studies*, ed. James D. Simmonds (Pittsburgh, 1973), pp. 3–37. The elements of romance which may be subsumed (and which distinguish romance from epic) include nonrealistic narratives and characters, such as knights errant; deliberate placement in a time past which is viewed through a scrim; digressions which are not treated as integral episodes (the possible source of Milton's extended similes which, however, are integrated into the whole); and extravagancies of story and imagery (which Milton turns into ironies—they never adhere to God).

6. See my discussion in "The Balanced Structure of *Paradise Lost*," *SP*, LXII (1965), 696–718.

7. *Milton's Brief Epic: The Genre, Meaning, and Art of "Paradise Regained"* (Providence, 1966). Numerous examples of other poems that fall into a tradition of shorter poetic works on a religious theme with similarities to the Jobean model are examined.

8. Lewalski sees Belial's speech as offering an analogous episode, which, of course, is not pursued in the basic action, thus emphasizing Milton's transformation and nonemployment of a staple of the diffuse epic. The nature of the history on which the episode is conceived is likewise significant: "Like *Paradise Lost*, *Paradise Regained* is conceived as a heroic poem grounded upon a true event; it is not a romance. In the brief epic, however, the romance allusions do not revalue the romance ethos so much as exalt it to the order of perfection." See her essay, "Milton's Revaluation of Romance," in *Four Essays on Romance*, ed. Herschel Baker (Cambridge, Mass., 1971), p. 70, but compare Annabel Patterson's discussion in the present collection.

9. Lewalski, *Brief Epic*, p. 106.

10. *Milton, A Biography* (Oxford, 1968), II, 1142.

11. "A Brief Epic: *Paradise Regained*," *SP*, LXVIII (1971), 223–43.

12. Ibid., p. 232.

13. Ibid., p. 240.

14. See his dissertation at Yale University in 1964, "The Brief Epic: Studies in the Styles and Structure of the Genre of *Paradise Regained*." An abstract was not published until 1971 in *Dissertations Abstracts, International*, XXXII (1971), 1464A. See also his "Sannazaro and Milton's Brief Epic," *CL*, XX (1968), 116–32. Lewalski discusses Sannazaro's poem in *Milton's Brief Epic*, pp. 60–61.

15. *"Paradise Regain'd:* The Interior Teacher," in Martz, *Poet of Exile: A Study of Milton's Poetry* (New Haven, 1980), Chap. XV, pp. 247–71. The chapter was previously printed in *The Paradise Within: Studies in Vaughan, Traherne, and Milton* (New Haven, 1967), Chap. IV, pp. 171–201, a revision of *"Paradise Regain'd:* The Meditative Combat," *ELH*, XXVII (1960), 223–47. See also Appendix 1 to *Poet of Exile*, *"Paradise Regain'd* and the *Georgics*," pp. 293–304.

16. Charles Dunster, ed., *Paradise Regained, a Poem, in Four Books* (London, 1795), p. 2n. He anticipated the tenor of recent criticism: "The Book of Job, which I have before supposed to have been our Author's model, materially resembles [*PR*] in this respect [a conclusion which rises in dignity and sublimity, thereby exciting the attention and admiration of the reader], and is perhaps the only instance that can be put in competition with it. . . . They who talk of our Author's genius being in the decline when he wrote his second poem, and who therefore turn from it, as from a dry prosaic composition are, I will venture to say, no judges of poetry. With a fancy such as Milton's it must have been more difficult to forbear poetic decorations than to furnish them; and a glaring profusion of

ornament would, I conceive, have more decidedly betrayed the *poeta senescens,* than a want of it. . . . The *PARADISE REGAINED* has something of the didactic character; it teaches not merely by the general moral, and by the character and conduct of its hero, but has also many positive precepts every where interspersed. It is written for the most part in a style admirably condensed, and with a studied reserve of ornament: it is nevertheless illuminated with beauties of the most captivating kind" (pp. 266–67n.).

17. Martz, *"Paradise Regain'd:* The Interior Teacher," p. 247.

18. "The Mental Pinnacle: *Paradise Regained* and the Romantic Four-Book Epic," in *Calm of Mind,* ed. Joseph Wittreich (Cleveland, 1971), p. 136.

19. As examples for the long epic I think of Joel Barlow's *The Columbiad* in heroic couplets, Hart Crane's *The Bridge* in "free verse," and William Carlos Williams' *Paterson* in mixed writing.

20. *Milton's Debt to Greek Tragedy in "Samson Agonistes"* (Baltimore, 1937).

21. "Milton's Hebraic Herculean Hero," in *Milton Studies,* IV, ed. James D. Simmonds (Pittsburgh, 1975), pp. 243–58.

22. A recent study by Jill Maurin, "A Stylistic Approach to *Samson Agonistes:* Poem or Play?", *Demarches linguistiques et poètiques,* XIX (Saint-Etienne, 1977), 235–52, concludes that it is indeed a poem, to be *reread;* Maurin bases her conclusions on the work's poetic unity (for example, in its imagery and structure), its distancing of thoughts and feelings and their expression, and its inner balance. As in a poem the inner drama is central: external causality, as in a play, is not. "[C]lose association between the writer and the work [is] more compatible with poetry than with drama" (p. 252). See also Roger B. Wilkenfeld, "Act and Emblem: The Conclusion of *Samson Agonistes,*" *ELH,* XXXII (1965), 161, and Anne D. Ferry, *Milton and the Miltonic Dryden* (Cambridge, Mass., 1968), pp. 130–37.

23. Anthony Low, "Milton's *Samson* and the Stage, with Implications for Dating the Play," *Huntington Library Quarterly,* XL (1977), 313–24, concludes, as the article title indicates, that *SA* is a play, on the basis of the references to plays in the prefatory discussion. The statement there that it was never intended for the stage dates the play late, Low argues, because in the 1640s Milton did intend to write a play for the stage.

24. *The Third Voice* (Princeton, 1966), p. 7.

25. Radzinowicz's classification of the poem into five acts and her constant view of the poem as a five-act play are not only interpretatively misleading but also inaccurate—not only because Milton says he has specifically eschewed such division. Her division of the poem into acts is illogical: Act I includes the *prologos,* the *parados,* and the first episode; Act II is the second episode; Act III is the third episode; Act IV is both the fourth and fifth episodes together; and Act V is the *exodos* and the *kommos.* See *Toward "Samson Agonistes": The Growth of Milton's Mind* (Princeton, 1978).

26. Ibid., p. 169.

27. See Richmond, *The Christian Revolutionary* (Berkeley and Los Angeles, 1974), p. 176, and Parker, *Milton,* II, 907–09.

28. The poem is included in David Erskine Baker's *The Companion to the Play-House: or, An Historical Account of all the Dramatic Writers (and their Works) that have appeared in Great Britain and Ireland* (London, 1764) unpaged. The author adds, however, a remark which indicates the difficulty of stage performance of the received text: "I remember to have seen in the Possession of a Gentleman in *Dublin* (one Mr. *Dixon*) an alteration of this Poem, said by himself to be his own, so as to render it fit for the Stage; and the same Gentleman also shewed me a Bill for the intended Performance (which was, through some Dispute among the Proprietors of the Theatre, entirely laid aside) in which,

from the Number of Characters, and the apparent Strength to support them, it appeared to have been cast to the greatest Advantage possible, every Performer of Importance, whether Actor, Singer or Dancer, having somewhat allotted to them, towards the illustration of it.—This Representation, if I mistake not, was intended for the Year 1741–2." Mr. Dixon is not identified, and such an altered version is otherwise unknown.

29. Perhaps it resulted from the kinds of criticism and discussion which prompted the statement concerning verse in *PL* (added in the second issue of 1668), which found its source in the controversy between Sir Robert Howard and John Dryden, memorialized in Dryden's *Essay on Dramatic Verse* (1668).

30. Talking of Tertullian's *De Spectaculis* in the Commonplace Book, f. 241, Milton mentions "poema dramaticum"; he refers to a performed literary work written by a poet: "he supports his obligation to bind with religious scruples the mind of a wary and prudent Christian from venturing to witness a dramatic poem, artistically composed by a poet in no wise lacking in skill" (CM, XVIII, 207); "he show[s] that he ought to fetter with scruples of conscience the mind of the careful and wise Christian so that he would not venture to see any dramatic poem composed by a poet by no means unskilled" (YP, I, 490).

31. Richard D. Jordan, in *"Paradise Regained:* A Dramatic Analogue," *Milton Quarterly* XII (1978), 65–68, suggests that the poems were seen as companion pieces by Milton because both are related to biblical drama. Jordan sees *PR* as being in the tradition of Jean Michel's *Le Mystère de la Passion*.

32. *Infernal Triad: The Flesh, the World, and the Devil in Spenser and Milton* (Princeton, 1974), p. 125. Cullen's remarks on the following pages and throughout the book wisely emphasize how the two poems are alike, for "companion poems" implies not only complementarity, which I and other writers have stressed, but similarity, which will heighten, and is indeed necessary to heighten, the contrastive and thus complementary nature of two works.

33. *Visionary Poetics: Milton's Tradition and His Legacy* (San Marino, Calif., 1979), pp. 191–2 and ff.

34. Radzinowicz, *Toward "Samson Agonistes,"* p. 229. See also her discussion of the poems as complementary works, pp. 227–60.

35. *Heroic Knowledge: An Interpretation of "Paradise Regained" and "Samson Agonistes"* (1957; rpt. Hamden, Conn., 1965), p. 205.

36. *Visionary Poetics*, p. 268, n. 295.

37. See my succeeding remarks, pp. 243–44.

38. *Visionary Poetics*, p. 207.

39. "Irony as Tragic Effect: *Samson Agonistes* and the Tragedy of Hope," in *Calm of Mind*, ed. Wittreich, p. 293. Further, "Samson is man fallen, man tempted, man regenerated, man saved. Samson *agonistes* is a player on the stage of the world in the endless drama of life which goes on and on in successive acts" (p. 294).

40. I think of Douglas Bush's comment that Milton "did not, certainly, have Samson's overwhelming sense of having betrayed God's cause . . . , but he had known the despair of witnessing the wreck of his and other men's hopes and labors for the nation" (*The Complete Poetical Works of John Milton* [Boston, 1965], p. 515).

41. The same point is to be seen in Milton's use of *sit* and *stand*; see my discussion in "A Metaphoric Approach to Reading Milton," *Ball State University Forum*, VIII (1967), 17–22.

42. It is by "MAN'S RENOVATION that he is BROUGHT TO A STATE OF GRACE AFTER BEING CURSED AND SUBJECTED TO GOD'S ANGER" (YP, VI, 453).

43. *Milton*, II, 1139.

THE DISTINCTIVE TRAGEDY OF *SAMSON AGONISTES*

Mary Ann Radzinowicz

THE BOLD design of *Samson Agonistes* takes one's breath away. The play opens with the strongest representation of tragic feeling it will afford, the kind of feeling Milton said in the prefatory essay "Of . . . Tragedy" was the feeling proper to the genre, "sadness and gravity" (CM, I, 332). At a stroke Milton deprives himself of the resources of emotional crescendo in constructing the remainder of his play. The tragedy commences where many might end, as if Milton meant to challenge Marlowe and Shakespeare, his two greatest English Renaissance predecessors, in the "disposition of the fable" as well as in those other aspects "much different from what among us passes for best" (ibid.). To match the pain and despair of Milton's fallen and suffering protagonist at his own irrevocable deed, who in an unbroken long opening soliloquy climactically confesses,

> O dark, dark, dark, amid the blaze of noon,
> Irrecoverably dark, total Eclipse
> Without all hope of day,   (80–82)

Macbeth would have to come on stage in the first scene speaking the lines

> To-morrow, and to-morrow, and to-morrow
> Creeps in this petty pace from day to day
> To the last syllable of recorded time;
> And all our yesterdays have lighted fools
> The way to dusty death,   (V, v, 19–23)

or Faustus open his tragical history with the words

> Ah, Faustus
> Now hast thou but one bare hour to live,
> And then thou must be damn'd perpetually!
> Stand still, you ever-moving spheres of Heaven
> That time may cease, and midnight never come.   (xiv, 74–78)

Dr. Faustus and *Macbeth* are the clearest Renaissance tragic analogs in that both, like *Samson Agonistes*, examine suffering as self-inflicted, arising from conscious and voluntary choice; both draw out the consequences of willful error in moral as well as psychological terms; both question the causes of evil so as to express grievous remorse and isolation; and both ask how justice or the affirmation of moral value can follow from willful wrongdoing. In terms of tragic feeling and tragic structure, however, *Samson Agonistes* begins almost at the end of the analogous plays by Marlowe and Shakespeare.[1] Not only does Samson suffer his intensest pain in the first and second episodes of the tragedy; the audience also responds there with its greatest pity and fear for him: the worthier the hero becomes of our regard, the less Milton makes him require our pity and fear.

Having presented his protagonist at a moral nadir, but a zenith of tragic passions, Milton concludes the first episode with a choral stasimon equally bold in its assertion of God's justice and of man's own responsibility for his suffering. At this second stroke, Milton apparently deprives himself of the dramatic resources of doubt or moral conflict:

> Just are the ways of God,
> And justifiable to Men;
> Unless there be who think not God at all,
> If any be, they walk obscure;
> For of such Doctrine never was there School,
> But the heart of a Fool,
> And no man therein Doctor but himself.   (293–99)

The authority of those lines over our response to the play is secured by their multiple echoes of the Psalms, principally Psalms xiv, liii, and cxix; and it is not challenged in what follows, however much the play is devised to ask and answer questions about the kind of justice God's is. To put the seal of finality, at the outset, on the justice of God's ways, Milton contrives the second episode so as to obtain Samson's full concurrence in it:

> all the contest is now
> 'Twixt God and *Dagon; Dagon* hath presum'd
> Me overthrown, to enter lists with God,
> His Deity comparing and preferring
> Before the God of *Abraham*. He, be sure,
> Will not connive, or linger, thus provok'd,
> But will arise and his great name assert.   (461–67)

And here again Milton disregards the structural strategies of his native tradition. The element of moral tension could have been more fully abjured in tragedy only had Malcolm opened *Macbeth* predicting:

> What's more to do
> Which would be plated newly with the time.
>
> . . . .
> this and what needful else
> That calls upon us, by the grace of Grace
> We will perform in measure, time, and place,   (V, viii, 64–73)

or Lucifer intruded into Dr. Faustus' opening lines to assure him, "Christ cannot save thy soul, for he is just" (vi, 90). Nor is such early assurance about justice a small matter. Concern with justice is so intrinsic to the genre as to be virtually definitive of tragedy.

These two structural decisions of breathtaking boldness are not, furthermore, a simple reversion to a classical model from Renaissance innovations. Although Milton binds his work to effect catharsis by quoting Aristotle and cites Aeschylus, Sophocles, and Euripides, "the three Tragic Poets unequall'd yet by any" as classical precedents for his form (CM, I, 333), his own plot is one which Aristotle explicity demotes: "The sound plot, therefore, must have a single, and not (as some maintain) a double issue. . . . Next comes the sort of plot which some put first: one with a double story, like the *Odyssey*, and an opposite issue for the good and bad personages. It is ranked first only because audiences are so weak; the poets simply follow their public, writing to suit its whims."[2] Milton is perfectly aware of Aristotle's put-down for poets who pander to audiences; he uses it to criticize "intermixing Comic stuff with Tragic sadness and gravity; or introducing trivial and vulgar persons, which by all judicious hath bin counted absurd; and brought in without discretion, corruptly to gratifie the people" (CM, I, 332). Yet he chooses a plot structure emphasizing distributive justice, the rewards and punishments meted to characters according to their deserts—for Samson "a death so noble" (1724), for the Philistian "Lords, Ladies, Captains, Councellors, or Priests" (1654) "thir own ruin on themselves [invited]" (1684).

Finally, Milton's architectonic boldness is capped, after the complication of the plot, by an emphatic separation of catastrophe from denouement into two distinct sections within the final episode so as to bring about a double catharsis—that of the protagonist and through him the onstage audience represented by the Chorus. It is too easy to imagine that Milton fashioned his dramatic poem so that the catastrophe was recounted, and not depicted, for essentially conservative neoclassicizing reasons, that endorsing Aristotle's view of "spectacle" as "the least artistic of all the parts . . . [having] the least connection with the art of poetry . . . more a matter for the costumier than the poet" (p. 15), he chose simply to work "after the Greek manner" (CM, I, 332). Since Aristotle thought that "even without seeing the things take place, he who simply hears the account of them shall be filled with horror and pity at the incidents" (p. 23), Milton, one might altogether too easily decide, took Samson offstage and brought on the Messenger. The Miltonic innovation is not the resort to reported action, however. It is the allocation of about 60 lines to the described catastrophe and then of a further 113 lines to the reactions of the Chorus as denouement. That structural boldness converts the reported action into a narrated play-within-the-play and the response to the reported action, rendered by the first and only antiphonal treatment of the Chorus in the play, into a surrogate audience response.

Among the various effects produced by Milton's disposition of his fable, these two—the formal and the thematic—make *Samson Agonistes* particularly potent and distinctive as philosophical tragedy. As to the first: the initial removal of the two common Renaissance sources of tragic intensity and the separation of catastrophe from denouement both create a spreading, dividing, and spacing of the effect of the various scenes between the opening and final episodes so that what one might call *dramatic suspension* replaces *dramatic suspense*. The efficacy of dramatic suspension is that it fixes attention upon intellectual conflict rather than physical action. When Milton described the preeminence of "that sort of Dramatic Poem which is called Tragedy" by calling it "the gravest, moralest and most profitable of all other Poems" and noting its favor with "Philosophers and other grave Writers" (CM, I, 331), he marked the philosophical and ethical thrust of his play. That thrust depends upon intense initial involvement followed by dramatic suspension. Dramatic suspension gave Milton a structure to which he called attention in the least noted sentence in "Of . . . Tragedy," again perfunctorily assigned to neoclassical conservatism: "The circumscription of time wherein the whole Drama begins and ends, is according to antient rule, and best example, within the space of twenty-four hours" (CM, I, 333). *Samson* takes places in a continuous present time; the action of the play in the present recapitulates in parallel incidents the protagonist's past life, not by disguised flashback but by gradually drawing the past with all its fatal and mistaken lessons into the present and toward a moment when the educated protagonist discovers a new meaning for his life involving a future for himself educative of the future for his audience.

Without dramatic suspension, the recapitulative structure would have no room to function. Much-rebuked Samuel Johnson, who complained erroneously that "the intermediate parts have neither cause nor consequence, neither hasten nor retard the catastrophe," was particularly erroneous in complaining that the play "wants that power of attracting the attention which a well-connected plot produces";[3] he simply ignored the recapitulative structure and its devices of dramatic suspension.

The second effect is thematic. The definition of catharsis as moderative and not extirpative—that is, tempering and not purging the passions—and the choice of a plot with an opposite issue for good and bad personages both combine in a double catharsis which itself constitutes the justification of God's ways toward men. Moderative catharsis in Milton is not solely a psychological by-product of tragedy—although it is that too; it is principally the image of God's Providence, his mercy and justice combined. Both effects, structural and thematic, are produced by a variety of extradramatic subgenres.

Dramatic suspension in *Samson Agonistes* makes room for a variety of specific local effects in the separate parts and subgenres of the play, while producing a firm unity of effect through the recapitulative structure of interlacement. In so strongly cast, brief, and unified a drama as *Samson Agonistes* is, varied delight properly depends upon the power of Milton to retard and fix his audience's attention upon the qualities which inhere in the subgenres he uses, while including in the subgenres themselves potent signals of repetition and prediction. In *Samson Agonistes* Milton deploys a number of literary kinds across and within the episodes of his recapitulative structure. Such delight from the whole, as Coleridge put it, "as is compatible with a distinct gratification from each component part"[4] arises from the distinctive qualities of the subsumed literary kind, of which four warrant attention: the "character"; the "*récit*" or lyric, particularly the threnody; the "debate"; and the narrated "play-within-a-play." Since, as Milton handles them, all these forms emphasize thinking, perception and mind changing, they are readily unified to induce philosophical speculation.

Finally, the double moderative catharsis has important thematic implications. A good number of critics have been reluctant to call *Samson Agonistes* a tragedy because of its Christian transcendence: Maurice Bowra may be allowed to speak for them all: "since all is best, there is nothing to regret."[5] More recently, some have refused to concede its transcendence because they have found the drama morally repugnant in it vengefulness.[6] By my reading, the tragedy is Christian, and the matter for serious and pained regret is the mystery of iniquity. To block the

reponse to his drama as less than moral, Milton took great pains to cleanse
his biblical text of all references to vengeance or retributive justice. He
made Samson accuse himself repeatedly of "impotence of mind in body
strong" against the scriptural indication of craftiness. He promoted Dalila
from Samson's concubine to his wife, although in *Paradise Lost* he exactly
followed the Book of Judges (*PL* IX, 1060), so as to raise the question of
matrimonial treason as urgently as the problems of outraged passions; and
in *Samson Agonistes* he not only stayed Samson's vindictive hand against
her, he precisely made the betrayed husband forgive her, if not graciously
in word at least clearly in deed: "At distance I forgive thee, go with that"
(954). He withheld from the play Samson's prayer in the Temple of Dagon, "O Lord God, remember me, I pray thee, and strengthen me, I pray
thee, only this once, O God, that I may be once avenged of the Philistines
for my two eyes" (Judges xvi, 28). He removed from the Temple all but
the "choice nobility" of the "sons of Caphtor," exacting no vengeance on
the Philistian populace: "The vulgar only scap'd who stood without"
(1659). In place of retributive justice, Milton emphasize distributive justice—the opposite issue of the action for the good and bad characters. He
showed God's grace to be consonant with his justice by rejecting any act
by any dramatic *deus ex machina*. In reaffirming distributive justice and
not retributive justice as the only justice satisfactory to human reason,
Milton further affirmed that distributive justice is accomplished only by
the free election of men themselves when they are most themselves by
virtue of having passed through moderative catharsis into a thoughtful
perceptivity. Through moderative catharsis Milton thus tells his audience
that "new acquist of true experience" creates "calm of mind," the only
form of transcendence the tragedy of human life affords—the mercy of
God-intended perspicuity, not savagely wrought triumph. And finally he
promises "peace and *consolation*"; after catharsis of remorse comes the
added note of forgiveness.

DRAMATIC SUSPENSION AND EXTRADRAMATIC SUBGENRES

The "Character"

The construction of the characters in *Samson Agonistes* owes a good
deal to Renaissance iconology, whatever it may owe to Protestant typology (and the tracing of that debt has been one of the most profitable
contributions of the last decade of scholarship to Milton studies).[7] The
fundamental principle of iconology is the rendering of the individual so as
to manifest the general and, through the general, to point toward abstract
interrelationships and truths. Samson, Manoa, Dalila, and Harapha are

all given iconic portraits deliberately enclosed and set forth to the audience by the Chorus in preliminary sketches which convey their abstract typicality. In their described appearances, the subjects are given a unified portrait not because the reader perceives them as psychological wholes but because their characterizers perceive in uniform modes, persistently attacking the question, What is to be thought of this kind of human being? Milton entrusts the role-typing sketches of his characters to the Chorus, but the manner in which the Chorus performs its task does not primarily develop the psychology of the Chorus; rather it reveals the abstracting nature of perception. The Chorus as a character represents a group of "brethren and men of Dan," "friends and neighbors not unknown" (180,332), but it draws the characters of others as a spokesman who clearly knows a good bit about the Renaissance art of portraiture as described by Puttenham, Foxe, Spenser, and the prose writers of the Theophrastian "character."[8] Working within that rhetorical tradition, the Chorus describes so as to entrench each figure in its conceptual value. A good bit of accidental detail is discarded in favor of abstraction; detail is not absent, of course, but the detail specified is not that which imitates one individual but rather such normative detail, drawn from well-known areas of allegory, mythology, martyrology, and biblical interpretation, as assigns essential rather than accidental value to its subject. In each portrait is given a configuration of unique but nearly timeless characteristics ordered consciously so that the iconic value of the portrait is emphasized more strongly than its personal value. Such topoi as race, citizenship, family, wondrous birth, early upbringing, appearance and temperament, profession and deeds, relatives and friends, fortune and destiny are deployed to float calculatedly in an arbitrary, not a naturalistic order, around the center of the icon. Milton shades these topoi by placing at the disposal of the Hebrew Chorus not simply the scriptural resources of the Book of Judges or the traditional Christian interpretations of that text but a number of literary and mythological parallels, pictorial emblems, details from contemporay hagiography and the like.[9] The introductory sketch of each character functions narratively, not dramatically, and aims at projecting its interpretation so as to elicit an intellectual as well as an emotional response. The "character" offers significance and meaning; its arrangement is not causal but normative and evaluative.

Naturally enough, Milton does not use the resources of the character or portrait at the expense of direct dramatic representation or self-characterization; he is much too great a dramatic poet for that. I have elsewhere shown how the rhetorical and dialectical patterning of Samson's opening soliloquy imitates the anguish of a laboring mind and

initiates a process of intellectual and personal change in the protagonist;[10] I repeat now that the most riveting speech in the entire
tragedy is that opening speech in which the hero, wrestling alone with
the painful meaning of his despair, both psychologically characterizes
himself and ethically measures his crime. Nevertheless, while retarda-
tion and suspension of the first choral ode is used to create a "character," setting forth Samson as abstract exemplar, its iconic design
establishes the moral terms the play will debate. Complementary processes work in the choral "character" of Harapha.

The "character" of Samson is given in lines 115 through 175. Naturally the biblical Samson active in history is represented by four references to the Book of Judges: he "tore the Lion, as the Lion tears the
Kid" (xiv, 6; cf. SA 127); "The bold Ascalonite / Fled from his Lion
ramp" (xiv, 9; cf. SA 138–39); he wielded "The Jaw of a dead Ass, his
sword of bone" (xv, 16; cf. SA 141); and "on his shoulders bore / The
Gates of Azza (xvi, 3; cf. SA 148–49). Those details appear in the Chorus' portrait in the order of their appearance in the narrative in the Book
of Judges, but the historical chronology of Judges does not determine
the arrangement of the portrait. The character neither commences nor
ends with the Judges sequence; the biblical references are not grouped
logically together; the Chorus does not mention other potent details in
Judges, not even three of the four Samson incidents Milton listed as
likely themes for tragedy in the Trinity manuscript—"Samson pursopho-
rus, Hybrites, or marrying"[11]—so that no picture is given of the arso-
nous, riddling, calculatedly vengeful historical Samson. Instead the Chorus draws the portrait of a hero of the people, an elect hero gifted with
the one talent of irresistible strength, who, fallen, presents an icon of
despair and a symbol of the lost leader cast down from fortune's wheel.
To the historical Samson, the Chorus adds literary allusions to Ovid's
self-portrait in exile ("see how he lies at random, carelessly diffus'd, /
With languished head" [118–19]; "languid limbs diffused over the bed,"
[Ex. Ponto III, iii, 8]); to Virgil ("chalybean temper'd steel, and frock of
mail" [133]; "the naked Chalybes give us iron" [Georgics i, 58]); and to
mythology ("Like whom the Gentiles feign to bear up Heaven" [150],
the Atlas myth). That classical dimension so commonplace in prosopopo-
eia is likewise introduced unsystematically. Instead this character of
Samson is governed by the twin insistences, at its moments of greatest
emphasis—the beginning and the ending—upon the depths of Samson's
present despair, indicated by references to the iconography of melancholy: the slumped figure, the downward-bending head, the careless
clothing, and upon the fallen hero as a man raised by his gifts, not by his

birth, indicated by the contempt for well-armed warriors and the insistence on virtue as definitive of greatness. That latter emphasis one might find in such differing places—to choose almost at random—as Spenser's introductory character of Satyrane (*Faerie Queene* I, vi, 20–28), where the boy, unequipped with courtly weapons, fearlessly pursues lions given both psalmic and mythological overtones (Psalm xxxv, 17: "Rescue . . . my darling from the lions," and a reminiscence of Thetis' fears when she sees Achilles molest wild beasts), or as John Foxe's characters either of Tyndale, "a special organ of the Lord appointed" whose simplicity and humility is compared with the pride and riches of the bishops, or of blind Zisca armed only with a poleaxe defeating the imperial army of Sigismond.[12]

I am far from urging any specific indebtedness to any particular "character" on Milton's part. My point is this: the literary kind, the character, throws emphasis upon the presentation of an abstract icon and demands an imaginative effort to discover or "read" the exemplary. The Chorus halts the action of the opening episode, which in the Argument Milton describes thus: "[Samson] happens at length to be visited by certain friends and equals of his tribe, which make the Chorus, who seek to comfort him what they can"; the Chorus then stands off and delivers a portrait containing a new definition of the tragic hero:

> For him I reckon not in high estate
> Whom long descent of birth
> Or the sphear of fortune raises;
> But thee whose strength, while vertue was her mate,
> Might have subdu'd the Earth,
> Universally crown'd with highest praises.   (170–75)

The Chorus' speech says that the symbolic meaning of the portrait drawn of "one past hope, abandon'd, / And by himself given over" (120–21) is the message "how the mighty are fallen":

> O mirror of our fickle state,
> Since man on earth unparallel'd
> The rarer thy example stands
> By how much from the top of wondrous glory,
> Strongest of mortal men,
> To lowest pitch of abject fortune thou art fall'n.   (164–69)

In brief, the portrait clusters its details around the abstract image of Samson as "The Dungeon of thy self" (156).

The portrait creates dramatic suspension but at the same time leaves Milton free to use it as instrumental to the unity of dramatic

effect. The imagination is asked to construct an exemplum. The implied
irrevocability of the example is tested by the action of the play. The
moral the Chorus draws of the wheel of fortune precipitating the mighty
low is challenged by Samson's self-evaluation: he says that the cause of
his fall was his "known offence" (1218), not the pitch of "fortune" (169).
The moral drawn by Harapha, who is the subject of the other "character" I shall discuss, about Samson is that Samson's God has rejected
him utterly and "delivered [him] up / Into [his] Enemies hand" as "good
for nothing else" but slavery (1158–59, 1163); that moral is refuted by
Samson's further self-evaluation: if he cannot be confident of himself or
his worthiness, he can be confident of his God, "Whose ear is ever open;
and his eye / Gracious to readmit the suppliant" (1172–73). The portrait
the Chorus draws of Harapha is so organized as to pick up from the
Chorus' previous portrait of Samson precisely the details ("Arms ridiculous," and "the forgery / of brazen shield and spear," 131–32) to present
in contrast to the man who was "Dungeon of thy self" (156)—a self-made
tower icon—a "pile high-built and proud" and by the contrast to prepare
for Samson's understanding that he need not remain self-imprisoned.
The whole Harapha character is given in only nine lines:

> Look now for no inchanting voice, nor fear
> The bait of honied words; a rougher tongue
> Draws hitherward, I know him by his stride,
> The Giant *Harapha* of *Gath*, his look
> Haughty as is his pile high-built and proud.
> Comes he in peace? what wind hath blown him hither
> I less conjecture then when first I saw
> The sumptuous *Dalila* floating this way:
> His habit carries peace, his brow defiance.   (1065–74)

Twice in those nine lines, which themselves retard action to deliver an
abstract entity, the Chorus looks back to its iconic portrait of Dalila
clustered about the commonplace symbol of proud woman as a gilt
galley blown seductively by the winds of self-will, deriving from classical
(Plautus, *Paenulus* I, ii), biblical (Psalm xlviii, 7), and contemporary
iconography (Jonson, *The Staple of News*, Lady Pecunia; Shakespeare,
Antony and Cleopatra, Enobarbus' description of Egypt and her barge)
and brought together by the logic of dominant perception, not by the
logic of psychological portrayal. The interrelationships among the static
"characters" contribute to the interlacing effect by which Milton makes
his dramatic suspension taut throughout the play. The principal abstracting effect of Harapha's portrait lies in the conjunction of "tongue" and

"pile high-built and proud." Not true but proud words, not good but self-regardful deeds come from the resistible giant; at first proud but then true words, at first self-regardful but then good deeds come not from Samson's gigantic mortal strength but from his clarified moral force. These icons are made to confront each other and to release into the richness of Milton's dramatic poetry the resources of an unexpected extradramatic kind.

The Récit

If the "character" makes an unexpected appearance in drama, the *récit* makes a less unexpected one, being a specialized form of the soliloquy in which by convention a character in monologue conveys directly to the audience information about his mood, intention, motives, and state of mind or directly acquaints the audience with expository information. Unlike the aside, another specialized soliloquy, the *récit* is not inaudible to the other characters on stage, if there be other such characters. Unlike some Elizabethan soliloquies, the *récit* is not expository (as, for example, the final monologue of Dr. Faustus is, when belatedly and frantically he tries to escape damnation). The *récit* is a lyrical speech on an abstract theme adaptable to utterance by a character in either his private role or his public capacity. An example is Macbeth's supreme *récit* quoted earlier; its purpose is to guide the audience thematically. Milton clearly conceived of his *récits* as odes, endowing them with the seriousness of stylistic elevation, musical complexity, and publicly proclamatory quality of classical odes, themselves modelled on the choral songs of tragedy. Naturally Milton's *récits* bear resemblance to the Greek *rhesus*, a set impassioned speech, but the threnody, the song of lamentation or dirge, was also a strong poetic influence upon them, and Milton found in the Psalms important models too. And yet by convention the seventeeth-century *récit*, like the Greek choral song, also enjoys a semidetachable status and extradramatic identity with respect to the play in which it occurs; it may become, as it were, a concert aria, much as Miriam Rooth auditions in *The Tragic Muse* before the French teacher to show her acting ability through the detached Racinian *tirade* and not through a fully developed dialogic scene. But whether the *récit* is unexpected in drama and detachable from it or the reverse, Milton's use of it, like his use of the "character," functions to increase the philosophical density of the play and to induce meditation quite as much as feeling.

I have written elsewhere of the dialectical power of Samson's soliloquies and of the density of reference to psalmic laments within them.[13]

Here I shall examine only two *récits*, neither by the hero: the choral stasimon, "Many are the sayings of the wise" (652), and Manoa's concluding *récit*, "Come, come no time for lamentation now" (1708). The latter opens with the lines:

> *Samson* hath quit himself
> Like *Samson*, and heroicly hath finish'd
> A life Heroic.   (1709–11)

With those lines Milton closes the circle of the action of his powerfully structured play. Dramatic suspension is seen in them not only to be consonant with the tightest and firmest plotting but positively to underscore it. The closure in Manoa's *récit* has precisely "that power of attracting attention which a well-connected plan produces." What was by Samson's disobedience lost has by his patience been restored: Samson's new heroism, the heroism of humiliation and sufferance, is not less but more heroic than the heroism of power. Samson has become the Samson who reveals and transcends the tragedy of wasted human power and misapplied human freedom. The audience hears in Manoa's *récit* a dispassionate and thoughtful speaker's—not primarily Manoa's—sense of Samson's fitness to be seen as heroic. To be sure, the *récit* ends in pure Manoa, as many have noticed:

> The Virgins also shall on feastful days
> Visit his Tomb with flowers, only bewailing
> His lot unfortunate in nuptial choice,
> From whence captivity and loss of eyes.   (1741–44)

When the circle of the action is closed, however, Manoa considers its philosophical meaning. The audience hears an abstract ode on death and suffering, where patience and grace are examined in terms which answer the questions abstractly posed by the choral *récit* in the second stasimon. The lofty and simple language of reassurance belongs not to Manoa, the Hebrew father, but to the voice which in the last of the three movements of *Lycidas* offered similar assurance and consolation:

> Nothing is here for tears, nothing to wail
> Or knock the breast, no weakness, no contempt,
> Dispraise, or blame, nothing but well and fair,
> And what may quiet us in a death so noble.   (1721–24)

(The expressive formulation "no contempt, / Dispraise, or blame" is not a Manoan device but a Miltonic signal of what is to be thought of Samson's self-transcendence in death).

The second choral stasimon has often and valuably been placed next to the fourth to weigh the values of action and patience. As an abstract *récit*, however, it asks the audience not to hurry ahead but to pause and consider the tragic mystery of iniquity. That mystery is universally a tragic mystery felt in the very doubleness of meaning in the word *iniquity* itself—that simultaneous sense of unrighteous action and public wrong together with unfair treatment and injustice; as Shakespeare reminded his audience, "Thus like the formal Vice, Iniquitee, / I moralize two meanings in one word" (*R3*, III, i, 82). The stasimon is quadripartite. The first fifteen lines are well suited to the chorus as a character. Samson's despairing prayer—"No long petition, speedy death, / The close of all my miseries, and the balm" (650–51)—must be given an answer; the answer is postponed to the final and fourth part of the *récit* and is a counter-prayer, "Behold him in this state calamitous, and turn / His labours, for thou canst, to peaceful end" (708–09). The arrival of Dalila in response to the counter-prayer ends the *récit* and begins the next episode.

The Chorus begins its *récit* obliquely: it ought to know what to say to despairing Samson. The ready-made panacea to suffering is surely "Patience as the truest fortitude" (654); however, the Chorus, decent and true-hearted, feel the very useless intrusiveness of the ready-made panacea "unless th' afflicted in his pangs feel within / Some source of consolation from above" (663–64), so they do not speak to Samson in their first words; with one voice they speak to each other and to the audience, contemplating a commonplace palliative and too nice in feeling to offer it. The second part of the *récit* turns away from medicating Samson's death wish to probe the source of tragic feeling itself—the near impossibility of resolving the mystery of iniquity; the Chorus asks the questions of Lear and Job about the felt disproportion between sinning and sinned against in the very nature of man's fate, stunned by having sinned but stunned equally at the completeness of suffering:

> God of our Fathers, what is man!
> That thou towards him with hand so various,
> Or might I say contrarious,
> Temperst they providence through his short course,
> Not evenly.   (667–71)

The twenty-two lines of part two of the *récit* express the human being's eternal bewilderment at such disproportion, not only by remarkable density of allusion to the Psalms but also by remarkable adaptation of psalmic rhythms. The Chorus refers again, as in its character of Samson, to the special kind of Puritan hero here tragically fallen:

such as thou hast solemnly elected,
With gifts and graces eminently adorn'd
To some great work, thy glory,
And peoples safety, which in part they effect.   (678–81)

Toward such heroes, however, God changes his countenance and hand
"with no regard / Of highest favours past" (684–85). The third section
moves toward its climactic and Jobean statement about iniquity—"Just
or unjust, alike seem miserable / For oft alike, both come to evil end"
(704–05)—by way of a range of specifications asking Milton's audience
to contain in mind disasters current in their own day, in Samson's day,
in the time of the Psalms, and in the rhythm of all human life from
strong youth to deformed age. God gave the bodies of his chosen people
to be "meat unto the fowls of the heavens, the flesh of [the] saint unto
the beasts of the earth" (Psalm lxxix, 2: cf, SA, "thir carkasses / To dogs
and fowls a prey" [693–94]; he gave his elect Englishmen at the collapse
of the Commonwealth "to the unjust tribunals under change of times, /
And condemnation of the ingrateful multitude" (695–96); he gives to all
men "crude old age," "causeless suffring," only just if it were "the
punishment of dissolute days" (700–02). The Chorus concedes that to
"degrade . . . or remit / To life obscur'd" were "fair" (687–88), but it
cannot tell what is the meaning of apparently merciless and unjust pain
piled on pain. It caps those eighteen lines of striking specification by
withdrawing its contemplation to the single case of Samson, the test case
of God's justice, to pray for him a "peaceful end" (709). The turn to
Samson so places the *récit* as an abstract consideration of the meaning of
tragedy as to inform the thoughtful audience of their responsibility for
discovering meaning: God "tempers" his Providence through man's
short course so as to temper his human creatures.

Manoa's final *récit* is a threnody pronouncing on Samson's case in
terms once more extending it to all human cases; "God not parted,"
Samson's suffering is offered as an instance of "honour . . . and freedom" to those who "Find courage to lay hold on this occasion" (1715–16,
1719). The great questions hanging over the poem and put in the choral
second stasimon are: Why does God act as he does? Why is the good so
easily lost? Why is it attained only by tragic suffering? Samson comes to
answer those questions, to show what kind of God God is and what kind
of meaning life bears. The final *récit* tells us that God is like the tragic
poet who moderates human passions, brings good in the tempering, and
teaches his people by the tragedy of human life.

The *récit* is not a naturalistic or realistic dramatic mode—it is a meditative mode. The contribution of its thought-extending effect to the dramatic suspension of the play is to prompt philosophy. The *récit* encourages a concentration upon Samson as an educating instance of God's ways toward men: the play occasions moderative catharsis in the hero and in the audience; the *récit* draws attention to the paideutic implications in the paradox of the Fortunate Fall. Manoa does not speak as a man bound to express a conviction applicable only to men under the Old Law. The imputation of evil to God has been removed by Samson's repeated urging of his own responsibility for what has befallen him. (He even briefly clears Dalila of responsibility for his, but not for her own, transgression in the debate I shall next examine: "true, / I to myself was false e're thou to me" [823–24].)

But what of God's justice and his mercy? Manoa's *récit* builds on Samson's own recognition in his exchange with Harapha that just as divine Providence does not annihilate free will or necessitate a *deus ex machina*, neither does free will betoken a *deus absconditus* or postulate an irreversible and fatal necessity governing human affairs. God's "ear is ever open; and his eye / Gracious to readmit the suppliant" (1172–73). Samson's awareness of "rouzing motions" (1382) disposing his thought to "something extraordinary" (1383) prompted the Chorus to commit him unchained to the officer with the words

> Go, and the Holy One
> Of *Israel* be thy guide
> To what may serve his glory best, & spread his name
> Great among the Heathen round.   (1427–30)

Now Manoa continues that line of thought:

> And which is best and happiest yet, all this
> With God not parted from him, as was feard,
> But favouring and assisting to the end.   (1718–20)

The *récit* is one of the long series of responses to Socrates' Protagorean question, Can man be educated and virtue taught? God is the supreme teacher and tragedy his strongest paideutic device, both just and merciful.

The Debate

To induce Socratic considerations Milton has recourse to a Socratic device, dialogic debate. Even as a young poet Milton thought of drama intended to be "doctrinal and exemplary to a Nation" (YP, I, 815) in terms of the *récit* and the debate. Outlines for tragedy in the Trinity manuscript show clearly that he then thought a proper tragic structure would be a first act of exposition delivered by a speaker other than the protagonist, followed by a choral commentary; a second act of complication with dominant roles assigned to allegorical characters, completed by a second choral ode; a third act of apparent resolution reported by authoritative abstractions, concluded by a chorus; a fourth act of renewed complication, again ended by the chorus; a fifth act of resolution, completed by a final choral dirge. In drafting the tragedy of "Paradise Lost," Milton listed just such five acts and choruses; he assigned to the abstract persons Justice, Mercy, Wisdom, and Heavenly Love both *récits* and debates; he specified "Justice and Mercie" in the first act "debating what should become of man if he fall" and the Chorus in that act in *récit* singing a "hymne of ye creation" (Trinity ms., p. 35). When Milton came to write *Samson Agonistes* as a vehicle of inner psychological change, with the protagonist on stage throughout "labouring [his] mind" (1298) and showing his changing conceptions of self, duty, and God in debate with opposing characters and in the presence of the Chorus, now made a participatory character to change along with the protagonist, he showed himself an artistic master of a very much more complex and striking structure than the Trinity manuscript would have predicted. Nonetheless he retained the *récit* and the debate, not as ossified remnants of an earlier conception of his art but as subgenres well adapted to carry the audience through an experience like the protagonist's and to extend its philosophical import.

The most striking of Milton's debates is that in Samson's encounter with Dalila, a debate assigning so few weak lines to Dalila that her modern defenders are of the opinion that she won it. In essence the subject of that debate is the criteria by which value, meaning, or truth are to be established—body versus mind, sensation versus reason, subjectivity versus objectivity—and the primary value at issue is the determination of human freedom. The general plot line of Dalila's argument is clear: she comes to compensate Samson with loving care for his present suffering, occasioned by his as much as her frailty and hence ascribable to weakness, forgivable (as weakness should always be mutually forgivable), a suffering inflicted by her patriotism and piety which opposed his enmity to Philistia, that enmity now defused so that she can solace him. The line of argument dictates a point-by-point rebuttal from Samson involving both their private or personal and their public or national relationships. The crux of the public debate is Dalila's reiteration of the wisely grounded and widely held maxim "that to the public good / Private respects must yield" (867). The issue is how the public good is to be decided. Dalila establishes the goodness of her version of public good by relativistic, numerical, subjective arguments which she abbreviates as she leaves Samson:

> Fame, if not double-fac't is double-mouth'd,
> And with contrary blast proclaims most deeds;
>
> . . . .
>
> in my countrey where I most desire,
> In *Ecron, Gaza, Asdod,* and in *Gath*
> I shall be nam'd among the famousest
> Of Women.   (971–83)

Against her position that good is established locally, in terms of personal wish and by force of numbers, Samson defines it essentially, ideally, and Platonically. His crucial argument runs:

> if aught against my life
> Thy countrey sought of thee, it sought unjustly,
> Against the law of nature, law of nations,
> No more thy countrey, but an impious crew
> Of men conspiring to uphold thir state
> By worse then hostile deeds, violating the ends
> For which our countrey is a name so dear;
> Not therefore to be obey'd. But zeal mov'd thee;
> To please thy gods thou didst it; gods unable
> To acquit themselves and prosecute their foes
> But by ungodly deeds, the contradiction
> Of their own deity, Gods cannot be:
> Less therefore to be pleas'd, obey'd, or fear'd.   (888–900)

Here Samson urges a familiar line of Miltonic argument: a country is defined by the ideal social ends it serves; it is not a majority compounding together in self-interest; a god is known by his creativity, power, excellence, and goodness to man, not by the blind or implicit faith of his believers; a marriage is the union of fit conversing mates, not a contract under ecclesiastical or other law; a priest is the feeder of sheep, not a hireling ordained by a church. Earlier in the personal area of the debate, Samson had heard Dalila define love as erotic feelings: "Here I should enjoy thee day and night / Mine and loves prisoner, not the Philistines" (807–08). He redefined her possessiveness as lust and not love in a similarly essential and not subjective manner. That exchange ended in Samson's angry tautology "Love seeks to have Love" (837) but his was no less for that an idealistic, rationalist stance. When Dalila offered her second line of defense to argue that she yielded to public good

("Virtue . . . truth, duty so enjoyning" [870]), she transferred the debate from a subjectively defined love to a subjectively defined piety and patriotism. Dalila's definitions are quite different from Samson's: a country is what I give allegiance to, a religion is what I profess, love is what I feel, and argument is what I accept, good fame is what I get from my people. All these definitions amount to the declaration that virtue is sincerity or volition; like Socrates, Milton thinks it is knowledge or reason.

The Dalila-Samson debate is intellectually crucial to reading *Samson Agonistes* as philosophical or moral tragedy. Those who find the play immoral seem to me to adopt Dalila's relativism. They appear to urge that the Philistines and Jews stand on the same footing of humanity: Samson believes in Jehovah, Dalila, in Dagon; Samson is a Nazarite, Dalila a Philistine; Samson knows his god by "intimate impulse" (223), it is open to Dalila to claim the same for her belief in Dagon. By the relative tests of authenticity and sincerity, their faiths equally validate their actions; Milton endorses Samson's faith and triumph in order to indulge his own desire for retribution. The tests of sincerity and authenticity are not those Milton applies, however; his are essentially reasonable: "gods unable / To acquit themselves and prosecute their foes / But by ungodly deeds . . . / . . . Gods cannot be" (896–99). Human beings, Milton makes clear in *De Doctrine Christiana*, are free to ask that sort of question about the nature of God: "In religion as in other things . . . God offers all his rewards not to those who are thoughtless and credulous, but to those who labor constantly and seek tirelessly after truth" (YP, VI, 120; cf. VI, 129: "Faith . . . does not mean that habit of believing, but the things which must habitually be believed.") Hence the debate between Samson and Dalila concerning the criteria establishing moral value specifically raises the question of human freedom. The justice and goodness of God is established in *Samson Agonistes* by the familiar argument of human responsibility: God made men free to form and then to answer to a conception of moral good; God did not dictate to man ungodly acts to advance his glory high.

The debate between Dalila and Samson circles persistently around the definition of liberty. Dalila views liberty, predictably, as an emotional, subjective, and physically registered state: "I knew that liberty / Would draw thee forth to perilous enterprises" (802–03); if Samson could but feel himself "love's prisoner, not the Philistines" (808) then he would feel free, then he could enjoy life's solaces "At home in leisure and domestic ease" (917) in freedom. Samson considers liberty a rational state of mind. He had told Manoa that when formerly he felt free, he had been truly in servitude:

> These rags, this grinding, is not yet so base
> As was my former servitude, ignoble,
> Unmanly, ignominious, infamous,
> True slavery, and that blindness worse then this,
> That saw not how degeneratly I served.   (415–19)

He now tells Dalila the same:

> This Gaol I count the house of Liberty
> To thine whose doors my feet shall never enter.   (949–50)

A definition of liberty in terms of sensations and feelings, he had warned the Chorus, was the sign of political corruption:

> But what more oft in Nations grown corrupt,
> And by thir vices brought to servitude,
> Then to love Bondage more then Liberty,
> Bondage with ease then strenuous liberty.   (268–72)

He now tells Dalila that a similar yielding to her "fair enchanted cup and warbling charms" (934) would be to repeat a personal corruption and create a renewed servitude, "To bring my feet again into the snare / Where once I have been caught" (931–32). Their debate catches up the strands of earlier debates and interlaces them within the dramatic suspension of the structure: at issue is the meaningfulness of freely and rationally considered moral judgment; the debate shows its evolution.

The Narrated Play-Within-the-Play

As an enactment in the "theatre of the soul" of what has happily been called "the drama of the soul,"[14] *Samson Agonistes* puns on or uses metaphorically the technical terms of the stage. Because his "part" was "from Heav'n assigned" (1217), Samson refuses to "shew [the Philistines] feats" (1340); have they not their own "Antics, Mummers, Mimics" (1325), that they "pick him out," "with shackles 'tir'd" (1326)? While offstage Samson performs his "great act" (1389), Manoa tells the chorus ironically that he is

> not at present here to find my Son,
> By order of the Lords new *parted* hence
> To come and *play* before them at thir Feast.   (1446–49; my emphasis)

The drama in Samson's soul reifies, externalizes, and then personifies those aspects of his inner nature which require harmonizing; his legalism, doubt, and fatalism into Manoa, his sensuality and romanticism into Dalila, his violence into Harapha. Conquering them as renewed tempta-

tions, he conquers himself. When that process is completed in the protagonist, Milton assures the catharsis of his audience by resort to the
narrated play-within-the-play. The final episode is not the first occasion
on which Milton used the device within his interlacing dramatic suspension. It is frequent in the play; one might instance Samson's self-con-
temptuously narrating his playing of the doting husband. Samson as "sole
Author" (376) of his fall dramatized his married life to Manoa, conveying
action ("thrice she assay'd" [392], "thrice . . . I turn'd to sport" [396]),
stage directions ("with blandisht parlies" [403], "when men seek most
repose and rest" [406]), and message ("servil mind . . . servil punishment" [412–13]).

The fullest of the narrated plays-within-the-play is, of course, the
Messenger's. He gives to Manoa and the Chorus an account of a "horrid
spectacle" (1542) which he still seems to "behold" in "dire imagination"
(1544), a spectacle Manoa says "no preface needs" (1554). The Messenger sets the stage, the "spacious theatre" (1605); he arranges the
audience, some with "seats . . . in order" (1607–08), most "on banks
and scaffolds under Skie" (1610); he presents the entrance of Samson
costumed in "state Livery" (1615), accompanied by "pipes and timbrels"
(1616–17), paraded in the midst of a military guard. He relates Samson's feats as a first act followed by "intermission" (1629). The thoughtful
silence of the actor is described, and then his words are given in direct
discourse. Those words continue the metaphor of the stage: Samson,
having offered his audience "wonder and delight" (1642), will now present a second act which "with amaze shall strike all who behold" (1645).
When the theatre comes down "upon the heads of all who sate below"
(1652), Samson is destroyed in their midst; "the vulgar . . . scap'd who
stood without" (1659).

A play-within-a-play reveals to the audience that the play as a whole
attempts to mirror reality by calling their attention to the artificial and
representational quality of what they have been seeing, reminding them
that they themselves are but audience watching a fiction to be interpreted, not unlike the onstage audience (the Chorus) but not thereby re-
lieved from interpreting the fictions themselves. A play-within-a-play,
that is, enforces the textuality of the whole play. It relates the play
reality to extradramatic reality by recalling to the audience its role: to
draw parallel constructions in its own world to those in the world shown
on the stage. Drama exemplifies truth; when the audience is made
self-conscious as audience, it is warned that the discovery and application of truth belongs to it. The audience sees an example; it sees in the
play-within-the-play that drama is shaped as example. The play meta-

phor, in short, hands over to the audience the playwright's thematic responsibility.[15]

In *The Reason of Church-Government*, Milton called the Book of Revelation a tragedy not as an eschatological dreamer or zealous millenarian might loosely, on the basis of its subject, but as a student of dramatic structure, describing it as "the majestick image of a high and stately Tragedy, shutting up and intermingling her solemn Scenes and Acts with a seven fold Chorus of Halleluja's and harping symphonies" (YP, I, 815); again citing Pareus on this point in "Of . . . Tragedy," he repeats the emphasis: "*Pareus* divides the whole book as a tragedy, into acts distinguished each by a chorus of heavenly harpings and songs between" (CM, I, 331). He recommended in the earlier work that the magistrates of the Commonwealth arrange "publick sports and festival pastimes" to procure "wise and artfull recitations" at "set and solemn Paneguries, in Theaters, porches, and what other place" (YP, I, 819–20). He actually looked forward to a Puritan stage, on which would be performed exemplary drama applicable to its hearers. Popular Puritanism regularly authorized the conversion both of scriptural and current events into dramatic edification and used the stage metaphor in that connection. Thomas Beard wrote of contemporary affairs under the title *The Theatre of Gods Judgements*, drawing attention to the link between medium and message.[16] Margot Heinemann has recently written of a striking reverse application: John Reynold's *The Triumphs of God's Revenge Against the Crying and Execrable Sin of Murther* became a plot source for Middleton's *The Changeling*, and was coupled with *The Theatre of Gods Judgements* and Foxe's *Book of Martyrs* by Henry Burton as able to "daunt the most professed Atheist, and reclaim the most incorrigible sinner."[17] Foxe's *Book of Martyrs* itself abounds in theater metaphor, latent when the stage of so many persecutions was amphitheater and open scaffold before the people, overt when the martyr is likened to a tragic protagonist. Of Elizabeth, Foxe wrote, for example, "there was nothing lacking to make a very Iphigenia of her but offering up upon the altar of the scaffold."[18] John Speed's *The Theatre of Great Britain* suggests the kind of political application which the play metaphor might urge.[19] The recognition by the offstage audience of its counterpart on stage in *Samson Agonistes*, which is the principal effect equally of the play metaphor, the theatrical imagery, and the play-within-the-play, allowed Milton to create the double moderative catharsis for which he had structurally divided catastrophe from denouement and then for the only time in the play to divide the chorus into two separate voices receiving and applying the ideas necessary for viewing catharsis itself as thematic.

While they reinforce a line of intellectual and philosophical consideration within the drama, all the devices I have examined are in some sense extradramatic. Even in the narrated play-within-the-play, the illusion of being present at a play-within-a-play is thoroughly restricted, contained, and controlled by the fact that the events are narrated, just as the theatrical imagery is restricted by the certainty that it is metaphorical. All the devices can be found in earlier English plays: characters who introduce themselves or are introduced iconically abound in mystery plays, admonitory extradramatic addresses abound in the moralities, debates in the interludes, and embedded plays in the inductions, prologues, frames, vices, and epilogues of the school, inns of court, and classically based pre-Shakespearean plays. All have a show of Greek precedent: choral characterizations, stage lyrics, dianoia presented in discussion, and reported actions are used by each of the greatest Greek playwrights, "the three Tragic Poets unequall'd yet by any."[20] What Milton achieved with these devices, however, was the structural incorporation of extradramatic forms within philosophical tragedy. His dramatic sophistication submerged and interlaced them into a recapitulative structure in which the hero in the present confronts his past as it reenters his present moment and then acts in the present. He made his play a tragedy of a defeated man exploring how he defeated himself, accepting responsibility for that defeat, finding a tragic triumph in his ability to accept defeat and responsibility, discovering in his acceptance a power to change and a moment of spiritual regeneration which cannot for him, but may for his people, his audience, lead to permanent enlightenment. The protagonist relives his past forward into a single present moment; he began with false assumptions about the past which made him see his present situation as permanent and irrevocable—he could not change, he had no future; the reliving initiates dramatic change; he concludes his tragedy in an act displaying his exemplary change for the permanent truth it may give the audience, not for the change it has made in their circumstances. The dramatic arc is as firm as possible. The recapitulative aspect of the plot line declares that the true heroic act of mankind is the achievement of "magnitude of mind" (1279); every extradramatic subgenre within the dramatic suspension of the structure reinforces mental labor and encourages a "rational libertie" (PL XII, 83).

MODERATIVE CATHARSIS AS THEME

In *Paradise Lost* Michael draws the moral of the Nimrod story, which was not far from Milton's mind in *Samson Agonistes* where Samson, God's champion, is contrasted to other versions of the mighty, fame-seeking hunter. Michael uses the story to examine God's justice and man's freedom: Nimrod is rightly detested for

> affecting to subdue
> Rational Libertie; yet know withall,
> Since thy original lapse, true Libertie
> Is lost, which alwayes with right Reason dwells
> Twinn'd, and from her hath no dividual being:
> Reason in man obscur'd, or not obeyd,
> Immediately inordinate desires
> And upstart Passions catch the Government
> From Reason, and to servitude reduce
> Man till then free. Therefore since hee permits
> Within himself unworthie Powers to reign
> Over free Reason, God in Judgement just
> Subjects him from without to violent Lords;
> Who oft as undeservedly enthrall
> His outward freedom: Tyrannie must be,
> Though to the Tyrant thereby no excuse.
> Yet somtimes Nations will decline so low
> From vertue, which is reason, that no wrong,
> But Justice, and some fatal curse annext
> Deprives them of thir outward libertie,
> Thir inward lost.   (XII, 81–101)

In the process Michael describes is found the theme of repeated tragic failure:

> Thus will this latter, as the former World,
> Still tend from bad to worse.   (XII, 105–06)

Michael plainly tells Adam that the burden of upholding liberty falls on man, that liberty cannot be distinguished from the rule of reason over the passions, that political enslavement to conquering tyrants follows upon personal enslavement to one's own desires, and that God's justice together with "some fatal curse" sometimes subjects whole nations. Michael's lesson is part of a search for a view of reality and human history which goes beyond the tragic to become epic.[21]

Samson Agonistes fits into Michael's lesson. To show that the play raises and answers the question why the good is so easily lost and so painfully reestablished and thereby vindicates God's ways, it is helpful to note what the play does not dramatize. The story it tells is of a man who permitted "unworthie Powers to reign / Over free Reason" (*PL* XII, 91–92), who was subjected "from without to violent Lords" (*PL* XII, 93), and "whose nation [declined] so low / From vertue" (*PL* XII,

97–98) that its people were deprived of "thir outward libertie, thir inward lost (*PL* XII, 83–84). As Milton tells that story, however, it is not God who "subjects" Samson nor a "fatal curse annext" which enslaves the Jews. Israel is brought to servitude "by thir vices" which cause them to "love Bondage more then Liberty" (*SA* 271); it lay in their power and would have been right to cast off that bondage first to luxury and then to Philistia by following Samson's lead. In almost the barest, and in their prose rhythm the simplest lines in the play, Milton defends a war of liberation when Samson replies to Harapha's charge that he is a "Revolter":

> My Nation was subjected to your Lords.
> It was the force of Conquest; force with force
> Is well ejected when the Conquer'd can.   (1205–07)

Like Milton, Samson can and does distinguish between a just and an unjust war, a Nimrod case of imperial aggrandizement and a Samson case of liberation. But Samson goes on to say that a "comely" and "reviving" instance of God's support in a just cause, a miracle of national revival, is not what his life dramatizes. He was given strength and command from heaven to free his country; in *Samson Agonistes* Milton uses the word *command* to signify both "orders" ("at our sending and command" [1397]) and "leadership" ("where wisdom bears command" [57]), and the second sense is more probable here. Samson's leadership was rejected:

> if their servile minds
> Me their Deliverer sent would not receive . . .
> Th'unworthier they; whence to this day they serve.   (1213–15)

The play ends with Israel still being urged to find their liberty. Liberty is still conditional on their own action; Samson has done his part by offering his nation "freedom, let but them / Find courage to lay hold on this occasion" (1716). I do not doubt the correctness of those who argue that Milton meant contemporary Englishmen to apply the drama to their own political condition and that the application would not have meant quiet acceptance of the status quo as "best," but I find no reason to think it would have prompted acts of terrorism.[22] Acts of ethical purification leading to a new political consensus, such as Milton desired in *Of True Religion*, seem to me implied by the allusions in Manoa's words, "let them but / Find courage to lay hold on this occasion" (1715–16) to St. Paul's "Fight the good fight of faith, lay hold on eternal life, whereunto thou art also called" and "Laying up in store for themselves a good foundation against the time to come, that they may lay hold on eternal life" (1 Timothy vi, 12, 19).[23]

Equally Milton tells us that the play does not involve "som fatal curse annext" (*PL* XII, 99). The Chorus may begin by thinking the hero a "mirror of our fickle state" (164) and the example of the "pitch of abject fortune" (169), but Samson rejects that version of reality: his "servil mind" was well rewarded with "servil punishment" (412). Of fate, the single use of the word in the play bears the strictly human meaning of "mortal," the "fatal harvest" (1024) of Samson's hair. Fortune is so discounted that the true hero is specified as *not* one "whom the sphear of fortune raises" (1972). The only necessity the play ever acknowledges is that of the uniform working of the law of gravity: under the falling roof of the Temple of Dagon Samson died with the Philistian leaders, "tangled in the fold / Of dire necessity" (1666). And most striking of all, the use made of the word *destiny* in the play is strictly a retrospective use, referring to the past habit of thought which the recapitulative structure of the play calls in doubt: "I was his nursling once . . . / His destin'd from the womb" (633–34). God's "promise" was as uncoercive as Samson's destiny; the two references to it are equally confined to past habits of thought in the opening episodes.

Finally, the play is not about the convenant of a national God with a special group of the faithful and does not prophesy the extension of that covenant to all people. Since the play asks what kind of God is God, the definition by which Samson proved Dagon no God must show God to be God:

> gods unable
> To acquit themselves and prosecute their foes
> But by ungodly means, the contradiction
> Of their own deity, Gods cannot be.   (896–99)

Has Jehovah engineered, more skillfully than Dagon could prevent, the ungodly deed of general slaughter? Milton puts a similar question in Dalila's last words to Samson, so that it amounts to the question, Was Dalila a Philistian Jael? with the implication that the Holy One of Israel does not much bother about ungodly means. But not only is no verdict given in favor of Jael's "inhospitable guile" (989), which "smote Sisera sleeping" (990), by either Samson or the Chorus; a hint of the very repugnance of such an action is contained directly after the Chorus in Samson's recollective horror at the Philistines' cowardly treachery:

> Nor in the house with chamber Ambushes
> Close-banded durst attaque me, no not sleeping.   (1112–13)

Nor does Dalila ask Dagon to pronounce upon his deed through her when she exults in future worldly fame. Nor does Samson claim that hand-to-hand combat with Harapha will prove God's superiority over Dagon until Harapha says that Samson's strength never had anything to do with God to start with:

> black enchantments, some Magicians Art
> Arm'd thee or charm'd thee strong, which thou from Heaven
> Feigndst at thy birth was giv'n thee in thy hair.   (1132–34)

Samson's denial of that calumny does not claim that God covenanted supernatural strength in exchange for service, but rather that Samson's strength was a gift from childhood and its lodgment in his hair was only "a pledge" of his human vow of obedience. Samson's demystifying view of his uncut hair as "pledge" is exactly like God's concept of the apple in *Paradise Lost* as "the pledge of [man's] Obedience and [his] Faith" (VIII, 325) against Satan's proposal that it is fruit of a sacred plant in which "the Gods" or something prior even to them "enclos'd / Knowledge of Good and Evil" (IX, 722–23). Signs are not sacraments: neither apples nor hairs contain mysterious properties. Finally, God's act is not identified with Samson's act but with Samson's agony. When the play asks whether that agony has been just, it shows that the agony has borne meaning, taught wisdom and knowledge of God and, most important of all, that it has carried Samson to a moderative catharsis. Samson's act is ascribed to Samson and to his own changed vision: "he though blind of sight . . . / His fiery virtue rous'd" (1689–90). Asking whether God's permission of agony was "just and justifiable to Men" (294), the play concludes that it was "best." It so concludes by illustrating the Christian humanist concept of exertion of mind and spirit in the epithet applied to Samson, *agonistes*.

Milton did not use any form of the word *agony* in its extended Platonic sense of moral exercise until he came to write *Samson Agonistes*. In *Paradise Lost* he reserved the word for mere human suffering: he synonymized it in the phrase "agony and pain" (*PL* II, 861) and twice made it accompany the disordered feverishness of postlapsarian love sickness (II, 861; IX, 858; XI, 482). But in *Samson Agonistes* he extended its meaning through its Greek associations to signify intellectual labor. (Milton secured a similar extension of implication for the word *suffering* in *Paradise Regained* when he distinguished between *suffering* and *sufferance*, between Christ's "Humiliation and strong Sufferance" [I, 160] as his ethical endurance and Socrates' "for truth's sake suffering death" [III, 98], as second only to Christ's perfectly knowing or faithful sufferance.) What makes tragedy "grave, moral and profitable" is its relationship to moral growth, its paideutic value. What makes God's mysterious ways toward men—ways they doubt and find unsearchable— both just and merciful is that they are both educative and moderative, yielding both "plain heroic magnitude of mind" (1279) and "calm of mind" (1758). As the preface promised, the drama concludes with "the mind purged of . . . passions": God "temperst his providence" so that human passions are "tempered and reduced to just measure" ("Of . . . Tragedy" CM, I, 331).

In *De Doctrina Christiana*, Milton wrote defending God's justice with respect to his unequal distribution of amounts of grace to human beings so as to remove any suggestion that God wills human punishment:

> If . . . God rejects none except the disobedient and the unbeliever, he undoubt-edly bestows grace on all, and if not equally upon each, at least sufficient to enable everyone to attain knowledge of the truth and salvation. I say not equally upon each, because he has not distributed grace equally. . . . For like everyone else, where his own possessions are concerned, God claims for himself the right of making decrees about them as he thinks fit, without being obliged to give a reason for his decree, though he could give a very good one if he wished. So God does not consider everyone worthy of equal grace, and the cause of this is his supreme will. But he considers all worthy of sufficient grace, and the cause is his justice. . . . It is unnecessary to give any cause or reason for the exercise of mercy, other than God's own merciful will. On the other hand, the cause of reprobation, which is followed by punishment, must, if it is to be just, be man's sin alone, not God's will.   (YP, VI, 192–95)

The destruction of the Philistines is the result of their choices—their vengeance, their exultation, their drunken frenzy. Samson's final act is his choice likewise, preceded by prayer and thought. Lest it be argued that God constrains the choices of the sinner, Milton cautions elsewhere,

> We should be wary of the common saying that God punishes sins with sins. . . . There is to be sure a proverb which says, he who prevents not when he can, commands. Men are bound by the principle as a moral duty, but not God. God says, speaking like a man, that he incites, when really he only omits to prevent, and this does not mean that he commands.   (YP, VI, 334)

When the first semichorus says that God sent a spirit of frenzy among the Philistines, it "speaks like men." When it finds the Philistines "In-sensate left, or to sense reprobate / And with blindness struck" (1685–86), however, it makes room for the ironic recognition that if the sighted were blind, the blind man achieved vision.

For the inequality of his grace, God "could give a very good [reason] if he wished." Milton gives God one such good reason when he discusses the concept of the good temptation:

Good temptations are those which God uses to tempt even righteous men, in order to prove them. He does this not for his own sake—as if he did not know what sort of men they would turn out to be—but either to exercise or demonstrate their faith or patience, as in the case of Abraham and Job, or to lessen their self-confidence and prove them guilty of weakness, so that they may become wise, and others may be instructed. (YP, VI, 338)

That Samson's "exercise" of "faith or patience" resulted in self-knowledge so that he became "wiser" is the second response of the first semichorus in the denouement; there is evidence of both his and their instruction:

> But he though blind of sight,
> Despis'd and thought extinguish't quite,
> With inward eyes illuminated
> His fierie vertue rouz'd
> From under ashes into sudden flame. (1687–91)

If some modern readers are not now perfectly happy with the imagery of the first two birds of revival in the semichorus' mounting praise of Samson's reviving power, the cause may lie in a modern inability to hear psalmic echoes. In the *kommos* the chorus and Manoa recognize the exemplary value of Samson's life; they express their own new vision by drawing on two psalms of communal thanksgiving, the paired psalms ciii and civ. Psalm ciii is a mixture of hymn and thanksgiving, praising God's guidance of man in history, by one who has personally experienced renewal. Psalm civ, now conjecturally ascribed to the same poet as ciii, treats God's wisdom and glory throughout creation. Among the most striking images of Psalm ciii is that of the eagle's revival; among the most striking of civ is that of God's hiding his face from men and then returning to them. When Psalm civ is cited in *De Doctrina Christiana* to prove God's eternal compassion to men, 1 Timothy vi, the moral "lay hold on eternal life" is also cited as revealing God's blessedness (YP, VI, 151). The third image of revival, the phoenix, by traditional iconography was an emblem of the triumph of eternal life over death and of virtuous constancy. That is the meaning the chorus gives to it, adding the note of good arising from pain, virtue from loss.

> So vertue giv'n for lost,
> Deprest, and overthrown, as seem'd,

> Like that self-begott'n bird
> In the *Arabian* woods embost,
> That no second knows nor third,
> And lay e're while a Holocaust,
> From out her ashie womb now teem'd,
> Revives, reflourishes, then vigorous most
> When most unactive deem'd,
> And though her body die, her fame survives,
> A secular bird ages of lives.   (1698–1708)

Milton's conception of tragedy differs from Aristotle's in several important respects (which is why Milton quotes *The Poetics* in "Of . . . Tragedy"). Milton aims at moderative, not extirpative catharsis, and his tragedy moderates passions other than simply those of pity and fear. His fable differs from Aristotle's preferred fables in proposing a double issue of the action. Aristotle wrote:

(i) a good man must not be shown as passing from happiness to misfortune; for that does not inspire pity or fear, but is an outrage upon our moral feelings. Nor (ii) must a bad man be seen passing from misfortune to happiness. That is as untragic as can possibly be; it makes no appeal either to our sense of poetic justice, or to our pity or to our fear. . . . Such a story may stir the human feeling in us but not our pity or fear; pity is reserved for undeserved misfortune, and fear for the misfortune of a man like ourselves. . . . The sound plot, therefore, must have a single and not a double issue; the hero's change of fortune must not be from misery to happiness, but the other way round; and it must be due not to any depravity, but to some grave mistake. (pp. 21–22)

Samson's is the story of a failed man who, after reassessing his nature, deeds, and failure becomes a good man, the passion faced in the encounters with other characters brought to a harmony under reason. While his regained happiness is only an inner quality of mind, a changed vision, the issue of the plot is double, emphasizing distributive and not retributive justice. The catharsis not only moderates passions, it bears a philosophical weight; it is not only a tragic effect, it is a tragic theme. The purpose of human life, like that of the imitation of human life, is man's education and tempering. God's purpose as the creator of human life is like the purpose of the tragic poet: he will bring good out of evil by strengthening the minds and sweetening the imaginations of human beings. Hence the catharsis not only brings "peace," it brings "consolation." The Chorus sought to give Samson council and consolation (189); they saw how necessary to him was a "source of consolation from above" (664); in the end the "peace and consolation" (1757) of his life's meaningfulness comes to them.

Milton ended his description of the good temptation noting, "Good temptation, then, is rather to be desired. . . . And God promises a happy outcome. . . . But the faithful are sometimes insufficiently aware of divine providence, until they examine the subject more deeply and become better informed about the word of God" (YP, VI, 339). That *Paradise Lost* as epic includes tragedy and the tragic vision no one doubts. No one doubts the capacity of epic to include history, encyclopedia, pastoral, and the like, and latterly few doubt its power to include prophecy. It is less usual to notice how tragedy overlaps with epic, how far the two genres—of which Aristotle wrote "All the parts of Epic are included in Tragedy, but not all those of Tragedy in Epic"—represent complementary responses to and complementary visions of the same kind of experience. An honorable exception is Thomas Vogler, who reminds us that the Book of Job can be read as tragic drama, or, as Milton read it, as "brief epic."[24] The *kommos* of *Samson Agonistes* enacting catharsis, paideia, and consolation moves tragedy toward epic. It describes the effect proper to tragedy—"true experience" (1756), "peace and consolation" (1757), "calm of mind all passion spent" (1758)— as a final transcendence: "All is best. . . . And ever best found in the close" (1745, 1748). The mind of the regenerated audience is shown in ultimate enlightenment, a mind itself made truly heroic. Epic is that composite genre in which ultimate enlightenment is proposed, critical of previous value structures but bearing the hope of a new and constant vision. My subject has been *Samson Agonistes* as tragedy, however, and I may only suggest and not pursue the notion that the enlightenment in its catharsis may "justly give Heroic name" as well as tragic to protagonist and to poem.

Cornell University

NOTES

1. The following books and articles are of particular interest to readers of SA as tragedy: Arthur E. Barker, "Calm Regained Through Passion Spent: The Conclusions of the Miltonic Effort," in *The Prison and the Pinnacle*, ed. Balachandra Rajan (London, 1975); Donald F. Bouchard, *Milton: A Structural Reading* (London, 1974); Una Ellis-Fermor, *The Frontiers of Drama*, 2d ed. (London, 1964); Anne Davidson Ferry, *Milton and the Miltonic Dryden* (Cambridge, Mass., 1968); William Haller, "The Tragedy of God's Englishmen," in *Reason and the Imagination*, ed. Joseph A. Mazzeo (New York, 1962); Christopher Hill, *Milton and the English Revolution* (London, 1977); Frank Kermode,

"Milton in Old Age", *Southern Review*, XI (1975), 513–29; Jon S. Lawry, *The Shadow of Heaven* (Ithaca, 1968); Barbara K. Lewalski, "*Samson Agonistes* and the Tragedy of the Apocalypse," *PMLA*, LXXXV (1970), 1050–62; Anthony Low, *The Blaze of Noon* (New York, 1974); Virginia R. Mollenkott, "Relativism in *Samson Agonistes*," *SP*, LXVIII (1970), 89–102; George N. Muldrow, *Milton and the Drama of the Soul* (The Hague, 1970); William Riley Parker, *Milton's Debt to Greek Tragedy in "Samson Agonistes"* (Baltimore, 1937); Lynn Veach Sadler, *Consolation in "Samson Agonistes"* (Salzburg, 1979); Irene Samuel, "*Samson Agonistes* as Tragedy," in *Calm of Mind*, ed. Joseph Wittreich (Cleveland, 1971); John M. Steadman, " 'Passions Well Imitated': Rhetoric and Poetics in the Preface to *Samson Agonistes*," and Raymond B. Waddington, " 'Melancholy against Melancholy': *Samson Agonistes* as Renaissance Tragedy," both essays in *Calm of Mind*, ed. Wittreich; A. S. P. Woodhouse, *The Heavenly Muse: A Preface to Milton*, ed. Hugh MacCallum (Toronto, 1972).

2. I quote Aristotle in the translation of John Warrington from Ingram Bywater's edition: *Aristotle's Poetics* (London, 1963), p. 22.

3. *Lives of the Poets* (New York, n.d.), p. 141.

4. *Biographia Literaria*, ed. George Watson (London, 1962), p. 172.

5. C. M. Bowra, *Inspiration and Poetry* (London, 1955), p. 112.

6. Here John Carey may speak for them all; see his *Milton* (London, 1969), pp. 138–46.

7. Some interesting reflections on this can be found in *Literary Uses of Typology from the Late Middle Ages to the Present*, ed. Earl Miner (Princeton, 1977).

8. An interesting and helpful summary of the iconic principles of Renaissance portraiture can be found in Wendy Steiner, *Exact Resemblance to Exact Resemblance: The Literary Portraiture of Gertrude Stein* (New Haven, 1978), pp. 51–52.

9. Milton's prose use of the character genre in the various characters in *The Second Defense* is well known; when preparing the text of *The History of Britain* for publication in 1670, a text he very probably worked on during the sixties, he deleted from it another such character, a "Character of the Long Parliament." His closest imitation of the popular seventeenth-century genre was perhaps his character of the religious conformist in *Areopagitica* (YP, II, 544; see also YP, V, i. xlii–xliii).

10. Mary Ann Radzinowicz, *Toward "Samson Agonistes"* (Princeton, 1979), pp. 15–61.

11. *John Milton, Poems, Reproduced from the Manuscript in Trinity College, Cambridge* (London, 1972), p. 36.

12. *Fox's Book of Martyrs*, ed W. B. Forbush (Philadelphia, n.d.), pp. 176, 147. On iconography, see Raymond Klibansky, E. Panofsky, and F. Saxl, *Saturn and Melancholy* (London, 1964), p. 288.

13. *Toward "Samson Agonistes,"* pp. 208–11.

14. Una Ellis-Fermor, *Frontiers of Drama*, p. 24; George Muldrow, *Milton and the Drama of the Soul*, pp. 166–67.

15. Anne Righter provides the classic examination of this subject in *Shakespeare and the Idea of the Play* (Harmondsworth, England, 1967), pp. 53–62.

16. Ibid., p. 19; Margot Heinemann, *Puritanism and Theatre* (Cambridge, 1980), p. 178.

17. Heinemann, *Puritanism and Theatre*, p. 178. The originality and firmness of the scholarship in this book are beyond praise.

18. Quoted in William Haller, *Foxe's Book of Martyrs and the Elect Nation* (London, 1963), p. 127.

19. Whether or not Milton was the author of the translation of George Buchanan's *Baptistes sive calumnia* under the title *Tyrannical Government Anatomised, or a Discourse concerning Evil Councellors*, ordered to be printed by Parliament in 1643, that play too drew upon and evidences the ability of an audience to make its own inferences from parallel constructions, from biblical instances to derive historical conclusions. The attribution to Milton was confidently dismissed by William Riley Parker, *Milton: A Biography*, 2 vols. (Oxford, 1968), II, 863; entertained as a possibility by Murray Roston, *Biblical Drama in England* (Evanston, 1968), p. 81; and is cautiously revived by Heinemann, *Puritanism and Theatre*, pp. 234–35.

20. William Riley Parker, *Milton's Debt to Greek Tragedy*, pp. 168–87, without specifically examining any of these substructures, usefully examines the construction of *Oedipus Coloneus* and *Prometheus* and the Greek idea of symmetry so as to imply at least the last three. The model for the recapitulative structure is likewise Greek and present in *Oedipus Rex*. Milton's distinctive tragedy involves a profound assimilation of his Greek sources and not a simple reversion to authority. Had not Parker and others made this point clear to us all, it would be necessary to say more about Milton's fully conscious decision to adopt his structure from Greek models.

21. Thomas A. Vogler distinguishes inner from outer form in epic and tragedy and writes suggestively on the differences and similarities between the inner forms of each. See *Preludes to Vision* (Berkeley and Los Angeles, 1971), pp. 5–6.

22. See Hill, *Milton and the English Revolution*, pp. 434–38, for the contrary view.

23. See also Hebrews x, 23: "Let us hold fast the profession of the faith without wavering," which verse is followed shortly by both the enrollment of Samson among the heroes of faith and the two comments "Let us run with patience the race that is set before us" and "Whom the Lord loveth he chasteneth." Milton quoted the Book of Timothy no less than 112 times in *De Doctrina Christiana*, particularly as evidence of God's desire that all men be saved.

24. *Preludes to Vision*, pp. 5–6.

"BEYOND THE FIFTH ACT":
SAMSON AGONISTES AS PROPHECY

John C. Ulreich, Jr.

S AMSON AGONISTES has generally, and no doubt rightly, been considered a Christian drama. Its precise Christian meaning, however, has proven somewhat resistant to critical definition. Many—though by no means all—of us think we know *that* the play is Christian, but we do not know *how* it is so. The reason for this elusiveness, I believe, is that the meaning of the play remains largely implicit in its dramatic form rather than being made explicit in its logical argument: both the shape of Samson's action and its final meaning remain mysterious, even at the close. In consequence, it seems to me useful to describe the metaphoric structure of Milton's play as essentially parabolic: like Samson's riddle in the Book of Judges, the story of Samson (as Milton tells it) is a parable of deliverance.

Furthermore, since parabolic discourse naturally lends itself to typological construction, we might suppose that such an approach to the play would assist us in formulating its Christian meaning. Unfortunately, however, *Samson* is peculiarly resistant to typological modes of interpretation; mythic analogies with the Crucifixion dash themselves against the rock of Samson's unremittingly Judaic consciousness. Here, I believe, we come to the crux of the matter: the essential difficulty of the play, its stubborn refusal to yield a "self-satisfying solution" (306), reflects Milton's persistent iconoclasm. He declines to allow any mere image to stand as true. And this radical iconoclasm leads me to call *Samson Agonistes* prophecy.

Iconoclasm, however, is the beginning of prophecy rather than its end. Samson's regeneration is a recreation, his death also a rebirth. And that rebirth ultimately reconstitutes the form of the play: what had appeared to be a classical tragedy, or perhaps a "Christian tragedy," must finally be seen as a work of tragic prophecy. When it is regarded generically, *Samson Agonistes* needs to be redefined along the lines suggested by Claudio Guillén: the "structural model" of Greek tragedy is "dialectically surpassed (and assimilated)" by a more comprehensive genre; as tragedy becomes prophecy, one "genre [is transformed] by a countergenre."[1]

Greek tragedy was not the only model available to Milton's imagination, however. And when we attempt to discover alternative models, it seems appropriate to consider the possibilities afforded by the prophets of the Old Testament. Among them, the tragic prophecy of Amos is conspicuous, not least because its quasi-dramatic form resembles rather closely the classical five-act structure of *Samson*. Even more to the purpose is the way in which each work projects tragedy into prophecy by transforming catastrophe into revelation.

In the case of *Samson*, however, that transformation is more radical than can be suggested by consideration of a single model. As a Christian prophecy, Milton's play becomes tragicomic; it subsumes not only the tragic prophecy of Amos but its generic counter-type, the comic prophecy of Jonah. By virtue of this twofold transformation, *Samson* comes to possess what Angus Fletcher has called "transcendental form": *Samson* is a "poetic structure that . . . includes more than its traditionally accepted generic limits . . . would allow it to include." And as Joseph Wittreich has shown, "Prophecy is the ultimate transcendental form: that is, tragedy is to epic what epic is to prophecy—the thing contained within a larger compass, contained not so that its vision of life will be affirmed but so that it may be subdued within a larger, more expansive vision."[2]

I

For the sake of argument, then, let us agree to call *Samson* a Christian play. As a point of departure we might take Anthony Low's suggestion that "*Samson Agonistes* is Greek in form; its story is Hebrew. . . . Yet the Greek and Hebrew in *Samson* are finally only veils for a deeply Christian meaning."[3] But how can that be? If the form of the play, its tragic action, is Greek, and its argument, the justification of God's ways to Samson, is Hebraic, in what sense can its significance be called Christian? In these terms, the structure of *Samson* seems incongruous because it juxtaposes two radically contradictory patterns of development: its apparently classical action is undercut by Hebraic argument. The action of the play presents the mythic development of active heroism: Samson *redivivus* rediscovers his "fierie virtue" even in the "ashes" of his ruin (1690–91). Roused by Manoa from his initial lethargy, provoked by Dalila into reaffirming his integrity, and finally goaded by Harapha into reasserting his heroic strength, Samson finally "Revives, reflourishes, then vigorous most / When most unactive deem'd" (1704–05). In classical terms, at least, "*Samson* hath quit himself / Like *Samson*, and heroicly hath finish'd / A life Heroic" (1709–11). In Hebraic terms, however, Samson's triumph over the Philistines represents God's providential conquest of Dagon. The argument of the play presents the ethical development of passive martyrdom: Samson *subjectus* bears "witness gloriously" to God's "uncontroulable intent" (1752, 1754). Preferring God's judgment to Manoa's mercy, asserting God's strength against Dalila's weakness, and choosing to fear God rather than Harapha, Samson justifies "the ways of God . . . to men" (293–94) by fulfilling "the work for which" he had been "foretold / To *Israel*" (1662–63). But these two patterns of development are not obviously congruous; although both converge on the same catastrophe, one presents this action as a triumph of Samson, the other as a triumph of God. The first pattern is intrinsic to the action, but its meaning seems merely literal and external, a "Proof of his mighty strength" (1602); the meaning of the second pattern seems relatively internal and spiritual, but the pattern itself is abstract, "tangl'd in the fold, / Of dire necessity" (1665–66), and seems largely extrinsic to Samson's action. It would appear, then, that the literal action of the play is not finally transformed by the spirit of its argument, so that letter and spirit remain irreconcilably opposed to one another: the "celestial vigour" (1280) of classical heroism and the "patience" (1287) of Hebraic martyrdom are ironically juxtaposed.

This irony is crystallized in the climax of the play: is Samson's destruction of the Philistines to be seen as an heroic act of "dearly-bought revenge" (1660), or is his self-destruction meant to seem self-sacrificial, an affirmation of God's "uncontroulable intent" (1754)? Either interpretation poses difficulties. If Samson's action is essentially vindictive, and if that motive is sanctioned by the form of the play, then we must reckon with Kenneth Fell's objection that the poem "fails to transcend the limitations inherent in its primitive story." As it happens, the play does transcend those limits; as John F. Andrews has shown, "The inner voice heeded by Samson is the voice of God, not the voice of misguided personal honor." Samson is, in the end, answerable only to God: "To me *belongeth* vengeance, and recompense" (Deuteronomy xxxii, 35).[4] But the Hebraic perspective is equally problematic, inasmuch as the deliverance of God's chosen people also entails the destruction of the unchosen—of whom Samson appears to be one. If the play remains focused on vengeance, as its violent catastrophe seems to suggest, then very little is gained by shifting the responsibility for Samson's "mighty strength" from the protagonist to God. The Hebraic vindication of Providence—if that is what the Chorus means by "dearly-bought revenge" (1660)—does not represent a very satisfactory alternative to classical self-affirmation.

Furthermore, the ethical basis of the play seems fundamentally confused by the unresolved tension between classical and Hebraic perspectives. The action of the play may affirm Samson's free will, his "celestial vigour" (1280) and "heroic magnitude of mind" (1279). But this free will seems to be denied by the providential argument; as G. A. Wilkes has argued, "the sovereignty of providence" is manifested by "the mode in which the divine impulsion is exerted—independent of Samson's volition and contrary to the course he proposed."[5] How, then, are we to interpret Samson's "rouzing motions" (1382)—as tragic impulse or providential compulsion? If we ignore the awfulness of the catastrophe itself, we can rationalize this dilemma by assuming that Samson elects his destiny, that the tragic form of the play subsists in an "inner tension between man's freedom and God's Providence," as A. S. P. Woodhouse argued. From this perspective, at least, Samson's regeneration seems to be defined by what Douglas Bush has called an "upward progression" from "self-centeredness, wounded pride, distrust of God's providence" toward "penitent humility, renewed faith . . . and, toward the end, untroubled exaltation of spirit." The humanist exaltation of Samson, however, is at best inferential—and at worst circular, since it assumes a providential direction, "steady, upward," which the action of the play does not realize. Stanley Fish has, at least, asked the crucial question: "What is the relationship between Samson's spiritual regeneration . . . and the act of pulling down the temple?"[6]

Fortunately, the very terms in which I have posed the dilemma suggest the form of its possible resolution. For if classical and Hebraic meanings are mutually incompatible, they may nonetheless be reconciled by, subsumed in, a more comprehensive, Christian meaning. The apparent impossibility of reconciling drama and argument suggests that we should explore the possibility of a third, figurative line of development. And because that development is essentially enigmatic, it seems useful to describe the form of the play as parabolic. In its simplest form, a parable is a way of saying one thing in order to mean something else; it is a story with a hidden, figurative meaning. But because of their equivocation between sign and signification, letter and spirit, parables are often radically enigmatic: in saying one thing and meaning another, parables may appear to say nearly the opposite of what they mean. Samson's riddle in the Book of Judges is a case in point. The riddle itself is palpably literal:

> Out of the eater came forth meat,
> and out of the strong came forth sweetness.

And the resolution of the paradox is also apparently literal:

> What is sweeter than honey?
> and what is stronger than a lion?   (xiv, 14, 18)

But this answer is also a question: how does that which consumes, as devouring strength, become instead that which nourishes? What is stronger than a lion? Samson. What is sweeter than honey? The deliverance of Israel. Thus the riddle begins to unfold its figurative possibilities: just as the lion which would devour Samson is devoured by him, so Samson, in seeking to destroy the Philistines, is himself destroyed; and as the death of the eater produces meat, so the destruction of Samson nourishes his people with the honey of deliverance. In this way the ancient riddle is transformed into a religious paradox, and the primitive fable of Samson the Destroyer becomes a parable of deliverance.

   Samson Agonistes, I believe, represents precisely this kind of parabolic transformation.[7] By juxtaposing classical action and Hebraic argument, Milton insists on their radical incongruity; he renders the literal surface of his play "inexcusable" in order to crystallize its figurative meaning. That meaning arises from the tension between the apparent, literal sense of the drama—Samson's heroic vengeance upon the Philistines—and its internal, spiritual meaning—Samson's heroic martyrdom: "At once both to destroy and be destroy'd" (1588).

   This notion of parabolic form can be clarified by analyzing the interrelation between the genetic constituents of *Samson:* its classical *mythos*, or tragic plot; its Hebraic *ethos*, or moral argument; and its Christian *psyche*, or spiritual form.[8] The first, immediately dramatic level reenacts the original Samson myth, the tale of "that invincible *Samson*" (341) whose tragic downfall is recorded in Judges. On this mythic level, the development of the drama corresponds closely to Aristotle's analysis of tragic action as a series of *agones* culminating in a *peripeteia*, or reversal of fortune: Samson "Revives, reflourishes, then vigorous most / When most unactive deem'd" (1704–05). On the second, ethical level, the argument of the play recapitulates a Judaic exposition of Providence. Samson's submission of his will to God's reflects Milton's characteristic attempt to "assert Eternal Providence, / And justifie the wayes of God to men" (*PL* I, 25–26). From this point of view, the development of the play suggests Aristotle's conception of tragic action leading to *catharsis:* "calm of mind all passion spent" (1758). The third, psychic, level of development is defined by the tension between concrete action and abstract argument, between active self-assertion and passive submission, free will and Providence. On this figurative level, the movement of the play represents neither self-assertion nor self-denial but self-discovery—the Aristotelian *anagnoresis:* a "new acquist / Of true experience" (1755–56). Samson's final self-realization both affirms and denies his previous existence: "This great Deliverer" (40) has indeed become God's "faithful Champion" (1751). Thus, if the external form of the play is classical, and if its subject matter is essentially Hebraic, its internal form—its soul *(psyche)* or first principle *(arche)*—is surely Christian. If the story is mythic and its ethos historical, then its spirit is perhaps typological, for it presents history as myth and Samson himself, in one aspect at least, as a type of Christ, "with God not parted from him" (1719). The pagan meaning of the play is individual, and its Hebraic meaning is communal, but its Christian meaning transcends these categories, for it is both concrete and universal, individual and superindividual: a feat of "strength, yet greater" (1644). The meaning of the play is symbolic: a classical myth of tragic self-realization through suffering is recast as an Hebraic history of deliverance through destruction and thereby transformed into a Christian parable of redemption through sacrifice. What had seemed at first to be an irreconcilable contradiction between classical letter and Hebraic spirit turns out, finally, to be a polarity, a productive tension between two sets of relatively literal meanings, classical *mythos* and Hebraic *ethos*, whose incongruity gives rise to a third, more fully spiritualized meaning; "Except a corn of wheat fall into the ground and die, it abideth alone: but if it die, it bringeth forth much fruit" (John xii, 24). Thus the kernel of classical myth falls into the fertile soil of Hebraic ethics in order to yield abundant fruit as Christian parable.

II

Furthermore, the subject of that parable would appear to be, not merely Christian, but Christ Himself. By refusing Manoa's suggestion that he turn the stones of his "loathsom plight" (480) into the bread of "self-preservation" (505), by declining to worship Dalila's power, and by finally asserting his "trust . . . in the living God" (1140), Samson prepares himself for the agony of Gesthemane: when he stands in darkness, inwardly illuminated, "as one who pray'd" (1637), Samson foreshadows Christ's anguished prayer for the strength to submit himself completely: compare "And being in an agony" (Luke xxii, 44) with Milton's "straining all his nerves he bowed" (1646). Christ "prayed more earnestly: . . . nevertheless not my will, but thine, be done. And there appeared an angel unto him from heaven, strengthening him" (xxii, 42–43) with "strength, yet greater" (1644). Speaking typologically, Samson prefigures the Son of God; his suffering is fulfilled in and redeemed by the Crucifixion: "And, behold, the veil of the temple was rent in twain from the top to the bottom; and the earth did quake, and the rocks rent" (Matthew xxvii, 51).

Unfortunately, however, the attempt to read Samson as a prefiguration of Christ seems to involve a fatal self-contradiction: Samson is not, he cannot be, conscious of himself as a type of Christ. (By definition, a type is the unconscious manifestation of meaning that is consciously revealed in the Christ.) But if Samson is merely a type, as William Madsen has argued, if he "remains blind to the spiritual significance of his sufferings,"[9] then he cannot *choose* to fulfill any purpose, for "Reason also is choice" (*PL* III,108), and his action is therefore devoid not only of ethical significance but of religious significance as well. For if Samson is merely an instrument, rather than an agent, of Providence, he cannot testify to that Providence. God's proposed deliverance would be a gruesome irony indeed, since rather than favoring and assisting Samson, God simply uses him—not for any obviously worthwhile purpose—and then abandons him. In thus externalizing Providence, we render the drama absurd, for we exclude Samson's free will, without which no regeneration is possible: "as for life, / To what end should I seek it?" (521–22)

That is, of course, precisely the question which Samson himself asks—and answers—before he goes to his end:

> Masters commands come with a power resistless
> To such as owe them absolute subjection;
> And for a life who will not change his purpose?   (1404–06)

As Joseph Summers has observed, "We know that Samson does not owe 'absolute subjection' to any nation or person; he owes it only to God; and we see (or will come to see) that . . . [Samson's] 'rousing motions' [1382] have come as a command from that 'master.' "[10] Summers is surely right in seeing Samson's swift change of purpose as a response to God's command. But how does that command act upon Samson's will—internally, as an "intimate impulse" (223) of "power resistless" (1404) or externally, as a "dire necessity" (1666) no less irresistible? Or does Samson freely choose both to destroy and be destroyed—and for what purpose? Samson offers no explicit description of his intent, no sign that he is conscious of what he will do or of what it might mean. If Samson has merely "quit" himself like Samson, ending his life as he began it, then the Christian meaning which we impute to his dearly bought revenge is simply what Madsen calls "an ironic counterpoint" to his literal blindness: Samson's "significance for the Christian reader lies primarily in his inability to measure up to the heroic norm delineated in *Paradise Regained*."[11]

Perhaps. But I choose not to think so, primarily because I believe that Samson's irony at the expense of his Philistine "master" must be truly his, and therefore a conscious expression of his "intimate," self-sacrifical purpose. Samson has himself precluded mere dramatic irony by insisting that the commands of the Philistines are not resistless:

> If I obey them,
> I do it freely; venturing to displease
> God for the fear of Man.   (1372–74)

When Samson speaks of "absolute subjection," therefore, he is being deliberately ironic. He has chosen to obey God, venturing to displease man and himself for the fear of Him, because he knows now who his Master is, whose power is resistless because He is life Himself. Furthermore, Samson's meaning cannot be consciously ironic without also being something more, since the irony of his words rests ultimately upon a paradox: "whosoever will save his life shall lose it" (Matthew xvi, 25). By articulating this paradox Samson bears conscious witness to the transformation of his will and hence to the ultimate freedom of that will: "Whosoever will lose his life for my sake shall find it" (ibid.). Samson does not simply "change his purpose"; his will is recreated by the "resistless" clarity of his insight. And so he "quits" himself (1709) to find himself, loses life to accomplish eternal life. *Samson Agonistes* is finally a Christian play, not so much because Samson is (on one level) a type of Christ as because he consciously enacts a parable of Redemption: "Except a corn of wheat fall into the ground and die, it abideth alone: but if it die, it bringeth forth much fruit" (John xii, 24).

To read the play in this way, parabolically, is not to identify Samson with Christ nor even to imply that his consciousness is in some anachronistic sense Christian. Samson's awareness of what life means is deeply rooted in the prophetic tradition of the Old Testament: "Man doth not live by bread only, but by every *word* that proceedeth out of the mouth of the LORD"(Deuteronomy viii, 3). "O LORD, by these *things men* live, and in all these *things is* the life of my spirit; so wilt thou recover me, and make me to live" (Isaiah xxxviii, 15–16). So also Samson: "he was sore athirst, and called on the LORD, and said, Thou has given this great deliverance into the hand of thy servant: and now shall I die for thirst, and fall into the hand of the uncircumcised? But God clave an hollow place that *was* in the jaw, and there came water thereout; and when he had drunk, his spirit came again, and he revived" (Judges, xv, 18–19).

The conflict in *Samson Agonistes* is not between God and Dagon, nor between Samson and his mortal antagonists, but between the creative and destructive forces of his own imagination: "within himself / The danger lies, yet lies within his power" (*PL* IX, 348–49).

But if that is really Milton's intention, if the transformation of Samson *Dagonistes* into a parable of deliverance is a meaning intrinsic to the text rather than one which we impute to it, why has Milton veiled his meaning in a "darke conceit" so that we catch the sense at two removes? Why has he perplexed his Christian theophany with the "sensuall Idolatry" of classical tragedy and the "old cast rudiments" of Jewish theodicy?[12] In a sense, of course, the question answers itself: poetry is essentially metaphor. Through its "unexpressive" silences, a poem utters meaning that cannot be communicated in any other way. Yet this hermeneutic solution does not answer to the extraordinary difficulty of this particular parable. The meaning I have educed from the play, though obvious enough in one sense, is extremely difficult to manifest and, as mysteries go, peculiarly rational.

Perhaps that is the heart of the mystery: the Logos who speaks through the play, whose word is Reason itself, incarnate in Samson's voluntary self-sacrifice. The transcendant Word becomes immanent in flesh when the I AM becomes also I am, "My self . . . my conscience and internal peace" (1334). And as Owen Barfield has observed, the Logos "is a Being who can be participated only in vigilance and freedom."[13] Samson's freedom to choose life is necessarily radical: although it is grounded in experience, it is not conditioned by circumstances. The freedom of Samson's will cannot be signified externally because it is internal. Free choice cannot be inspired by any form of impulsion, whether subconscious or supernatural, nor can it be imposed by compulsion, and it is in that sense "rational," because it has its seat in reason. As Milton says in *Areopagitica*, "reason is but choosing" (YP, II, 527), not because reason is merely choosing, but because real choice, the election (or rejection) of the Creator by the creature, can have no other ground than the Logos Himself, in Whom we live. Choice is growth and transformation. Love—the rational form of desire—also is choice; it "refines / The thoughts, and heart enlarges" (*PL* VIII, 589–90). This self-enlargement is a conscious process; it arises not out of ungoverned impulse, the slavery of the self to the self, or from unresisted passion, the slavery of the self to another (which other is really a projection of the self), but from reason. Choice subsists in right reason, which is *reasoning*, a process of becoming rather than a quality or a state of being.

For this reason, the Logos in whom we participate, the divine process in whom we become, can be imagined but cannot be rationalized; it can be imaged—as in "the radiant image of his Glory" (*PL* III, 63)—but it cannot be transfixed by imagery—unless imagery is also crucified. Milton's poetry of choice is therefore radically iconoclastic; as he observes in *On Christian Doctrine*, "not teeth but faith is needed to eat [Christ's] flesh" (YP, VI, 553). The process of Samson's regeneration is essentially a struggle to free himself from the vain idols of his own imagination—the false deliverance offered by his earthly father, the false forgiveness of his own violent passion for Dalila, and his false pride in himself as a great deliverer. Just before Samson is finally redeemed by God's "rouzing motions" (1382), Harapha presents him with the idol of himself as God's "faithful Champion" (1751). Samson spurns this "Haughty . . . and proud" image of himself (1069) and reaffirms his "trust . . . in the living God" (1140); at the same time, however, by offering to prove "whose God is strongest" (1155), Samson threatens to turn that God into an idol—the mere image of his own physical strength rather than its ultimate source. And idolatry is death, not life.

That self-destructive impulse is always present in Samson, threatening to unmake him; it is a grisly parody of the self-sacrifical choice which finally remakes him. And the parody is all the more demonic because it can be mistaken for the reality. To the literal-minded all things are literal: the tendency to idolatry is inherent in the very nature of language itself and can be resisted only by a strenuous effort of will. And so Milton refuses to represent the mysterious transformation of Samson's will; he avoids the problem of rationalizing Samson's choice by voiding his drama of imagery that would externalize that choice. Samson himself speaks to us most powerfully through his silence. He conspicuously does not pray, like the Old Testament Samson, to be "avenged of the Philistines" (Judges xvii, 28). Instead, as Arnold Stein has observed, Samson simply "withdraws in thought and spirit before the final redemptive act which is to end the long process of redemption."[14] Of his final burst of iconoclasm, his symbolic destruction of Dagon, Milton tells us only that we cannot "see" its meaning unless our vision has been radically transformed, "With inward eyes illuminated" (1689). This generation of Milton readers naturally "seeketh after a sign; and there shall no sign be given to it, but the sign of" Samson (Matthew xii, 39). Yet behold, one greater than Samson is here. For as Charles Huttar has shown, Samson's self-discovery is "self-transcending and at [the] same time self-authenticating." Like Jacob-Israel, the Supplanter whose second name means 'strives with God' (Genesis xxxii, 28), Samson *agonistes* wrestles with

God. But "as Job discovered, God will not spar with men. He is beyond
their comprehension. A parable." And a parable, like the "ashy womb"
of the phoenix (1703), and like the prophetic form of *Samson* itself, "is
an accommodation to human finitude."[15] "God has revealed only so
much of himself as our minds can conceive and the weakness of our
nature can bear," Milton says in *On Christian Doctrine,* "not as he
really is but in such a way as will make him conceivable to us" (YP, VI,
133).

By virtue of its parabolic iconoclasm, *Samson Agonistes* declares
itself as a work of the prophetic imagination. Though it deliberately
resists formulation as an oracle, its spirit is essentially embodied in the
word of the LORD to Amos: "Seek the LORD, and ye shall live" (Amos v,
6). In calling the work "prophetic," however, I mean to emphasize its
vocation rather than its inspiration, the way in which it speaks to us
rather than its possible sources in Scripture or in Milton's vatic relation
to his muse.[16] The mission of the prophet is not simply to inspire visions
but to purge vision itself, so that the life-giving energies of poetic faith
are not reduced to mere idolatry. And for this reason, the word of the
prophet is uttered parabolically, as a direct assault on the idolatrous,
literalizing imagination: "Therefore speak I to them in parables: because
they seeing see not; and hearing they hear not, neither do they understand" (Matthew xiii, 13). That is precisely Samson's condition at the
beginning of the play: "dead more than half" (79), Samson is a virtual
idol, "a living death" (100), deaf to everything but the tumult of his own
"restless thoughts" (19) and blind to the reality of his own condition:
"Light the prime work of God to [him] is extinct" (70). And "Since light
so necessary is to life, / And almost life it self" (90–91), "So much the
rather" must "Celestial light / Shine inward, and the mind through all
her powers / Irradiate" (*PL* III, 51–53), so that the prophet's fit audience, as well as Samson himself, may learn "Of things invisible to mortal
sight" (55). From this perspective, Samson's blindness is prophetic
rather than merely ironic. Dramatic irony defines the limits of human
perception in order to manifest God's Word, "th' unsearchable dispose /
Of highest wisdom" (1746–47).[17] To those who glimpse this wisdom,
because their "inward eyes" have been "illuminated" (1689), purged by
the "fierie virtue" (1690) of God's saving grace, *Samson Agonistes* represents, not the triumph of Samson over his enemies, nor the triumph of
God over Dagon, but the triumph of Samson over himself, the triumph
of the divine spirit within man over the vain idols of his own imagination. Samson's regeneration is therefore an actual (though not a literal)
rebirth. To those who read it parabolically, the tragedy of Samson does

indeed present a "new acquist / Of true experience" (1755–56): "And the eyes of them that see shall not be dim, and the ears of them that hear shall hearken" (Isaiah xxxii, 3).

"In that day every man shall cast away his idols . . . which your own hands have made unto you for a sin" (xxxi, 7). "And the LORD shall cause his glorious voice to be heard" (xxx, 30). "And the Word was made flesh, and dwelt among us" (John i, 14). Thus, when Samson is finally delivered "Home to his father's house" (1733), we catch the echo of *evangelium:* "In my Father's house are many mansions. . . . I go to prepare a place for you" (John xiv, 2). Samson is thus associated with Christ prophetically, not so much because he is a "shadowy type" of the Redeemer as because, in giving his life to God, he redeems himself. In purging himself of his idolatry, freeing himself from the "dungeon" of himself (156), Samson fulfills in himself the typological paradigm articulated in *Paradise Lost*. Even under the very shadow of the Law, he progresses

> From shadowie Types to Truth, from Flesh to Spirit,
> From imposition of strict Laws, to free
> Acceptance of large Grace, from servil fear
> To filial, works of Law to works of Faith.   (*PL* XII, 303–06)

Milton's Samson thus becomes a type of

CHRISTIAN LIBERTY . . . whereby WE ARE LOOSED . . . THROUGH CHRIST OUR DELIVERER, FROM THE BONDAGE OF SIN . . . TO THE INTENT THAT BEING MADE SONS INSTEAD OF SERVANTS . . . WE MAY SERVE GOD IN LOVE THROUGH THE GUIDANCE OF THE SPIRIT OF TRUTH.[18]

In *Samson Agonistes* the Word Himself dies in order to be reborn. And the crucial figure in this imaginative crucifixion is not the Christ of *Paradise Regained*, whose virtue is exemplary without being wholly communicable, but Samson, last of idolators and first of iconoclasts, in whom the Word becomes fully incarnate, whose merely human will is absolutely transformed by realizing the divinity within himself: "And for a life who would not change his purpose?" (1406)

III

Once again, however, we must ask ourselves, "How can that be?" To speak of Samson as the Word made flesh implies, not merely that he is a type of Christ, but that he has himself become a son of God. And if that is so, then the form of *Samson Agonistes* is not merely parabolic but radically prophetic. For although Samson himself does not obviously attain to anything like prophetic strain, the play as a whole speaks to us in the voice of Revelation—as the self-renewing conflagration of "that self-begott'n bird" (1699) foreshadows a "new heaven and a new earth" (Revelation xxi, 1). Considered structurally, therefore, the spiritual regeneration of Samson's will must be answerable to a generic transformation of tragedy into prophecy. Accordingly, my purpose now is to explore the formal implications of that hypothesis: that the parabolic recreation of Samson renders Milton's play translucent to Christian meaning by transforming classical tragedy into tragic prophecy.

Milton establishes the structural basis for this generic transformation by his prefatory allusion to Paraeus, whose commentary on Revelation "divides the whole Book as a Tragedy, into Acts distinguisht each by a Chorus of Heavenly Harpings and Song between" (CM, I:2, 331). To this "highest dignity" *Samson* may also aspire, for if, as Milton says in *The Reason of Church-Government*, "the Apocalyps of Saint *John* is the majestick image of a high and stately Tragedy" (YP, I, 815), then tragedy may also become an image of prophecy. If we take seriously the argument that Milton advances in his prefatory note, that tragedy is "the gravest, moralest, and most profitable of all other poems," then we should also entertain the possibility that his own "endeavor to write tragedy" is in fact an instance of transcendental form. For what Angus Fletcher has said of *Comus* is at least equally true of *Samson:* "As containing form this [transcendent] structure will apparently be held together by an immanent order"—by *decorum*, the generic limits of classical tragedy, and by *verisimilitude*, the fidelity of the play to its Hebraic subject. "As a symbolic matrix, however, this closed and immanent order will display a countering activity of all its details, exploding out from the containing frame, transcending limits formally accepted." Insofar as Milton established new generic limits for his poem, by "modeling" it after the image of the Apocalypse, *Samson* becomes a work of prophetic form. What Joseph Wittreich says about "visionary form" in Milton's epics and in *Lycidas* is equally applicable to Samson: "By Milton prophecy is made to subsume [tragedy] in a dialectic that also restores prophecy to its original preeminence." And the end of this prophetic recreation is liberation: the visionary structure of *Samson* "is an agent in the process that culminates in our seeing all things anew."[19]

To be seen as a prophetic structure, a visionary rather than a merely spectacular form, *Samson* must be "produced beyond the fifth act." The allusion to neoclassical theory—the Horatian dictum that "a play should have five acts, no less, no more"[20]—is less a concession to modern bondage than a gesture of defiance on behalf of ancient liberty recovered. The fact that *Samson* can be rationalized into five acts, in accord with ancient rule, should not blind us to the structural possibilities afforded by Milton's best example, the Apocalypse of St. John. In *The Reason of Church-Government*, Milton heartily endorsed Paraeus' analysis of Revelation as a sevenfold dramatic structure, "shutting up and intermingling her solemn Scenes and Acts with a sevenfold *Chorus* of halleluja's and harping symphonies" (YP, I, 815). Wittreich quotes Paraeus to show that in Revelation, "what begins as an epistolary form becomes in Chapter 4 a 'plainly . . . *Dramaticall* forme, hence the Revelation . . . may truely be called a *Propheticall Drama*,' its closest literary analogue being with 'humane Tragedies'."[21] In its analogy with "*Dramaticall* forme," Revelation possesses a sevenfold structure:

Prologue	i, 1–9
1 Vision	i, 10–iii
2 Vision	iv–vii
3 Vision	viii–xi
4 Vision	xii–xiv
5 Vision	xv–xvi
6 Vision	xvii–xix
7 Vision	xx–xxii, 6
Epilogue	xxii, 7–end

Now, when *Samson Agonistes* is measured against this model, it becomes immediately apparent that the five-act dramatic scheme of the play adduced by William Riley Parker (and generally accepted by subsequent critics) is equally susceptible to analysis as a sevenfold visionary structure:

I.	*prologos*	1–114 (114 lines), Samson's soliloquy
	parodos	115–75 (61 lines), Chorus ("aside")
II.	1st *epeisodion*	176–292 (117 lines), Samson and Chorus
	1st *stasimon*	293–325 (33 lines), Chorus
III.	2nd *epeisodion*	326–651 (326 lines), Samson and Manoa
	2nd *stasimon*	652–709 (58 lines), Chorus
IV.	3rd *epeisodion*	710–1009 (300 lines), Samson and Dalila
	3rd *stasimon*	1010–60 (51 lines), Chorus
V.	4th *epeisodion*	1061–1267 (207 lines), Samson and Harapha
	4th *stasimon*	1268–99 (32 lines), Chorus
VI.	5th *epeisodion*	1300–1426 (127 lines), Samson and the Officer
	5th *stasimon*	1427–40 (14 lines), Chorus
VII.	*exodos*	1441–1758 (318 lines), Manoa, Messenger, and Chorus including
	kommos	1660–1758 (99 lines) Manoa and Chorus[22]

If we further choose to regard Milton's defense "Of Tragedy" together with his prefatory Argument to *Samson* as an epistolary prologue, and if we take the Chorus's final speech—the last fourteen lines of the play (1745–58), like the last fourteen verses of Revelation (xxii, 8–21)—as epilogue, so that Parker's *exodos* and *kommos* (through 1744) become the seventh vision, then the structural parallelism between Milton's play and Revelation becomes extremely close. When *Samson* is reflected in and seen through the dark glass of Revelation, the play takes on the visionary aspect of a prophetical drama.

In itself, thus baldly asserted, this structural possibility is suggestive rather than definitive; it invites further exploration from a variety of perspectives.[23] Among the perspectives opened up by the visionary form of the play, the generic possibilities seem paramount: if *Samson Agonistes* can no longer be seen as *merely* "the finest imitation of the ancient Greek drama that ever had been, or ever would be written,"[24] then some way must be found to represent (to the critical imagination, at least) the new dimensions of its prophetic form. The term *Christian tragedy*, which has enjoyed some currency since Woodhouse's essay first appeared, no longer seems adequate. A work may be both tragic and (at least ironically) Christian, as *Dr. Faustus* now seems to many of us, without possessing the internal structure of a prophetic poem. Woodhouse proposed to read *Samson* as an "adaptation" of "classical . . . form to a Christian content"; as I have tried to show, however, the violence of the catastrophe and the absence of any demonstrable connection between it and Samson's regeneration precludes any such ready and easy translation from classical form to Christian meaning. Woodhouse's formulation of the play as "a classical tragedy with a Christian theme and outlook" must therefore be taken as provisional—as an imperfect shadow of the perfect form revealing itself in Milton's scriptural tragedy.[25]

As I have also tried to show, an analysis of *Samson* as "Christian" can help to reveal the dialectical process which informs its *dianoia*—the "process of speech" (*PL* VII, 178) through which the play expresses its discursive content. Classical heroism is a thesis to which Hebraic martyrdom stands as antithesis; from the dialectical interpenetration of these opposites emerges the synthesis of Christian heroism, "the better fortitude / Of . . . Heroic Martyrdom" (*PL* IX, 31–32). When we attempt to transpose this formula to *Samson Agonistes*, however, it suffers a loss of perspicuity and resonance, precisely because of the violence which the external form of the play seems to sanction. We must not "dream . . . of thir fight, / As of a Duel" (*PL* XII, 386–87); yet the external structure of the tragedy—both its classical decorum and its Hebraic verisimilitude—

seems to demand such a catastrophe. To resist this consummation, we must find some way to express our intuition of the play's internal form, a form at once tragic and more than tragic. Toward that end, Fletcher's conception of "transcendental form" and Wittreich's analogous idea of "visionary poetics" are instrumental. For our present purpose, however, these formulations need to be more specifically defined. Accordingly, by analogy with Wittreich's conception of *Paradise Lost* as "epic prophecy" and of *Lycidas* as "pastoral prophecy," in which "through prophecy, the pastoral world" is subsumed in prophetic vision and "reestablished in human history,"[26] I venture to offer the term *tragic prophecy* as a means of suggesting the analogous process at work in *Samson*—of suggesting, that is, the dialectical process by which tragic form is subsumed in the more comprehensive form of prophecy.

The oxymoron "tragic prophecy" is deliberately chosen, both to suggest an essential likeness between tragedy and prophecy as vision-ary forms and to emphasize the radical difference between tragic rec-ognition and prophetic revelation. As poetic structures, both tragedy and prophecy are defined by anagnorisis, "a change from ignorance to knowledge"; in both, suffering implies "the 'agonized unfolding of perception'."[27] The substance of this perception, however, and the manner in which it is embodied differ radically in the two forms. Whereas tragedy enforces the recognition of limits, prophecy is in-spired by a revelation of possibility. What Joan Webber has said of epic applies equally to tragedy—serves, in fact, to define the specifi-cally tragic aspect of the more comprehensive epic form: the tragic hero "is a person with godlike longings or capabilities, who must paradoxically accept his limitations and his limited context in order to be heroic. . . . With self-consciousness come suffering, the knowledge of separateness, and a sense of loss and guilt. The formation of self proceeds by recognition of negatives (I am not that) and opposites." Prophecy, however, subsumes this limited recognition by revealing the possibility of self-transcendence; like the epic hero, the prophet "forces a way for people to a new dimension of awareness." Like "the story of every epic," the history of prophecy "is that of the hero allowing himself to accept definition as a mortal being . . . and then learning to transcend his own definition."[28] And just as the substance of the tragic vision, the recognition of limits, is subsumed by the prophetic vision of transcendental possibility, so the form of tragedy is contained in the more comprehensive architecture of visionary form. Considered archetypally, tragedy represents what Northrop Frye has called "a mimesis of sacrifice." The tragic hero suffers a "Dionysiac" *sparagmos*—"Orpheus torn to pieces by the Bacchantes, Balder murdered by the treachery of Loki, Christ dying on the cross and marking with the words 'Why hast thou forsaken me?' a sense of his exclusion, as a divine being, from the society of the Trinity."[29] The prophet suffers a similar *sparagmos*—an *agonized* unfolding of perception. Isaiah is "purged" by "a live coal" from the hallowed fire of God's altar (vi, 6–7). Jeremiah is "a terror" to himself: God's "*word* was in mine heart as a burning fire, shut up in my bones" (xx, 4–9). The psalmist is crucified: "My God, my God, why hast thou forsaken me?" (xxii, 1). For the prophet, however, death and dismemberment are a means to spiritual rebirth; for God "will swallow up death in victory: and the LORD God will wipe away tears from off all faces" (Isaiah xxv, 8). As the Crucifixion is transcended by the Resurrection, tragic form is subsumed in prophecy. In Frye's terms, the prophetic vision "sees tragedy as an episode in the divine comedy, the larger scheme of redemption and resurrection."[30]

In other words, borrowed from the analogy that Milton draws in *Christian Doctrine*, prophetic form contains the tragic as "spirit, being the more excellent substance, virtually, as they say, and eminently contains within itself what is clearly the inferior substance." As the "more excellent" and more comprehensive form, prophecy subsumes the "inferior" genre of tragedy. At the same time, however, prophetic form presupposes the tragic matter which it actualizes: "not even God's virtue and efficiency could have produced bodies out of nothing" (YP, VI, 309). Prophecy demands tragic recognition as an essential ground of revelation, not simply because the redemption of the righteous implies the destruction of the wicked, but because the achievement of righteousness presupposes the destruction of wickedness in the prophet himself. Even in their morphology, the words *re*birth, *re*creation, and *Re*surrection imply their logical opposites—death, destruction, and Crucifixion; and in this case, at least, the logic of grammar faithfully reflects the *Logos* of Creation: recreation entails annihilation. As Webber has shown, for Milton's "revolutionary consciousness" even God is "subject to the same limitations or requirements that beset other conscious beings," and since "the process of creation [itself] . . . requires the realization of opposites, including death, the opposite of life," the "price of consciousness, of creativity, is knowledge of and participation in death."[31]

Seen in this perspective, as an "encyclopedic form,"[32] prophecy may be regarded as a realization—both a refutation and a recreation—of tragedy. For tragedy "as it was anciently composed" contains a profound structural paradox: the very anagnorisis which leads to the hero's annihilation reaffirms precisely those communal values which the agonized unfolding of the hero's more comprehensive perception had called into question. Thus, for example, the enigma of *Oedipus Rex;* in accepting his role as scapegoat, Oedipus reaffirms the destiny which has virtually destroyed him: "I have been preserved / For some unthinkable fate." Oedipus can achieve selfhood only by accepting responsibility for actions he could not have avoided, by choosing to be what he already is: Apollo "brought my sick, sick fate upon me. / But the blinding hand was my own." Oedipus leaves his life in Thebes, but Thebes lives on, and the tragic *mythos* of the community is reaffirmed by the conventional wisdom of the Chorus:

> Let everyman in mankind's frailty
> Consider his last day, and let none
> Presume on his good fortune until he find
> Life, at his death, a memory without pain.[33]

Prophecy resolves this paradox by inverting it: the community dies, but prophecy lives on—and, if it chooses to renew itself in the prophetic spirit, the community is reborn: "My salvation shall be for ever, and my righteousness shall not be abolished" (Isaiah li, 6). The essential task of prophecy is not to reaffirm the past but to recreate it, "to transform the past into the future," as Webber suggests; therefore, although the prophet preserves a tradition which he inherits, "he obviously must in some way reject the past as unequal to . . . the future."[34] The tradition of prophecy is therefore radically iconoclastic, in its generic transformations not less than in its assault on consciousness; prophecy must perpetually renew itself by destroying and recreating the forms which it inherits.

Where tragedy ends, prophecy begins, making all things new, recreating itself by rediscovering and remaking its generic as well as its cultural origins. And if tragedy is thus original to prophecy, its generic limits cannot be circumscribed by the "ancient rule" of classical tragedy; if we seek "the majestick image" of tragedy itself, our definition must comprehend not only "what the lofty grave Tragœdians taught" but "the more excellent substance" of "*Sion's* songs, to all true tasts excelling" and of "our Prophets . . . / As men divinely taught" (*PR* IV, 261, 347, 356–57). Accordingly we direct our attention now, not to the classical models which Milton transformed nor to the biblical subject matter which he transubstantiated, but to the composite order of biblical prophecy, "those frequent Songs throughout the law and prophets," which, as Milton explains in *The Reason of Church-Government,* "not in their divine argument alone, but in the very critical art of composition may be easily made appear over all the kinds of Lyrick poesy, to be incomparable" (YP, I, 816).

IV

When we seek to focus the specifically tragic aspect of scriptural prophecy and to define its generic basis, we need to discover some locus of organization which may serve as a structural model. One such locus is already conspicuous; as Wittreich has shown, the Renaissance imagination conceived the prophetic drama of Revelation as "the prototype for all true prophecy."[35] Another possible starting point, however, is the dramatic prophecy of Amos. Within the context of the prophetic tradition as a whole, Amos and Revelation are juxtaposed as Old Testament type and New Testament antitype; Amos figures the tragedy of the Law, "the mystery [*sacramentum*] of the Old Testament, in which the New was hidden."[36] In generic terms, therefore, the tragic prophecy of Amos stands, for both Milton and John of Patmos, as a "structural model," in Guillén's terms, "a principle of construction or organization" which serves the poet as "an invitation to form," assisting him in the "process of [re-]formulation, [re-]making, *poiēsis*."[37]

As a possible generic model for *Samson Agonistes,* the Book of Amos is especially useful because of its apparently tragic form. As tragedy, Amos implies the Mosaic paradox: "I the LORD thy God *am* a jealous God, visiting the iniquity of the fathers upon the children unto the third and fourth *generation* of them that hate me; And shewing mercy unto thousands of them that love me, and keep my commandments" (Exodux xx, 5–6). This paradox and the apparent inability of God's mercy to redeem his wayward people—"yet have ye not returned to me" (iv, 6, 8–11), "Therefore . . . prepare to meet thy God, O Israel" (iv, 12)—constitutes the tragic vision of Amos. It is also the tragic vision of Milton's *Samson:* "captivity and loss of eyes" (1744). Notwithstanding his bravery about "Heroic" vengeance (1711) and "death so noble" (1724), Manoa and Israel cannot see beyond the ruin of their hope because their eyes are blinded by tears.

Even more crucial for our present investigation, however, is the fact that Amos is almost unique among the prophetic books of the Old Testament in possessing a coherent external form, an apparently self-satisfying structure of incidents. Furthermore, that structure is, up to a point, closely analogous to the classical form of Greek tragedy discerned by Aristotle and redefined by critics like Kenneth Burke, Elder Olson, and Francis Fergusson as a psychic development:

from *purpose:*   "the Lord GOD hath spoken, who can but prophesy?"
                       (iii, 8);

through *passion:*   "But ye . . . commanded the prophets, saying,
                       Prophesy not" (ii, 12);

to *perception:*   "I will send a famine in the land, not a famine
                       of bread, nor a thirst for water, but of hearing
                       the words of the LORD" (viii, 11).[38]

As is so often the case in classical tragedy, and so conspicuously in *Oedipus Rex,* the crime *is* the punishment. And in Amos this recognition satisfies the Aristotelian desideratum that recognition be coincident with a reversal of the situation.[39] Amos apparently fulfills his own prophecy when he is silenced and driven from the temple at Bethel: "Thou sayest, Prophesy not against Israel" (vii, 16). But Amos' self-discovery turns Amaziah's foolishness against himself, who will "die in a polluted land," and against all of Israel, which "shall surely go into captivity" (vii, 17). In that day, Amaziah's prohibition will redound upon him as the fulfillment of a curse: "they shall run to and fro to seek the word of the LORD, and shall not find it" (viii, 12).

Tragic ironies of this sort abound in the work, not only in its action but in the structure of its imagery. The Lord who "roar[s] from Zion" (i, 2) becomes a hungry lion whose appetite will shortly be slaked: "Will a lion roar in the forest, when he hath no prey?" (iii, 4). The lion of Judah thus signifies both the fearful inevitability of the prophetic vocation— "The lion hath roared, who will not fear? the LORD God hath spoken, who can but prophecy?" (iii, 8)—and the more awful inevitability of ruin, "as the shepherd taketh out of the mouth of the lion two legs, or a piece of an ear" (iii, 11). Again, judgment ought to "run down as waters, and righteousness as a mighty stream" (v, 24); instead, the earth "shall be drowned, as *by* the flood," for God "calleth for the waters of the sea, and poureth them out upon the face of the earth" (ix, 5–6).

Such patterns of imagery are reinforced by the dramatic structure of the action, even in its technical aspect. For Amos can be rather easily fitted to a five-act neoclassical structure:

    I.   Oracles against foreign nations and Israel (Chaps. i–ii)
            "For three transgressions . . . and for four" (i, 3, 6, 9, 11, 13; ii, 1, 4, 6)
            "Ye gave the Nazarites wine to drink" (ii, 12)
    II.   Sermons and oracles against Israel (Chaps. iii–vi)
            "They know not to do right" (iii, 10)
            "Yet have ye not returned to me" (iv, 6, 8, 9, 10, 11)
            "Therefore . . . prepare to meet thy God, O Israel" (iv, 12)

"I hate, I despise your feast days" (v, 21)
"Ye have turned judgment into gall" (vi, 12)

III. Three visions (vii, 1–9)
"By whom shall Jacob arise?" (vii, 2, 5) *grasshoppers eating*
"The LORD repented for this" (vii, 3, 6) and *fire devouring*
"I will not again pass by them anymore" (vii, 8) *a plumbline*

IV. Climax: Amos versus Amaziah (vii, 10–17)
"Prophesy not again any more" (vii, 13)
"The LORD said unto me, Go, prophesy" (vii, 15)

V. Two visions (viii, 1–ix, 8a) . . . and a vision of the end (ix, 8b–15)
"A basket of summer fruit . . . famine" (viii, 1, 11)
"I saw the LORD standing upon the altar" (ix, 1)
"The plowman shall overtake the reaper" (ix, 13)

This structure seems adequate to the tragic form of Amos and to the rigor of God's justice. If the doubtful verses in Amos (ix, 11–15) are in fact a later addition, then the final note of Amos's prophecy is unremittingly tragic: "All the sinners of my people shall die by the sword" (ix, 10).

Even in these words, however, there is implicit a promise of hope in the qualification "the sinners." Perhaps not all may die if God purposes to spare a "remnant" (ix, 12; cp. v, 15): "I will restore the fortunes of my people Israel" (ix, 14). Though this whole apocalyptic passage seems radically incongruous with the overall tone of Amos's prophecy, its triumphant affirmation of Yahweh's faithfulness—"I will plant them upon their land" (ix, 15)—is in fact implicit in the very structure of God's judgment. For besides being a tragic condemnation of evil, Amos's Word is also a call to repentance: "See the LORD, and ye shall live. . . . Seek good, and not evil, that ye may live. . . . Hate the evil, and love the good, and establish judgment in the gate: it may be that the LORD God of hosts will be gracious unto the remnant of Joseph" (v, 6, 14–15). The destiny of Israel is all the more tragic for being radically juxtaposed to its prophetic alternative: "let judgment run down as waters, and righteousness as a mighty stream" (v, 24). The vision of the remnant is an appeal for reformation and renewal. God will not revoke the punishment for transgression, but an end to wickedness may be also the beginning of righteousness; even death may bring forth the renewal of life. What Amos promises is not a stay of execution but a restoration. The "day of the LORD" will still be "darkness, and not light" (v, 18). But light may be made to issue from the darkness itself: "the earth was without form, and void; and darkness *was* upon the face of the deep. . . . And God said, Let there be light: and there was light" (Genesis i, 2–3).

To be comprehended as a whole, therefore, the Book of Amos must be "produced beyond the fifth act" of the catastrophe, the immanent captivity of Israel. As prophecy, Amos possesses a twofold structure: tragic self-recognition is subsumed in prophetic revelation. Prophecy begins where tragedy ends. In their sinfulness, God's people have incurred a tragic destiny: "ye gave the Nazarites wine to drink; . . . ye have planted pleasant vineyards, but ye shall not drink wine of them" (ii, 12; v, 11). But if they will hear the Word of their God, they may be renewed: "they shall plant vineyards, and drink the wine thereof" (ix, 14). If the people "seek good, and not evil" (v, 14), the terrible "flood" of God's wrath (ix, 5) will become a "mighty stream" (v, 24) of living waters: "and the mountains shall drop sweet wine and all the hills shall melt" (ix, 13). Once again, the covenant that was given to Abraham—"in thy seed shall all the nations of the earth be blessed" (Genesis xxii, 18)— is renewed: "And I will plant them upon their land, and they shall no more be pulled up out of their land which I have given them, saith the LORD thy God" (ix, 15). To those who will not see, "the day of the LORD is darkness, and not light" (v, 18). But even that day may bring light to those "that walked in darkness," "with blindness internal struck," if "With inward eyes illuminated" (SA, 1686–89) they "have seen a great light" (Isaiah ix, 2; Matthew iv, 16), for on that day they shall be brought "out of darkness into marvellous light" (1 Peter ii, 9).

Milton's tragic prophecy implies an analogous *peripeteia:* "for a life who will not change his purpose?" (1406). For Milton's play possesses a similar twofold structure, a similar providential irony subsuming tragic irony as prophetic subsumes tragic form, and a similar parabolic transformation of catastrophe into apocalypse.

If we look now at the form of Milton's play in its technical, neoclassical aspect, and especially if we circumscribe its action by the catastrophic ending of the tragedy, its five-act structure closely parallels the dramatic scheme of Amos. (A slight reformulation of Amos and a conflation of choric interludes with episodes in *Samson,* makes the parallelism more emphatic:)

Prologue: "Eyeless in *Gaza*" (SA 41; A i, 6)
   Samson 1–175: "In power of others, never in my own" (78)
   Amos i, 1–ii, 5: "I will not turn away the punishment" (i, 3)
Act I: *Nazarites* (318; ii, 11)
   Samson 176–325: "The work to which I was divinely call'd" (226)
   Amos ii, 6–iii: "You only have I known" (iii, 2)
Act II: *Sacrifice* and *Solemn Assemblies* (436; v, 21)
   Samson 326–709: "This day the *Philistines* a popular Feast" (434)
   Amos iv–v: "I despise your feast days" (v, 21)

Act III: The *evil* day (736; vi, 3)
    Samson 710–1060: "To light'n what thou suffer'st, and appease" (744)
    Amos vi: "Woe to them *that are* at ease in Zion" (vi, 1)
Act IV: *By the Sword* (1165; vii, 9)
    Samson 1061–1299: "Yet despair not of his final pardon" (1171)
    Amos vii, 1–9: "O LORD God, forgive, I beseech thee" (vii, 2)
Act V: *Captive* (1393; vii, 11)
    Samson 1300–1440: "Our Law forbids at thir Religious Rites" (1320)
    Amos vii, 10–17: "Prophesy not again" (vii, 13)
Exode: *Lamentation* (1708; viii, 10)
    Samson 1441–1686: "The vulgar only scap'd" (1659)
    Amos viii, 1–ix, 10: "All the sinners of my people shall perish" (ix, 10)
Dubia: His Father's *House* (1717; ix, 9)
    Samson 1687–1758: "Like that self-begotten bird" (1699)
    Amos ix, 11–15: "I will raise up his ruins" (ix, 11)

The very closeness of the external parallelism, and its manifest inadequacy to the internal form of either work, emphasizes the underlying twofold structure in each. As tragedy, each work ends in catastrophic destruction: "At once both to destroy and be destroy'd" (1587). But this vindication of God's purpose turns out to be hollow, even pointless. If God should "utterly destroy the house of Jacob" (ix, 8), none would be left to know Him or to sing His praise. Conversely, the death of the Philistines will not necessarily mean the liberation of Israel from oppression. And so a "remnant" (ix, 12) will be spared: "The vulgar only scap'd" (1659). And this tragic kernel, falling into the ground of history, brings forth prophetic fruit. Prophecy re-produces tragedy beyond the catastrophe: Israel will be redeemed from "captivity" (ix, 14), and Samson will become God's "faithful champion" indeed (1751). Just as Israel's destruction becomes the basis for its renewal, as self-recognition and self-annihilation are the indispensable precondition for revelation and renovation, so Samson's (virtual) destruction is essential to his rebirth; literal blindness is the parabolic basis for spiritual insight.

    Each work is pervaded by a similar tragic irony: Amaziah, who silences Amos, is himself silenced, and the Philistines, who blind Samson, are themselves blinded. And in each work tragic irony is subsumed in prophetic paradox: even in death, and only in death, can Israel "seek the LORD, and . . . live" (v, 6), and "for a life who will not change his purpose?" (1406). When each work is produced beyond its external catastrophe, so that the end is seen as a beginning, we begin to perceive the internal working of its parabolic form: just as literal famine—"clean-

ness of teeth . . . and want of bread" (iv, 6) becomes first a figurative
famine—"of hearing the words of the LORD" (viii, 11)—and then spiritual abundance—"they shall also make gardens, and eat the fruit of
them" (ix, 14)—so Samson's "impotence of mind" (52) becomes not
merely a "strength, yet greater" (1644), as it seems, but a renewal of life
itself, which "Revives, reflourishes, then vigorous most / When most
unactive deem'd" (1704–05).

The basis of parabolic form, the radical transformation of appearance into reality, is incongruity: "surface disorder stands in marked
contrast to an ordered interior." Parabolic form may appear to be
superficially coherent, but that surface is in fact discontinuous: as
Wittreich suggests, "linear movement is disrupted" so that external
form may become a means to the achievement of "a new level of
comprehension."[40] Classical tragedy demands surface plausibility,
even at the cost of truth: "Within the action there must be nothing
irrational. . . . Accordingly, the poet should prefer probable impossi-
bilities to improbable possibilities."[41] Prophecy, however, will have
truth, even at the sacrifice of logical coherence; Samson Agonistes
"has a Beginning and an End, which Aristotle himself could not have
disapproved, but it must be allowed to want a Middle, since nothing
passes between the first Act and the last, that either hastens or delays
the Death of Samson."[42] Wittreich carries Johnson's objection to its
metalogical conclusion: like "the literal sense of the Apocalypse," the
surface of Samson "may operate 'without constancy and coher-
ency' "—or with a merely classical illusion of coherence, a plausible
absurdity; "but, says Henry More, 'in the Propheticall sense there is
no such incongruity.' "[43] In Samson as in Amos, the generic tension
between tragic recognition and prophetic revelation gives rise to visionary form. What appears in Amos as an abrupt transition from the
destruction of all to the salvation of a few and as an absolute reversal
of tone, from tragic despair to prophetic optimism, manifests itself in
Samson as a radical incongruity of letter and spirit, literal destruction
and typological recreation, and as a twofold Apocalypse, foreshadowing both Daniel and Revelation: "many of them that sleep in the dust
of the earth shall awake, some to everlasting life, and some to shame
and everlasting contempt" (Daniel xii, 2). "This is the first resurrection. . . . [But] I saw [also] a new heaven and a new earth: for the
first heaven and the first earth were passed away; and there was no
more sea" (Revelation xx, 5; xxi, 1): sic exeunt Philistinii, the People
from the Sea. So also Samson foretells the resurrection to eternal life:

To *Israel*
Honour hath left, and freedom, let but them
Find courage to lay hold on this occasion,
To himself and Fathers house eternal fame.   (1714–17)

For "though [his] body die, [his] fame survives" (1706), "Revives, reflourishes, then vigorous most / When most unactive deem'd" (1704–05).

V

Samson Agonistes does not merely imitate the Book of Amos, however, any more than it does the "ancient rule" of *Oedipus Rex*. In
"modelling" his work on Amos's tragic prophecy, Milton subsumes the
mystery of the Old Testament in the Revelation of the New: Amos's
vision of Israel "planted" in the Promised Land is *transplanted* in
Christ, "As from a second root . . . restor'd" (*PL* III, 293, 288). And just
as all who "are restor'd . . . Receive new life . . . And dying rise" in
Christ (289, 294, 296), so Samson *Phoinizein* "Revives, reflourishes"
(1704) from the "ashy womb"/"Tomb" (1703, 1742) of his "Holocaust"
(1702). As Amos has transformed the prophetic oracle against the nations
into a tragic prophecy of Israel's judgment, so *Samson* transforms the
tragic-prophetic vision of Amos into the perfect form of tragic prophecy:
as the "propos'd deliverance" (292) of God's chosen people becomes the
salvation of the elect, all those "whom God hath chosen once" (368) are
"overcome" (365) in order that they may become the seed through
whom "His servants" are blessed "with inward eyes" (1755, 1689). Amos
and *Samson* are thus not so much instances of a single genre or of
"genres fronting on one another . . . in a common mode" as they are
"countergenres—twinned yet opposite."[44]

As tragic prophecies, Amos and *Samson* are twinned, "inmixt inevi-
tably" (1657). Even in their catastrophes, however, they are opposed, as
tragic prophecy *simpliciter* is to the composite order of tragicomic prophecy. (Though I have hitherto resisted this Apollonian and Polonian
term, "tragic prophecy" does not quite adequately suggest the generic
mixture of Milton's play.) The Chorus sees in the death of the Philistines
only the possibility of Israel's future deliverance; that promise, unful-
filled in the Old Testament, is redeemed only by the New, as yet
unimagined by Amos or by Manoa but shadowed typologically by the
figure of Samson. For when the death of Samson is produced beyond
the fifth act, redeemed by the prophetic vision of one greater man, it
becomes also a rebirth, not the survival of a remnant, or a mere renew-

al, but an actual recreation, made possible by the "Holocaust" (1702) of self-annihilation and self-sacrifice.[45] Amos cannot finally accept that consummation, the utter destruction of Israel (ix, 8), and so his prophetic vision is framed by tragic irony, even as the Old Testament is framed by the New (framed in this case, however, by comic irony), as the type is consumed by as well as subsumed in the antitype. *Samson* begins where Amos ends, with a vision of Israel "Captiv'd" (33); its end is a new beginning, looking forward, beyond the deliverance of Israel to the redemption of time itself, when all things shall be made new in Christ, the God-begott'n Son, "Divine Similitude" (*PL* III, 384), whose "second" and "third" are the Father and the Holy Ghost (1699, 1701).

Even the idea that the Book of Amos and *Samson Agonistes* are counter-genres, however, does not quite do justice to Milton's radical transformation of prophetic tradition, for *Samson Agonistes* is both a refutation and a fulfillment of Amos. *Samson* is not merely the opposite of Amos; rather, as both fully tragic and fully prophetic, it contains both Amos and its opposite, both tragedy (into which Amos collapses when it is seen in New Testament perspective) and its counter-genre, comedy.

Within the Old Testament, the clearest generic antithesis of Amos is the Book of Jonah, whose comic structure embodies the archetype of reintegration and renewal. Amos enforces judgment: "All the sinners of my people shall die" (ix, 10). Jonah promises salvation: "yet hast thou brought up my life from corruption" (ii, 6). Amos articulates one half of the Mosaic paradox, God's unfailing condemnation of sin: "a jealous God, visiting the iniquity of the fathers upon the children unto the third and fourth *generation* of them that hate me" (Exodus xx, 5; also xxxiv, 7). Jonah redefines God's mercy: "I knew that thou *art* a gracious God, and merciful, slow to anger, and of great kindness, and repentest thee of the evil" (iv, 2; cf. Exodus xxxiv, 6–7). Jonah's God does "repent" (Amos vii, 3, 6), and repentant Nineveh is spared: "should not I spare Nineveh, that great city, wherein are more than six score thousand persons that cannot discern between their right hand and their left hand; and also much cattle?" (iv, 11). The brilliant anticlimax underscores a comic irony which is also potentially tragic, for Jonah himself may be incapable of redemption. The book ends not in comic resolution but with a parabolic question: "Doest thou well to be angry?" (iv, 9). For God's mercy "displeased Jonah exceedingly, and he was very angry . . . *even* unto death" (iv, 1, 9). Jonah is a most peculiar prophet, faithful only in his militant self-righteousness—"Wilt thou condemn me, that thou mayest be righteous?" (Job xl, 8)—heroic only in his fanatic obstinacy, "*even* unto death." Jonah's wrath is comic only because it is annulled by God's patient mercy. Jonah is saved once, "vomited out . . . upon the dry *land*" (ii, 10); "this *is* the first resurrection" (Revelation xx, 5). But his second resurrection remains doubtful: "Doest thou well?" Whereas the tragic hero redeems society and himself by sacrifice and the comic hero reintegrates society in himself, Jonah recreates Nineveh without redeeming himself or integrating himself into society; he remains wholly alienated, as much from Israel's life and prophetic vocation as from the Ninehvites whom he hates.

So also Samson, whose tragic isolation is virtually absolute, notwithstanding his father's pathetic efforts to redeem his corpse.

> Yet so it may fall out, because thir end
> Is hate, not help to me, it may with mine
> Draw thir own ruin who attempt the deed.   (1265–67)

Unlike the Ninehvites, the Philistines remain unrepentant. *Samson* exploits the comic perspective of Jonah by subsuming its irony. Jonah's heroic self-righteousness is embodied in the seriocomic effort of Milton's Chorus to find "self-satisfying solution" (306), in what C. A. Patrides calls its "regressive" movement of thought toward "the stunning affirmation that the universe is under the control of an alarmingly authoritarian and capricious deity, 'Who made our laws to bind us, not himself.' "[46] Yet even this comic inversion of the Law contains (as Jonah contains) the seed of possible redemption: "that he may dispense with me or thee . . . For some important cause, thou needst not doubt" (1377–79). That important cause, however, is not the tragic destruction of the Philistines or the comic deliverance of Israel but the prophetic salvation of Samson himelf. Jonah ends with an explicit question: "Doest thou well?" Can Jonah himself be redeemed? *Samson* begins where Jonah ends, with the question of Samson's deliverance: "O wherefore was my birth from Heaven foretold?" (23). And *Samson* ends with an implicit answer to that question, the hope of Samson's redemption, who "Revives, reflourishes, then vigorous most / When most unactive deem'd" (1704–05).

And as that hope is not merely tragic neither is it simply comic; as prophecy, *Samson Agonistes* embraces both possibilities in the "more perfect" form of tragicomedy. The tragic vision of Amos-Manoa, "captivity and loss of eyes" (1744), is dialectically juxtaposed to the comic vision of Jonah-Chorus, "th' unsearchable dispose / Of highest wisdom" (1747), and subsumed in the tragicomic and prophetic vision of the phoenix, "self-begott'n" (1699), self-consumed, and finally self-transcendent.

Aristotle argues that tragedy and comedy diverge from a single source, and this identification is confirmed by Plato: "The chief thing

[Aristodemus] remembered was Socrates compelling . . . [Aristophanes and Agathon] to acknowledge that the genius [hence also *genus*] of comedy was the same with that of tragedy, and that the true artist in tragedy was an artist in comedy also. To this they were constrained to assent, being drowsy, and not quite following the argument."[47] Whatever the actual history of tragedy and comedy, their archetypal affinity is profound. As Wittreich notes, the normal tendency of Renaissance exegesis is to regard the Apocalypse as a "tragicall Comedie," tragic in what it records, comic in its promise, balanced on itself in "a delightsome coherence"; "Rosalie Colie has described pastoral 'as *the* mixed dramatic genre,' and thus regards it 'as the official locus of tragicomedy.' Another locus, this one having scriptural sanction, is prophecy."[48] Whichever locus we choose to explore, the archetypal conclusion is the same: tragedy and comedy are yoked as two contrary forces of a single power. Recalling Frye's discussion of tragic and comic archetypes, we see their interpenetration: disintegration/destruction versus integration/creation gives rise to *re*integration/creation. Thus tragicomedy "can contain a potential tragedy within itself."[49]

Most actual tragicomedies do not quite fulfill this polar archetype, however. As a rule, because tragicomedy circumvents the possibility of actual tragedy, transposing rather than transcending the forces which seek to destroy the community, it reaffirms the idols of the tribe, as tragedy and comedy do, rather than recreating them as prophecy seeks to do. Tragicomedy imitates the prophetic moment—"that critical juncture when the prophetic order of history is revealed"[50]—but never quite achieves the perfect form of prophetic vision. The practical tendency of tragicomedy is to subvert tragedy rather than subsume it: the tragic possibility is always present but never realized. In *The Winter's Tale,* for example, Hermione does not die, although she must seem to do so; Perdita-Persephone is never actually ravished. Snow White is only *Sleeping* Beauty. As a consequence, Galatea is never really brought to life. No statue, no transformation. Strictly speaking, the miracle of restoration wrought by tragicomedy is sheer illusion, for nothing has been lost to be restored, nothing destroyed to be recreated anew. In *The Tempest,* God's efficacy may be unable to produce bodies from nothing but Prospero's can, or can seem to do so:

> These our actors
> (As I foretold you) were all spirits, and
> Are melted into air, into thin air,
> And like the baseless fabric of this vision,
> The cloud-capp'd tow'rs, the gorgeous palaces,

The solemn temples, the great globe itself,
Yea, all which it inherit, shall dissolve,
And like this insubstantial pageant faded
Leave not a rack behind. We are such stuff
As dreams are made on; and our little life
Is rounded with a sleep. (IV.i.148–58)

That is perhaps as close as tragicomedy comes to a tragic vision of
the world as futile stage play. Tragicomedy aspires to the possibility of
actual regeneration only when it becomes self-consciously prophetic—
when Prospero abandons the illusion of myth for the reality of history:
"Now my charms are all o'erthrown" (epilogue, 1). It is far from certain, however, that history has been redeemed; like Jonah, *The Tempest* ends, not in revelation but with a question (which may or may not
be an occasion for revelation): "As you from crimes would pardon'd be,
/ Let your indulgence set me free" (epilogue, 20). In a sense, of
course, *Samson Agonistes* ends with a similar, parabolic question. How
are we to interpret Manoa's enigmatic affirmation that Samson "hath
quit himself / Like *Samson*" (1709–10)? Has Samson merely acquitted
himself heroically, ending as he began, or has he actually yielded up
his former life to gain eternal life? Both meanings are possible, but
only the latter could justify the final affirmation of the play, that "All is
best" (1745). The first, merely comic possibility is virtually foreclosed
by the dire necessity of Samson's tragic death, which demands nothing
less than an actual revelation.

Among extant tragicomedies before *Paradise Regained*, perhaps the
brief epic of Job comes closest to achieving the perfect form of Revelation. Job possesses a sevenfold, five-act structure:

I.	Prologue
II. ⎫	
III. ⎬	Acts I–III: Job's three debates with his three comforters
IV. ⎭	
V.	Act IV: Job's complaint and Elihu's (redactive) answer
VI.	Act V: God's answer, the humiliation which exalts Job
VII.	Epilogue

Within that structure, moreover, the tragicomic anagnorisis of Job prepares the way for both Revelation and *Samson:* "I [had] heard of thee by
the hearing of the ear: but now mine eye seeth thee" (xlii, 5). But Job
also ends with a comic reversal that distances and even threatens to
subvert Job's tragic humiliation: "So the LORD blessed the latter end of
Job more than his beginning" (xlii, 12). If the latter end of Job is not to

become mere fairy tale, these words must be taken in their parabolic rather than in their literal sense.

In general, the parabolic dimension of particular works requires delicate assessment. In *Samson*, however, a parabolic reading seems virtually forced, if not by the violence of the catastrophe itself then by the radical disparity between Samson's tragic death and the Chorus's comic reaffirmation of God's Providence. If all is best, how is it best for Samson? Where tragicomedy sublimates, tragicomic prophecy subsumes the actual crucifixion of the hero: Samson's death is no mere illusion of stagecraft. Moreover, as the tragic possibility of Samson's death is fully realized by the play, so is the comic potential of his rebirth. The tragicomic vision of the play is won not by denying but by realizing as fully as possible its own tragic impulses: only the denial of life itself brings the hope of eternal life. Where *The Tempest* merely hints at regeneration, *Samson* affirms the Resurrection. Milton's play ends not with a question but with the radical transfiguration of a prophetic moment: the phoenix transcends death by dying, "then vigorous most / When most unactive" (1704–05). Like the story of Job, or the parable of Lazarus, or the Resurrection itself, Milton's image of "that self-begott'n bird" (1699) signifies a resurrection. At the same time, it suggests the interpenetration of tragic disintegration and comic reintegration. The latter end of Job is like his beginning; the comic reversal of Samson's fortunes, however, implies a new beginning.

The tragicomic structure of Milton's play is crucial to the revelation of its prophetic form. *Paradise Lost* was more than once conceived along generally dramatic and specifically tragicomic lines, and even when due allowance is made for a medieval rather than a classical inspiration, the projected play, "Adam unparadiz'd," sketched in the Cambridge manuscript, presents a curious generic mixture. The drama intermingles persons real (Adam, Eve, Gabriel, Lucifer) with figures allegoric (Justice and Mercy, Faith, Hope, and Charity) and further perplexes this medieval Morality with a classical chorus and (in one draft) a neoclassical five-act structure.[51] The result seems to be a hybrid cross between a Mystery and a Morality—a cruciform conflation of *Everyman* and the *Second Shepherd's Play*. And *Samson Agonistes*, though in subtler form, presents a similar generic mixture. Its characters are both real and allegorical; Manoa, for example, is scriptural and literal father, but he is heavenly Father as well. In its external form *Samson* is both a Morality and a Mystery. In the structure of its moral dialectic, Samson's search for a "guiding hand" (1) echoes *Everyman*: "Eueryman, I wyll go with the, and be thy gyde." And in the inverted, invisible *pieta* with which the play ends, Manoa's pathetic consolation echoes the Wakefield *Cruci-fixion*. As Manoa comforts himself, "Come, come, no time for lamentation . . . Nothing is here for tears, nothing to wail" (1708, 1721)—so Christ consoles his comforters: "Cease with sorrow thy soul to sear, / It weighs my heart with heavy care. . . . Woman weep thou right nought!"[52] The copresence of these complementary kinds in Milton's play sharpens our awareness of the comic archetype: "The theme of the comic is the integration of society, which usually takes the form of incorporating a central character into it."[53] Samson is incorporated in this sense—"Let us go find the body where it lies . . . To fetch him hence" (1725, 1731)—rather than exiled (as Oedipus is), and the values of the Hebrew community are thus reaffirmed: "Thither shall all the valiant youth resort" (1738). Though the Chorus often doubts, and never knows quite what to expect, it seems confident now that "All is best . . . And ever best found in the close" (1745–48).

Thus *Samson* folds in upon itself, and unfolds itself to the spirit of the reader, whose judgment equal or superior must produce its visionary form beyond the fifth act. As tragic, so also comic form is ultimately unanswerable to the true experience of prophecy. *Samson* does not affirm the values of the Hebrew Chorus—glorious vengeance and doubtful liberty; rather, the play contains this possibility as a contending perspective to be transcended. And where comic form denies the tragic annihilation of the hero, prophetic form demands this holocaust. Yet none of these generic options is finally foreclosed by the composite order of *Samson*, whose encyclopedic form encompasses them all.

Once again, the crucial issues are focused, not by the external "catastrophe . . . wherewith the tragedy ends" but by the internal climax of visionary form, the new beginning of the prophetic moment: "And for a life who will not change his purpose?" (1406) To whose "resistless" power does Samson owe "absolute subjection" (1404–05)? Faced with the catastrophe itself, we stand "full of doubt . . . Whether . . . [to] repent . . . of sin / . . . or rejoyce / Much more, that much more good thereof shall spring" (*PL* XII, 473–76). Inspired by the comic vision of the Chorus we do rejoice, at least momentarily. Joseph Summers retells

Rachel Trickett's story of how C. S. Lewis used to tease a pious young academic friend by asking, 'Don't you rejoice with that chorus,

> While their hearts were jocund and sublime,
> Drunk with idolatry, drunk with wine,
>
> . . . .

> Among them he a spirit of frenzy sent,
> Who hurt their minds
> And urged them on with mad desire
> To call in haste for their destroyer?'   [SA 1669–78]

The young friend would protest, 'No! No!, I don't! It's unchristian,' and Lewis would reply, 'Oh, come now! Rejoice! You're supposed to, you know.'[54]

If we fail to rejoice at God's and Samson's triumph, our apathy probably bespeaks some deep-rooted hypocrisy in us, a refusal to acknowledge our own capacity for violence. Such impulses, the play may tell us, are better faced than suppressed, so that, as Milton remarks in "Of Tragedy," we may "purge the mind of those and such-like passions . . . and reduce them to just measure" (CM, I:2, 331). To admit such motives, however, is not to sanction them. The particular mode of comic relief that might be called "gloating"—alien to the spirit of classical tragedy though not to the spirit of Judges—is here foreclosed by tragic impulses still more powerful in their operation. Any trivial comfort we might receive from the destruction of a hated enemy is absolutely nullified by Manoa's tragic desolation: "captivity and loss of eyes" (1744). Only the promise of eternal life could redeem such a loss, and so the catastrophe drives us back upon the climax, as prophetic form folds in upon itself: whose commands? whose "rouzing motions" (1382)? The form of the play moves us to such questions.

EPILOGUE

The final chorus of Milton's play echoes the close of *Oedipus Rex*, proffering a similar, albeit more optimistic wisdom, rooted in the ethos of the Hebrew community:

> All is best, though we oft doubt,
> What th' unsearchable dispose
> Of highest wisdom brings about,
> And ever best found in the close.
> Oft he seems to hide his face,
> But unexpectedly returns
> And to his faithful Champion hath in place
> Bore witness gloriously; whence *Gaza* mourns
> And all that band them to resist
> His uncontroulable intent,
> His servants he with new acquist
> Of true experience from this great event

With peace and consolation hath dismist,
And calm of mind all passion spent.   (1745–1758)

But we can accept that dispensation only provisionally, still searching God's "unsearchable disclose." For the choric vision of God's triumphant vindication is neither adequate to the tragic catharsis which it seems to subvert nor answerable to the prophetic force of Milton's vision, the illumination of our "inward eyes" (1689). Such consolation as we find "at the close," therefore, results not from our assent to the vindictive, self-asserting vision of the Chorus or from "the catastrophe . . . wherewith the tragedy ends," but from the epiphany of Samson's self-sacrifice to that Master who "commands . . . absolute subjection" (1404–05).

Where tragedy ends, prophecy begins, making all things new, re-creating itself by rediscovering and remaking its generic origins. In *Samson Agonistes*, however, this prophetic recreation remains implicit, a potential to be realized by Milton's fit audience rather than a conclusion of the poem. The internal form of the play lies hidden beneath its surface, masked both by the decorum of classical form and by the verisimilitude of Hebraic subject matter; as a consequence, the final meaning of the play lies "all before [us], where to choose" (*PL* XII,646). It is still barely possible to read Milton's Samson as a mirror of his own fickle state or "as a symbol for the revolutionary cause"[55]—although such possibilities are discouraged by the perspicuous order of the play. *Samson Agonistes* does include political apologetic among its *genera mixta*, but the poem is not primarily "about Milton himself, and *a fortiori* about current politics."[56] The composite order of the play demands a more comprehensive critical perspective.

Even when we have begun to establish that perspective, however, and have generally agreed about the relevant contexts for the play, the range of interpretive choices remains extremely broad. Is Samson the Antichrist? Is *Samson Agonistes* a demonic parody of the Apocalypse? Or is Samson the antitype, the Word made flesh, of which Samson's holocaust is the type? I am not sure that this choice can be determined from the evidence of the play; indeed, my own attempt to find a "self-satisfying solution" to this crux convinces me that it cannot be externally resolved. It remains, therefore, an occasion for choice—in effect a parabolic question: "Doest thou well?" Stanley Fish chooses to be consumed by the "unexpressive" spirit of the play; I prefer to find myself in the Word. Each metaphor offers its own angle of vision, without offering any ground to justify itself. But then, that seems to me as it should be, for radical indeterminacy is also an aspect of parabolic form—an aspect that I would emphasize, if possible, even more than Wittreich does: visionary form is always an occasion for choosing. The prophetic moment is a crisis: it demands that the prophet perpetually renew himself, reshaping all human traditions—words as vehicles of spirit—to the divinely inspired purpose of the Word. And that purpose demands an analogous response from the prophet's fit audience: we must choose the prophet's meaning not capriciously, but freely, within the form of his vision, which is also a liberation from form. In this way we become responsible for producing the action of the prophecy "beyond the fifth act," shaping and reshaping our response in accord with the cumulative vision of the poem itself and with our own unfolding perception. And by this voluntary participation in the poet's making, we shape for ourselves not a mere "mirror of our fickle state" but "the majestick image of a high and stately Tragedy."

University of Arizona

NOTES

1. *Literature as System: Essays Toward the Theory of Literary History* (Princeton, 1971), p. 146.

2. Fletcher, *The Transcendental Masque: An Essay on Milton's "Comus"* (Ithaca, 1971), pp. 116–17; Wittreich, *Visionary Poetics: Milton's Tradition and His Legacy* (San Marino, Calif., 1979), p. 76.

3. *The Blaze of Noon: A Reading of "Samson Agonistes"* (New York, 1974), p. 33.

4. Fell, "From Myth to Martyrdom: Towards a View of *Samson Agonistes*," *English Studies*, XXXIV (1953), 154; Andrews, " 'Dearly Bought Revenge': *Samson Agonistes, Hamlet,* and Elizabethan Revenge Tragedy," in *Milton Studies*, XIII, edited by James D. Simmonds, (Pittsburgh, 1979), p. 101. Unless otherwise noted, all biblical quotations are from the Authorized, King James version of 1611.

5. "The Interpretation of *Samson Agonistes*," *Huntington Library Quarterly*, XXVI (1963), 378.

6. Woodhouse, "Tragic Effect in *Samson Agonistes*," *UTQ*, LIII (1959), 206; Bush, ed., *Complete Poetical Works of John Milton* (Boston, 1965), p. 514; Fish, "Question and Answer in *Samson Agonistes*," *Critical Quarterly*, XI (1969), 237.

7. This is essentially the argument I have advanced in " 'This Great Deliverer': *Samson Agonistes* as Parable," *Milton Quarterly*, XIII (1979), 79–84. I have explored the parabolic meaning of Judges itself in another essay, "Samson's Riddle: Judges 13–16 as Parable," *Cithara*, XVIII, ii (1979), 3–28.

8. At various times, each of the three cultural perspectives available has been singled out for critical attention. William Riley Parker, *Milton's Debt to Greek Tragedy in "Samson Agonistes"* (Baltimore, 1937), pp. 238–39, was the first to argue systematically that the

spirit of *SA* as well as its form is essentially classical. Parker's exposition had in part been a response to Sir Richard Jebb's assertion, in "*Samson Agonistes* and the Hellenic Drama," *Proceedings of the British Academy*, III (1903), 341, that the spirit of the play is Hebraic. More recently, Christian apologists have advanced similarly exclusive claims. G. A. Wilkes, for example, "The Interpretation of *Samson*," p. 377, has argued that both classical and Hebraic perspectives are irrelevant to Milton's Calvinist "conception of grace as operating beyond human capacity and effort."

9. *From Shadowy Types to Truth: Studies in Milton's Symbolism* (New Haven, 1968), p. 202. For the dubious scheme linking Samson's temptations with those of Christ, see F. Michael Krouse, *Milton's Samson and the Christian Tradition* (Princeton, 1949), and for the link between Samson's agony and Christ's see T. S. K. Scott-Craig, "Concerning Milton's Samson," *Renaissance News*, V (1952), 45–53.

10. "The Movements of the Drama," in *The Lyric and Dramatic Milton*, ed. Joseph Summers (New York, 1965), p. 172.

11. *From Shadowy Types to Truth*, p. 198. In a similar vein, John Shawcross, "Irony as Tragic Effect: *Samson Agonistes* and the Tragedy of Hope," in *Calm of Mind: Tercentenary Essays on "Paradise Regained" and "Samson Agonistes" in Honor of John S. Diekhoff*, ed. Joseph Wittreich (Cleveland, 1971), p. 291, has argued that "Samson should be viewed ironically as one who, acting entirely out of his faith, commits an act whose meaning and consequences he does not understand."

12. See *Of Reformation*, in YP, I, 520.

13. *Saving the Appearances: A Study in Idolatry* (New York, 1957), p. 185.

14. *Heroic Knowledge: An Interpretation of "Paradise Regained" and "Samson Agonistes"* (Minneapolis, 1957), p. 197.

15. "Samson's Identity Crisis and Milton's," in *Imagination and the Spirit: Essays in Literature and the Christian Faith Presented to Clyde S. Kilby*, ed. Charles A. Huttar (Grand Rapids, Mich., 1971), p. 151.

16. William Kerrigan, *The Prophetic Milton* (Charlottesville, 1974), p. 261, is certainly right in asserting that "Milton believed himself to be divinely inspired." As Kerrigan himself is aware, however, and as William Empson pointedly reminded us, in *Milton's God*, rev. ed. (London, 1965), p. 226, the trouble with unconscious illumination "is that you may get very bad results, and that they are not open to public scrutiny." *Pace* Empson, however, Milton does not allow Samson (or the reader) to indulge in the false security of "divine instinct" (526). As Mary Ann Radzinowicz has shown, in *Toward "Samson Agonistes": The Growth of Milton's Mind* (Princeton, 1978), p. 354, Milton moves "away from . . . a passive role in uttering dictated truths and towards the assertion of reason, the tempering of the passions, the superiority of rationality in the saving remnant towards whom he would address himself."

17. As Balachandra Rajan has observed, in *The Lofty Rhyme: A Study of Milton's Major Poetry* (Coral Gables, Fla., 1970), p. 131, *SA* "is so deeply ironic that dramatic irony seems to become a paradigm of providential irony." Rajan's suggestion is confirmed by Edward W. Tayler, "Milton's *Samson*: The Form of Christian Tragedy," *English Literary Renaissance*, III (1973), 306, 320: "Milton's distinctively Christian use of dramatic irony . . . has invested Sophoclean irony with providential force."

18. *CD* I, xxvii. I here prefer Sumner's translation to Carey's and quote from *John Milton: Complete Poems and Major Prose*, ed. Merritt Y. Hughes (New York, 1957), p. 1012b. As Arthur Barker has argued, in "Structural and Doctrinal Pattern in Milton's Later Poems: *Samson Agonistes*," in *Twentieth Century Interpretations of "Samson Agonistes*," ed. Galbraith M. Crump (Englewood Cliffs, N.J., 1968), pp. 75, 82, *SA* reflects Milton's

"preoccupation with redemption and the process of regeneration and the Christian liberty resulting from the process": "in his way and time, Samson is the type of what the Christian may be the type of in his way and time."

19. Fletcher, *The Transcendental Masque*, pp. 116–17; Wittreich, *Visionary Poetics*, pp. 76, 43. The ending "end / Of all yet done" (*PL* VII, 505–06) is of course Sidney's "virtuous action" (*An Apology for Poetry or the Defence of Poesy*, ed. Geoffrey Shepherd [London, 1965], p. 104).

20. Horace, *The Art of Poetry* (189, 228), trans. John G. Hawthorne, in *Latin Poetry in Verse Translation*, ed. J. R. Lind (Boston, 1957), p. 134. Milton's "not . . . produced beyond the fifth act" is a literal translation of *neu sit quinto productior actu*, quoted from *Q. Horati flacci epistulae*, ed. Augustus S. Wilkins (London, 1923), p. 67.

21. Pareus, *A Commentary upon the Divine Revelation of the Apostle and Evangelist John*, trans. Elias Arnold (Amsterdam, 1644), p. 20; cited by Wittreich, *Visionary Poetics*, pp. 40–41, whose structural summary I reproduce.

22. *Milton's Debt to Greek Tragedy*, p. 17. Parker himself concedes that his "analysis may be thought . . . arbitrary" (p. 17n.) and suggests the possibility of a sevenfold structure: if "act divisions are determined by the choral odes" (as in Pareus' *Commentary*), then "*Samson Agonistes* has perhaps six acts—or, if the parodos be counted as an ode, seven" (p. 14).

23. The most obvious perspective, of course, is that afforded by a direct comparison between *SA* and Revelation as sevenfold composite orders.

24. Samuel Taylor Coleridge, *Seven Lectures on Shakespeare and Milton*, ed. J. Payne Collier (London, 1856), p. xxvii; cited by Parker, *Milton's Debt to Greek Tragedy*, p. 55.

25. "Tragic Effect," pp. 206, 222.

26. *Visionary Poetics*, p. 131.

27. Aristotle, *Poetics* XI, 1, in *Aristotle's Theory of Poetry and Fine Art*, ed. and trans. S. H. Butcher, 4th ed. (New York, 1951), p. 41; Wittreich, *Visionary Poetics*, pp. 6, 219n., cites both William M. Ryan, *William Langland* (New York, 1968), p. 13, and Elizabeth D. Kirk, *The Dream Thought of Piers Plowman* (New Haven, 1972), pp. 2, 205, to show that *Piers Plowman* is, like the Book of Revelation, "a cumulative structure reflecting the 'agonized unfolding of perception.' "

28. *Milton and His Epic Tradition* (Seattle, 1979), pp. 60–62.

29. *Anatomy of Criticism: Four Essays* (Princeton, 1957), pp. 214, 36.

30. Ibid., p. 215. Frye argues that "the ritual pattern behind the catharsis of comedy" is not the Dionysiac *sparagmos* but the Apollonian "resurrection that follows the death, the epiphany or manifestation of the risen hero."

31. *Milton and His Epic Tradition*, pp. 112, 115.

32. This term is taken from Rosalie Colie's discussion of *PL* as a cultural summary in *The Resources of Kind: Genre-Theory in the Renaissance*, ed. Barbara K. Lewalski (Berkeley and Los Angeles, 1973), pp. 119–22. Though my specific concerns have led to more frequent citation of other kindly "auctoritee," my attempt to apprehend *SA* as an instance of *genera mixta* and "even of the *genus universum*" (p. 123) should suggest something of my indebtedness to Colie's seminal study.

33. *Oedipus Rex*, in *Sophocles: The Oedipus Cycle*, trans. Dudley Fitts and Robert Fitzgerald (New York, 1939), pp. 74, 70, 78.

34. *Milton and His Epic Tradition*, p. 8.

35. *Visionary Poetics*, p. 5.

36. Augustine, *De Civitate Dei* VII, xxxii; *The City of God*, trans. Marcus Dods (New York, 1950), p. 238.

37. *Literature as System*, pp. 118–19, 111–12; Milton, *Of Education*, YP, II, 405.

38. On the shape of the Aristotelian *energeia*, the tragic rhythm of *praxis, pathos, theoreia*, see Burke, *Counter-Statement*, 2d ed. (Chicago, 1953); Olson, *Aristotle's "Poetics" and English Literature: A Collection of Critical Essays* (Chicago, 1965); and Fergusson, Introduction, *Aristotle's Poetics* (New York, 1961).

39. Aristotle, *Poetics* XI, 2, in *Aristotle's Theory*, p. 41. Like the catharsis of pity and terror, this coincidence of recognition and turning point should arise from "the inner structure" of the work (XVI, 1, in *Aristotle's Theory*, p. 49).

40. Wittreich, *Visionary Poetics*, pp. 44, 41.

41. Aristotle, *Poetics* XV, 7; XIV, 10, in *Aristotle's Theory*, pp. 57, 95.

42. Samuel Johnson, *Rambler* no. 139, p. 832; cited by Parker, *Milton's Debt to Greek Tragedy*, p. 23.

43. Wittreich, *Visionary Poetics*, p. 41; Wittreich (p. 232) cites More, *An Exposition of the Seven Epistles to the Seven Churches* (London, 1669), p. 179.

44. Colie, *Resources of Kind*, p. 67.

45. A *holocaust* is, of course, a sacrifice wholly consumed by flame; this nonscriptural word does not appear elsewhere in Milton's poetry. It is perhaps also worthy of note that the word *remnant*, which occurs with some frequency in Milton's prose, is not found in his poetry.

46. "The Comic Dimension in Greek Tragedy and *Samson Agonistes*," in *Milton Studies*, X, ed. James D. Simmonds (Pittsburgh, 1977), p. 16. As Patrides also notes, however, "in time the Chorus's regressive movement is inverted" (p. 17).

47. Aristotle, *Poetics* IV, in *Aristotle's Theory*, pp. 15–21; Plato, *Symposium*, in *The Republic and Other Works of Plato*, trans. Benjamin Jowett (Garden City, N.Y., 1960), p. 365.

48. Wittreich, *Visionary Poetics*, p. 37, cites Richard Bernard, *A Key of Knowledge for the Opening of the Secret Mysteries of St. Johns Mystical Revelation* (London, 1617), p. 130, and Colie, *Shakespeare's Living Art* (Princeton, 1974), p. 244.

49. Frye, *Anatomy of Criticism*, p. 215. Frye suggests that "the death of Samson" would not "lead to 'calm of mind, all passion spent,' if Samson were not a prototype of the rising Christ, associated at the appropriate moment with the phoenix."

50. Angus Fletcher, *The Prophetic Moment: An Essay on Spenser* (Chicago, 1971), p. 45.

51. According to the Outlines for Tragedies set down in the Trinity manuscript (CM, XVIII, 229–30), the five-act structure of draft 3 corresponds approximately with the five-act structure of SA (assuming the appropriate choral interludes):

Prologue	Moses *prologizei*	Samson *prologizei*	(1–114)
I.	Justice-Mercy-Widsom debate	Samson and Chorus	(176–292)
II.	Marriage of Adam and Eve narrated	Samson and Manoa	(326–651)
III.	Lucifer contriving	Samson and Dalila	(710–1009)
IV.	Adam and Eve fallen	Samson and Harapha	(1061–1267)
V.	Adam and Eve unparadised	Samson and Officer	(1300–1426)
Epilogue	Chorus briefly concludes	Narrative and choric finale	(1441–1758)

52. *Everyman* I, 522, in *Chief Pre-Shakespearean Dramas*, ed. Joseph Quincy Adams (Cambridge, Mass., 1924), p. 296; *The Crucifixion*, in *Wakefield Mystery Plays*, ed. Martial Rose (Garden City, N.Y., 1963), p. 407.

53. Frye, *Anatomy of Criticism*, p. 43.

54. "Response to Anthony Low's Address on *Samson Agonistes*," *Milton Quarterly*, XIII (1979), 106.

55. Christopher Hill, *Milton and The English Revolution* (Harmondsworth, England, 1977), p. 435.

56. Empson, *Milton's God*, p. 217. In his unremitting antipathy for all things Judeo-Christian, Empson forgets what Wittreich remembers in *Visionary Poetics*, p. 197, citing Abraham Heschel, *The Prophets: An Introduction* (1962; rpt. New York, 1969), p. 166: "The prophets were the first men in history to regard a nation's reliance upon force as evil." To which one might apend, "Would God that all the Lord's people were prophets" (Numbers xi, 29).